OUT OF THE BLUE

Photo by Vitaly Lazarenko, Moscow, 1995.

OUT OF THE BLUE

Russia's Hidden Gay Literature
An Anthology

Edited by Kevin Moss

Introduction by Simon Karlinsky

Gay Sunshine Press
San Francisco

First Edition 1997

EDITOR'S ACKNOWLEDGMENTS

I am indebted to Middlebury College for supporting my research on this collection. I am grateful to my translator colleagues for the new translations/essays done for this volume: Vitaly Chernetsky, Tolya Vishevsky, Michael Biggins, Tony Vanchu, Gerald McCausland, Dan Healey, Michael Green. My thanks to the following for their assistance and suggestions: Valery Tugolukov, Kevin Gardner, Zhenya Bazanov, Pavel Yashchenkov, Dima Kuz'min, Helena Goscilo, Simon Karlinsky, Tanya Kotys, Melissa Zahniser, Dima Lytchev, Roman Kalinin, Gena Krimenskoi, Alexander Shatalov. And special thanks to my partner, Ernie McLeod, for his patience and literate advice.

The following translations are copyright © 1997 by Gay Sunshine Press Inc.: All translations by Vitaly Chernetsky: Lermontov's poems; V. Ivanov's poems; Ivnev's poem; Esenin's four poems; G. Ivanov's "The Third Rome"; Pereleshin's Twelve Sonnets; Dmitry Kuz'min's poems; Mogutin's "The Death of Misha Beautiful" and "Army Elegy"; Bushuev's poem and "Echoes of Harlequin." Leontiev's "Khamid and Manoli," translated by Gerald McCausland. All translations by Kevin Moss: Tolstoy's "The Ivins" and "Pages from Diaries"; Trifonov's "Open Letter"; "Letters to the Editor of *Tema* and *1/10*; Four stories by Kharitonov (Russian text of Kharitonov copyright © The Estate of Yevgeny Kharitonov, used by permission of Serpent's Tail, London); and "Editor's Preface." "Letters About Prison Life," translated by Dan Healey. Makanin's "Prisoner of the Caucasus," and Rybikov's "Lays of the Gay Slavs," translated by Anatoly Vishevsky/Michael Biggins. Past's "No Offense in Love," translated by Diane Nemec Ignashev. Gubin's three poems, translated by J. Kates. Yeliseev's "The Bench," Yasinsky's "A Sunny Day at the Seashore," and K.E.'s "The Phone Call," all translated by Anthony Vanchu.

The following translations are under the copyrights stated: Simon Karlinsky's Introduction ("Russia's Gay Literature and History") is from *Gay and Lesbian Literary Heritage* by Claude J. Summers. Copyright © 1995 by New England Publishing Association, Inc. Reprinted by permission of Henry Holt and Co., Inc. The following translations/articles copyright © 1997 by Michael Green: Pushkin's "Imitation of the Arabic," "A Pushkin Puzzle," Kuzmin's stories and poems, "Mikhail Kuzmin: Past and Present" and "Mikhail Kuzmin's Diaries." Gogol's "Nights at the Villa" is reprinted with permission from *The Sexual Labyrinth of Nikolai Gogol* (pp. 192–196), University of Chicago Press, 1992. Copyright © 1976 by Simon Karlinsky. Sologub's "The Petty Demon" (selections), translated by S.D. Cioran, is reprinted with permission of, and copyrighted by, Ardis Publishers. The following translations are copyright © 1997 by Simon Karlinsky: Klyuev's two poems; Pereleshin's three poems and three sonnets and Trifonov's four poems. Rozanov's "People of the Moonlight" (selections) is reprinted with permission from *Four Faces of Rozanov*, © 1978 by Philosophical Library. Ivnev's Diary selections and Trifonov's "Two Ballets by George Balanchine," translated by Michael Molnar, are reprinted from and copyrighted © 1995 by *Index on Censorship*, London. Anatoly Steiger's Ten Poems are reprinted from: Simon Karlinsky, Alfred Appel Jr., *Bitter Air of Exile: Russian Writers in the West 1922–1972* (pp. 336–338), University of Calif. Press. Copyright © 1977 The Regents of the University of California. "Around Dupont" is copyright © 1995 by Vassily Aksyonov. Kolyada's "Slingshot" is copyright © 1997 by San Diego Repertory Theatre. Thanks to Glagol, Moscow, agent for Ivnev, Kharitonov and Trifonov, for facilitating permissions.

GRAPHICS: Photos by Vitaly Lazarenko (front cover and pp. 2, 234, 244) copyright © 1997 by Gay Sunshine Press Inc. All other photos, drawings remain under the copyright of the artists/photographers named, except for those in public domain. Photos by Alexei Sedov (back cover, pp. 257, 392, 402) and O. Kaminka (p. 352), originally published in *Ty* (Moscow), are used with permission of Harlow Robinson and Gennady Krimenskoi. Drawings (pp. 27, 67, 157, 233) by Victoria Urman-Kuslik are from the Russian magazine *Risk* (photographed there by Pavel Smirnov-Belozertsev).

LIBRARY OF CONGRESS CATALOGUING-IN-PUBLICATION DATA

Out of the blue : Russia's hidden gay literature : an anthology / edited by Kevin Moss ; introduction by Simon Karlinsky.
    416 p. 6 × 9 in.   cm.
    Includes bibliographical references.
    ISBN 0-940567-19-9 (cloth : alk. paper).—ISBN 0-940567-20-2 (paper : alk. paper)
    1. Gay men—Russia (Federation)—Literary collections. 2. Gay men's writings, Russian. 3. Homosexuality in literature. I. Moss, Kevin, 1955– . II. Karlinsky, Simon
PG3205.H65094 1996   96-24504
891.708'09206642—dc20   CIP

Gay Sunshine Press Inc., P.O. Box 410690, San Francisco, CA 94141
Write for free catalogue of books available, including how to order additional copies of this book.

PG
3205
.H65
O94
1997

CONTENTS

III. HIDDEN FROM VIEW UNDER THE SOVIETS: UNDERGROUND AND EMIGRE LITERATURE (1920–1980)

       Front cover photo by Vitaly Lazarenko, 1995
       Back cover photo by Alexei Sedov

GRAPHICS

Page 2: photo by Vitaly Lazarenko; p. 14: photo of Vyacheslav Ivanov and Mikhail Kuzmin; photo of Alexei Apukhtin; pp. 27, 67, 157, 233: drawings by Victoria Urman-Kuslik; p. 28: drawing of Alexander Pushkin by Heitman; self-portrait drawing by Pushkin; p. 29: self-portrait drawing by Pushkin; p. 48: drawing by Victor Putintsev; p. 68: photo of Mikhail Kuzmin; p. 155: photo of Sergei Esenin and Nikolai Klyuev; p. 158: photo of Yevgeny Kharitonov; p. 226: photo of Gennady Trifonov; p. 234: photo by Vitaly Lazarenko; p. 244: photo by Vitaly Lazarenko; p. 257: photo by Alexei Sedov; p. 262: photo by Vitaly Lazarenko; p. 306: scene from the play Slingshot; p. 345: drawing by Imas Levsky; p. 352: photo by O. Kaminka; p. 379: drawing by Imas Levsky; p. 392: photo by Alexei Sedov; p. 402: photo by Alexei Sedov; p. 412: photo of Dimitri Bushuev.

EDITOR'S PREFACE

Kevin Moss

G IVEN THE pervasive sexophobia in Soviet culture, it is no wonder gay people and gay literature appeared to be completely absent. Yet the material in this collection shows that Russian gay writing was nothing new in the 1990s. As Simon Karlinsky demonstrates in the essay that follows, same-sex love appears in some of the earliest documents of Russian culture. Nevertheless, years of Soviet censorship of any mention of homosexuality and criminalization of sex between men rendered gay-themed writing invisible even to most Western observers.

If asked where to look for gay themes in Russian literature, most Slavists could probably point to the work of Mikhail Kuzmin, the openly gay poet of the Silver Age and author of the first gay novel in Russian, *Wings*. Many also know Karlinsky's ground-breaking essay, "Russia's Gay Literature and History" first published in *Gay Sunshine* in 1977 and reprinted, in its revised version, as an introduction to the present volume. But for most, that would exhaust their knowledge. In part our blind spot has been due to the conservatism of older emigré scholars who disapprove of women's and gender studies. Many more recent emigrés raised on Soviet puritanism were no more open-minded, especially when it came to homosexuality. And in Russia until the repeal of Article 121 in 1993, it was potentially danger-ous to study gay topics. Gay Americans rightly feared the KGB could blackmail them or at the very least forbid them to reenter the Soviet Union if they were found out.[1] One of the first accounts of gay life in Soviet Rus-sia was published by an American professor under a pseudonym.[2] And to this day researchers can gain access to gay material in some archives only by disguising their real interests.

The situation has changed with the gradual liberalization in Russia itself. For most of the Soviet period, criminalization of homosexuality ensured that gay topics were silenced. Founding of a gay rights group in Leningrad in 1984 proved premature: it was disbanded by the KGB.[3] It was not until glasnost relaxed the restrictions on all topics that discussion could begin again. The Sexual Minorities Association was founded in Moscow in 1989; the next year it became the Moscow Union of Lesbians and Homosexuals, and its newspaper *Tema* was officially registered in 1990. With the help of the newly-founded International Gay and Lesbian Human Rights Commis-sion the Moscow activists planned to "Turn Red Squares into Pink Tri-angles" in the summer of 1991. The international conference and film

---

[1] Masha Gessen, The Rights of Lesbians and Gay Men in the Russian Federation (San Francisco: IGLHRC, 1994), p. 19.

[2] "G," "The Secret Life of Moscow," *Christopher Street*, June 1980.

[3] Igor S. Kon, *The Sexual Revolution in Russia* (tr.) (New York: Free Press, 1995), p. 252.

festival were a success in both Leningrad and Moscow, even if only a handful of activists were willing to appear on television or use their real names in print. When, later that same summer, reactionary forces staged a coup, the new gay activists knew where their bread was buttered: they rallied to Yeltsin's side, printing his proclamations on their new Xerox machines and helping to defend the barricades.

Gay publications proliferated: *Tema* was joined by *1/10*, *Ty* (You), *Risk*, *Gay Slaviane!*, *Kristofer*, *Argo*, and others (of these, *1/10* has proven to be the most resilient, with a reputed distribution of 50,000 copies). These journals included international and Russian gay news, personal ads, and translations of gay works from the West. But they also published new Russian writing and works by Russian authors previously unavailable in Russia. Increased visibility, however, led to an increased backlash from the ever-more-virulent right wing.

In culture as well as politics, same-sex love and homoeroticism have come out of the closet: there are gay art exhibits, gay plays, and an all-male ballet troupe. Still, the recent boom has its roots in the 70s and 80s. The films of Sergei Paradzhanov, who was imprisoned for several years under Article 121, were distinctly homoerotic. Roman Viktiuk directed increasingly homoerotic plays through the late 80s: his productions sexualized the males and always included handsome shirtless men. If in 1989 Viktiuk's production in San Diego of Kolyada's openly gay-themed *Slingshot* risked scandal at home, by the mid-90s he was directing "M. Butterfly" and the same *Slingshot* in Moscow.

In literature as well, gay topics have become increasingly acceptable. Eduard Limonov was perhaps the first to use sex between men to shock his readers in *It's Me, Eddie*. But in 1979 his novel was of course only published abroad. When post-perestroika authors exhausted the shock-value of straight sexuality, many of them too turned to gay sex, among other "scandalous" topics, to improve their sales. While this collection includes a few modern straight authors, their works do not exploit homoeroticism or gay themes merely to titillate.

This anthology was conceived as a collection of homoerotic and gay-themed writing in Russian by Russians. It includes a broad range of genres: novel, short story, poem, diary, letter, and essay forms are all represented. We made a conscious decision early in the compilation to include some homoerotic stories from the new gay journals that may not qualify as high literature. These, like some of the letters to the editors of the gay journals, help flesh out the context of gay life in Russia.

We also decided to include only gay male materials. There is a wealth of material on lesbians in Russia that awaits a similar compilation: major authors like Tsvetaeva, Zinovieva-Gannibal, Parnok, and the more recent studies by Diana Burgin, Olga Zhuk, and Masha Gessen, to name a few, should be made more accessible to the wider English-speaking audience.

The sections of the anthology are divided chronologically. The divisions correspond roughly to traditional literary periodization, but they also parallel political changes that affected gay life and changes in the ways gay Russians conceived of themselves.

Part One covers Russian literature's Golden Age, the 19th century, and includes several of its most famous authors. Pushkin and Lermontov are the creators of the Russian verse tradition, and with Gogol and Tolstoy they are among the greatest masters of Russian fiction. None of them was gay in the modern sense of the word. Pushkin and Lermontov's casual treatment of homosexuality show that it was not as stigmatized in early 19th century society as one might expect. Gogol and Tolstoy both reveal their own romantic attachments to men, yet it is unlikely either ever acted on them. Leontiev seems to have been bisexual and probably took advantage of his diplomatic postings in the Near East to indulge his taste in men.

Not surprisingly, many of the materials in this section have been marginalized in various ways: Pushkin and Lermontov's verses published here are not considered central to their canon, Gogol's and Tolstoy's diary selections are buried in obscure volumes, and Leontiev's "Khamid and Manoli" has apparently never been published previously in English. Several of these selections also marginalize homosexuality by setting it in another culture (Pushkin's "Imitation of the Arabic," Leontiev's story set in Crete) or restricting it to a childhood phase (Lermontov's cadet school, Tolstoy's "Childhood").

Part Two, The First Flowering of Gay Culture, demonstrates the explosion of gay literature in the Silver Age (early 20th century). This section too contains major writers, but their works are now more openly gay and they are central, not marginal. In Kuzmin, for example, we find the first gay voice in Russia describing a gay world. Kuzmin wrote both poetry and prose, has a place in the Russian canon, and cannot be read as anything but gay. Sologub, another Silver Age writer associated with Decadence, writes about a sado-masochistic attachment between a schoolteacher and his pupils in his best-known novel of the period. And Rozanov, whose theory that homosexuality is central to Christian asceticism will strike modern Western readers as bizarre, remains an influential figure in Russian philosophical thought.

The flowering of gay culture at the beginning of the 20th Century was to be short-lived. While some argue that homosexuality was decriminalized when the Revolution of 1917 eliminated all laws, there does not appear to be a positive reaction in gay life at the time. Many elite or intellectual homosexuals emigrated, and in 1933 homosexuality was criminalized anew with a vengeance under Stalin. Given the strict censorship applied to all writing under the Soviets, it is not surprising that no gay-themed works were published in Russia until glasnost relaxed the controls. Instead, homosexuality became one of the many themes relegated to underground and emigré writing.

In Part Three: Hidden from View, authors' biographies compete in their tragic twists with their writings. Trifonov spent 4 years in prison under Article 121. When a gay friend of Kharitonov's was murdered, the writer was brought in and threatened by the KGB, and the resultant stress eventually led to Kharitonov's death. Pereleshin, like many Russians in Siberia, emigrated to China and then to Brazil. In China he was harassed and incarcerated by the Chinese Communists for his homosexuality. All three are major gay writers. Kharitonov, who died in 1981, was virtually unknown until 1993, when his works were finally published in Moscow. Pereleshin, unfortunately, remains little-known in Russia.

Gay Life Reborn (Part Four), which shows the post-Soviet proliferation of gay-themed materials, is the most eclectic. Here we have a wealth of material from the first gay journals: literature, erotic stories, letters to the editor. Compulsory army service for men meant that for many gay men the army was an important place of discovery. And the criminalization of sex between men compounded with the large population of the prison system as a whole under the Soviets meant that prison sexuality played a more central role in the gay imagination than in perhaps any other country. Both of these issues are covered in letters and stories.

If we compare Russian and Western gay writing in the 90s, we find several differences. For one thing, there is hardly any discussion of the impact of AIDS in Russia. Here AIDS appears in "The Phone Call" by K. E. and in one letter. The story in which the disease plays the most central role, Aksyonov's "Around Dupont," is set in the U.S. The epidemic has come late to Russia, and its effects have yet to percolate into literary form. As we would expect, there are coming out stories, but they deal only with the issue of the individual coming to terms with his own homosexuality, not with coming out to others. There is little treatment of gayness as a political issue or of the place of gay people in Russian society as a whole. For decades under Soviet rule Russians took refuge in the private sphere and avoided involvement in state politics. The legacy of this separation is reflected here: for most Russian gays, the personal is not yet political.

Perhaps what is most striking is that, for all the differences, the emotional landscape covered in these writings is so familiar, running the full gamut from self-hatred to righteous anger, from passionate love to unrequited lust, from sentimental self-pity to camp wit. They show the range and richness of the gay experience for Russians over the past two centuries.

Out of the Blue owes its very existence to the constant commitment of its publisher, Winston Leyland, to supporting worthwhile projects. The anthology was his long before it was ours, and over the course of our collaboration it was clear that it was a labor of love for him. I am very grateful for his professional advice and commitment to quality, his willingness both to be flexible and to bring intellectual rigor to this project.

PUBLISHER'S NOTE

Winston Leyland

THE GENESIS OF *Out of the Blue* goes back fifteen years. At that time I decided to research, edit, and publish an anthology of Russian gay literature in English translation. In my twenty-two years as publisher of Gay Sunshine Press I've had a special interest in bringing to readers collections of gay writing in translation from other cultures and societies: to date these include the two Latin American gay anthologies (*Now the Volcano*, *My Deep Dark Pain Is Love*), a medieval Arab anthology (*The Delight of Hearts*), a Japanese gay anthology (*Partings at Dawn*), as well as individual books in translation, such as *Adonis Garcia*, *Bom Crioulo* and *Crystal Boys*; and in progress is an Israeli gay anthology.

In the mid 1970s I had already published in *Gay Sunshine Journal* Professor Simon Karlinsky's pioneering, in-depth article on Russian gay literature—reprinted in a revised version in the present anthology—as well as his translations of poetry by Ivanov, Klyuev, Esenin, Sophia Parnok and Valery Pereleshin. In the early 1980s I located a translator who agreed to take on the anthology project, and we began to research material from the Golden and Silver ages of Russian literature (19th to early 20th centuries). Due to personal circumstances, however, the translator soon had to withdraw from the project, and I shelved it, intending to return to it in a later year. That decision proved to be most fortuitous. In the intervening years Russia underwent its *glasnost* and *perestroika*, and innovative gay writing began to appear in newly established alternative gay journals—similar to the process which followed our own Stonewall in 1969. It became obvious to me that this was the right time to resume the project and to incorporate a generous sampling of the new writing into the anthology. The result, dear reader, is in your hands.

I am convinced that this is a remarkably pioneering book. I would like to thank all those who have made it possible: first and foremost the editor, Professor Kevin Moss. The editor and I would also like to thank all the living authors and translators included for their enthusiastic cooperation. Our special thanks to Professors Vitaly Chernetsky, Michael Green, Simon Karlinsky, Anatoly Vishevsky and Anthony Vanchu for their suggestions and assistance, as well as their superb translations; also to the Russian editors who so generously cooperated with the project (see copyright page for a more detailed list of acknowledgments). My own very personal thanks is due to those who were supportive of my vision in coordinating this anthology during the many years in which it was "in progress"— especially Michael Green.

Vyacheslav Ivanov (1866–1949), left, and Mikhail Kuzmin (1872–1936) in a photo of ca. 1908. From a private collection, Moscow. Ivanov and Kuzmin were housemates but apparently not lovers. See Kuzmin's work on pp. 69–114 and Ivanov's on pp. 140–141 of this book.

Alexei Apukhtin (1841–1893), poet, was a one-time classmate and lover of the composer Peter Ilyich Tchaikovsky.

INTRODUCTION:
RUSSIA'S GAY LITERATURE AND HISTORY

Simon Karlinsky

L ike Russian history, Russian literature can be conveniently divided into three periods: the Kievan (tenth to thirteenth centuries A.D.), the Muscovite (fourteenth to seventeenth centuries), and modern (eighteenth century and later). Kievan history began with the unification in the 860s of twelve East Slavic tribes (ancestors of the modern Russians, Ukrainians, and Belarussians) into a nation with its capital in Kiev. The country's rulers were converted to Christianity in 988. The new religion, which came from Byzantium, brought with it the Slavic alphabet, devised earlier by Byzantine missionaries. The earliest Russian literature, which was also the literature of other East and South Slavic peoples, consisted mainly of historical (chronicles) and religious (prayer books, sermons, lives of saints) genres.

As Vasily Rozanov pointed out in 1913, instances of homosexual love can be found in certain lives of saints (*vitae*) that date from the Kievan period. For example, "The Legend of Boris and Gleb," written by an anonymous monk at the turn of the eleventh century, enjoyed a wide circulation not only in Russia, but also in other Eastern Orthodox countries, such as Bulgaria, Serbia, and even the non-Slavic-speaking Rumania. (Religious literature was written in all these countries in Old Church Slavic, a medieval South Slavic dialect that had the same function in Orthodox countries that Latin had in Catholic ones.) Combining features of history, hagiography, and lyric poetry, "The Legend" told of the assassination of two young Kievan princes for dynastic reasons. Prince Boris had a favorite squire, George the Hungarian. He had a magnificent golden necklace made for George because "he was loved by Boris beyond all reckoning." When the four assassins pierced Boris with their swords, George flung himself on the body of his prince, exclaiming: "I will not be left behind, my precious lord! Ere the beauty of thy body begins to wilt, let it be granted that my life may end!" Through the standard life-of-saint format, imported from Byzantium, the author's sympathy for the mutual love of Boris and George comes unmistakably through.

George's brother Moses, later canonized by the Orthodox Church as St. Moses the Hungarian, was the only member of Boris's retinue to survive the massacre. His later fate is told in a section devoted to him in *The Kievan Paterikon*, a compilation of monastic lives dating from the 1220s. Moses was taken prisoner and sold as a slave to a Polish noblewoman who became enamored of his powerful physique. For a year, she tried to seduce him, offering him his freedom and even her own hand in marriage, but Moses preferred the company of her other male slaves. Finally, his mocking refusals exasperated the noblewoman and she ordered that Moses be given

15

one hundred lashes and castrated. He found his way to the Kievan Crypt Monastery, where he lived for another ten years. The story of Moses the Hungarian is clearly influenced by the biblical account of Joseph and Potiphar's wife. But it can still be read (as Vasily Rozanov maintained) as a tale of a Russian medieval homosexual, punished because he would not enter a heterosexual marriage.

The culturally rich Kievan period ended in 1240, when Kiev was occupied and virtually destroyed by an army of nomadic Mongol invaders. The invasion was followed by 250 years of Mongol captivity. When Russia regained its independence, it had a new capital in Moscow. The Muscovite period may have been the era of the greatest visibility and tolerance for male homosexuality that the world had seen since the days of ancient Greece and Rome. During the fifteenth, sixteenth, and seventeenth centuries, foreign travelers and ambassadors, coming from countries where "sodomites" were subjected to torture, burning at the stake, and life-long incarcerations, repeatedly registered their amazement and shock at the unconcealed manifestations of homosexual behavior by Russian men of every social class. Among the numerous testimonies to this visibility in travel and memoir literature are the books by Sigismund von Herberstein and Adam Olearius and an amusing poem by the Englishman George Turberville, "To Dancie." Turberville visited Moscow with a diplomatic mission in 1568, the time of one of Ivan the Terrible's worst political purges. The poet was struck not by the carnage, however, but by the open homosexuality of the Russian peasants.

But homosexuality existed not only among the lower classes; it also extended to the ruling monarchs as well. Grand Prince Vasily III of Moscow (reigned from 1505 to 1533) was homosexual throughout his life. He went to the extent of announcing this fact to other gay men of his time by shaving off his beard when his twenty-year marriage to his first wife was terminated—being beardless was a sort of gay password at the time. During Vasily's second marriage, he was able to perform his conjugal duties only when an officer of his guard joined him and his wife in bed in the nude. The son of Vasily III's second marriage, Ivan IV, better known as Ivan the Terrible, was married no less than seven times. But he was also attracted to young men in female attire. One of the most ruthless chieftains of Ivan's political police, Feodor Basmanov, rose to his high position through performing seductive dances in women's clothes at the tsar's court. The nineteenth-century poet A. K. Tolstoy (1817–1875) wrote a historical novel, *Prince Serebriany* (1862), set during the reign of Ivan the Terrible, where he described with great frankness the paradoxical character of Feodor: a capable military commander; the scheming initiator of murderous political purges; the tsar's bed partner; and an effeminate homosexual who discussed in public the cosmetics he used to improve his complexion and hair.

Also bisexual was the False Dmitri, the runaway monk who claimed to be the youngest son of Ivan the Terrible and who overthrew Tsar Boris Godunov to reign for less than a year in Moscow. During the pretender's wedding to the aristocratic Pole Marina Mniszek in 1606, he was waited upon by his lover, the eighteen-year-old Prince Ivan Khvorostinin. The latter, a scion of a noble family of ancient lineage, was attired for the occasion in a dazzling brocaded outfit, which he managed to change to two other equally dazzling ones in the course of the festivities. In his later life, Khvorostinin repeatedly got into trouble with the authorities, not because of his homosexuality or his involvement with the pretender, but because of his satirical writings in prose and in verse (doggerel, really). His satire was aimed at Russian backwardness and lack of culture. He repeatedly asserted the superiority of Western Protestant countries, their fashions and their high intellectual level. Such praise for the West was considered the height of heresy. The young prince was repeatedly denounced by his friends and servants. But he was quite good at talking his way out of incarceration or confiscation of his property. He never got to realize his great dream of going to live in Holland or Italy; he died of natural causes at the age of thirty-seven.

The main reflection of homosexuality in the literature of Muscovite Russia survives in the writings of Orthodox churchmen who denounced the practice. "Sermon No. 12" by Metropolitan Daniel, a popular Moscow preacher of the 1530s, offers an extended panorama of various homosexual types of his time, both effeminate and not. Archpriest Avvakum was the leader of the Old Believers during the religious schism of the 1650s. (The Old Believers broke away from the Orthodox Church because of the reforms in the ritual and in corrected spelling of biblical names instituted by the Patriarch Nikon; in the eighteenth and nineteenth centuries, Old Believer communities gave rise to numerous lesser religious dissenter sects.) In his *Autobiography* (1673), much admired for its style by later writers, Avvakum states that he refused to hear confession of any man who shaved off his beard. On one occasion, Avvakum enraged a provincial governor by refusing to bless his son, who, by shaving his beard, must have tried to look seductive to other men. The father responded by having the churchman thrown into the river Volga. Apart from clerical admonitions, nothing else restrained the homosexual behavior among the men of Kievan and Muscovite Russia.

Beginning with the earliest known Russian legal code, *Russkaia pravda* (*Russian Justice*), promulgated during the reign of Iaroslav the Wise (who ruled from 1019 to 1054) and up to the military regulations of Peter the Great early in the eighteenth century, no Russian legislation prohibited "the sin of Sodom" or any other homosexual practice. As Eve Levin has shown in her book *Sex and Society in the World of Orthodox Slavs, 900–1700*, unlike Western Europe, which often had laws based on Old Testament interdictions, Eastern Orthodox Christianity considered various forms of sexual deviance not as crimes, but as sins, subject to religious jurisdiction. What Eve Levin established was that in this area the main concern was not so much the sex of the participants or the organs involved, but the *relative position* of the partners during the sex act. The woman below and the man above was permitted as the "natural" way; reversal of this position was "unnatural" and a sin. Homosexual and lesbian contacts were thus sinful, the sin being of the same magnitude as the reversal of positions in heterosexual intercourse. It was of no concern to civil authorities and it could be expiated by going to confession, doing an assigned number of prostrations, and abstaining from meat and milk products for several months. Summing up the testimony of foreign and native observers of Muscovite Russia, the authoritative nineteenth-century historian Sergei Soloviov wrote: "Nowhere, either in the Orient or in the West, was [homosexuality] taken as lightly as in Russia."

Only after the increase in travel of Russians abroad during the reign of Peter the Great was it understood that the practices the Russians had taken for granted for almost a millennium were regarded with horror or with fury by those who lived in the supposedly more civilized countries in the West. In the eighteenth century, the open homosexuality of the Muscovite period had to go underground. Yet, at the same time, it made a renewed appearance in the religious dissenter sects that split from the Old Believers during that same century. Two of these sects, Khlysty (a distorted plural form of Christ) and Skoptsy (Castrates) had recognizable homosexual and bisexual strains in their culture, folklore, and religious rituals. The major gay poet of the early twentieth century, Nikolai Klyuev, incorporated much of these sects' lore into his visionary poetry.

By the middle of the eighteenth century, Russian literature caught up with the current West European literary forms. The end of that century was in Russia, as elsewhere, the Age of Sentimentalism. The leading Russian Sentimentalist poet was Ivan Dmitriev (1760–1837). He wrote clever satires, saccharine love songs, and didactic fables. Dmitriev was a government official who eventually rose to the position of Minister of Justice in the reign of Alexander I. In his government career, he was nepotistic, surrounding himself with handsome young assistants, some of whom owed their advancement to the fact that they were Dmitriev's lovers. In his poetry, however, he wore a heterosexual mask, pretending to pine for some neoclassical Chloe or Phyllis. The exceptions are his adaptations of La Fontaine's fables "The Two Pigeons" and "The Two Friends," which he turned into unequivocal depictions of love affairs between males.

With ALEXANDER PUSHKIN (1799–1837), Russian literature acquired its first major figure of international significance. A happily adjusted heterosexual, Pushkin viewed alternative forms of sexuality with an amused tolerance that was not otherwise typical of Russian nineteenth-century writers.

In the fall of 1823, while Pushkin was in exile in the south of Russia, he addressed a remarkable letter to the memoirist Philip Vigel (whose subsequently published memoirs described Vigel's orientation and the homosexual circles of his time). In this letter and an attached witty poem, Pushkin commiserated with Vigel for having to live in Kishinev (now the capital of Moldova) rather than in the civilized city of Sodom, "that Paris of the Old Testament." He mentioned three handsome brothers in Kishinev who might be receptive to Vigel's advances, and invited him for a visit in Odessa, but with the proviso: "To serve you I'll be all too happy/With all my soul, my verse, my prose,/But Vigel, you must spare my rear!" In his poems that imitated the Greek Anthology or Muslim poets, Pushkin assumed the persona of a man attracted to adolescent boys, a literary stratagem that had no correlates in his life.

Pushkin's younger contemporary MIKHAIL LERMONTOV (1814–1841) wrote of homosexual love in the cycle of poems known as his "Hussar" or "Cadet" poems. Written when he was twenty and a student at a military academy, two of the five poems of this cycle depict the sexual encounters between other cadets. Though the theme is treated with clear distaste, the details are so concrete that Lermontov must have personally witnessed the incidents he described. NIKOLAI GOGOL (1809–1852), only ten years younger than Pushkin, was one of the most harrowing cases of sexual self-repression to be found in the annals of literature. Totally and exclusively gay, Gogol spent his life denying this fact to himself and to others, mainly for religious reasons. His stories and plays are permeated with fear of marriage and other forms of sexual contact with women, but Gogol enveloped this theme in such a cloud of symbols and surrealistic fantasies that his contemporary readers failed to discern its presence. A sketch for his second play, *Marriage* (a headlong attack on the entire institution of matrimony), mentioned an official who so loved his subordinate that he slept in the same bed with him, a passage that was removed from the finished version of the play. This brilliant writer committed suicide at the age of forty-three, after confessing his true sexuality to a bigoted priest who ordered him to fast and pray day and night if he wanted to escape hellfire and brimstone.

The two giants of Russian nineteenth-century literature, Tolstoy and Dostoevsky, were men of the Victorian age who regarded all forms of sexuality as impure, distasteful, and dangerous. The theme of homosexuality in the life of LEO TOLSTOY (1828–1910) deserves a special study that will undoubtedly be written one day. In his childhood, Tolstoy kept falling in love with both boys and girls, and recorded such experiences in the first two novels of his early autobiographical trilogy *Childhood* (1852), *Boyhood* (1854), and *Youth* (1857). While serving in the army in the 1850s, Tolstoy was strongly attracted to several of his fellow soldiers. But he noted in his diaries that he rejected same-sex love because his attraction to men was purely physical—he was drawn only to very handsome men whose characters were usually not admirable—while his love for women was based on their personalities and good qualities and not exclusively on their looks. In his later novels, Tolstoy showed male homosexuality in a negative light.

Anna Karenina (1877) contains a brief vignette of two inseparable army officers, whom Anna's lover Alexei Vronsky and his friends avoid, suspecting them, not without reason, of having an affair with each other (Part Two, Chapter XIX). In *Resurrection* (1899), the aged Tolstoy wanted to indict the inequities and corruption of Tsarist Russia. The novel contains an episode about a high government official who gets convicted for violating paragraph 995 of the criminal code. (Criminalization of male homosexuality for the entire population was enacted in the code of 1832–1845, promulgated during the reign of the most repressive of the Romanovs, Nicholas I. The law was hard to enforce and was very rarely applied.) The convicted homosexual arouses the warm sympathy of St. Petersburg high society and, since his sentence calls for resettlement in Siberia, he arranges a transfer to one of the major Siberian cities, keeping the same rank. Later in the novel, a reptilian government-employed lawman (who spitefully railroads the novel's heroine, Maslova, to a Siberian penal colony) defends equal rights for homosexuals and proposes that marriage between men be legalized. Both of these characters were meant to suggest the country's moral decay.

FYODOR DOSTOEVSKY (1821–1881) was far less interested in homosexuality than Tolstoy. In an early novel, *Netochka Nezvanova* (1849), Dostoevsky depicted a passionate lesbian infatuation between two adolescent girls. In *Notes from the House of the Dead* (1862), a semifictionalized account of Dostoevsky's own experiences in a Siberian hard-labor camp, there are veiled indications that homosexuality was practiced by some of the convicts. But in the curious episode that involves the violent and hardened professional criminal Petrov, the narrator seems perplexed about the reasons for Petrov's fondness for his own person. Petrov seeks the narrator out, plies him with meaningless questions just to be in his presence, and constantly does him favors. In recompense, all Petrov wants is to undress the narrator at the communal baths and to soap and wash his body while seated at his feet. The narrator (who clearly stands for Dostoevsky) offers several tentative psychological explanations for Petrov's behavior but finds them all unsatisfactory. The most obvious explanation of all, which is that Petrov found the narrator physically attractive and desirable, just did not occur to Dostoevsky.

Some of the less-known Russian writers of the second half of the nineteenth century also touched on homosexual themes. Ivan Kushchevsky (1847–1876) was a radical writer who lived only long enough to write a volume of stories and the satirical novel *Nikolai Negorev, or The Prosperous Russian* (1871). The title character belongs to a coterie of idealistic young revolutionaries, all of whom he eventually drops. At the end of the novel, looking for opportunities to start a new career, Negorev encounters an apparent homosexual named Stern, who has "prohibited relationships with several young men." Through Stern, Negorev meets a group of aristocratic young men, who refer to each other as "countess" or "princess," brag of their conquests of other men, and are much given to shrieking. Negorev decides to investigate this group, hoping to blackmail one of them —for homosexuality, the modern reader expects. However, the author becomes confused: The fellow does get blackmailed, but for having gotten pregnant the daughter of a powerful official and trying to obtain an illegal abortion for her. By denouncing the couple to the young woman's father and offering to marry her himself so as to cover up her condition, Negorev sets himself up for a major career in the government bureaucracy. (Unlike in Germany or England of the time, blackmail for homosexuality seems to have been unknown in nineteenth-century Russia.)

Homosexuality became somewhat more visible in Russian life and literature after the momentous reforms initiated by Tsar Alexander II in the early 1860s, which abolished serfdom, replaced an archaic legal system with trials by jury open to press and public, and reduced the censorship of books and periodicals. KONSTANTIN LEONTIEV (1831–1891) was an ultraconservative political philosopher, a literary critic, and novelist, who spent much of his life in consular service in the countries of the Near East. Bisexuality was a theme he often treated in his fiction. In his early novel *A Husband's Confession* (1867), the husband loves his young wife, but he also falls in love with a mustachioed Turk taken captive during the Crimean War. To give expression to this second love, he encourages his wife to become the Turk's mistress and to run away with him to Turkey. Such simultaneous infatuation of a man with a well-bred but drab female and with a robust and colorful male is also the situation in Leontiev's best-known novel, *The Egyptian Dove* (1881). His story "Hamid and Manoli," published in 1869, is an account of a love affair between two men, a Turk and a Cretan, which ends in a bloody tragedy because of the prejudices of the Cretan's Christian family. It is the only piece of Russian literature of the nineteenth century that denounces the ugliness of homophobia.

One of the greatest Russian celebrities in the second half of the nineteenth century, both at home and abroad, was the explorer and author of travel books Nikolai Przhevalsky (1839–1888). His accounts of his travels and adventures (such as his famous discovery of the undomesticated horse, *Equus przevalskii*) were best-sellers in Russia and were widely popular in translation in England and America. A recent biography by Donald Rayfield showed that each of Przhevalsky's expeditions was planned to include a young male lover-companion. The great love of his life was Piotr Kozlov, who spent Przhevalsky's last years with him and who later became a noted explorer in his own right. The literary qualities of Przhevalsky's books were greatly admired by Anton Chekhov, who in his obituary of the explorer called him "a hero as vital as the sun." Vladimir Nabokov, in the most personal and perfect of his Russian novels, *The Gift*, based the character of the protagonist's father on Przhevalsky (minus his homosexuality). Nabokov's description of the father's expeditions to the remote regions of Central Asia is a set of variations on themes from Przhevalsky's writings.

The decade of the 1890s saw a mass emergence of lesbians and gay men on the Russian cultural scene. There were several quite visible gay grand dukes (brothers, uncles, or nephews of the last three tsars). The most overt of them was the Grand Duke Sergei Alexandrovich (1857–1905), brother of Alexander III and uncle of Nicholas II, who appeared with his current lover at official functions and at the theater and opera. Close to the tsar's court was the reactionary publisher Prince Vladimir Meshchersky. When the latter got involved in a scandal because of his affair with a bugle boy from the imperial marching band in the late 1880s, Tsar Alexander III ordered the case to be quashed and the witnesses silenced. An associate of the Grand Duke Sergei and of Meshchersky was the poet Alexei Apukhtin (1841–1893), author of flashy salon lyrics and a classmate and one-time lover of Peter Tchaikovsky. Apukhtin's and Tchaikovsky's orientation was generally known, as was that of the liberal lesbian publisher Anna Yevreinova (1844–1919) and the poet and editor Polyxena Soloviova (1867–1924). Both of these women lived openly with their female partners, arrangements that were accepted by their families and by society. The association of critics and artists, "The World of Art," headed by Sergei Diaghilev, which in 1898 launched their epochal journal of the same name, was predominantly gay. It was on the pages of that journal that the Symbolist poet ZINAIDA GIPPIUS (1869–1945) published in 1899 her travelogue "On the Shores of the Ionian Sea," where she described in detail the homosexual colony at Taormina in Sicily, which was grouped around Baron Wilhelm von Gloeden, the pioneer photographer of male nudes. Elsewhere, Gippius published an extended account of a gay and lesbian bar that she had visited in Paris.

The massive, nationwide uprising known as the Revolution of 1905 forced Nicholas II to issue his October Manifesto, which authorized a parliamentary system, legalized all political parties, and virtually abolished preliminary censorship of books and periodicals. From 1906 onward, there appeared in Russia lesbian and gay poets, fiction writers, and artists who saw in the new freedom of expression a chance to describe their lifestyles in an honest and affirmative manner. MIKHAIL KUZMIN (1872–1936), the most outspoken, prolific and well-known of Russia's gay writers, made his literary debut in 1906, when the prestigious art journal *Vesy* (Libra) serialized his autobiographical novel *Wings*.

Published in book form one year later, *Wings* used the format of the *Bildungsroman* (novel of self-education), following the example of such Western classics as Goethe's *Wilhelm Meister* and Flaubert's *Sentimental*

Education. The young Ivan (Vanya) Smurov's growing attraction to his older friend Larion turns to fear and revulsion when he learns that Larion moves in St. Petersburg's gay circles and patronizes a gay bathhouse. Vanya learns to accept his own feelings after he stays with an Old Believer family on the Volga who tell him that any form of love is better than repression and hatred. Vanya discovers that he cannot respond sexually to women; then he takes an eye-opening trip to Italy. The novel ends with Vanya accepting Larion's offer to live and travel together, a decision that makes him feel as if he had grown wings.

On its first appearance, *Wings* was attacked as pornographic by both the conservative and left-wing publications. But the novel's acclaim by the leading poets and critics of the day soon put Kuzmin beyond the reach of journalistic sniping. It was as a poet that Kuzmin soon acquired the stature of a major figure. Despite the themes of gay love and gay sex that permeated his poetry, it was extolled by the greatest poets of the age, from Alexander Blok to Vladimir Mayakovsky. Between 1906 and the early 1920s, Kuzmin wrote and published several other novels, many short stories, plays, and a great deal of poetry. His plays on gay themes, such as *Dangerous Precaution* (1907) and *The Venetian Madcaps* (1914) were performed at professional theaters and at amateur theatricals. A whole generation of Russian gay men in the decade before the October Revolution saw Kuzmin as their spokesman. His poetry and *Wings* became their catechism.

Much gay literature was published in Russia during the first two decades of our century. The leading Symbolist poet VYACHESLAV IVANOV (1866–1949) brought out in 1911 his much-acclaimed book of verse *Cor Ardens*, which contained a section called "Eros" about the married poet's homosexual experiences. Ivanov's wife, LYDIA ZINOVIEVA-ANNIBAL (1866–1907), specialized in the topic of lesbian love. Her short novel *Thirty-Three Freaks* and her collection of stories *The Tragic Zoo* (both 1907) were much discussed in the press and made lesbian love a better-known phenomenon. Around 1910, there appeared in Russia a group of poets called "peasant," not so much because of their origins, but because the survival of the peasant way of life in the twentieth century and a sort of peasant separatism from the rest of society were their central concerns. The undisputed leader of this group was NIKOLAI KLYUEV (1887–1937). Born in a peasant family that belonged to the Khlysty sect, Klyuev learned (and taught his followers) how to combine his native village folklore with the modernist style and versification developed by the Russian Symbolist poets. Klyuev's undisguised homosexuality did not prevent most critics and intellectuals of the time from considering him the leading literary spokesman for the whole of Russian peasantry.

Klyuev's poetry, with its crowded imagery and a tone akin to magic spells and incantations, served as a model for a whole school of poets and fiction writers. The most notable of his disciples was SERGEI ESENIN (1895–

1925), much better known in the West because of his brief marriage to the dancer Isadora Duncan. For about two years (1915–1917), Klyuev and Esenin lived together as lovers and wrote about it in their poetry. Although married during his short life to three women, Esenin could write meaningful love poetry only when it was addressed to other men.

His last poem, which was also his suicide note, was addressed to a young Jewish poet who had spent the night with him a few days earlier. Because Esenin's poetry was an object of a veritable cult in the last decades of the Soviet system, all references to his homosexuality, in his poetry and in memoirs about him, were banned. Most Russians today respond with stupefaction or rage when this aspect of his life and writings is mentioned.

The February Revolution of 1917 brought to power moderate democrats and libertarian Socialists and it turned the country into a democracy for the next eight months. But the seizure of power by Lenin and Trotsky in October led to the negation and reversal of all the rights that homosexual and lesbian writers and artists had gained through the revolutions of 1905 and February 1917. Because the most visible homosexuals of the prerevolutionary decades belonged to royalty or aristocracy (the grand dukes, Meshchersky) or were politically ultraconservative (Leontiev, Przhevalsky, Tchaikovsky), the Bolshevik government assumed from the start that homosexuality was the vice of upper-class exploiters. Lenin himself, who had set out to create the Soviet Union in his own image, was a blue-nosed Puritan in sexual and cultural matters. Lenin was shocked that in Germany women were allowed to read Freud and he declared unequivocally that he saw *any* kind of sexual liberation as antisocial and non-Marxist.

Much has been written in Germany and England in the 1920s and in America from the 1970s on about the supposed abrogation by the Bolsheviks of all antihomosexual laws after they came to power. What they actually abrogated was the entire Criminal Code of the Russian Empire, of which paragraphs 995 and 996 were a very small portion. A new criminal code was promulgated in 1922 and amended in 1926. This new code did not mention sexual contacts between consenting adults, which meant that male homosexuality was legal. (Lesbianism was never criminalized in Russia.) But as discovered recently, there were two show trials staged right after the appearance of the 1922 code. One trial was of a group of Baltic Fleet sailors who had rented a large apartment in which to receive their gay lovers and friends. The other one involved a lesbian couple, one of whom had changed her name to its masculine form and took to wearing male clothes so that she and her lover could be seen as spouses. The trials were publicized only locally; internationally, the Soviet Union pretended to have the most liberal legislation on sexuality in the world until the late 1920s. The local press accounts recognized that homosexuality did not violate any Soviet law, but stressed that overt homosexual behavior should be punished because the condition is contagious and might lead young people to imitate the behavior of the gay sailors or the lesbian couple.

The flowering of gay and lesbian poetry, fiction, drama, and art that existed during the decade that preceded the October Revolution was gradually stifled in the 1920s. The right to print gay-affirmative works, won after the Revolution of 1905, did not become extinct until the late 1920s. Such acclaimed figures of earlier times as Kuzmin and Klyuev were doing their best work during that decade. But their books could no longer be advertised or receive favorable reviews in the Soviet press. One of the worst casualties of these new conditions was the fine lesbian poet SOPHIA PARNOK (1885–1933). Her two most important books of verse, *Music* (1926) and *In a Hushed Voice* (1928), were greeted by total silence in the press, and no one but the poet's friends knew that these books were published. (In the 1970s, the Soviet scholar Sophia Poliakova wrote the biography of Parnok and prepared an edition of her poetry, which she sent abroad to be published. This brought Parnok the recognition she was denied in her lifetime.)

Among the numerous talented poets and fiction writers who made their debuts in the 1920s, there was not a single openly lesbian or gay figure. By 1922, numerous noted writers had emigrated to the West, among them the great bisexual poet MARINA TSVETAEVA (1892–1941), who did her most important writing while in exile; also, the openly gay critic GEORGY ADAMOVICH (1894–1972) and gay poet ANATOLY STEIGER (1907–1944); while gay poet VALERY PERELESHIN (1913–1992) emigrated to China and later to Brazil. The most important novelist produced by the Russian emigration, Vladimir Nabokov (1899–1977), later an American writer, had homosexual characters in many of his fictions, though he usually wrote of them in a sarcastic tone.

Of the gay writers who stayed in Russia, Kuzmin and Parnok could no longer publish their work after the late 1920s. Esenin was driven to suicide in 1925, and Klyuev was sent to a gulag camp, where he died. Stalin's criminalization of male homosexuality in 1933 led to the worst stigmatization and persecution of homosexuals in Russia's history. The mass arrests in 1934 and periodic crackdowns since that time led to the virtual invisibility of gay men and lesbians in Russian life and literature for the next four decades. Only in the 1970s did there appear underground gay writers, such as the poet GENNADY TRIFONOV (b. 1945), who served a hard labor sentence from 1976 to 1980 for privately circulating gay poetry in manuscript; and the fiction writer YEVGENY KHARITONOV, who died at the age of forty in 1981, but was published to great acclaim in 1993. With the coming of *glasnost*, gay figures of the past, such as Leontiev and Kuzmin, have been reprinted; a number of gay periodicals have appeared; and foreign gay novels by Marcel Proust and James Baldwin have been translated. Despite the present chaotic conditions in Russia, the recent decriminalization of homosexuality by Boris Yeltsin's government suggests that the future of Russian gay literature might well turn out to be promising.

BIBLIOGRAPHY

Burgin, Diana Lewis. "Laid Out in Lavender: Perception of Lesbian Love in Russian Literature and Criticism of the Silver Age, 1893-1917." *Sexuality and the Body in Russian Culture*. Jane T. Costlow, Stephanie Sandler, and Judith Vowles, eds. Stanford: Stanford University Press, 1993: 177-203.

G. R. "Protsessy gomoseksualistov" [Legal proceedings against homosexuals]. *Ezhenedel'nik sovetskoi iustitsii* [*Soviet Justice Weekly*] 33 (1922): 16-17.

Herberstein, Sigismund von. *Description of Moscow and Muscovy*. Bertold Picard, ed. J. B. C. Grundy, trans. London: Dent, 1966.

Hopkins, William. "Lermontov's Hussar Poems." *Russian Literature Triquarterly* 14 (1976): 36-47.

Karlinsky, Simon. *Marina Tsvetaeva. The Woman, Her World and Her Poetry*. Cambridge: Cambridge University Press, 1987 or 1988.

———. "Russia's Gay Literature and Culture: The Impact of the October Revolution." *Hidden from History. Reclaiming the Gay and Lesbian Past*. Martin Bauml Duberman, Martha Vicinus, and George Chauncey, Jr., eds. New York: New American Library, 1989: 348-364.

———. "Russia's Gay History and Literature. (11th-20th Centuries)." *Gay Sunshine* 29/30 (1976): 1-7. Reprinted in *Gay Roots. Twenty Years of Gay Sunshine*. Winston Leyland, ed. San Francisco: Gay Sunshine Press, 1991:81-104.

———. *The Sexual Labyrinth of Nikolai Gogol*. Cambridge: Harvard University Press, 1976. Paperback reissue, Chicago: University of Chicago Press, 1992.

Kozlovskii, Vladimir. *Argo russkoi gomosek-sual'noi subku'ltury* [*The Slang of Russian Homosexual Subculture*]. Benson, Vt.: Chalidze Publications, 1986.

Levin, Eve. *Sex and Society in the World of Orthodox Slavs, 900-1700*. Ithaca, N.Y.: Cornell University Press, 1989.

Moss, Kevin (Editor). *Out of the Blue: Russia's Hidden Gay Literature—An Anthology*. San Francisco: Gay Sunshine Press, 1997.

Olearius, Adam. *The Travels of Olearius in Seventeenth-Century Russia*. Samuel Baron, ed. Stanford: Stanford University Press, 1967.

Poznansky, Alexander. *Tchaikovsky. The Quest for the Inner Man*. Boston: Schirmer, 1991.

Rayfield, Donald. *The Dream of Lhasa: The Life of Nikolai Przhevalsky, Explorer of Central Asia*. Athens: Ohio University Press, 1976.

Rozanov, Vasilii. *Liudi lunnogo sveta* [*People of lunar light*]. 2d ed. St. Petersburg: Ivan Mitiurnikov, 1913.

Turberville, George. "To Dancie." *Rude and Barbarous Kingdom*. Lloyd E. Berry and Robert O. Crommey, eds. Madison: University of Wisconsin Press, 1968.

Zen'kovskii, Sergei. "Drug Samozvantsa, eretik i stikhotvorets. Kniaz'Ivan Khvorostinin" [The Pretender's friend, heretic and poet. Prince Ivan Khvorostinin]. *Opyty* 6 (1956): 77-88.

Zlobin, Vladimir. *A Difficult Soul. Zinaida Gippius*. Simon Karlinsky, ed. Berkeley: University of California Press, 1980.

I

GAY THEMES IN GOLDEN AGE LITERATURE
(19th Century)

The adolescent Pushkin—from an engraving by E. Heitman that suggests Pushkin's black ancestry (he was an octoroon).

Self-portrait drawing by Pushkin with caricature aspects.

Alexander Pushkin (1799–1837)

ALEXANDER PUSHKIN (1799–1837) is the greatest and best-loved figure in Russian letters. His poetry, prose, and drama set the standard for Russian literature and in many ways created the modern literary language. He was one of the first to make a living by his writing, and his Romantic political verse often got him into trouble with the authorities. Later in his life, Tsar Nicholas I acted as his personal censor. As Michael Green points out, Pushkin was not gay, but he was what we would call gay-friendly, as can be seen from a joking letter Pushkin wrote to his wife about his gay friend Wiegel: "Tell Princess Viazemskaya that she need not worry about the portrait of Wiegel and that *from that side* my honest conduct is above suspicion; but out of respect for her request I will place his portrait *behind* all the others." (to N. N. Pushkina, 21 October 1833)

IMITATION OF THE ARABIC

[Podrazhanie arabskomu, 1835]

Translated by Michael Green

Sweet lad, tender lad,
Have no shame, you're mine for good;
We share a sole insurgent fire,
We live in boundless brotherhood.

I do not fear the gibes of men;
One being split in two we dwell,
The kernel of a double nut
Embedded in a single shell.

Self-portrait drawing by Pushkin (bottom). The other head (top) is probably that of Nikolai Rayevsky ("we loved each other," Pushkin says in a dedication addressed to him).

29

A PUSHKIN PUZZLE

Michael Green

for Gore Vidal

THE POEM "Imitation of the Arabic" (printed on the previous page) is likely to take the non-Russian reader by surprise. Such sentiments are not expected of so confirmed a womanizer as Alexander Pushkin, whose great "novel in verse," *Eugene Onegin*, might well be said to have set the pattern for the fictional treatment of relations between the sexes in nineteenth-century Russian narrative: a lyrical, noble-spirited heroine disappointed by a caddish, if brilliant, hero. What are we to make of it?

This "Imitation of the Arabic" dates from 1835; its author was killed in a duel in January 1837. The poem is to be found in the third volume of a Soviet "complete" (if censored) edition of his work. Although in general liberally supplied with scholarly notes, the edition has no more to tell us about this particular poem than that it did not appear in print during the poet's lifetime—not a word about Pushkin's acquaintance with Arabic literature, no suggestion of a poem on which it might have been modeled. Can this enigmatic little piece be no more than a literary exercise? It would, of course, be as absurd to recruit Pushkin for gay liberation as it would be, on the strength of his Abyssinian great-grandfather Annibal, to claim him as a precursor of black nationalism—even if he did refer to his "nigger profile" as well as to "the skies of my Africa." This said, though, let us not ignore the poem's uncanny anticipation of the mood of a gay pride manifesto: "Have no shame . . ."; "I do not fear the gibes of men . . ."

Soviet scholarship, at once provincial and prudish, was more than a little uncomfortable with this aspect of Russia's supreme national genius. Pushkin's attitude to the physical expression of desire between males (to avoid such an anachronism as "homosexuality") seems to have been one of cheerful and benign acceptance. A friend from the scapegrace underground literary clubs of his student days was Filipp Filippovich Wiegel, a career diplomat, later Vice-Governor of Bessarabia, and the author of some fascinating reminiscences that have yet to be published in full. Wiegel made no secret of his sexual preference, and Pushkin, in response to his old pal's invitation to pay him a visit in "the accursed town of Kishinev," where he had just completed three years exile, delivered himself of a missive (it survives in a rough draft) that is unique in the correspondence of one of Russia's most entertaining letter writers. Here are some passages of interest:

> You are bored in the godforsaken hole where I was bored for three years. I want to distract you if only for a minute—so I'll pass on the information you asked me for in your letter to Shvarts. Of your three acquaintances, the smallest could

be put to good use; N.B. he sleeps in the same room as his brother Mikhail, and what they get up to really makes the whole place shake—that should enable you to draw certain conclusions, which I entrust to your experience and good sense. The oldest brother is as stupid as a bishop's crosier, as you have already noted. Vanka jacks off.

Which of this well nigh anonymous fraternal trinity can Vanka be? Or is he some other available lad? We shall never know. Odd that Wiegel has requested this rather specialized information in a letter to Dmitri Maximovich Shvarts, an official in the service of the governor of southern Russia, Pushkin's anglomane bugbear Count Vorontsov. Could a surreptitious pederastically-predisposed cabal have been flourishing under the count's very nose? But let us give Pushkin his due: the Sodom mentioned toward the end of the letter to Wiegel is associated with incest rather than the "vice" for which its name has become a byword:

I drink like Lot of Sodom, and regret that I don't have a single daughter with me. The young folk got together the other day. I was chief carouser—we all got drunk and made the rounds of the brothels.

The prose portion of the letter is preceded by a rhymed diatribe against a town of which a lengthy involuntary sojourn had given him a cordial detestation. Here are the concluding lines:

But in Kishinev, as you know all too well,/You won't find any lovely ladies,/ Or a madam, or a bookseller./I lament your sad fate!/Toward evening, perhaps/ three handsome lads will come your way;/But anyway, my friend,/As soon as I have some free time/I shall present myself;/I'll be happy to be of service to you/ With verse, with prose, with all my heart,/But, Wiegel—have mercy on my ass!

Pushkin follows this outrageous—and of course famous—final line with something in the nature of an apology: "This is verse, and consequently not to be taken seriously—don't be cross but give us a little smile, dear Filipp Filippovich." It is curious, and somehow very Pushkinian, that the poet does not address his correspondent in the *tu* form (except in the poem) but in the more formal second person plural: Wiegel was not a close friend.

Pushkin was to give his most ambiguous expression of the theme of sexual nonconformism in a poem of a mere three lines published in 1826. Titled "Sappho," this poetic jotting is concerned, as the editorial note informs us, with the love of the Greek poetess for Phaon:

O happy youth, you've captured me with all:
Your spirit proud and ardent and urbane,
And with the girlish beauty of first youth.

Sappho, whose name and the name of whose island, Lesbos, were later to denote the form of love of which she is the most famous exemplar, is made to praise the beauty ("girlish," naturally) of a young man. Pushkin would not have been a whit put out—rather the reverse, it is safe to assume—by the assertion of modern scholarship that "the familiar story of Sappho's love for Phaon, and suicide by leaping into the sea from the Leucadian cliff is a transparent later forgery." An attempt to clean up the lady's act?

A decade later, in the last year of his creative life, Pushkin was to hymn the decidedly ungirlish beauty of a stripling in an epigram in the style of the Greek Anthology, using the elegiac meter that is as artificial in Russian as it is in English (yes, another literary exercise). The poem is one of a pair of quatrains that appeared in the December 1836 number of the *Art Gazette* as adornment to an article by the obsequiously patriotic drama-turge Nestor Kukolnik (*The Hand of the Almighty Saved the Fatherland*) titled "A St. Petersburg Exhibition at the Imperial Academy of the Arts." The more memorable of these two quatrains, each of which is inspired by a statue of a Russian peasant youth demonstrating a Russian peasant sport, "On the Statue of a player at *Svaika*" (a heavy nail that has to be cast into a ring) connects the Russian youth with the classical Greek ideal of the discus thrower:

Full of beauty, full of tension, to effort a stranger, a stripling,
　　Slender, sinewy, light as air—is reveling in the nimble sport!
Here's a fitting companion for you, O Discobulus! Worthy, by my oath,
　　When sporting's done with, to rest beside you, locked in amicable
　　　　embrace.

In an erudite article, "Pushkin's Anthological Epigrams," published in 1986, S. A. Kibalnik, a Soviet scholar, observes drily that the four late Pushkin epigrams (of which our *Svaika* poem is one) are all addressed to a "Youth," adding that:

Epigrams either addressed to youths or describing them are extremely rare in the Russian anthological tradition and very frequent in the Greek. . . .

We shall follow Mr. Kibalnik's admirable reticence and make no further comment. And what of the remaining two epigrams addressed to youths? Both were unpublished during Pushkin's lifetime. The first, which dates from January 1833, offers the Russian urchin a couplet's worth of sensible advice:

Be moderate at the feast, O youth, and Bacchus' sibilant brew
Mingle with water's temperate stream as well as with sagacious talk.

The second, dating from January 1835, mates masculine indifference (or satiety) with feminine perseverance in a roseately sentimental cameo: the youth has suddenly fallen asleep, his head resting on the shoulder of the girl who has been bitterly upbraiding him. She smiles at the sleeper, not wishing to wake him, shedding quiet tears.

Let us turn from the poet's works to his life—or rather to his death. Georges-Charles d'Anthès was the dashing young guardsman (he was twenty-three years old when he exchanged shots with Pushkin) who killed the poet in a duel in January 1837. Prince Alexander Trubetskoi was d'Anthès's army messmate (they shared a billet), and the short memoir "Account of the Relations between Pushkin and d'Anthès," written more than fifty years after the tragic events of 1837, is certainly not intended to blacken the character of the man who had extinguished the luminary of Russian letters—on the contrary, Trubetskoi is evidently much impressed with his companion's worldly success and by his triumphs with the fair sex. It is equally evident that he has no reverence for the memory of Pushkin (whose character is pronounced "unbearable" more than once in the course of this memoir). As a member of the "high society" of which he is writing, the prince is untroubled by the sexual relations he alleges to have existed between d'Anthès and his patron and foster-parent; such relations merit no more than a shrug and the lifting of an eyebrow. Tone and intention are *not* denunciatory:

> He was an excellent comrade, a model officer. He was guilty of a few pranks, but they were all quite innocent, the usual harmless tricks that young folk get up to—apart from one thing, that is, which we only found out about much later. I don't quite know how to put it: did he live with Heckeren or did Heckeren live with him? . . . In the high society of those days there was nothing unusual about buggery [Trubetskoi resorts to a word derived from the French—*bugrstvo*—that is not to be located in the seventeen volume Academy dictionary of the Russian language]. Judging by the fact that d'Anthès was constantly in pursuit of the ladies, one has to suppose that in his relations with Heckeren he played the passive role only. He was very handsome and had been spoiled by his unfailing success with the ladies: his attitude toward them was very much that of a foreigner—bolder and freer than that of us Russians.

What Alexander Trubetskoi is saying here is that the man whose name is familiar to every Russian schoolboy as Pushkin's killer was, not to put too fine a point on it, the kept boy of his adoptive father, the Dutch ambassador at the court of St. Petersburg, Jacob Theodore Derk Borchard Anne, Baron van Heckeren, to give him his full name. Could this really have been so? A distinguished French biographer of Pushkin discounts the story: "If Heckeren had been known as a homosexual, Pushkin would have been only too happy to add that charge to the list of accusations in his final letter of insult. . . . Even more significant is the fact that throughout the long and brilliant careers of both men, no such allegation was ever made about either of them. . . .''

One somehow fails to be convinced by Henri Troyat's certainties. Can there really have been not so much as a breath of scandal concerning the relations between the middle-aged antique-collecting bachelor "known throughout St. Petersburg for his malicious tongue" and the strapping young horseguardsman with whom he had contrived a domestic partnership? And this in a city where, to repeat Trubetskoi, "there was nothing unusual about buggery"? (a free translation of "V vysshem obshchestve bylo razvito bugrstvo": buggery was developed in high society). Troyat somewhat undermines his own case by quoting the words of one of Pushkin's closest friends, Prince Peter Viazemsky: "Baron Heckeren was known for his immorality; he surrounded himself with shamefully depraved young men. . . ." Why then did not Pushkin make use of Heckeren's homosexuality, of which it is difficult to believe he could have been unaware, as serviceable ammunition? But Heckeren was a foreign dignitary of noble birth; it is inconceivable that Pushkin would have even considered—as Troyat would have him do—alluding to unsubstantiated rumor of so "unmentionable" a nature in a missive to such an adversary. Pushkin was a gentleman.

Pushkin was not incapable of resorting to the poison dart of the pen in such a case—if the context was purely literary and Russian. Let us examine a squib from the poet's pen that made the rounds of the St. Petersburg of Nicholas I:

> To make the Academy complete
> Dondook the prince has claimed a seat.
> Such honor ill befits, we're told,
> Dondook—how come he sits so high?
> The answer, friends, I'll not withhold:
> Because he has a butt—that's why.

Let us cite the note on this poem in our Soviet edition of Pushkin's collected works, which is unusually forthcoming:

The epigram was passed from hand to hand. It was directed against the Vice President of the Academy of Sciences M. A. Dondukov-Korsakov, who had no scientific publications and who owed his position to the patronage of S. S. Uvarov. The poem hints [!] at the vice linking Uvarov and Dondukov-Korsakov. Thanks to Pushkin's epigram the name "Dunduk" has become a common term.

The Soviet edition, of course, presents a "cleaned-up" version of the final line ("Because he has something to sit down with") in order to avoid the printing of the dreadful word "butt" (*zhopa*). Not only was Prince Dondukov-Korsakov (it is Pushkin who emends the first syllable of his name, our own version of which is an attempt to find an Anglo-American sonic equivalent) vice president of the Academy of Sciences, he also occupied—thanks to his affair with Count Uvarov, the minister of education—a post in which he could be far more of a threat to Pushkin the writer, that of chairman of the board of censors. It was as a writer—and Pushkin the proud aristocrat of ancient lineage was first and foremost a *writer*—that our poet suffered from the attentions of this loving couple. In 1834 Pushkin succeeded in obtaining from the government (= Nicholas I: *L'état c'est moi*) a grant of 20,000 roubles toward the publication of his study of the leader of a peasant revolt some sixty years previously, in the reign of Nicholas' beloved grandmother Catherine the Great (true, at the expense of changing his original title from *History of Pugachev* to *History of the Pugachev Rebellion*: as Nicholas succinctly observed, "A rebel can have no history"). The book was not a success, and a furious diary entry for February 1835 might be read as a footnote to the squib englished above:

> The public is very critical of my Pugachev—and, what's more, they're not buying it. Uvarov is a scoundrel. From his yelling about this book of mine, you'd think it was something reprehensible. His creature Dundukov [sic] (a fool and a profligate) is persecuting me with those censors of his. . . . Uvarov, incidentally, is a scoundrel and a fraud. He is a man of notorious depravity. . . .

Pushkin then recounts how a respected former minister encountered Uvarov walking arm in arm with Vasily Zhukovsky, renowned poet as well as tutor to the tsarevich. The minister takes the poet aside: "You should be ashamed to promenade in public with an individual of that ilk."

Are we justified in labeling a vituperative reference to a literary foe, a hated representative of the powers-that-be—a reference that was certainly not intended for the printed page—"homophobic," to use a term much in vogue in this concluding decade of the millennium? Can the confidant and auxiliary of Filipp Wiegel's games with the likely lads of Kishinev have really been transformed into a "homophobe" in the space of a decade? Let us not forget that 1835, the year of the furious diary entry, is also the year, to bring these musings full circle, Pushkin wrote (but did not publish) "Sweet lad, tender lad," the year that precedes a (published) pair of epigrams in the style of the Greek Anthology, both addressed, in a manner unhallowed by Russian tradition, to the sculptured forms of handsome peasant lads, including the stripling "slender, sinewy, light as air" who is now familiar to us. Did the abounding "African" sensuality of a man who kept a "Don Juan catalogue" of his affairs with women brim over into "forbidden" regions? Did it find complete fulfillment in the penning of an occasional poem, perhaps in an archaic form, engendered by a tradition (Arabic, Greek) with a strong pederastic component?

Our conclusion can only be a series of questions.

Mikhail Lermontov (1814–1841)

TWO POEMS

Translated by Vitaly Chernetsky

MIKHAIL LERMONTOV was Russia's second great Romantic poet. Like Pushkin, he wrote both poetry and prose, and like Pushkin, he was killed in a
duel. Some of his poems dating from his years in the Cavalry Cadet School
are quite bawdy and pornographic. "Ode to the John," and "To Tiesen-
hausen" date from this period.

ODE TO THE JOHN

[Oda k nuzhniku, 1834]

Oh you, the stinky temple of an unknown goddess!
To you I speak . . . to you I appeal from the desert
Of noisy crowds where for so many days I have
Been looking—but in vain—for real human beings.
Accept my humble gifts of incense, volatile and free,
Our nation's poetry's weak and unripe early blossoms.
You are our true protector, and inside your walls
I'm not afraid of any envious evil foes;
Under your cover neither Mikhailov's gaze
Nor Schlippenbach's loud voice will cause our fear.

Just when the cadets rise after the supper,
And grab their pipes, and run, and shout "It's time!"
The crowd busily gathers right behind your doors.
The long pipe has appeared snake-like from a sleeve,
Your hospitable safe haven is finally opened then
With utter care, and fire covers the tobacco,
And then the pipe receives the sweet and cherished smoke.
And when Laskovsky's formidable eye appears,
You safely hide us from his oh so dreaded search,
And then again the white ass of a youthful beau
Courageously appears inside you with no cover.

But then the dark of night envelopes our school,
Cleron has finally made his usual nightly rounds,
And no more music's heard from our old school piano . . .
At last the final candle next to Beloven's bed

36

Has gone out. Now it is the moon that sheds pale light
Onto white beds and onto lacquered hardwood floors.
But suddenly rustling, a weak noise, and two light shadows
Glide over all the way to your desired cover;
They've entered . . . and a kiss resounds through the silence,
And a reddening cock has risen like a hungry tiger;
Now it is being groped by an immodest hand,
While lips are pressed against the lips, and words are heard,
"Oh be with me, I'm yours, oh dear friend, please hold
Me stronger, I am melting, I'm on fire . . ." And one
Cannot recount all the impassioned words. But here
The shirt is being pulled up, and one of them has bared
His satin ass and thighs, and the admiring cock
Is towering and trembling over the plump ass.
Now they get closer . . . And in just a moment they . . .
But here it's time to close the curtain over the picture;
It's time, so that the inexorable fate would not
Transform its praise into a caustic reproach.

TO TIESENHAUSEN

[Tizengauzenu, 1834]

Do not move your eyes in languor,
Do not twist your round ass,
Stay away from wilful joking
With voluptuousness and sin.
Do not go to the beds of others,
Don't let others close to yours,
Do not offer tender handshakes
Either jesting or for real.
You must know, our charming Finn boy:
Youth does not shine for too long
(Even though your lover gives you
Golden coins every time).
When the hand of God unleashes
Storms above your poor head,
All of those who now are begging
At your feet, stretched on the ground,
Will not quench your melancholy
With the sweet dew of a kiss—
Although then just for a cock's tip
You would gladly give your life.

Nikolai Gogol (1809–1852)

NIGHTS AT THE VILLA

[Nochi na ville, 1839]

Translated with commentary by Simon Karlinsky

NIKOLAI GOGOL (1809–52) was a great comic writer and a master of Russian prose. In *The Sexual Labyrinth of Nikolai Gogol* (Harvard University Press 1976), Simon Karlinsky argues convincingly from Gogol's prose and biographical materials that he was a repressed homosexual who may never have had sex with anyone. "Nights at the Villa" is a diary entry describing an affair Gogol had with Iosif Vielhorsky while he was living in Italy.

IT WAS AT Zinaida Volkonskaya's[1] villa that Gogol first met Iosif Vielhorsky on December 20, 1838. The meeting marked the beginning of what seems to have been the happiest and most fulfilling period in Gogol's life. Throughout January and February of 1839, Vasily Zhukovsky [poet and tutor to the future tsar Alexander II] was in Rome, and Gogol acted as his guide. In March, Zhukovsky was replaced by Pogodin. Gogol's pleasure at the company of these two old and admired friends and his gradually growing closeness with Iosif Vielhorsky are reflected in some of his letters of the period and in Pogodin's memoir "A Year Abroad." Pogodin was introduced to Vielhorsky and was highly impressed by his potential as a historian. "The young Count Vielhorsky showed me his materials for a bibliography of Russian history," Pogodin wrote in his memoir. "He's doing fine work, but will the Lord allow him to bring it to completion? The red color in his cheeks bodes no good. Nevertheless, he's working continually."

With the turn of Vielhorsky's illness for the worse in April, Gogol moved in with him at Volkonskaya's villa in order to devote his entire time to nursing him. "I learned at that time that [Gogol] was on terms of intimacy with the young Vielhorsky," wrote Alexandra Smirnova in her memoirs, "but I saw him rarely then and did not try to find out how and when this rela-

---

[1]Princess Zinaida Volkonskaya (1792–1862) was one of the most remarkable Russian women of the age. A celebrated beauty and one-time mistress of Tsar Alexander I, she was also a gifted poet, composer and singer. In 1829 she was converted to Roman Catholicism and thereby incurred the wrath of Nicholas I. The tsar allowed her to keep her property, but forbade Volkonskaya to reside in Russia. She decided to settle in Rome, where her magnificent villa soon became an important literary salon and a magnet for all resident and visiting artists and intellectuals.

tionship came about. I found their intimacy *comme il faut*, most natural and simple." There is a tinge of defensiveness or perhaps justification in Smirnova's tone that implies, as Henri Troyat has pointed out, that the arrangement may have raised a few eyebrows. But for once, Gogol was beyond caring for appearances. He had at last found a friend whose need for shared closeness and affection was equal to his own. His love was reciprocated; but he fully realized that the days of his loved one were numbered. "I live now only for the sake of his dwindling days," Gogol wrote to Maria Balabina on May 30, 1839. "I catch his every minute. His smile or his momentary joyous expression make an epoch for me, an event in my monotonously passing day." And in the postscript of a letter to Stepan Shevyryov, also at the end of May: "I spend my days and nights at the bedside of the ailing Iosif, of my Vielhorsky. The poor boy cannot bear to spend a minute without me near him."

Gogol kept a journal of his vigils at Volkonskaya's villa. Two manuscript fragments from his journal were eventually discovered in Mikhail Pogodin's archive. They are usually printed in complete editions of Gogol's works in Russian under the title "Nights at the Villa." Russian critics, both pre-revolutionary and Soviet, often refer to "Nights at the Villa" as a fragmentary work of fiction.[2] It is, however, clearly a part of a larger personal diary, the remainder of which, given the explicit nature of the surviving portions and the attitudes of the Victorian age, may well have been destroyed. Here is the text of these fragments:

They were sweet and tormenting, those sleepless nights. He sat, ill, in the armchair. I was with him. Sleep dared not touch my eyes. Silently and involuntarily, it seems, it respected the sanctity of my vigil. It was so sweet to sit near him, to look at him. For two nights already we have been saying "thou" to each other. How much closer he has become to me since then! He sat there just as before, meek, quiet, and resigned. Good God! With what joy, with what happiness I would have taken his illness upon

---

[2]The Russian custom of considering "Nights at the Villa" a work of imaginative fiction, and of ascribing the love scenes between men that it contains to sensibilities peculiar to the Romantic age, has its exact parallels in the English tradition of explaining away the similar scenes and sentiments in Shakespeare's sonnets in terms of Renaissance sensibilities rather than homosexuality. In his introduction to the sonnets in the 1974 edition of the *Riverside Shakespeare*, Hallett Smith writes: "The attitude of the poet toward the friend is one of love and admiration, deference and possessiveness, but it is not at all a sexual passion. Sonnet 20 makes quite clear the difference between the platonic love of man for man, more often expressed in the sixteenth century than in the twentieth, and any kind of homosexual attachment" (p. 1746). For a commentator of this type, nothing short of an explicit physical seduction will ever qualify as an expression of homosexual sentiment. And yet, were it a question of a relationship between a man and a woman, no one would have dreamt of denying that an attitude that involved love, admiration, and possessiveness constitutes a bona fide heterosexual attachment.

myself! And if my death could restore him to health, with what readiness I would have rushed toward it!

* * *

I did not stay with him last night. I had finally decided to stay home and sleep. Oh, how base, how vile that night and my despicable sleep were! I slept poorly, even though I had been without sleep for almost a week. I was tormented by the thought of him. I kept imagining him, imploring and reproachful. I saw him with the eyes of my soul. I hastened to come early to him and felt like a criminal as I went. From his bed he saw me. He smiled with his usual angel's smile. He offered his hand. He pressed mine lovingly. "Traitor," he said, "you betrayed me." "My angel," I said, "forgive me. I myself suffered with your suffering. I was in torment all night. My rest brought me no repose. Forgive me!" My meek one! He pressed my hand. How fully rewarded I was for the suffering that the stupidly spent night had brought me! "My head is weary," he said. I began to fan him with a laurel branch. "Ah, how fresh and good," he said. His words were then . . . what were they? What would I then not have given, what earthly goods, those despicable, those vile, those disgusting goods . . . no, they are not worth mentioning. You into whose hands will fall—if they will fall— these incoherent, feeble lines, pallid expressions of my emotions, you will understand me. Otherwise they will not fall into your hands. You will understand how repulsive the entire heap of treasures and honors is that attracts those wooden dolls which are called people. Oh, with what joy, with what anger I could have trampled underfoot and squashed everything that is bestowed by the mighty scepter of the Tsar of the North, if I only knew that this would buy a smile that indicated the slightest relief on his face.

"Why did you prepare such a bad month of May for me?" he said to me, awakening in his armchair and hearing the wind beyond the window-panes that wafted the aroma of the blossoming wild jasmine and white acacia, which it mingled with the whirling rose petals.

* * *

At ten o'clock I went down to see him. I had left him three hours before to get some rest, to prepare [something] for him, to afford him some variety, so that my arrival would give him more pleasure. I went down to him at ten o'clock. He had been alone for more than an hour. His visitors had long since left. The dejection of boredom showed on his face. He saw me. Waved his hand slightly. "My savior," he said to me. They still sound in my ears, those words. "My angel! Did you miss me?" "Oh, how I missed you," he replied. I kissed him on the shoulder. He offered his cheek. We kissed; he was still pressing my hand.

THE EIGHTH NIGHT

He did not like going to bed and hardly ever did. He preferred his armchair and the sitting position. That night the doctor ordered him to rest. He stood up reluctantly and, leaning on my shoulder, moved to his bed. My darling! His weary glance, his brightly colored jacket, his slow steps—I can see it all, it is all before my eyes. He whispered in my ear, leaning on my shoulder and glancing at the bed: "Now I'm a ruined man." "We will remain in bed for only half an hour," I said to him, "and then we'll go back to your armchair." I watched you, my precious, tender flower! All the time when you were sleeping or merely dozing in your bed or armchair, I followed your movements and your moments, bound to you by some incomprehensible force.

How strangely new my life was then and, at the same time, I discerned in it a repetition of something distant, something that once actually was. But it seems hard to give an idea of it: there returned to me a fresh, fleeting fragment of my youth, that time when a youthful soul seeks fraternal friendship with those of one's own age, a decidedly juvenile friendship, full of sweet, almost infantile trifles and mutual show of tokens of tender attachment; the time when it is sweet to gaze into each other's eyes, when your entire being is ready to offer sacrifices, which are usually not even necessary. And all these feelings, sweet, youthful, fresh—alas! inhabitants of a vanished world—all these feelings returned to me. Good Lord! What for? I watched you, my precious, tender flower. Did this fresh breath of youth waft upon me only so that I might suddenly and irrevocably sink into even greater and more deadening coldness of feelings, so that I might become all at once older by a decade, so that I might see my vanishing life with even greater despair and hopelessness? Thus does a dying fire send its last flame up into the air, so that it might illuminate with its flickering the somber walls and then disappear forever.

Iosif Vielhorsky died in Rome on May 21, 1839. His last moments were darkened by Zinaida Volkonskaya's ill-advised efforts to effect a deathbed conversion to Catholicism. Gogol's opposition to this move earned him Volkonskaya's subsequent enmity. On June 5, Gogol wrote to Alexander Danilevsky: "A few days ago I buried my friend, one whom fate gave me at a time of life when friends are no longer given. I speak of my Iosif Vielhorsky. We have been long attached to each other, have long respected one another, but we became united intimately, indissolubly, and utterly fraternally only during his illness, alas." The relationship left Gogol with some of the most cherished memories of his life. It apparently also saddled him with a lasting sense of guilt.

Leo Tolstoy (1828–1910)

"THE IVINS": SELECTIONS FROM *CHILDHOOD*

[Detstvo, 1852]

Translated by Kevin Moss

COUNT LEO TOLSTOY is a renowned figure in world literature, author of such famous novels as *War and Peace* and *Anna Karenina*. He devoted his later years to social reform, espousing a type of Christian anarchism. Basically heterosexual, Tolstoy clearly had homosexual leanings, although his temperament led him to take a jaundiced view of all sexuality. "The Ivins" from Tolstoy's *Childhood* (1852), and excerpts from his diaries of the previous year, show that he was open (at least in confessional autobiography) about his attraction to men as well as women.

"VOLODYA! VOLODYA! The Ivins!" I shouted when I caught sight of three boys out the window in blue overcoats with beaver collars as they followed their young foppish tutor from the sidewalk across the street to our house.

The Ivins were related to us and almost the same age; we had met them soon after our arrival in Moscow and had taken a liking to them.

The second Ivin, Seryozha, was a dark-skinned, curly-headed boy with a little turned up nose, very fresh red lips, which only rarely completely covered his white upper teeth, beautiful deep blue eyes, and unusually lively expression. He never smiled, but either looked completely serious or laughed wholeheartedly with his ringing, distinct, and extremely infectious laugh. His unusual beauty struck me the first time I saw him. I was irresistably attracted to him. Merely to see him was enough to make me happy; for a time all the powers of my soul were concentrated on this desire; when I had to spend three or four days without seeing him I would begin to pine and become sad to the point of tears. All my thoughts, waking and sleeping, were of him: as I lay down to sleep I desired that I should dream of him; as I closed my eyes I saw him before me, and I cherished this image as my greatest delight. I would have dared entrust no one with this emotion, so dear was it to me. Perhaps because he grew tired of feeling my restless eyes constantly fixed on him, or perhaps it was that he felt nothing towards me, but he clearly preferred playing and talking with Volodya, rather than with me; still I was happy, desiring no more, demanding no more, and was ready to sacrifice everything for him. Aside from the passionate attraction he inspired in me, his presence aroused in me another feeling, equally strong—the fear of disappointing him, of offending him somehow, of not pleasing him: perhaps because of his haughty expression, or because despising my own appearance I placed too much store in the advantages of beauty, or most likely (because it is a sure sign of love) because I felt as much fear of him as love. The first time Seryozha spoke to me I became so muddled from this unexpected happiness that I blanched, blushed, and could not answer. He had a bad habit, when he was deep in thought, of staring at one spot and constantly winking, twitching his nose and eyebrows. Everyone thought this habit spoiled his appearance, but I found it so lovable that I unwittingly started doing the same thing, and a few days after we met grandmother asked if my eyes hurt, since I was blinking them like an owl. Not a word of love was spoken between us; but he felt his power over me and unconsciously, but tyrannically used it in our childish relations; no matter how I might wish to tell him everything in my soul, I was too afraid of him to risk a confession; I tried to appear indifferent and obeyed him without a murmur. Sometimes his influence seemed to me difficult, unbearable; but to escape from under his power was beyond my strength.

I am sad to recollect this fresh, beautiful feeling of disinterested and boundless love that died without ever being expressed or returned.

Strange: why is it that when I was a child I tried to be like a grown-up, and ever since I have ceased to be a child, I have often wanted to be like one? How often in my relations with Seryozha did this desire not to be like a child stop the feeling that was ready to be expressed and instead make me pretend? Not only did I not dare kiss him, which I sometimes wanted very much to do, to take his hand, to say how happy I was to see him: I did not even dare call him "Seryozha," but rather "Sergei" without exception, as everyone else did. Every expression of emotion was proof of one's childishness and anyone who permitted himself such emotion was still a "little boy." Without ever having been through the bitter trials that make adults cautious and cold in their relations, we deprived ourselves of the pure delights of tender childhood attachments solely because of a strange desire to imitate "grown-ups."

I met the Ivins in the entrance, said hello, and rushed headlong to grandmother: when I informed her that the Ivins had come my expression showed this news should render her utterly happy. Then, without taking my eyes from Seryozha, I followed him into the drawing room watching his every move. When grandmother said how much he had grown and directed her piercing gaze at him, I felt the same feeling of terror and hope an artist must feel as he awaits the sentencing of his work by a respected judge.

Having asked grandmother's permission, the Ivins' young tutor, Herr Frost, went out with us into the garden, sat on a green bench, colorfully crossing his legs with his bronze-handled walking stick between them, and with the air of a man satisfied with his actions, lit a cigar.

Herr Frost was a German, but of a completely different sort than our good Karl Ivanich: first, he spoke Russian correctly, spoke French with a bad accent, and had the reputation—particularly among the ladies—of a very educated man; second, he had a reddish mustache, a big ruby pin in his black satin scarf, the ends of which were stuck under his suspenders, and light blue pants with straps; third, he was young, had a handsome, self-satisfied appearance, and extraordinarily striking muscular legs. One could see that he was particularly proud of the latter: he considered their effect irresistible with respect to persons of the female sex, and probably with this in mind, always tried to put his legs in plain view, flexing his calves whether he was standing or sitting. He was the type of young Russian German who aspires to be a fine fellow and a lady's man.

It was fun in the garden. The game of robbers was going better than ever; but one circumstance nearly spoiled it all. Seryozha was the robber: while chasing after the travelers he tripped and at full speed hit his knee against a tree so hard I thought it would be smashed to pieces. In spite of the fact that I was a gendarme and my duty was to catch him, I went up to him and asked, concerned, if he had hurt himself. Seryozha got angry with me: he clenched his fists, stamped his foot, and shouted at me in a voice that clearly showed that he had hurt himself badly,

"Well, what's this? After this there can't be any game! Why aren't you catching me? Why aren't you catching me?" he repeated several times, glancing sideways at Volodya and the eldest Ivin. They were playing travelers, jumping and running down the path, and he suddenly let out a yelp and ran to catch them with a loud laugh.

I cannot describe how this heroic act astonished and captivated me: in spite of his terrible pain, not only did he not cry, he did not even show he was in pain and did not forget the game for a minute.

Soon after this, when Ilinka Grap also joined our party and we went upstairs before lunch, Seryozha had the opportunity to captivate and astonish me even more with his surprising manliness and firmness of character.

Ilinka Grap was the son of a poor foreigner who had once lived at my uncle's, was somehow indebted to him, and felt obliged to send his son to visit us very often. If he thought that acquaintance with us could give his son some kind of respect or pleasure, he was thoroughly mistaken, because not only were we not friendly with Ilinka, we paid attention to him only when we wanted to make fun of him. Ilinka Grap was a boy of about thirteen, thin, tall, pale, with a face like a bird and a good-naturedly submissive expression. He was dressed very poorly, but he was always so copiously pomaded that we assured each other that on a sunny day Grap's pomade melted on his head and ran down under his jacket. When I recall him now, I remember him as a very obliging, quiet, and kind boy; then he seemed to me a despicable creature unworthy of pity or even a second thought.

When the game of robbers ended, we went upstairs and began to carry on and show off with various gymnastic stunts. Ilinka watched us with a shy astonished smile, and when we suggested he try the same, he refused, saying he had no strength at all. Seryozha was amazingly charming; he took off his jacket—his face and his eyes lit up—he laughed incessantly and kept thinking up new tricks: he jumped over three chairs in a row, did cartwheels around the whole room, stood on his head on Tatishchev's dictionaries, which he had placed as a pedestal in the middle of the room, and at the same time did such hilarious things with his legs that it was impossible not to laugh. After this last stunt he thought a moment, blinking his eyes, and suddenly, with a perfectly serious expression, went up to Ilinka. "You try to do it; it's really not hard." When he noticed all the attention was focused on him, Grap blushed and, in a voice that was barely audible, assured us there was no way he could do it.

"Really, why doesn't he want to show us anything? What kind of girl is he? He absolutely must stand on his head!"

And Seryozha took his hand.

"He must, he must stand on his head!" we all cried, surrounding Ilinka, who then noticeably took fright and went pale. We took him by the hand and led him to the dictionaries.

"Let me go, I'll do it myself! You'll rip my jacket!" cried the unfortunate victim. But these desperate cries only inspired us more; we were dying laughing; the green jacket was splitting at the seams.

Volodya and the oldest Ivin bent his head down and put it on the dictionaries; Seryozha and I grabbed the poor boy by his thin legs, which he was waving in various directions, rolled his pants up to his knees, and with a loud laugh threw the legs up, while the youngest Ivin checked the balance of his body.

After our noisy laughter, we all suddenly became silent, and the room got so quiet that only the heavy breathing of the unfortunate Grap could be heard. At that moment I was not completely convinced that all this was so funny.

"Attaboy!" said Seryozha, slapping him with his hand.

Ilinka remained silent and kicked his legs in various directions, trying to break free. With one of his desperate movements he kicked Seryozha in the eye so hard that Seryozha immediately released his legs and grabbed his eye, from which unwilled tears had begun to flow, and he shoved Ilinka with all his might. Ilinka, who was no longer supported by us, fell lifelessly to the ground with a thud and through his tears could only say,

"Why do you bully me?"

We were all struck by the pitiful sight of poor Ilinka, his face in tears, his hair mussed, his pant-legs rolled up showing the dirty boot-tops; we stood in silence, attempting to smile casually.

Seryozha was the first to recover.

"What a girl! What a crybaby!" he said, touching him lightly with his foot: "you can't joke with him. . . . All right, get up."

"I told you, you're a good-for-nothing," Ilinka said angrily, and turning away, he began to sob.

"Aha! Kicks me with his heels and still curses me!" cried Seryozha, grabbing a dictionary and waving it over the head of the poor unfortunate, who did not think of defending himself, but only put his arms over his head.

"Take that! Take that! . . . we'll leave him, since he can't take a joke. . . . Let's go downstairs," said Seryozha, laughing artificially.

I felt bad for the poor fellow as he lay on the floor, his face buried in the dictionaries, crying so hard that it seemed he might die of the convulsions that racked his whole body.

"Hey, Seryozha!" I asked him, "Why did you do that?"

"That's great! . . . I hope I didn't cry today when I hit my leg almost down to the bone."

Yes, that's true, I thought, Ilinka's nothing but a crybaby, while Seryozha's a great guy . . . what a great guy!

I did not understand that the poor fellow was crying probably not so much from the physical pain as from the thought that five boys, whom he perhaps liked, had for no reason at all decided to hate and persecute him.

I cannot explain to myself the cruelty of my action. How is it that I did not go to him, defend him and console him? Where did my compassion go, the compassion that sometimes made me break into sobs at the sight of a baby jackdaw thrown out of its nest, a puppy thrown over a fence, or a chicken being carried by the cook for soup?

How could it be that this beautiful feeling was stifled in me by my love for Seryozha and my desire to seem to be the same kind of hero he was? That love and that desire to seem a hero were not enviable qualities! They left the only dark spots in the pages of my childhood recollections.

Leo Tolstoy (1828–1910)

PAGES FROM TOLSTOY'S *DIARIES*
[Iz dnevnika]

Translated by Kevin Moss

29 November 1851. Tiflis

I was never in love with women. —There was only one strong feeling like love that I felt when I was 13 or 14; but I [don't] want to believe that this was love; because the object was a plump maid (though with a very handsome face), and furthermore from 13 to 15 is the most muddled time for a boy (youth): you don't know what to throw yourself on, and voluptuousness, in this period, acts with unusual force. —I fell in love very often with men, the 1st love was the 2 Pushk[ins], then the 2nd—Sab[urov?], then the 3rd Zyb[in] and Dyak[ov], the 4th Obol[ensky], Blosfeld, Islav[in], then Gauthier and many others. —Of all of these people I continue to love only D[yakov]. For me the main symptom of love is a fear of offending or [not] pleasing [the love object], simply fear. —I was falling in love with m[en] before I had a concept of *pederasty*; but even learning of it, the idea of the possibility of intercourse never entered my head. —Gauthier is a curious example of a liking that can't be explained by anything. —Not having any kind of relations with him at all except for buying books. I was thrown into a fever when he entered the room. —My love for Is[lavin] ruined 8 whole m[onths] of my life in Petersb[urg]. —Though it was unconscious, I didn't think about anything except pleasing him. —All the people I loved could feel it, and I noticed that it was hard for them to look at me. —Often when I couldn't find the moral prerequisites that reason required in my love object, or after some unpleasantness with him, I felt hostility toward them; but this hostility was based on love. —I never felt this kind of love for my brothers. —I often was jealous of them with women. —I understand that the ideal of love is complete sacrifice of oneself to the love object. And this is exactly what I felt. —I always loved people who were cool towards me and only valued me. The older I get the more rarely I experience this feeling. —And if I do feel it, not so passionately and for people who love me, i.e. the reverse of the way it was before. Beauty always had much influence on my choice; take the example of D[yakov]; but I never will forget the night we were driving from P[irogov?], and I wanted to hide under the sleigh blanket and kiss him and cry. —There was voluptuousness in this feeling too, but how it got there I can't decide; because, as I said, my imagination never drew lubricious pictures, quite the contrary, I have a terrible repulsion.—

[L. N. Tolstoi. Polnoe sobranie sochinenii, t. 46 (M/L: Khudozhestvennaia literatura, 1934), 237–38.]

47

Drawing by Victor Putintsev, 1994.

Konstantin Leontiev (1831–1891)

KHAMID AND MANOLI

(A Cretan Greek Woman's Story about True Events of 1858)

[Khamid i Manoli, 1869]

Translated by Gerald McCausland

KONSTANTIN LEONTIEV (1831–91) was a writer, philosopher, and critic. He served as a diplomat in the Turkish Balkans and in Crete, where the story "Khamid and Manoli" is set. Conservative and religious, Leontiev was also gay. One wonders what kind of relations he had with the Turks, whom his orientalizing discourse casts as the debauched other (in this respect Leontiev follows the general European tendency of the day). It is likely "Khamid and Manoli" is based on Leontiev's experiences in the consular service.

I

WE WERE TWO children in the family, my brother Manoli and myself. Our house was in Anerokourou. From the road to Soudha you've probably seen two villages on the mountainside. One of them is called Skalaria and the other is Anerokourou. Our home. It is all hidden by vegetation and remains intact to this day. No matter how much those damn Turks robbed and plundered the people, they left the area around Khania pretty much alone, no doubt from fear of the consuls.

Our house has long since been sold and I have no refuge, good Sir. Our whole family was born to a bitter lot. My father was a fisherman and drowned in the sea when my brother was but ten years old, and I a little bit older. For a long time our poor mother provided for us as well as she could on her own by sewing socks or cleaning floors or serving in the monastery. Once in a while she would gather the most fragrant jasmine, string it out on a twig and sit on the road and wait. Some bey would come riding by or rich Turkish women would come walking along or a consul or some other rich Frank with his wife under his arm out on a stroll showing themselves off. My mother would bow to them and give them the jasmine, and they would always give her something in return. I must be honest and tell you that the Turks almost never refused. That's just how they are. Others gave as well and would joke with my mother, "So Elena, you're poor now, are you? Sacrificing yourself for your children? How long ago was it that you were the leading beauty of our neighborhood? Wasn't it about you that they wrote the verses:

Queen of all our girls,
You, Elena, the soul of beauty and goodness!''

These jokes would often come from one particular seller, Stavraki, whenever he caught sight of my mother and he would never leave her empty handed. They say that he wanted to marry my mother despite his youth and poverty, but his relatives talked him out of it. His fate turned out otherwise: the daughter of his master, in whose shop he served, fell in love with him. When the rich father saw that his daughter was pregnant by Stavraki, he beat the youth, but nevertheless gave his daughter in matrimony along with his fortune. And my mother married a fisherman.

Those Franks are worse than all the others. What shall I say, good Sir? If it were up to me, I would tie the Franks to the tails of horses and have the horses tear them to bits. The Turks are dull and uncultured and are taught all kinds of evil. This is why we believe in Orthodoxy rather than in their religion. Once my mother gave the jasmine to a French woman, who yelled, ''Get out of here! I don't like that smell! How shameless all these Greeks are. They just don't want to work!'' Can you believe that? The Greeks are lazy? They don't want to work? Go to hell, you Frankish witch! So, it's shameful for a poor woman to sell flowers? What about your husband, you Frankish bitch! He dragged all kinds of rotten trash from Austria into his shop and now he fleeces our poor simple folk. That's not shameful? Someone buys a rug from your husband, thinking that it's of European quality. A year later and you'll see that the worthless piece of trash has been thrown out. I've seen all kinds of evil from the Franks, my good Sir! And my poor brother Manoli perished at the hands of the Turks. Soldiers crushed him on the Pasha's stairs in front of all the people. That was his fate! He made friends with the Turks, embraced with his soul the whole great shame and sin and perished because of it.

Misfortune has always followed our entire family.

II

About myself there's not a whole lot to say. Three years after my father drowned I got married and was left a widow just a year after that. My husband, Ianaki, was a stonemason and was crushed by rocks that collapsed onto him while he was working.

Things went well during the half-year we were betrothed, and we lived well during our marriage also. I saw him for the first time at a wedding in our village. He had come from another town. He came and stood leaning against a wall with his broad shoulders, laughing and looking at us. It was carnival time, the Maltese porters in Khania sang and danced and the Italians taught our youth to get dressed up—one as a bear, one as a doctor, one as a consular guard in an Arnautian kilt. Our lads called to Ianaki,

"You get dressed up as well!" but he just answered, "Childish nonsense, I'm certainly not going to get dressed up!" And he glanced over at me out of the corner of his eye. I took a liking to him. He found work in our Anerokourou and then came to visit my mother. We served him coffee and it seemed to me that fate was smiling on me. Although he was just a stonemason he had his own house and on holidays he dressed up very neatly in fine light blue cloth. He liked to show off. Being a schemer myself and knowing what road he took in the evenings from work I would just happen to take that same road every third day or so.

"Good evening, Katerina," he would say and if there was no one around he would take my hand. He was handsome without trying to be so, and everybody liked him. I should say that our Cretans are all good looking. Ianaki's face was not as nice as many, but I loved him anyway!

Once he was going past us and showed me that a button had come off his sleeve. "I'm like an orphan here, Katerina, who in Anerokourou will sew it back on for me?" I told him, "I'll sew it back on!" And I did. And when I bent over his arm to bite off the thread his hand shuddered and he said to me, "I love you with all my heart, Katinko, more than anything on God's earth!"

We told my mother who was naturally pleased. "Thank God, fortune has smiled on my daughter!" Ianaki began coming over to our place every day, gave me silver watches, a silk dress, and more silk scarves than I could count! He fixed up our house by himself. On holidays we would invite the girls, he would bring the other guys and we would all dance on the terrace. We're quite free in that way. I remember how my father would say that the Ianinese girls would not appear on the street and would take communion at night. During the day they would not even go to church so that the men would not see them, but nevertheless they say that there was a lot of debauchery around there. It's not like that in our town—you can go out and dance and talk and laugh—just know how to guard your virtue. If you don't maintain your virtue they'll either kill you or you'll be dishonored for life.

Ianaki and I had fun before our wedding and once married we also lived happily. But once we were married, he said to me, "I am jealous, Katerina. Like the line from that song you all like to sing in Anerokourou: I'll kill you, you bitch, Katerina!"

"Don't be jealous," I would say. "I'll never even look at another man." And we began to live like a pair of turtledoves. He bought me a mule and on holidays took me to the monastery and we went together to pray. I cleaned our yard and planted flowers there. We had a little dog and I enjoyed her. She had been born with no tail but was nonetheless a smart dog. We called her Arkuditsa which means little bear cub.

Momma was happy for us and moved in with us to live. When I became pregnant Ianaki fell in love with me even more. And everyone said about us, "What a good family, they are poor but still live well." Only my brother Manoli worried us. He was not a bad youth, but simply foolish and dissolute. He perished thanks to his foolishness! May the Lord God forgive him!

III

At first Mother gave my brother Manoli over to a painter. They went together from house to house painting doors and ceilings. Manoli, poor though he was, still loved his family back then and whenever anyone gave him baksheesh he wouldn't spend it all but always brought something for our mother. He grew into such a handsome lad that he would always turn heads when he walked along the streets. And me? Next to him I always looked like some gypsy and my husband would joke with my mother, "If I weren't so sure that you were faithful to my deceased father-in-law, I would look at every old Gypsy and Arab and wonder to myself, which one of them had been your lover and fathered my dark-skinned wife!"

"Shameless!" my mother would respond, "How shameless to talk that way!" But she never took the least offense.

The three of us lived together peacefully. Manoli was as light skinned as an English lady. His dark curls, his walk, his stature and his hands were all as in a painting. And his eyes were as blue as the sea on a hot day and would become so pretty whenever he would lose himself in thought. But he was not only without guile but also without common sense. He would believe anyone. If one of the rich merchants shook hands with him at the bazaar, he would run home and report, "A great guy! He shook my hand and asked how I'm doing!"

A "great guy" simply because he shook the boy's hand! But of course it would turn out that this "guy" needed something from Manoli and had sent him on some sort of mission. The boy would claim, "No one can fool me. I can see right through them! Everyone tries to watch out, but my eyes are the sharpest of all!" And he would fix his gaze on us as if to prove the truth of his words.

My husband would say, "Don't look at us like that! You'll scare us."

Manoli would take offense.

He was both hot-tempered and timid. Should the least thing go wrong he would respond, "Huh? Where? What? What is it?" run here and there and accomplish not a thing. We often felt sorry for him and often scolded him. That's why his relationship with my husband got bad. It was better while he was living with the painter. The painter was a strict old man, he himself worked a lot and kept a tight reign on the boy. Manoli was afraid of him.

The trouble started when he met a young Turk, Khamid, who ran a tobacco stand in Khania. The Turks themselves called this Khamid "Deli-Khamid" which in their own language could mean either "Crazy Khamid" or "Khamid-the-Daredevil." Khamid was a good and honest businessman. No one ever accused him of cheating in his tobacco dealings. He was a Cretan Turk, from the Selinon area, and he spoke and wrote Greek well. He was no fanatic and in fact he visited the mosque rarely. What did he need the mosque for? Life for him was singing, drinking wine, dressing well and racing around on his horse in front of all the girls. He would pomade his blond mustache to curl upward, throw on a carefully selected hooded cloak, dress himself in trousers of the most delicate and colorful fabric, and decorate his horse in red tassels. He would ride as if he were the child of the best family, the son of some rich bey with the tassels bouncing around on the horse. He had studied with an Italian and played both the violin and the flute. He would go hunting and take the flute along. Having killed some birds he would make his way home joyfully playing his flute. He had no desire to marry although he was already twenty-seven years old. "A wife is a burden," he would say. "The way you have to go and pay court to her family. You can't even buy a simple slave these days, it's already against the law. It's all the fault of the Franks."

Khamid liked wine and drank a lot, but he hated making a fool of himself when drunk. He would sing, enjoy himself and then fall asleep. The other Turks asked him, "Why do you drink with Greeks? The Prophet forbad drinking." As an answer Khamid always had the following story ready.

During the reign of Sultan Murad there lived in Constantinople a drunkard named Birki-Mustafa. Sultan Murad strictly punished all Turks caught drinking and would condemn even those whose breath but smelled of wine. The Sultan himself never tried wine until he met Birki-Mustafa. Once the Sultan was walking at night, looking around the city. He had a guard with him. They came upon Birki who demanded, "Make way for me!"

"I am the *Padishah*!" said the Sultan.

"And I am Birki-Mustafa," answered the drunkard, "and I will buy Constantinople from you and will buy you as well, if you wish." The Sultan ordered that he be taken to the palace and when he finally sobered up on the second day, the Sultan had him summoned and asked, "Where is the treasure, with which you intend to buy both me and my capital city?" Birki took out from under his robe a bottle of fine wine and said, "O *Padishah*! Here is the treasure that makes a beggar into a conquering emperor, and makes the least fakir the equal of Two-Horned Iskender. (They say that there was once such an emperor in Macedonia—the Two-Horned—who conquered the whole world. My brother Manoli had a book about him.) The Sultan was surprised, tried the wine and from that moment on was himself the greatest drunkard in the land and brought Birki-Mustafa into the palace as his personal friend.

Khamid would tell everyone about Birki. The other Turks would shake their heads in wonder and leave him saying, "Without a doubt—Crazy Khamid."

This is how he met Manoli. My brother was painting the door of a coffee house. It was a Friday and many Turks were sitting in front of the coffee house on chairs. Khamid was among them, smoking a hookah. He was smoking and looking at my brother. He watched him for a long time and suddenly cried out: "My God and my faith you are, *boyaci*!" *Boyaci* means painter. He took such a liking to my brother that he called him his God and faith. The Turks murmured to themselves, took Khamid by force and brought him to the religious judge. The judge commanded, "Lock him up in jail. Tomorrow we will investigate the affair." Khamid wasn't worried in the slightest and through the night carefully thought out how he would answer in his defense.

They led him into court. The judge asked, "Is it true, that you called the young Greek painter a God?"

"No," answered Khamid, "I did not call the painter a God, but called God a painter."

"What is that supposed to mean?" asked the judge in surprise.

"Have the boy brought in," asked Khamid. They brought in poor Manoli who was crying in terror.

"Look, Your Honor!" said Khamid. "Look at the eyes of this young Greek. Even full of tears they are so beautiful! Last night these eyes were laughing and their color was even clearer. Who gave them this heavenly color? Who was the painter of these eyes? Must it not be Allah, who alone is all powerful and all good? Who other than He could create such eyes? That is why I called God a painter!"

The judge burst out laughing and all of the Turks said to Khamid, "You are a crafty fellow and you have a lot of daring!" They released him together with my brother.

As soon as Khamid was alone with my brother he began telling him, "Give up your craft my dear child. You walk around with your beauty all covered in paint and it makes me sad. I'm sure you are smart. If you are able to keep accounts accurately, then come to work in my shop. I'll make you a new cloak and buy you a Persian sash and give you a watch. Working for me will be easy. You'll sit in the shop and weigh the tobacco and collect the money when I am not there myself. You can handle money, can't you Manolaki?"

"Yes, my eyes are very sharp, no one can fool me!" answered Manoli.

We tried to convince him not to leave the painter. We were afraid to let Khamid have him. At first he listened to us, but one day he hid his paint and took off without permission and left no word of where he went. The next morning his master began to beat him. It was a Sunday. After a couple of blows Manoli ran out of the house. The master followed behind him and easily caught up with him at the corner. Manoli backed up against a wall and awaited his punishment. His master approached him, stood silently before him for a time and then struck him so that my brother's fez fell from his head. He struck him a second time and blood flowed from Manoli's mouth. There were many Arabs and Turks there. They rushed to my brother's aid and pulled him away from the old man. One old Arab said, "You should be ashamed to beat the child like that. And today is one of your holidays, it is simply a sin!"

The old man saw that there were many ready to defend the boy. He left my brother alone but as he left he said to the Turks and Arabs, "My sin is not your affair but it is the degradation of your mind that makes you feel sorry for the young!" For these words to the Muslims the old man spent two weeks in jail. Manoli stopped obeying us after this incident and he moved in with Khamid. In his new clothes and with his silver watch chain he sat pretty as a picture in the shop of the dissolute Turk.

IV

I always wonder why our family has had so much more than its share of unhappiness. In the course of one year my mother passed away, and my husband was felled by a stone and the Turks killed my brother in Khania. The Father Superior of the Most Holy Mother of God Monastery counseled me by quoting the Apostle James: "You must rejoice in all grief and temptation. It is in grief and temptation that human endurance becomes manifest." The Father Superior was a young man and had studied in Athens. He preached in a very high style and he kept strict order in the monastery. People said that he was proud and loved fancy clothes and money. I don't know about that. I only know that in '66 he went into the mountains to the Sphakians where he fought together with the common people against the Turks. Then he disappeared without a trace. I don't know whether he was killed or whether he hid somewhere. I could tell that he spoke to me from the heart and that he himself did not fear grief or death and that he was not afraid to risk his high position and his security. I remember him as still young and cutting an impressive figure in his golden chasuble looking down from his high throne during the service. I felt so sorry for him, perhaps more sorry for him than for my husband and for my whole family. His words helped me get over my grief. I now save all that I earn so that when I die my daughter will inherit only half of it and the other half will go to erect a large silver candelabra on the island of Tinos. This gives my soul peace. I live and await my hour, whenever it should arrive.

But back then I was not at peace. First my mother got sick and passed away. We felt sorry for her. She had always looked after my baby and helped us in all kinds of ways and we never once heard her utter an angry word! But then she died and we buried her. Manoli came out from the city to the funeral but he didn't seem to grieve much. His head had been completely turned by the kindness and gifts of the Turks and he completely forgot his family.

Around this time there was an uprising of the local Greeks against Veli-Pasha. The people began taking up arms, coming together in mobs and moving toward Khania.

I saw Veli-Pasha myself rather often; he had his summer home in Khaleppa near Khania. The English consul also lived in Khaleppa back then with his wife. The consul was great friends with Veli-Pasha. They invited each other to dinner and took walks together, the Pasha arm in arm with the consul's wife and the consul walking along nearby. We would see this and wondered that a Turk could walk with an English lady on his arm. As if he weren't a Turk but had been born a Frank! We had never had such a Pasha before. Veli-Pasha was from Crete like us. His father had been called Mustafa-Kiritli-Pasha. Kiritli's father held many estates in Crete—they have been sold off only very recently. He owned the largest villa and had the most magnificent gardens near Sersepilia. The moment you walked into them it was like being in paradise! The blooming violets spread their fragrance along the paths. Orange, lemon and poplar trees stood so tall they seemed to reach the sky. The flowing water of the fountains was stocked with red fish. And all around the garden, wherever you looked, you saw wide olive trees, cool shade, singing birds. Spending time there was like finding eternal happiness and peace.

And Veli-Pasha would have lived among us in Crete for a long time if he had not been so afraid to offend anyone.

Political people who understand such things claim that he was not a bad person and had a good education but simply decided to rule independent of the Sultan like an Egyptian pasha or like Prince Aristarkhi had been on the island of Samos. But it hardly matters. I don't know if that is all true or not; but for whatever reason the people began to get restless.

There is a coffee house in our settlement. At the time it was owned by a Greek from Cherigo. This Cherigote (God help us!) was such a patriot. His mustache was incredibly large as were his shoulders, eyes and everything else about him. He could get along with the Turks to his own advantage although above the doors of his coffee house there was painted in blue a kind of flower bouquet that just about anyone with an education or simply with a sharp mind could see portrayed not flowers at all but a Byzantine two-headed eagle. And this Cherigote was also able to get hold of newspapers that the Turks would normally strictly forbid. He would never even say "Crete" but always "the Homeland of Minos" (Minos was our Emperor in Crete long before the Turks arrived). He was great friends with my Ianaki. When there were no Turks in the room the Cherigote would poke my husband in the chest and say, "Such a strong man with such shoulders . . . who never went to war!"

"I'll go to war when the need arises," Ianaki would answer.

Our people began to gather at this Cherigote's place and talk about politics and about the way rights were once given to the Cretan people and then taken away again. These people also began spending evenings at our house. I would be falling asleep in the corner while Kafedzhi would be going on, "Tell me about rights and about Metternich . . . that Austrian Metternich caused the Greeks a lot of trouble. Now in this place a Muslim judge in a turban judges you according to the Koran, but you should have your own demogerontia, your archbishops and elders to judge you. . . ."

"The people are arming themselves," our people would tell him.

"Words are one thing," shouted Kafedzhi, "all words. You Cretans are all liars. Even the Apostle Paul said that you are all liars."

To that my husband answered, "Many years have passed since the Apostle Paul lived. We have become a different people!"

And truly the people began to gather in Sersepilia even from far off villages and my Ianaki said, "It's time for me to go as well, my dear Katerina."

A lump rose in my throat and I began to cry, but I did not try to talk him out of it. A good man cannot shirk from danger in defense of his homeland while others are coming forward. But he never even got to clean his father's gun. Two days after our conversation he was killed at work by a rock. They feared for me and did not bring his body back home but took him directly to the churchyard. It was there that I saw his poor body.

Of course, my good Sir, even a widow's tears must have an end. I cried for a long time for my Ianaki, but I also had to provide for myself and my daughter. I took my daughter and went into the city to find work as a servant.

V

I told you, good Sir, that I went to Khania looking for work in some house. They told me that there was a Catholic woman who just lost a servant. I went to see her and agreed to serve there for a half-lira per month. They wouldn't allow my daughter to move in with me so I took her back to the village and left her to be cared for by one of my relatives.

I lived in that house for only one month, I just couldn't stand it. There was a lot of work, much more than my strength could bear, and they abused me terribly without end. "Why do you take such care to dress well? What are you, some kind of lady? Dressing up with that ugly mug of yours! You look like some kind of whore. You want the men leering at you, huh?" Guests would come . . . and mother and daughter would start at it:

"How are you feeling? How are things?"

"How are we? Well, how are we supposed to be in these barbarous lands? From the servants alone there is no end to the troubles."

"You have a new maid? A Greek?"

"Yes, unfortunately a Greek. The common folk are evil brutes in any country, but nowhere is there a people worse than the Greeks! The uppityness of these people is beyond belief!"

"Indeed, an evil people. They hate us with their very souls and among themselves and even to the Russians they call us Frankish dogs. The Turks are right to beat them!"

And I would stand there holding a tray with coffee or jam and listen to all this.

Both the mother and daughter were filthy! Whenever there were no guests the place was filled with dirty old junk, but just let someone knock on the door! "Jesus and Mother of God! Visitors! Visitors!" they would cry, "Give me this, give me that, open the door, all at once!"

"We are important people," they would say. "Gentility!"

"Ha!" I would think to myself. "Real gentility has nothing to do with people like you. I know, I've been around!"

They were miserly and mean to such extremes. They would have a dessert cake brought to them and the mother would count the pieces herself and lock them in the cupboard. They couldn't eat such a huge cake themselves but wouldn't think of giving it to the household help. Once the mice and insects had gotten to it they would throw it away.

The old man of the house was somewhat nicer but also much more depraved. When he began to toy with me I left. I was sick to death with despair. Where was I to go? I didn't want to go to the Turks, but there was nothing else to do. I won't hide the truth—I received more kindness from the Turks. One good merchant, Selim-Aga, took me into his harem. "Bring your daughter with you," he said, "and let her play and sleep together with our children." There was less work here and I never heard an insulting word. Selim-Aga was a grim and strict old man, but he never called me anything but "my daughter." His wife sat me beside herself at their table and would not allow her children to insult my daughter in any way. If her son pushed my daughter or said anything unkind to her, she would take brazier tongs and give him a lesson in manners.

I had been raised to eat with forks, but they ate with their hands. That was the only hard thing for me. Otherwise everything was fine!

My brother Manoli would visit me often. He had begun to fight with Khamid. Manoli had now become friends with a certain young Morean. In spite of his being a Christian, the Morean was worse than Khamid. A depraved and despicable person! His kilt was always dirty and his face was thin and evil. His world consisted of drinking, fighting, chasing loose women, thievery, and banditry. His name was Khristo Papadaki. I have no idea what he lived on. He himself claimed, "We Moreans are bandits! Clever fellows! One of our villagers goes to Athens with a dirty kilt and a soiled fez and bows to all."

"Where are you from, friend?"

"From Morea (the Peloponnese), my Lord!"

Before you know it he has remade himself heaven knows how! Now he's dressed in a newly tailored jacket and well-made fez and he's standing at the coffee house leaning against the wall. And if the King himself should ask "Where are you from?" he would answer, "Where from? Where are we from?! Why, from the Peloponnese!" and march off prouder than a government minister!

The Turks had chased Khristo out of Crete a number of times for rowdiness and disorderly conduct, but he would always return. The Greek consuls tried sending him to jail by accusing him of murder. But as soon as he began to feel persecuted he would threaten them, "I'll come and show you what a Turk is really like!" And they would leave him alone. This is the kind of bandit that my poor Manolaki became friends with.

Khristo took him to visit those Turkish women who walk unveiled in public and to other nasty places. Khamid learned about this and began to berate my brother and argue with him. Nevertheless he loved him so much that he could never drive him from his shop.

My new master Selim-Aga told me all about this. "*Aman*! (Alas!) Poor Katerina," he said, "what a shame to bring bad news to an orphan and a widow, but your brother will perish. Deli-Khamid's love is an evil thing, but the friendship of a bandit like Khristo is even more dangerous! Manoli will either end up in jail or he will be killed! I heard how Khamid threatened to slash him to pieces if he continued to accompany Khristo to these disreputable places. It's shameful for an old man like me to say such things, but the truth must be told! This friendship makes Khamid terribly jealous and he claims, 'I will never give you up, but will kill you and will myself perish!' This has been told to me by well-meaning people!"

I wept and wailed but the old Aga said, "Call him, together we will talk some sense into him." We called Manoli, and Selim-Aga and I tried to persuade him. But the old man spoiled everything, God forgive him. His talk became heated and he began to insult and frighten the boy.

"Your father was honest and your mother was honest and your sister lives honestly in my home! But you are a deceiver, a depraved bandit! You cannot be admitted into a good house. If you don't reform yourself, I'll eventually have to take this stick and crack your skull, because I knew your father and loved him and I feel sorry for you!"

Aga felt so sorry for my brother he wanted to beat him! He was a simple man and thought that he was doing good, but he just made things worse. Manoli was mortified and when I saw him to the door he said, "Katerina, I will no longer come here! Damn the religion of that old devil and his entire house, and damn his father and mother as well! It seems that any old ass can order me around! He is neither father nor brother to me! Good bye!" And he left red in the face with rage. He walked away from me quickly with only his trousers and the tassel of his fez rustling as he walked. I stood at the door thinking. How he's learned to swear and damn people to hell with his poor little face so pretty and good as the Archangel Michael, whose icon was brought from Russia by our Father Superior! The very image of the icon we all used to go and admire!

Since that time I have not laid eyes on my brother! The hour of his death was near, but none of us knew anything at all.

VI

Our Christians were arming themselves at that time and gathering at the environs of Khania, near Sersepilia and Perivilia. There were about ten thousand of them from different dioceses and villages. Their leaders were many, but the first among them was one young man, Mavroghenni. Even now, when people speak about the time of Veli-Pasha or the time of Mavroghenni, they mean the same thing. They stood around in gardens and under olive trees neither spoiling nor so much as touching anything even in the Turkish gardens and houses. They sent messengers to all the Turkish villagers in Kissamos and Selinon and other settlements and told them not to leave their work and not to be afraid. "We are at war with Veli-Pasha and have no quarrel with you. You are Cretan people like us and have nothing to fear from us."

Nevertheless the foolish rural Turks didn't believe our assurances but rather believed Veli-Pasha. The Pasha sent people to them to say, "Go and save yourselves in the cities, don't believe the Greeks, there are more of them in the villages and they will massacre you there."

He wanted to cause such confusion in Crete that the Sultan would say, "Only you can bring order back, Veli-Pasha! Without you there is no hope."

Our people said that the English consul also intrigued against the Christians.

The Turks fled in hordes from the villages into the city. Women and children rode on donkeys and mules, carting their belongings with them while the men went on foot nearby with their weapons. They all gathered in Khania tired, angry and hungry. They had all left their work in the fields and had nothing to live on. There was no work for them in the city. As you know, our city is crowded, the streets are narrow and the walls around the city are thick. The gates of the fortress are closed at night and there is nowhere to flee unless you want to throw yourself into the sea. The Christians in the city became frightened. When night fell there wouldn't be a soul around, as if brutal death lurked in the streets! What was there to do? Where could you flee?

Our people from the gardens of Sersepilia sent messengers to the Pasha insisting, "The Sultan should return to us the rights we were promised!" But the Pasha was waiting for military forces from Constantinople and wouldn't budge. I saw that the Turks in the city were hungry and angry and that with the crowds there was no place for them to live. Those who lived with relatives made the cramped conditions that much worse and God only knows what those without relatives were to do. Not to mention the heat that had to be endured that summer with small children and the sick and the elderly all living together wherever they could.

Whatever the conditions in their villages the houses were all clean and well-kept. They began to threaten us daily. It became dangerous for Greeks to walk around the bazaar. The Turks harassed our women. Once, on a feast day, we followed the Bishop when he came out of the cathedral. The Turks started harassing the Greek women and the Bishop stopped and shouted at them, "Don't touch the women as they come from prayer! That is forbidden by your own laws and customs!" One Kissamian fellow hid a knife underneath his cloak and wanted to attack the Bishop. The Pasha ordered that the young man be clapped in irons. This enraged the Turks even more.

Our men continued to send their threats from Sersepilia. "If anyone touches the Christians in Khania, we will cut off the water supply and the entire city along with the Pasha will perish from thirst." The city was supplied with good water from Sersepilia and the area even had the name *I manou tou nerou* which means the Water Mother. Where else were the Turks to go for water? In the city there was no other supply of drinkable water and they were afraid to go into the surrounding villages with so few soldiers.

So we suffered like this for a long time. I thought of fleeing the city from fear and the crowds. I thought that it would be better just to eat bread in some village and get by without being paid anything. In the city the nights were the worst. It just got scarier and scarier. When it would be time to lock the city gates and you saw yourself surrounded on all sides by those thick walls that seemed to reach the sky and the Turks were all around you with their grim faces and huge mustaches, the terror was enough to make you weep! As if you had been buried alive along with your innocent child. The Turkish women in the house comforted me and tried to reassure me.

"Don't be afraid, *morè* (silly) Katerina! We won't let anyone get at you! You are safe in our harem, don't be afraid!"

In spite of my gratitude to them I was nevertheless getting ready to leave. "Stay just until tomorrow," said my mistress. "Wash this one dress of mine and then tomorrow you can be on your way."

So I stayed for one more night. My daughter had fallen asleep long ago and I was getting ready for bed myself. Selim-Aga was at the coffee house and had not yet come home. It was near midnight and everything was dark and quiet in the city. Suddenly someone in our household nearby let out a shout. "Slaughter the infidels! Cut them down! Slaughter all the infidels! They are killing us!" In less than a minute there were Turks running from all directions. Fire and shouts and the sounds of weapons and the doors of the houses slamming. Women were crying and children screaming. My legs would have given out from under me had I not thought of my daughter. I grabbed her and ran for the door. I wanted to flee to the Italian consulate since I remembered the consul, Monsieur Matteo, to be a good old gentleman.

My mistress shouted at me, "Don't go out, you fool! We will wrap you in a rug and hide you underneath the couch. Who among the Turks would come here to a harem to kill you?!" But I was not in my right mind. I broke away and ran out into the street. My sleepy daughter was crying with fright as I ran along carrying her.

I don't even remember the faces of the people I ran across. I remember Turkish soldiers running, and officers, and Greeks, and half-dressed Turkish townspeople, and screams.

One thing I saw clearly. A crowd of soldiers had gathered in one place. I stopped and wondered what to do. I saw how one of our neighbors, an old Turkish bey, dashed out of a doorway half-naked and with a hatchet in his hand. "They're killing us! Slaughter them! Slaughter the Greeks!"

A *nizam* (regular army) colonel grabbed him by the throat and struck him in the face. "You're lying! They're not killing anyone!" The colonel took the hatchet from him and pushed him back into the house, locked the door and went on further with the soldiers. They didn't even look at me. But I saw that in the next street Greeks with women and children were running in a mob. I ran behind them and reached the French consulate along with them. We still didn't have a Russian consulate in Crete and the Greek consulate was even further away than the French one. I understood, after all, that France was a great European power and that in their consulate it would not be so dangerous. I knew that although the Franks might despise us they would not allow the Turks to slaughter us without any reason. It wasn't because they felt sorry for us (heaven save us from their pity!), but because they wanted to show the world that there was law and order in Turkey. Every child among us understood these elementary political games. So I ran into the French consul's house with the others. His house was already full of Greeks. At that hour every consul except the English one opened his doors to our people. I don't know whether the English consul was simply out of town or whether he decided to refuse us. Whatever the reason, his doors were closed to us.

The French consulate was filled with groans and weeping. Pale guards were walking around and whispering. The consul himself was also walking around deep in thought, he strode across our legs, he smoked silently. He walked out onto the balcony and stood there listening. He then came back inside.

"Do any of you have weapons?" he asked.

"Yes," the people answered.

He called over the guards and had them collect our weapons from us.

"God help you if one of you should by chance shoot off your gun," he said. "The Turks will think that we are shooting at them from here and then who knows what will happen. Just sit quietly and don't be afraid, you are under the flag of the Emperor of France!"

We calmed down at least a little bit and began to speak softly among ourselves. "What happened?" we asked ourselves.

One Greek told us what had happened. We all listened to his story along with the dragomans and guards and the consul himself. I listened as well and had no idea that his story was about my poor brother. A young Christian knifed a Turk in his bed and wanted to rob him. But his attack was awkward and he ran into the street covered in blood while the bleeding Turk still managed to get to the door of the house and call to the other Turks for help. The Turks all concluded that the Greeks had begun to slaughter them.

"Thank God!" we all thought and crossed ourselves. "Then everything will be alright." We could hear that things had already started to quiet down in the city. We could hear the footsteps of soldiers marching along near the consulate. Obviously a regular regiment had arrived and we became less afraid. We waited a half-hour, and then an hour at the consulate and everything remained quiet. The consul had sent out one of his dragomans, a Jew, to the *Porta*. The Jew returned pale and shaking and whispered something to the consul. They went out together.

Then gunshots began to ring out. More and more frequently they came! We could only lift our arms to heaven and pray for the forgiveness of our sins. The gunfire got ever louder. A guard ran in and said, "The Greek kid that murdered the Turk has been caught by the police and they've taken him to the Pasha in his villa. Thousands from among the Turkish populace have gathered in front of the villa along with the beys and Hadjis and are demanding of Veli-Pasha, "Either turn the Greek over to us to be torn to pieces or we will massacre every Christian in Khania!"

The Pasha didn't want to give him up and insisted that he must be judged in court rather than killed in such a way. When the Turks heard this answer they began to shoot at the windows of the Pasha's house. The situation was at a crisis! The dragoman once again ran off somewhere with a guard.

And we said among ourselves, "They would do better to release that Greek to the people so that the rest of us can be saved! He's a murderer, but what have we done?" And the people began to pray and I too (God forgive me!), began to pray, "Let the Pasha release the murderer to be executed!"

I had no idea that I was praying for my own brother's death! Because it was none other than he who had done the deed and the victim was his very own Khamid. I cry bitter tears to this day when I think back on it!

VII

Have patience now and I will tell you how it all happened that our Manoli murdered Khamid. I learned the whole story later on. It was obvious that Khamid loved him very much and at first Manoli was satisfied with his lot. But then, when Khristo Papadaki and the other Greeks began to tease him on account of Khamid and laugh at him, it became difficult for him. At this Khamid began to threaten him in various ways. "I'll kill myself and you along with me!" Khamid would say.

"Leave him," advised Khristo. "Let's leave for Greece. It is a land of enlightenment and freedom there, but here it is like in Turkey."

"I'll kill you if you try to leave me," insisted Khamid.

My brother began to cry, but Khristo just continued, "Let's leave for Greece. You're a handsome fellow and my younger sister in Patras is even prettier than you. Fair as a carnation she is! No man has ever seen her so much as smile. You will be the first! If you'll just be a man, you'll get her along with a house as a dowry."

"What? Are you saying I am not a man?" asked my brother.

"What kind of a man are you? If you were a man you would have long ago gotten rid of this Khamid who has taken advantage of your childish stupidity and covered you in shame. Kill him and we'll run away together. Take all his money from the cash box and come directly to me once he is dead. I'll hide you on a Greek ship."

That evening Khamid was somewhat drunk. He counted his money right in front of Manoli, seemingly on purpose, so that Manoli wouldn't think of leaving him. He forgot to lock the money up and went to bed. My brother rose and stabbed him in the chest. But his attack was awkward. He got confused and scared and ran from the shop. There arose a commotion among the neighbors and some police on the corner arrested him and took him to the villa.

And what happened was this. When Veli-Pasha saw that they were beginning to shoot into his villa and that the windows were breaking from the bullets and shattering, he became thoughtful. Everyone advised him, "Release the damned Greek kid, he's a murderer."

And the Turks continued to shoot at the villa and shouted like wild animals, "Release him to us! Give him up!"

There was nothing else for the Pasha to do. Should he let all perish for the sake of one? Furthermore, he had very few soldiers and police!

However, he did not release Manoli to be tortured and killed, but he had the police lead the boy up a high staircase. Down below the people seethed like an angry sea. They threw themselves at the staircase and climbed onto it. The police quickly suffocated Manoli with a noose and threw his body down from the staircase to the people below.

The Turks rejoiced. They became barbarians. They tied ropes to the chains binding Manoli's feet and, grabbing the ropes, they ran with shouts and curses through the streets. In front of every consulate they stopped and shouted insults and curses at the Greeks and at all who they considered infidels. And they insulted the consuls themselves most shamefully. In front of the French consulate the crowd stood for a long time shouting insults. The brave ones among us ran to the window.

"The time of your infidel rule over us is coming to an end! It will soon end, you dogs! You costumed jesters! You filthy pimps! We'll tear you all to bits! All of you!"

Surely you yourself understand, my good Sir, how frightful it all was.

The consul, however, went out onto the balcony and convinced the Turks to leave while, at the same time, he looked to see who the major instigators were. The Pasha also noticed these people later and had them all sent to jail. The longest time prison terms were served by one hunchbacked dervish and one old bey. The latter was one of our own from Khaleppa who was always seen wearing silver glasses. He served six months in prison for the uprising.

The Turks finally had their fill of shouting and dragged Manoli's corpse further with the chains clinking against the stones. The crowd followed behind the corpse hollering and laughing. We all crossed ourselves and relaxed. Some began to cry for joy and we all thanked the consul. The Turks threw the body of my brother into a ditch and dispersed to the coffee houses, smoked their hookahs, calmed down and made merry until dawn and boasted about how they had terrified even the consuls.

That was how it all ended. Soon after that Sami-Pasha arrived from Constantinople to replace Veli-Pasha. Troops arrived with him. Sami-Pasha promised to grant the Greeks many things for which they had been asking (he was lying, of course, as you know). The young Mavroghenni also arrived in Khania. Sami-Pasha rode in on horseback, and Mavroghenni walked beside him so that all would see how the Cretan Christians had made up with the Turkish authorities.

After that the Greeks from Perivilia and Sersepilia dispersed to their homes and the village Turks all left Khania. Everyone was glad that things had quieted down and they praised the consuls. Only that Cherigote Kafedzhi with the mustache, the one who had been friends with my deceased husband, did not boast and did not rejoice.

"What a shame, a real shame," he would say, "that the Turks massacred neither you nor the consuls. Then Turkey would have perished immediately. You think that the western consuls cared about you? What foolish people! They too are conducting their political intrigues against each other. They were all acting against the English consul, so that they would have more influence with Veli-Pasha. What bumpkins you all are! What I'm supposed to do with you, I just don't know!"

I don't know whether Kafedzhi was telling the truth or whether he was just talking out of his hatred for the Franks.

Once things quieted down my spirit was much more at peace. For a long time I did not shed a single tear. I felt as if someone, with a single breath, had extinguished my soul like a lamp. I wandered around wanting nothing, seeing everything but looking at nothing. For a year I lived at home practically on bread alone and never went out anywhere except to church. My heart had turned to stone, but such a stone is heavier than my complaints or tears! I forced myself to think about my brother and my husband and my mother and waited to see if I would cry. I deliberately began to dote on my daughter, "O my poor orphan! My unhappy little one!" And still the tears would not come!

When the spring came I finally cried, and things became much easier for me. It happened this way. My daughter had started to doze off in my arms and I sat remembering different songs with which people lull children to sleep. And I remembered one song from some foreign region. My father had taught it to me when he returned from Epirus.

> Our little one, our spoiled one
> We washed him and combed him and sent him to school . . .
> The teacher awaits him with paper in hand;
> And the woman teacher awaits him with a gold quill pen.
> O my child, where is your lesson, where is your mind?
> My lesson is on the paper, and my mind is far, far away.
> Far, among those black-eyed girls,
> Their eyes are like olives and their brows like braided thread.
> And their hair blond—and forty-five yards long!

My daughter had already fallen asleep, but I sat there and began to sing this song to myself. I remembered how I had carried my brother around when I myself had been but a little girl! I remembered how in the evenings I would carry him from the gates up to the house and sing this song and the moon would light up his little face and with his deep blue eyes he would look up into my eyes in silence. And as I remembered all this my soul opened up and at that moment my tears began to flow.

Please believe, good Sir, that I am telling you the whole truth!

I listened carefully to Katerina's story. The sky above us was clear and already a pink glow illuminated the old peach tree by which we were sitting. The sea was quiet and snow glistened peacefully from the far away Sphakia Heights.

I believed and felt Katerina's sufferings, but somehow both suffering and joy in this marvelous land seemed better to me than those sufferings and joys by which people live among the fetid luxuries of European capitals.

II

THE FIRST FLOWERING OF GAY CULTURE
(Early 20th Century)

Mikhail Kuzmin (1872–1936) as a young man.

Mikhail Kuzmin (1872–1936)

AUNT SONYA'S SOFA

[Kushetka teti Soni, 1907]

Translated by Michael Green

MIKHAIL KUZMIN (1872–1936) is the first major figure in gay literature in Russia. He was a symbolist poet, prose writer, and playwright. Openly gay, he wrote the first celebrations of gay themes in Russian literature, and the first Russian coming-out novel, *Wings* (1907). Presented here are two of his stories, two cycles of poems (a total of 22 poems in all), and selections from his poetry cycle "Alexandrian Songs." These are followed by two essays on Kuzmin's life and writings.

I dedicate this true story to my sister

IT'S SO LONG that I've been standing in the storeroom, surrounded by all kinds of junk, that I have only the dimmest recollections of my young days, when the Turk with a pipe and the shepherdess with a little dog scratching itself for fleas, hind leg raised, all of them embroidered on my spine, gleamed in bright hues—yellow, pink and sky-blue—as yet unfaded and undimmed by dust; and so what occupies my thoughts now more than anything else are the events to which I was witness before once more being consigned to oblivion, this time, I fear, for ever. They had me covered in a wine-colored silken material, stood me in the passageway and threw over my arm a shawl with a pattern of bright roses, as if some beauty from the days of my youth, disturbed at a tender tryst, had left it behind in her flight. I should add that this shawl was always carefully draped in exactly the same way, and if the General, or his sister, Aunt Pavla, happened to disturb it, Kostya, who had arranged this part of the house to his own taste, would restore the folds of the soft, gaily-colored stuff to their former exquisite casualness. Aunt Pavla protested against my disinterment from the storeroom, saying that poor Sophie had died on me, that someone or other's wedding had been upset because of me, that I brought the family misfortune; however, not only was I defended by Kostya, his student friends and the other young people, but even the General himself said:

"That's all prejudice, Pavla Petrovna! If that old monstrosity ever had any magic power in it, sixty years in the storeroom should have taken care of that; besides, it's standing in the passageway—no one's likely to die or propose on it there!"

Although I wasn't very flattered to be called a "monstrosity," and the General proved to be less than a prophet, I did at any rate establish myself as part of the passageway with the greenish wallpaper, where I stood faced by a china cabinet, over which hung an old round mirror, dimly reflecting my occasional visitors. There lived in General Gambakov's house, in addition to his sister Pavla and his son Kostya, his daughter Nastya, a student at the institute for young ladies.

*　*　*

The next room had a westerly outlook, and so admitted into my passageway the long rays of the evening sun; they would strike the rose-patterned shawl, making it glint and shimmer more enchantingly than ever. At this moment, these rays were falling across the face and dress of Nastya, who was sitting on me; she seemed so fragile that I almost thought it strange that the ruddy light did not pass through her body, which hardly seemed a sufficient obstacle to it, and fall on her companion. She was talking to her brother about the Christmas theatricals, as part of which they were planning to put on an act from "Esther"; it seemed, however, that the girl's thoughts were far from the subject of the conversation. Kostya remarked:

"I think we could use Seryozha too—his accent is pretty good."

"Are you suggesting that Sergey Pavlovich should play a young Israelite girl—one of my handmaidens?"

"Why that? I can't bear *travesti* roles—not that he wouldn't look good in a woman's costume."

"Well, what other part is there for him to play?"

I knew at once that they were talking about Sergey Pavlovich Pavilikin, young Gambakov's friend. To me he had always seemed an insignificant boy, in spite of his striking good looks. His close-cropped dark hair emphasized the fullness of his round, strangely bloodless face; he had a pleasing mouth and large, pale-gray eyes. His height enabled him to carry off an inclination to plumpness, but he was certainly very heavy, always collapsing onto me and scattering me with ash from the *papirosy* with very long mouthpieces which he smoked one after another; and nothing could have been more empty-headed than his conversation. He came to the house almost every day, notwithstanding the displeasure of Pavla Petrovna, who could not abide him.

After a silence the young lady began hesitantly:

"Do you know Pavilikin well, Kostya?"

"What a question! He's my best friend!"

"Is he? . . . But you haven't been friends all that long, have you?"

"Ever since I began attending university this year. But what difference does that make?"

"None, of course. I just asked because I wanted to know. . . ."

"Why do you find our friendship so interesting?"

"I would like to know whether one can trust him. . . . I'd like to . . ."

Kostya's laughter interrupted her.

"It depends what with! In monetary affairs I wouldn't advise it! . . . All the same, he's a good friend, and no skinflint when he's in funds—but you know he's poor. . . ."

Nastya said after a pause:

"No, I didn't mean that at all—I meant in the matters of feeling, affection."

"What nonsense! What on earth do they put into your heads at those institutes? How should I know?! . . . Have you fallen for Seryozha or something?"

The young lady continued without answering:

"I want you to do something for me. Will you?"

"Is it to do with Sergey Pavlovich?"

"Perhaps."

"Well, all right—though you'd better not forget that he's not much of a one for wasting time on young ladies."

"No, Kostya, you have to promise me! . . ."

"I've said I'll do it, haven't I? Well?"

"I'll tell you this evening," announced Nastya solemnly, looking into her brother's uneasily shifting eyes, eyes which, like hers, were hazel flecked with gold.

"Whenever you like—now, this evening," said the young man unconcernedly, as he got up and readjusted the rose-patterned shawl which the girl had released as she too rose.

But no ray of the evening sun gleamed on the tender roses because Nastya had gone into the next room and taken up a position at the window, as impenetrable to the ruddy light as before; she stood there gazing at the snow-covered street until the electric lights were lit.

* * *

Today I simply haven't had a moment's quiet—such comings and goings all day, and all through my passageway! And what's the point of all these amateur theatricals—that's what I'd like to know. A swarm of young misses and young men—lord knows who they all are—bustling about, yelling, running, calling for some peasants or other to saw through something or other, dragging about furniture, cushions, lengths of cloth; it's a mercy they didn't start taking things from the passage—why, they might even have carried off my shawl! At last things quieted down and a piano began to play somewhere far off. The General and Pavla Petrovna emerged cautiously and sat down beside each other; the old maid was saying:

"If she falls in love with him, it will be a family misfortune. Just think of it—a mere boy, and worse than that—with no name, no fortune, absolutely nothing to offer! . . ."

"It seems to me you're very much exaggerating all this—I haven't noticed anything. . . ."

"When did men ever notice such things? But I, for one, will fight against it to the bitter end."

"I shouldn't think things will ever reach the point where you have to be for or against."

"And he has absolutely no morals at all: do you know what they say about him? I'm convinced that he's corrupting Kostya too. Nastya's a child, she doesn't understand anything," fulminated the old lady.

"Well, my dear, and whom don't they talk about? You should hear the gossip about Kostya! And it wouldn't surprise me if some of these fairy tales didn't have a grain of truth in them. Only age can protect you from gossip—as the two of us ought to know! . . ."

Pavla Petrovna blushed crimson and said curtly:

"You do as you wish; at least I've warned you. And *I* shall certainly be on my guard—Nastya is my blood too, you know!"

At this moment Nastya herself entered, already dressed in her costume for the play—pale blue with yellow stripes, with a yellow turban.

"Papa," she began breathlessly, turning to the General, "why aren't you watching the rehearsals?"—and without waiting for a reply she rushed on, "What about lending our emperor your ring? It has such a huge emerald!"

"You mean this one?" asked the old man in surprise, showing an antique ring of rare workmanship, set with a dark emerald the size of a large gooseberry.

"Yes, that one!" answered the young lady, not at all disconcerted.

"Nastya, you don't know what you're asking!" her aunt intervened. "A family heirloom which Maksim never parts with, and you want him to let you take it to that madhouse of yours where you'll lose it in no time? You know your father never takes it off his finger!"

"Well, it's only once or twice, and even if someone does drop it, it's sure to be somewhere in the room. . . ."

"No, Maksim, I absolutely forbid you to take it off!"

"You see, Aunt Pavla won't let me!" said the old General with an embarrassed laugh.

Nastya stalked out crossly without the ring, and Pavla Petrovna set about comforting her brother, who was upset to see his daughter disappointed.

And again there was hubbub, rushing about, changing of clothes, leavetaking.

Mr. Pavilikin remained in the house a long time. When he and Kostya came into my passageway it was nearly four o'clock in the morning. Coming to a standstill, they kissed each other good-bye. Sergey Pavlovich said in an embarrassed voice:

"You don't know how happy I am, Kostya! But I feel so uncomfortable that this should have happened today of all days, after you had let me have that money! Lord knows what awful things you might think. . . ."

Kostya, pale, his eyes shining with happiness, his hair rumpled, again kissed his friend, and said:

"I won't think anything at all, you idiot! It's simply coincidence, chance—something that could happen to anyone."

"Yes, but I feel awkward, so awkward. . . ."

"Don't say another word about it, please—you can let me have it back in the spring. . . ."

"It was just that I needed those six hundred roubles desperately. . . ."

Kostya made no rejoinder. After a little while he said:

"Good-bye, then. Don't forget you're going to "Manon" with me tomorrow."

"Yes, of course! . . ."

"And not with Petya Klimov?"

"O, *tempi passati*! Good-bye!"

"Close the door gently, and tread softly when you go past Aunt Pavla's bedroom: she didn't see you come back, and you know she doesn't much care for you. Good-bye!"

The young men embraced once more; as I said before, it was nearly four o'clock in the morning.

* * *

Without taking off her rose-trimmed fur hat after the ride, Nastya sat down on the edge of the chair, while her escort kept racing up and down the room, his cheeks faintly pink from the frost. The girl was chattering gaily away, but underneath the bird-like twitter there lurked a certain unease.

"Wasn't that a glorious ride! Frost and sunshine—that's so nice! I adore the embankment! . . ."

"Yes."

"I love to go horseriding—in the summer I disappear for days on end. You've never visited our place at Svyataya Krucha, have you?"

"No. I prefer to ride in a car."

"You do have bad taste. . . . You know, don't you, that Svyataya Krucha, Alekseyevskoye and Lgovka are all my personal property—I'm a very good match. And then Auntie Pavla Petrovna is going to leave me everything. You see—I'm advising you to think things over."

"The likes of us mustn't be getting ideas above our station!"

"Where do you pick up these gems of shop-assistants' wisdom?"

Seryozha shrugged and continued his steady pacing back and forth. The young lady made one or two more attempts to start up her twittering, but each time more halfheartedly, like a broken toy, until she at last fell silent; when she spoke again, it was in a sad, gentle voice. Without taking off her hat, she sank back in the chair; as she spoke in the darkened room, she seemed to be addressing a plaint to herself:

"How long it's been since we put on our play! Do you remember? Your entrance. . . . What a lot has changed since then! You've changed too—I have, everyone has. . . . I didn't really know you then. You've no idea how much better I understand you than Kostya does! You don't believe it? Why do you pretend to be so slow on the uptake? Would it give you pleasure if I came out and said what is considered humiliating for a woman to say first? You're tormenting me, Sergey Pavlovich!''

"How dreadfully you exaggerate everything, Nastasya Maksimovna—my dimness of wit, my pride, and even, perhaps, your feelings for me. . . ''

She stood up and said almost soundlessly:

"Do I? Perhaps. . . .''

"Are you going?''—he was suddenly alert.

"Yes, I have to change for dinner. You're not dining with us?''

"No, I'm invited somewhere.''

"With Kostya?''

"No. Why do you ask that?''

She was standing by the table with the magazines, reluctant to leave the room.

"Are you going to him now?''

"No, I'm leaving straight away.''

"Are you? Good-bye, then! And I love you—there!'' she added suddenly, turning away. No word came from him in the darkness which hid his face from her, and she threw in laughingly (or that was the effect she intended), "Well, are you satisfied now?''

"Surely you don't think that's the word I would choose?'' he said, bending over her hand.

"Good-bye. Go now,''—the words came from her as she left the room.

Seryozha turned on the light and began walking in the direction of Kostya's room, whistling cheerfully.

*   *   *

The General was pacing about holding a newspaper; he seemed very upset about something. Pavla Petrovna was following him about the room in a rustle of black silk.

"You mustn't let it upset you, Maksim! It happens so often these days that you almost get used to it. Of course, it's dreadful, but what can we do about it? It's no good kicking against the pricks, as they say.''

"It's no good, Pavla, I just can't reconcile myself to the thought of it:

all that was left was his cap and a mess of blood and brains on the wall. Poor Lev Ivanovich!''

"Don't think about it, brother! Tomorrow we'll have a funeral mass said for him at Udely. Put it out of your mind, think of your own well-being— you have a son and daughter of your own to worry about."

The General, red in the face, sank down onto me, letting fall his newspaper; the old lady, nimbly picking it up and placing it out of her brother's reach, made haste to change the subject:

"Well, did you find the ring?"

The General again displayed signs of uneasiness:

"No, no, I haven't. That's another thing I'm terribly worried about."

"When do you last remember having it?"

"I showed it to Sergey Pavlovich this morning on this very sofa; he seemed most interested. . . . Then I dozed off—when I woke up it had gone, I remember that. . . ."

"Did you take it off?"

"Yes. . . ."

"That was ill-advised of you. Quite apart from its cash value, as a family heirloom it's priceless."

"I'm sure it means some misfortune is in store for us."

"Let's hope that Lev Ivanovich's death is misfortune enough for the time being."

The General heaved a deep sigh. Pavla Petrovna pressed on relentlessly:

"Did Pavilikin take it with him, I wonder. That's just the sort of thing I'd expect of him."

"Why should he have? He had such a good look at it—and he asked how much a dealer would give for it and all that."

"Well, perhaps he just took it."

"Stole it—is that what you're trying to say?"

Pavla Petrovna had no chance to reply: the conversation was interrupted by Nastya, who came rushing excitedly into the room.

"Papa!" she cried, "Sergey Pavlovich has proposed to me; I hope you're not opposed to the idea?"

"Not now, not now!"—the General waved her away.

"And why not? Why put it off? You know him pretty well by now," said Nastya, reddening.

Pavla Petrovna rose to her feet:

"I have a voice in this matter too, and I am opposed to the match under any circumstances; at the very least I demand that we postpone this discussion until Maksim's ring is found."

"What has papa's ring to do with my fiancé?" asked the girl haughtily.

"We think Sergey Pavlovich has the ring."

"You think he has committed a theft?"

"You could put it like that."

Nastya turned to the General without answering her aunt, and said:
"And do you believe this fairy tale?"

Her father said nothing, redder in the face than ever.

The girl again turned to Pavla:

"Why are you standing between us? You hate Seryozha—Sergey Pavlovich—and you invent all sorts of nonsense! And you're trying to set
father against Kostya too. What is it you want from us?"

"Nastya, don't you dare, I forbid you! . . .." said her father, gasping
for breath.

Nastya paid him no attention.

"What are you getting in such a rage about? Why can't you wait until
the matter is cleared up? Can't you see that it's a matter of principle?"

"I can see that where my fiancé is concerned no one should dare even
to suspect such a thing!" shouted Nastya. The General sat in silence, turning redder and redder.

"You're afraid—that's the truth isn't it?"

"There can only be one truth, and I know what it is. And I advise you
not to oppose our marriage—or it'll be the worse for you!"

"You think so?"

"I know!"

Pavla gave her a searching look.

"Is there any reason for this hurry?"

"What a nasty mind you have! Kostya!"—Nastya threw herself toward
her brother, who had just entered, "Kostya darling, you be the judge! Sergey Pavlovich has proposed to me, and father—Aunt Pavla has him completely under her thumb—won't give his consent until we clear up this
business about his ring."

"What the devil is all this?! Do you mean to tell me you're accusing
Pavilikin of theft?"

"Yes!" hissed the old lady. "Of course you'll stand up for him, you'll
even redeem the ring. There are a few things I could tell about you too! I
can hear the doors squeaking from my room when your friend leaves and
what you say to each other. Be grateful for my silence!"

Never in all my life have I heard such an uproar, such a scandal, such
a torrent of abuse. Kostya banged with his fist and shouted; Pavla appealed
for respect to be shown to years; Nastya screamed hysterically. . . . But
all at once everyone fell silent: all the voices, the noise and the shouting,
were pierced by the strange animal-like sound emitted by the General, who,
silent to this moment, had suddenly risen to his feet. Then he sank back
heavily, his face between red and blue, and began to wheeze. Pavla threw
herself toward him:

"What's the matter? Maksim, Maksim?"

The General only wheezed and rolled the whites of his eyes, now completely blue in the face.

"Water! Water! He's dying—it's a stroke!" whispered the aunt, but Nastya pushed her aside with the words:

"Let me see to him—I'll undo his collar!" and sank down on her knees before me.

* * *

Even the passageway was not free of the pervasive smell of incense from the old General's funeral mass; the sound of chanting too could be faintly heard. More than once I had the feeling that they were singing a farewell to me. Ah, how close I was to the truth!

The young men came in, deep in conversation; Pavilikin was saying:

"And then today I received the following note from Pavla Petrovna"— and taking a letter from his pocket, he read it aloud:

"Dear Sir, for reasons which I trust there is no need to go into here, I find your visits at this time, a time so painful to our family, to be undesirable, and I hope that you will not refuse to comport yourself in accordance with our general wish. The future will show whether former relations can be resumed, but in the meantime, I can assure you that Anastasia Maksimovna, my niece, is fully in agreement with me on this matter. Yours, etc."

He looked inquiringly at Kostya, who remarked:

"You know, from her point of view my aunt is right, and I really don't know what my sister will have to say to you."

"But, I mean to say, all because of such a little thing! . . ."

"Is that what you call papa's death?"

"But it wasn't my fault!"

"Of course it wasn't. . . . You know, not long ago I read a story in the 'Thousand and One Nights': a man is throwing date stones—a perfectly harmless occupation—and happens to hit a Genii's son in the eye, thus bringing down on his head a whole series of misfortunes. Who can predict the results of our most trivial actions?"

"But the two of us will still see each other, won't we?"

"Oh certainly! I shan't be living with the family any more, and I'm always delighted to see you. What's between us is a bit more permanent than a schoolgirl crush."

"And doesn't have to be afraid of date stones?"

"Precisely. . . ."

Seryozha put his arm round young Gambakov, and they went out of the room together. I was never to see Pavilikin again, as I was to see little of any of the people I had grown familiar with during my final period of grace.

* * *

Early next morning some peasants came tramping in; "This one here?" they asked Pavla Petrovna, and set about lifting me. The oldest of them lingered, trying to find out if there was anything else to be sold, but on being assured that there wasn't, he went out after the others.

When they turned me on my side to get me through the doorway, something struck the floor (the carpets having already been taken up in anticipation of summer). One of my bearers picked up the fallen object and handed it to the old lady, saying:

"Now there's a fine ring for you, ma'am. Someone must have dropped it on this here couch, and it must have gone and rolled down inside the covers."

"Good. I'm very much obliged to you!" said Aunt Pavla, turning pale; hastily dropping into her reticule a ring with an emerald like a large gooseberry, she left the room.

June, 1907

Mikhail Kuzmin (1872–1936)

VIRGINAL VICTOR: A BYZANTINE TALE

[Devstvennyi Viktor, 1914]

Translated by Michael Green

To Arthur Lourier

THE HOLY CHURCH commands us to take pity on orphans. In the imperial city of Byzantium a vast orphanage had been established; for both private individuals and public institutions it was held to be a great desert in the eyes of the Almighty to nourish and rear infants deprived of their parents. If nothing can restore to a child its mother's tenderness, at least there is always the possibility of providing it with food, shelter and instruction in Christian conduct.

Although Victor, son of Timothy, had lost his parents, he had no need to have recourse either to private or state charity, since he had inherited a commodious house, one of the city's finest libraries, three dozen house slaves, splendid stables and a sizeable country estate in the north. The sister of his deceased mother, the widow Pulcheria, took up residence in his household, not in the capacity of a guardian, as the youth had already reached his nineteenth year, but merely so that the management of the household should be under a woman's eye. She established her quarters in the upper part of the house, next to the private chapel, from which the gulf and the shore of Asia Minor could be seen in the distance. In her rooms there was always semi-darkness and the whisper of holy discourse. Priests in soft slippers slid noiselessly by, stopping at the drawn door-curtains to murmur a prayer, the servants were elderly women, yesterday's incense hung in the air, and through the window, instead of sea and boats, one saw painted branches, beasts and birds. Sometimes hermits would come, hulking fellows dressed in goatskins, as simple-hearted and dirty as shepherds.

Victor often listened to their tales. Pulcheria, as befitted a Christian matron, did not expose her sparse, graying hair, swathing it with a fillet sewn with the modest amethysts and emeralds of widowhood: by family tradition the widow belonged to the "Green" faction. Her face was immobile from the thick layer of ceruse, rouge and stibium, her puffy yellowish fingers were unable to bend from their multitude of rings, the folds of her robe, smoothed out by her slaves, seemed carved of stone, her neck and waist were festooned with crosses, incense pouches, rosaries, miniatures of saints, fragments of holy relics and amulets; in one hand she held a scarlet kerchief fringed with gold lace, in the other a sprig of lavender, which from time to time she would raise to her whitened nostrils to rid herself of the goat smell of some hermit. Now and then her eyebrows would quiver, and then the maid attending her would drive a somnolent fly from her mistress's face or hands with a fan. Beside her stood her household priest, explaining to her in an undertone the words of the anchorite, who mingled barbarian expressions with Greek ones, waved his arms about, sighed and stammered.

Afterwards Victor would dream of sand and trees, birds and deer similar to those patterned on his robe, for it was on cloth that he most frequently saw these things. Of course, in the nearby countryside birds flew, poppies and burdocks flourished, but the youth did not go any further from Byzantium than the Monastery of Olympus, whither each year in all kinds of weather he would make a pilgrimage in memory of the five holy martyrs of the thirteenth of December. Their house had a small garden, but the pious gardener had given all the bushes and trees the form of Christian emblems: the barberry bushes were clipped in the shape of hearts and anchors, the limes resembled fish with their tails pointed upward (as is well known, their very name is made up of the first letters of the following words: Jesus Christ, Son of God, Saviour), while close by the apple tree, the boughs of which had been lopped in the form of a cross, were placed two poles, painted in red lead, representing a spear and a stave.

The most Christian city of Byzantium wafted its fragrance to the Creator, not like a lily of the field, but like a precious oil, poured into a vessel wrought by cunning goldsmiths, stooped in their dark cells, their short-sighted eyes accustomed to envisioning sky, flowers and birds in an improved, a more brilliant, a more fantastical guise than nature, that guileless simpleton, presents them to us.

The widow Pulcheria had long been yearning for monastic life, but she was reluctant to leave her nephew until he had given the house a new young mistress. But here her intentions met with an unexpected obstacle, and the good woman had to recognize that even virtue itself can present certain inconveniences. There was no shortage of brides. Although Victor had no official post and no rank, his wealth and beauty made him a desirable husband and son-in-law for all. But the youth himself felt no inclination to marry and to all appearances his heart was free; consequently he responded evasively to all attempts at matchmaking. Enquiries made among servants and friends revealed no love affair to tie the young man, so that the lady Pulcheria didn't know what to think. At last she decided to have a frank talk with him.

When Victor entered the woman's quarters, the widow was holding in her arms a white long-haired cat, a gift from the Archbishop of Antioch, which she was combing with a small gilt comb. Having spoken of the allegedly deteriorating state of her health, of household matters, of the recent storm, Pulcheria said:

"Well, nephew, have you thought about which of the maidens I have proposed to you you would prefer as your wife, so that I may begin discussions with her parents?''

"I have, lady Pulcheria."

"Well, and on whom has your choice fallen?"

"I have decided to wait awhile yet."

"But why wait? You're a grown man, I'm growing weaker with every month, it's time to think of the future."

"My heart feels no inclination toward any of them."

The widow angrily removed the resisting cat from her knees and exclaimed:

"What nonsense! Surely, nephew, you don't imagine that life is a pastoral novel or the 'Ethiopian Tales'? What's this 'inclination of the heart' you're talking about? If a girl is worthy and of noble birth, and you can rely on me to see to that, it follows that the blessing of Heaven and the Church will be on your house."

But to all his aunt's arguments, Victor kept repeating only one thing— that he didn't want to marry. Pulcheria listened to his reply, knitting her brows, as far as the ceruse permitted her to, and at last announced enigmatically:

"Remember that there is no secret that will not be revealed in time."

"I have nothing to hide, I assure you."

"So much the better," replied his aunt, and with that put an end to the conversation. Afterwards, when her nephew had left, she heaved a sigh and sent for the household confessor.

On the Tuesday of the fourth week in Lent, the priest received a country gift: a clay pitcher of honey and two dozen red-cheeked apples in a golden dish. The widow wrote briefly that she begged him not to disdain her modest gift and to accede to her request. By Friday, in all likelihood, the mission had already been accomplished, since the confessor appeared in the lady Pulcheria's quarters, and as soon as the customary greetings had been exchanged and the servant sent away, said:

"He is pure in the sight of God."

A faint mocking smile parted the lady's painted lips.

"Can that be? Victor—a virgin?"

"Your nephew is a stranger to carnal sin."

"And my suppositions have proved groundless?"

"The Lord be praised, my lady, you were mistaken."

Seeing that Pulcheria expressed no particular joy, but sat frowning and motionless, the confessor went on soothingly:

"You should thank heaven for such a mercy, for without grace from above, it is hard to keep one's purity, as the young master has kept his."

Seeing that Pulcheria maintained her gloomy silence, after a pause the priest began cautiously:

"Of course, my lady, this calls for further investigation. What has not been subjected to temptation cannot be considered virtue, anger may find no external expression, but nonetheless a man who has anger in his heart remains privy to that sin."

To this the lady listened attentively.

"Perhaps your nephew is too timid, has little knowledge of the world, his passions sleep that they may with greater fury gain possession of him when it will already be too late. We might put his resolve to the test."

"What can we do?"

"Neither you nor I, my lady, is likely to be experienced in these matters, but I too have a nephew, whom I have kept at a distance because of his unworthy behavior, but it would seem that the ways of fate are inscrutable. Even a muddy path sometimes leads to salvation. He has a wide acquaintance in the circles needful to us, and I am confident that he and his lady friends will willingly take upon themselves the task of putting the young master to the test."

It was clear that the priest's plans were to Pulcheria's liking; she turned the conversation to the empress, whom she had seen at a service, remarked that in her next conversation she would not fail to mention him as a loyal and devoted man, asked whether the apples she had sent had been tasty, and at last lowered her blue-painted, hen-like lids, as if to convey that the audience was at an end. Only in parting did she add, again becoming somewhat animated:

"As long as my nephew doesn't get into the gaming habit! Another thing—I don't wish in the least that Victor should remain in this company forever."

"Set your heart at rest, my lady, set your heart at rest. It will be no more than a trial, and then we'll marry the noble youth."

The good priest had some trouble finding his scapegrace nephew, but in the end he was extracted from some nocturnal eating house. It took some time to comprehend what was demanded of him, but having grasped it, he willingly agreed to help the widow and take her nephew in hand. Among those ladies who might put Victor's virginity to the test, Pancratius (as the priest's nephew was called) moved, so to speak in the middle circles, knowing by name but having no access to those women who had already attained riches and fame, and who imitated noble matrons in their dress and manner of painting their faces, mimicking strenuous piety and occasionally turning their hand to erotic verses in the form of acrostics, which often became confused with *eirmosa* and *kontakia*. Knowing the inconstancy of fate, and meeting a great many people—courtiers, grooms, bishops and conspirators—these women dreamed of being raised up to the throne, for in this world, and particularly in the imperial city, all things are possible. Dull, ambitious and malevolent thoughts crept across the standing pools of their eyes, as they sat in state, like idols in the circus, gazing enviously at the seats reserved for matrons of noble blood. When they were borne away in their litters, the dark-skinned, flat-breasted flowersellers would gaze after them no less enviously.

With these ladies Pancratius was not acquainted, and besides they were of no interest to Pulcheria's virginal nephew, closely resembling those who were proposed to him as brides. But the acquaintances of the priest's kinsman were not street harlots either, lying in wait for stray sailors—they were gay, carefree creatures, mocking, sentimental and heartless. But apparently Pancratius too met with no particular success, for when he appeared before his uncle a month later he had an embarrassed and somewhat astonished air.

"What news?" asked the priest, not turning from the desk at which he was composing a sermon for the following day.

"Nothing good, uncle. The Lord Victor is in the same condition as he was on the day you acquainted us."

A learned starling called out "Peace be unto you," but the master of the house flapped his sleeve at him and inquired anxiously:

"The Lord Victor, you say, remains chaste?"

"Yes—an odd young man!"

"Perhaps you're wanting to ask more money from me so that you can carry on with your merry life on the pretext that the virtue of the respected Pulcheria's nephew has not yet been sufficiently tested?"

"You can be sure that I wouldn't refuse, but unfortunately I have to confess defeat."

Uncle gazed at nephew, not knowing whether to marvel at his moderation or Victor's resolve. In the silence the starling again called out "Peace be unto you," but no one took the slightest notice of him. That very evening the lady Pulcheria received a report of the state of affairs.

It is hard to say whether the youth himself guessed that the widow's questions, the confessor's admonitions, the sudden appearance of a new friend, so apparently attached to him and so eager to accompany him to various houses—that all these things were closely connected, and had something to do with his spiritual qualities. He did not consider his condition out of the ordinary, and lived quietly, dividing his time between library and church. Of course, the most natural thing for him would have been to contemplate the seclusion of a monastery, which, after all, differed but little from his present way of life—but perhaps for this very reason such dreams did not particularly attract him. What future prospect might have attracted him was difficult to imagine, and he revealed it to no one, not even to his favorite slave, Andrew the Hungarian, who accompanied him everywhere, and when his master read, sat drowsing nearby or with his eyes fixed unwaveringly upon him. He had recently been brought from the north and bound in service to Victor, who soon grew fond of him. He knew only about a dozen words of Greek, and so it was not possible to have long conversations with him. It was not, then, for his conversation that his young master became attached to him; perhaps it was for his quietness and piety, perhaps for his strange, wild air or for his devoted tenderness and meekness.

Andrew would always accompany his master to church, to all services, praying decorously and devoutly, looking neither right nor left, or raising his eyes to the choirs curtained at the sides, where the female parishioners were. From above, nevertheless, more than one feminine gaze was directed on master and servant, and impressions, marvellings, conjectures were passed to the opposite wall in whispers, as if in some kind of game.

One day, as Victor and the Hungarian were returning from Mass, they found their way barred by a large crowd which surrounded a tall man in a loose robe and a nightcap; the man laughed, capered about and spat, slapping his ribs and mouthing incoherently to the tune of a street song. Catching sight of the approaching youths, he paused in his capers for a moment and, leaning on his long staff, seemed to be waiting, then he began to whirl even faster. He stopped once more, wrinkled his nose and frowned. Everyone waited to hear what he would say.

"Faugh, faugh! What a stench of devils!"

They all began looking about them, wondering whether the exclamation might refer to them, but the holy fool went on:

"You think it smells of musk? Hellish brimstone, that's what! See that demon dancing—he's blowing his pipe, the foul fiend, he's pulling faces, grinning, trying to trip me up."

Suddenly the man of God buried his face in his hands and began moaning like a woman; "Oh! Oh! Oh! Woe is me, would that my eyes could not see!

Mizra, Mizra, full of guile
What made you journey to the Nile?"

A smiling woman's face, heavily painted and surmounted by towering ginger coiffure, looked down from an upper window. The holy fool withdrew his hands from his cheeks and yelled to the whole street:

"And you laugh, you filthy whore! I shall fight—and I shall not yield!"

And without further ado he leaped in the air, pulling up his robe, and, naked as he was, assumed an indecent pose. The green window-shutters were slammed shut, and uncontrolled laughter came from behind them, while the old man, having adjusted his clothes, suddenly began to speak in a preceptorial manner:

"Do not imagine, brothers, that this Herodias, this Jezebel, is worse than any of you. And besides, you witnessed how easily she was subdued. I tell you that those two over there" (here he pointed his stick at Victor and Andrew) "are a hundred times worse than she. There's as many devils on them as fleas on a dog."

Everyone turned toward the youths, and, flushing, Victor went up to the fool and asked humbly:

"Reveal to us, O father—by what devils are we possessed?"

The fool clicked his tongue and answered:

"What I say to you is: 'Not on your life!' Find out for yourselves!"

And again he began babbling something incomprehensible.

Victor never spoke to Andrew of this incident, but the fool's words often came to his mind, particularly during hours of insomnia to which he was subject. Meanwhile the Hungarian fell sick and as his health failed, so his piety grew stronger. Rarely leaving his narrow bed under the stairs, he was forever whispering prayers, his eyes fixed on the sombre icon in the corner. Victor spent all his time in his servant's cramped quarters, holding his dry and burning hand in his and listening to his rambling speech, which sometimes turned to outright delirium. One day he was sitting there, the sick man had dozed off, and Victor, as he gazed at the dusky, sweating brow and the dark eyes, which, for all their sunkenness, seemed to start from his head, suddenly recalled the day the fool stopped them. What had he meant, and to which of the two of them had his words been directed? As if sensing his master's gaze, Andrew opened his eyes, and, feeling his hand in the hand of the other, began softly:

"My hour has come. My soul's anguish is twofold. It is parting with the body and it is taking its leave of you; to me, sweet Victor, you were not a master but a brother and friend."

The sick man wanted to say something else, but clearly it was beyond his strength. He only signed to Victor to bend over him, twined his arms about his neck and pressed his lips to his master's lips. Suddenly his mouth grew cold, and his arms weighed more heavily. Carefully Victor unclasped Andrew's fingers, and the Hungarian fell back lifeless on the pillows.

Only after his servant's death did Victor understand how dear he had been to him. It would have been easier, so it seemed, if his right hand had been cut off, or he had been thrown into a dungeon for life. Only now did he realize how tenderly he had loved the dead man, without whom even his beloved books came to seem dull and devoid of interest. Church services alone attracted him more than before; besides, circumstances themselves compelled him to intensify his piety, for, apart from the customary memorial services, he would pray alone every night for the repose of his friend's soul, never ceasing to wonder what the fool's words of long ago had meant and what it was that Andrew had wanted to say to him before his death. He could not forget the lips grown suddenly cold, and that kiss, the only kiss of his life, apart from the casual salutations of greeting and farewell. This had also been a kiss of farewell, but forever; a kiss of eternal separation.

One day Victor prayed for a long time before the icon-shelf in his room, as emotion, tears and heavy thoughts had kept him awake, even in bed. Turning his face to the wall, where the tiger on the carpet glowed red in the light of the icon lamp, he whispered over and over again:

"Lord! O Lord! Grant my soul peace, assuage my sorrow; if my brother Andrew cannot be brought back, then reveal to me what has befallen his soul, its wanderings and its place of rest, that I may know whether to shed more tears or rejoice."

Victor said all this with his gaze fixed on the tiger, and he felt a desire to look at the Saviour, the Mother of God and Victor the Martyr, who stood in the row on the middle shelf. Quickly he turned over on the bed and saw . . .

By the lintel of the door stood his brother Andrew, quite naked except for a cloth about his loins. At first Victor did not recognize him in this guise, having never seen his slave stripped of his clothes. Then he knew him; gave a joyful cry of "Andrew!" and even reached out his arms; then all at once he began to make the sign of the cross over his visitor, muttering, "May the Lord rise again." Andrew did not vanish, but smiled calmly and pointed to the cross that hung about his neck.

"Have no fear, Victor, my brother, and do not turn away in horror! I am no ghost and no demon, but your beloved brother. You summoned me, you wished to learn of the sorrowful path beyond the grave, and so I have come to you. I am no ghost, you can take me by the hand if you wish."

He reached out his hand. Its shadow loomed vast on the wall and touched Victor's feet. He tucked them under the blanket, which he drew up to his throat, and said:

"I believe you and I thank you. Tell me brother, of the dark path beyond the grave."

Again his visitor smiled, and began his tale; it seemed to Victor that Andrew did not open his mouth and that his words did not echo in the room, but rather as if someone inserted them into his, Victor's ears.

"Bitter is the final hour! When noseless death appears with her spears, saws, forks, sabres, swords and deadly scythe—you don't know where to hide yourself, you rush hither and thither, you groan, you implore, but she has no ears and no eyes—she is inexorable. She sunders bone from bone, she cuts through all your sinews and tendons, and pierces your very heart. The angel of death waits gloomily while the noseless one goes about her business. On either side stand angels and demons with thick books, waiting. More bitter than vinegar with mustard is the last hour. And bitterest of all is the last breath. And with the last breath the soul leaps from the body, and the Angel of Death gathers it up. How it cowers, how it clings, how it weeps, the poor little naked soul! The Angel of Death turns its head about and says: "Look at your body, your envelope, your comrade. You will enter it again at the last resurrection." And the body lies white, motionless, voiceless, like a log. Friends and kinsmen stand over it and weep, but there is no restoring to it the precious breath of life! The soul buries its face in its hands and cries out: "I don't want to enter it!" But the Angel of Death answers: "You will when the time comes!" and carries it further. Fair youths and dark demons follow them. And now they mount a long bridge, two weeks it takes to cross it. On the far bank you can glimpse the green of meadows, fields and groves, and little white flowers. They move about, and every now and then they fly up in a swarm like dandelion down. These are angels and the souls of the righteous in radiant paradise. The bridge passes above dense fog. If you look hard, you can make out what look like fiery mineshafts with a great many divisions and subdivisions. Only the coarse terrestrial mind fails to see the difference between, let us say, lying and untruthfulness, calumny and slander, hardness of heart and mercilessness, pride and arrogance. But the subtle minds of heaven know all the differences and distinctions and assign everything its proper place. You will not be sent where you ought not to be, be assured of that. The bridge is the place of ordeals. It's a bit like our tollgates or excise houses, where taxes are collected. Angels sit at high tables; in their hands they hold the most precise scales and measures, and everything is written in a book; your slightest thought, desires that you yourself have forgotten, stand there as if alive, each one docketed. The soul is filled with terror and trembles, recalling all its sins and remembering nothing good; but the angels have everything written down, not a jot escapes them. The demons unroll their scrolls, the angels open their books; they weigh, they measure and either let the soul proceed or cast it from the bridge; and the youths weep, while the demons bare their teeth, kick up a racket and cheer like a mob at the races. In this way I passed through the ordeals of untruthfulness, slander, envy, lying, wrath, anger, arrogance, intemperate speech, lewd speech, idleness, sloth, vanity and came at last to the twentieth ordeal."

Here Andrew fell silent.

"Well, and what is the twentieth ordeal?" asked Victor, apparently not noticing that his visitor was no longer standing by the lintel, but was sitting on the bed, all rosy with the light of the icon lamp, looking down at him with starting eyes.

"What is the twentieth ordeal?"

"Do not question me, sweet brother, do not question me. I am with you now. The fire of hell has not extinguished the blood and the heart within me. I am cold . . ."

Victor had forgotten his fear, he was ready to cover his visitor with anything at hand, to warm him with his own breath, his own body, if only he would tell him about the twentieth ordeal. Whereas before Andrew's lips had grown cold in a kiss, now they burned, searing Victor, as if infusing him with the flame that had not been extinguished in the fire of hell. Terrible and sweet it was, and this sweetness, this terror, would have made him forgetful of Andrew's final ordeal, had the latter not said to him in parting:

"And now, brother, you too know the yearning of the twentieth ordeal —take care lest it destroy you."

Often it happens that words of warning, constantly called to mind, push us toward the very thing they would guard us against. And so now Victor thought only of his dead friend's visitation and the tale he had told; he would have given anything only to bring him back. It seemed to him that everything life had to offer him grew dim before what had been revealed to him. Not knowing how to express his longing, he prayed that he might once again hear the tale of the twentieth ordeal. But all was in vain, and he wandered flushed, vacant-eyed, distraught, exalted, not knowing what to do with himself. At last he revealed these strange prayers of his to his confessor, who having heard him out, was silent for a long time, and said at last:

"It is from meekness, lord Victor, that you resort to such prayers—you are too pure. But often meekness turns into boundless pride, and of this you should beware. I advise you always to keep to the prayers that are to be found in the prayerbook. They were assembled by the holy fathers— and, rest assured, they knew better than you or I what is needful to man."

That very day the priest hastened to the widow Pulcheria and said:

"Your nephew must be married at all costs. Use force, appeal to the emperor and let him issue the command, but marriage is essential for the lord Victor. His virginity is not from God."

Pulcheria agreed and, glancing down the list of eligible brides, said:

"I'll send matchmakers to Leucadia, the daughter of Demetrius, the chief scribe"—then she gave a sigh and became thoughtful.

"Why do you sigh, my lady? It will be for your nephew's good."

"I know. As a woman I sigh for poor Leucadia, that's all."

Mikhail Kuzmin (1872-1936)

TWO POETRY CYCLES:

A SUMMER AFFAIR

[Liubov' etogo leta]

and

A STORY INTERRUPTED

[Prervannaia povest]

Translated by Michael Green

"A Summer Affair" was written in 1906 and published in the symbolist journal, *Vesy* (The Scales) in 1907 and later in Kuzmin's first collection of poetry, *Nets* (1908). "A Story Interrupted" was written in 1906 and first published in the literary almanac, *White Nights* (1907), and then also reprinted in *Nets*.

I

A SUMMER AFFAIR

For P. K. Maslov*

1

Where shall I find a style to catch a stroll,†
Chablis on ice, a crisply toasted roll,
The agate succulence of cherries ripe?
The sunset's far, the ocean's splashing cool
Can offer solace to a sunburnt nape.

---

*"For P. K. Maslov." Pavel Maslov was a young army officer who was close to Kuzmin in 1906. In a letter to Walter Nouvel dated July 20, 1906 Kuzmin wrote: ". . . I love him more than before, more than I thought I did, more than I ever loved anyone."

†"Where shall I find a style to catch a stroll." This *"art poétique,"* this "manifesto" poem came as a revelation to Kuzmin's contemporaries. In the context of Russian Symbolism, with its metaphysical airs, this poem is both a challenge and a triumphant demonstration of its stated "program." This apotheosis of the small, the concrete and the downright frivolous (not to forget its rediscovery of the eighteenth century of Marivaux and Mozart) is a deliberate flouting of literary orthodoxy. In this poem alone—an "important" one in the development of Russian verse—I have attempted to adhere as closely as possible to the meter and rhyme scheme of the original.

The sly come-hither of your velvet gaze
Is like the darling prattle in some plays,
Like the capricious pen of Marivaux.
Your Pierrot nose, your mouth's befuddling gash
Put my head in a whirl like Mozart's "Figaro."

Spirit of aery and delicious trifles,
Of a night of love that pampers us and stifles,
Of the weightless joy of life's unthinking mirth!
Ah I am true, remote from docile miracles,
To your flowers and none other, O gay earth!

2

Serpent eyes and coilings serpentine,
Play of light on motley tissues,
Unexampled sultry motions . . .
From the bashful to the shameless,
Kisses of all shades and scope,
Heady scent of ashen roses . . .

Hot embraces, heart's wild beating,
Of snake-like arms the intertwinings,
Of limbs the practiced palpitations,
Of lips on flesh the practiced ardour,
Buoyancy of a promised tryst
And leavetaking across the threshold.

3

Oh lips kissed by so many,
By so many other lips.
You pierce the heart with bitter arrows,
With bitter arrows, hundreds of them.

Blossom you will in confident smiles,
Like radiant burgeoning of bushes in springtime,
Recalling caresses of delicate fingers,
Of fingers delicate and cherished.

Pilgrim or impudent desperado—
Not a single kiss is kept at bay.
Be he Antinous or be he vile Thersites,*
Each man will find a fitting fortune.

A kiss that's pressed upon your flesh
Sets on that flesh a lasting mark:
Who of loved lips takes communion
Is made kith and kin with all lovers past.

Prayerful gaze on icon fixed
Is held there fast with powerful fetters:
The ancient countenance, prayer-glorified
With those fetters binds the worshiper.

Thus do you walk in perilous places,
In perilous and holy places—
Oh lips kissed by so many,
By so many other lips.

---

*Antinous, Thersites. Antinous was the beautiful Bithynian favorite and constant companion of the grecophile Hadrian (117–138), one of the most civilized of the Roman emperors. He died by drowning in the Nile during Hadrian's visit to Egypt (130). Hadrian founded a city named after him (Antinoopolis), deified him, and set up temples for his cult. Antinous was important to Kuzmin, both as an ideal of male beauty (many statues of the emperor's beloved survive) and a symbol of human divinity. In the semi-autobiographical "gay novel" *Wings* (1906), Vanya's Greek teacher Daniil Ivanovich allots a sacred corner of his room to "a small head of Antinous," while the Catholic canon Mori toward the end of the novel embarks on a disquisition on the relations between Hadrian and his favorite (of which he does not *wholly* approve), and the "religion of the deified man" (of which, as a good Catholic, he approves thoroughly). The "Fragments" section of Kuzmin's first collection, *Nets* (1908) dedicates a beautiful poem to an unnamed but unmistakable Antinous (see this poem on p. 113 of the present anthology).

"Vile Thersites"—or "rank Thersites," as Shakespeare prefers to dub him—is quite another matter. Thersites is the professional slanderer of Book II of the *Iliad*: "He was the ugliest man of all those that came before Troy—bandy-legged, lame on one foot, with his two shoulders rounded and hung over his chest." Thersites' calumnies against Agamemnon arouse the anger of Odysseus, who "beat him with his staff about the back and shoulders till he dropped and fell a-weeping."

4

We washed ourselves and then got dressed,
After the night we kissed each other,
After the caress-filled night.
Using the lilac tea service,
As if with a brother, as if with a guest,
We drank tea, keeping on our masks.

They smiled, those masks of ours,
And our glances did not meet
And our lips said not a word.
We sang from "Faust," played the piano,
As if we had not known that night;
We are not they, those night ones, we.

5

A parched rose drooped in doleful fashion
From a basket left behind by someone,
And they sang for us that aria of Rosina's:
"Io sono docile, io sono rispettosa."

Candles burned, a warm and drowsiness-
Diffusing rain dripped scarcely heeded from the trees,
Pesaro's swan,* voluptuous and stately,
With gaiety capped his briefest bar.

Friends' tales of bygone wanderings,
Disputes fine-pointed where the mind takes wing.
But all this while in expectation vain
My tender friend in solitude roams the garden.

Ah radiant are the kisses of Mozartian tones,
Like the remote distances of Raphael's "Parnassus,"†
But they can't make me forget the meeting
I haven't had with you since four o'clock.

---

*"Pesaro's swan." Gioacchino Rossini (1792–1868) was born in the central Italian city of Pesaro. Rosina's aria "Io sono docile, sono rispettosa" is from the second act of *Il barbiere di Seviglia* (1816).

†"Raphael's 'Parnassus.' " One of a set of four Raphael frescoes (1509–1511) in the Vatican.

6

Why does the newly risen moon grow roseate
And the wind, filled with warm sweetness, breathe?
And the skiff seem unmindful of the snake-skinned surge
When my spirit is locked in fasting for your sake?

When I do not eye your eye,
I am seared by memories of nights of love—
I'm resting—but even now keeps jealous watch
The enchantment of dear, delicious trifles:

The calm look of the river's distant windings,
The rare light in an unsleeping window,
The broken threads of cloud soft-gleaming
Won't drive away my sad and tender thoughts

Of other gardens' shadowy paths—
And dawn's uncertain glimmering . . .
The lanterns glitter with a final flame . . .
Love's devices have a winning zing . . .

The soul flies to abandoned pleasures,
The mildest poisons have a potent suture,
And it's not for summer's meek and simple herbs
To drown the fragrance of the rose.

7

I cannot sleep: my spirit pines,
My head is going round and round
And empty is my bed—
Where are the shoulders, where the arms,
Where the broken sentences
And the lips that I adore? . . .

The sheet had twisted about me,
My sweltering body burned,
Night was black against the pane . . .
My heart is pounding, dry my hands.
To drive away love's longing
I have no strength, I am too weak . . .

We held each other tight, we kissed,
Each with the other intertwined
Like paladin and serpent . . .
The smell of mint came drifting in,
And the pillow's rumpled quite,
And I'm alone, I'm all alone.

8

Every evening I look out from the steep*
At the smooth waters glittering afar;
I note which steamer's going past:
The Kamensk one, the Volga one or the one for Liubim.
The sun is very close to setting,
And always I keep steady watch to see
If there's a star above the steamer's wheel.
That's when it passes my vantage point.
If no star's visible—must be a mailboat,
Could be bringing letters addressed to me.
I rush down to the landing-stage,
Where the mailcoach stands ready and waiting.
Oh ye leather bags with massive locks,
How ponderous you are, how elephantine!
And surely there must be letters from those dear to me,
Which they would have written with their own dear hands?
So beats my heart, so sweetly does it ache
While I stand waiting at the mailman's back:
Will there be a letter there for me or not?
And this delectable riddle tortures me.
Oh my, the mountain road's already decked with stars.
To be alone, without a letter!
The road's a direct one.
A light burns here and there, houses nestle in their gardens.
And here it is, a letter from my friend: "I'm always calling you to mind,
No matter who I'm with, be it this one or that one."
So there you are, exactly the way he is
I love him and accept him.
The steamers will pull out, borne by the waves,
And I gaze sadly after them—
O my friends, my dear ones,
When will I set eyes on you again?

---

*"Every evening I look out from the steep . . ." What Kuzmin is referring to here
is a steamship route by way of the rivers Volga and Kostroma to the district town of
Liubim in Yaroslavl province, north of Moscow.

9

I'm sitting reading fairy tales and true ones,
Looking at portraits of the dead in ancient volumes,
They say, the portraits of the dead in ancient volumes:
"You've been forgotten, you've been forgotten . . ."

—What can I do about it if I've been forgotten,
What's to be done about it, ancient portraits?—
That's what I'm asking you, ancient portraits,
Will threats, or oaths, or entreaties do me any good?

"You too will forget the shoulders you have kissed,
Be then like us, be a portrait ancient and enamoured:
You'd make a good enamoured portrait
With languishing look and uttering no word."

—Of love beyond measure I am drooping and dying!
Can you not see that, O portraits I treasure?—
"We see it, we see it," the portraits assured me,
"What are you—a lover that's faithful and true?"

Thus sat I reading fairy tales and true ones,
Looking at portraits of the dead in ancient volumes.
And I wasn't sorry when the portraits whispered:
"You've been forgotten, you've been forgotten."

10

I am so weary, tired to death.
What yesterday still held my dreams
Has suddenly lost all sense and worth.
I cannot escape the vasselage
To certain shoulders, certain eyes,
To certain passionate and tender trysts.

Like a wounded man in the grass I lie,
Gazing at the infant moon.
The changing of the long-drawn hours
Brings no betrayal of unchanging love.
How alien, how vacant is the world to me
If I catch no glimpse of the lips that I love!

O gladness of the heart, O love,
When again shall I behold you.
When again with entrancing poison
Shall that sly gaze of yours imbue me,
And tenderness of familiar hands
Once more bring back my faithful friend?

I lie here haunted by a single thought:
There's the distant town, there's our house,
There's the garden where the gymnasts leap,
To which we made our way so often.
O house I love! . . . O threshold dear!
I'm tired to death, so weary I . . .

11

No matter the drizzle has soaked my clothes:
It has brought with it a precious hope.

Soon I'll be leaving, be leaving this town,
This dreary picture I shall see no more.

I count remaining days and hours,
No longer do I write, or go for walks, or read.

I'll soon be on my way—no point in settling down.
Tomorrow, tomorrow morning I'll get the packing done!

Long road ahead, you are unbearable and longed-for,
Day of departure, you are so remote, so strange!

I'm eager to be off, yet filled with fear and trembling,
I dare not believe our tender meeting's near.

Villages, mountains, rivers—they'll all go flashing by,
Maybe I will never set eyes on them again.

And I don't see anything, know nothing—
Dreaming only of the lips and eyes I love.

The tenderness I'll hoard in separation
Will make our kiss of greeting sweeter still.

So I'm glad the drizzle has soaked my clothes:
It has brought with it a precious hope.

12

The chugging steamer's in a hurry,
Its measured chugging seems to say:
"Be calm, my friend, for very soon
You'll glimpse the sweetness of that gaze,
From tedious torments you'll find rest
In caresses of the hands you knew."

My sleep's uneasy; light repose
Brings to me dreams of my dearest friend:
Now leavetaking, now clasps of greeting,
A fresh encounter, more embraces.
A parting of so many days
Adds passion to the hour of love.

I'm lying under a window now,
And scarcely bothering to take a peek.
The coastline slips by playfully,
As if it were a melody of Mozart's,
And through the clefts of lustrous cloud
A ray of sunlight softly glows.

I'm like one drunk with happiness.
Everyone is dear to me: captain,
And passenger, and matelot;
Casual roadway questioning is all
I fear: I do not wish my mind
To lose its clarity of thought.

The chugging steamer's in a hurry,
Its measured chugging seems to say:
"Be calm, my friend, for very soon
You'll glimpse the sweetness of that gaze,
From tedious torments you'll find rest
In caresses of the hands you knew."

II
A STORY INTERRUPTED*

1
MY PORTRAIT†

When you painted this portrait
Love was guiding your hand.
From no one now will I hide my face,
No one will say: "No, that one never loved."

With the brand of love my features
by your hand were eternally imprinted;
Made captive by a single dream the eyes gaze out,
And their dead calm is void of rest.

A wreath behind my head, open my lips,
Two useless angels at my back.
Neither thunder nor trumpet will assault my ear,
Nor the soft call hence to another land.

Only your voice I hear, I dream of you,
On you is fixed the gaze of my unmoving eyes.
I blaze, grow cold, I melt
Only in coming closer to you, touching you.

And, mindless of interdiction, everyone will say,
Looking at my swarthy, languid oval:
"In painting the portrait, one was guided by love—
The other enchanted him by love."

---

*"A Story Interrupted" made its first appearance in *White Nights: A St. Petersburg Almanack* in 1907. The same almanac also contained a story by Kuzmin, "The Cardboard House" that is clearly related to the cycle.

†"My Portrait." The portrait in question was painted by Sergei Sudeikin (1882–1946), who worked as scene painter and set designer for both Meyerhold and Diaghilev.

2
AT THE THEATRE*

Passageways, corridors, dressing-rooms,
A winding staircase, half-dark;
Conversations, stubborn arguments,
Over doors are curtains hiding nothing.

It smells of dust, and bleach, and turpentine,
In the distance, sounds of an ovation.
There's a little balcony with shaky breast-rails,
From which to look at the scenery below.

Long hours of waiting,
Chitchat with little actresses,
Wandering through dressing-rooms, through lobbies,
Now in the workshop, now in the wings.

You will arrive quite unexpectedly,
Stamping through the corridor resoundingly—
Oh, the depths of meaning attached
To your walk, to your smile, to your gaze!

How delightful to be embraced in sight of all.
With a greeting apparently quite casual,
To heed with heart enchained
The words indifferent and dear.

How I love the damp-stained walls
Of the white auditorium,
The dusty hangings on the stage,
The sting of jealousy!

---

*"At the Theatre." The theatre referred to is that of Vera Komissarzhevskaya. Her new theatrical enterprise, in collaboration with Vsevolod Meyerhold, which opened in November, 1906 on Ofitserskaya Street, marked a new experimental, anti-naturalistic epoch in the Russian theatre. In his "Reminiscences of N. N. Sapunov" Kuzmin noted that the new theatre was "a unifying center for painters, writers, and actors." Kuzmin wrote the music for the Komissarzhevskaya Theatre's most famous and controversial production—music that was, at least to the ears of one listener, "piquant, highly spiced, disturbing and voluptuous"—that of Aleksandr Blok's *Puppet Show*, which opened in December, 1906.

3
AT A PARTY*

You and me and the fat lady,
Discreetly closing the door behind us,
Have made our escape from the din of the crowd.

I play my "Seasons of Love" for you,
Every moment the door kept creaking—
Ladies of fashion and dandies arriving.

I understood what your eyes were hinting,
And we manoeuvred behind the door together,
And all those people were remote in a second.

The fat lady didn't move from the grand piano,
The dandies were herding at the door,
A slim, stylish lady was laughing her head off.

In the dark we mounted the stairway,
Threw open those doors so familiar,
Your smile became more languorous.

Our eyes were curtained with love,
We'd locked the other doors already . . .
If only they happened more often, nights like this!

---

*"At a Party." We are informed in the memoirs of Johannes von Guenther that the "fat lady" was Serafima Pavlovna Remizova-Dovgello, the spouse of A. M. Remizov, while the "slim, stylish lady" was Liudmila Nikolayevna Vilkina—the wife of N. M. Minsky and a poetess, prosaist and translator in her own right. "Seasons of Love" (1906), a cycle of poems set to music by Kuzmin himself, was first published in *The Scales* in 1909.

4
A LUCKY DAY*

Today we'll be spending the whole day together!
Hard to believe such luck could come our way!
We'll follow each other around in carriages or on foot:
You'll be wearing that Dutch cap of yours and your plaid.
Paying calls as a team—just think of all the mud . . .
We're so lovey-dovey, so entrancingly bourgeois!
We are faithful to the rules of a life that's gay and carefree—
And "Chablis on ice" is a motto we haven't forgotten.
A shame you don't care for the "Vienna,"
But why do I tremble at some kind of treachery?
Today you are sweeter than ever I've known you,
To find someone better than you I'd be lucky.
Come see me tomorrow, and bring Sapunov with you—†
Dear friend, every meeting with you is a first one!

---

*"A Lucky Day." "Chablis on ice": Kuzmin is quoting the famous phrase from his own "manifesto" poem that opens "A Summer Affair." The restaurant that Sudeikin doesn't care for is the "Vienna" on Gogol Street—a popular gathering place for St. Petersburg bohemians.

†". . . bring Sapunov with you." Nikolai Nikolayevich Sapunov (1880–1912) is "The painter long sea-slain" who "Stamps a capricious heel" in the Second Prologue to *The Trout Breaks the Ice*. Sapunov had been drowned when the rowboat in which he was sailing to Terioki on the Gulf of Finland, together with Kuzmin and some other participants in the lively experimental theatre at Terioki, had overturned. It was Sapunov who had painted the sets for Meyerhold's production of Blok's *Puppet Show*. In 1910 he furnished the decor for Kuzmin's one-act musical comedy *The Dutch Girl Lise* at Meyerhold's House of Interludes.

5
THE CARDBOARD HOUSE*

My friend has gone away without a good-bye,
Leaving me a cardboard house.
Precious gift, are you a hint or a prediction?
Is my friend a heartless prankster or a tenderhearted loon?
What's to be done with you, singular offering?
I shall light a candle behind your windows of colored paper.
Do you not promise me the joy of a birth?
Are they not close—the Wise Men?
You are light, transparent and of many colors,
And you glow when I put a flame inside you.
Without a flame you are cardboard and gloomy:
Do I understand your hint correctly?
And this is your prediction:
A star will arise and the Wise Men will come with gold, frankincense
    and myrrh.
What meaning can it possibly have
Except that money will be coming our way, that love and world-wide
    fame are ours to win?

---

*"The Cardboard House." This poem was published together with Kuzmin's identically titled story in *White Nights*. Both poem and story are autobiographical. Sudeikin had given Kuzmin a cardboard house at their meeting on December 3, 1906 and then left for Moscow the following day. In the final paragraph of the short story version, the composer Demianov (who shares his first name and the initial of his patronymic with Kuzmin) finds that his friend Miatlev has left him a parting gift:

   The little house was the kind peddlars sell before Christmas, made of thick cardboard
   with cut-out doors and windows with sashes on both floors; red and green transparent
   paper was inserted in the windows, so as to shine gaily when a candle was lit inside
   the house.

The "Christmas motif" is a powerful one in the poem.

6
AN UNLUCKY DAY

I know you have your own little ways:
Going off without a good-bye, returning unannounced,
Unpredictable behavior is a whim of yours—
But how to find a way of telling you you're wrong?

To be in the same town, nearby, just round the corner—
And not to catch a glimpse of you, not hear your voice, not touch you,
Going down to the porter a score of times a day.
Looking to see if that long-awaited note has come.

No good, no good, it's just no good! Strangers keep you company
And talk to you, listening without much interest—
Things that would have plunged me into quivering ecstasy—
And your hand is shaken by indifferent hands.

Cabbies, actors, drivers of autobuses—
There's no hiding from them, they see you when they like.
So be it, I must offer no offense to love:
I will be patient, devoted, continent.

7
DREAMS OF MOSCOW

The pink house with the sky-blue gates;
That Dutch cap of yours with its earflaps:

The hands so dear, the untrue eyes,
Beloved lips (could they possibly dissemble?);

The room has a wardrobe and a double bed,
A distant street is visible from the workshop window;

In your dining-room with its inside stairway,
How delightful to drink tea or morning coffee;

We're together days on end, few close friends visit,
High spirits, laughter, singing, well-aimed wit;

Wanderings together through snow-crammed alleyways,
The long kiss that launches and concludes the night.

8
THE CONSOLATION

With a pathetic delight I will console myself,
Buying myself a cap that's just like yours;
With a sigh, I'll hang it on a peg,
And think of you each time I do so.

Catching in passing my own reflection,
I'll be surprised it isn't you I'm seeing,
And in a trice imagination will sketch in
Beneath that cap the glance of those dear, faithless eyes.

And chancing to stroll through the hallway,
I'll suddenly fall captive to a foolish dream,
A strange delusion will enthrall me:
"He's turned up unexpectedly, he must be in his room."

The familiar figure is before my eyes,
I can hear your voice—it is no dream—
A moment more, and once again I'm downcast,
Beguiled but briefly by an empty dream.

And I cast a glance about the empty hall:
Alas, that deceitful diamond was but glass!
And all I can do is to sadly kiss the pleat
Of the cap just like the one you used to have.

9
ALL DAY

I'm going to stay home all day today;
Other people I just don't want to see.
Sad weariness possesses me,
And I've lost count of unlucky days.

It's frosty, clear, the sun shines through the window,
From the nursery come the children's din and laughter;
I'm quietly writing in my room
A letter to which he won't reply.

I'll sit for a while in Seriozha's room,*
Then with my sister,† in the dining-room, in my own—
You are dearer to me with every moment,
You who have forgotten me, despise me, do not love me.

I'm reading a book, not understanding a word of it,
And one thought again and again repeats itself:
"In wintertime May's blossoming is still far off,
Who'll venture with parting to affirm love?"

Two candles' light does not disperse half-darkness,
Stubborn and dull my melancholy mood.
I sing to myself that ditty of Dalayrac's‡
"Mon bien-aimé, hélas, ne revient pas!"

Time for supper, tea, and a cold cutlet,
The lazy arguing of the domestics—I hold my tongue;
And having performed the ceremony of toilette,
I hasten to blow out the mournful candle.

---

*". . . Seriozha's room." Seriozha is Sergei Abramovich Auslender (1886–1943?), Kuzmin's nephew, who was a writer of fiction and a dramatist.

†". . . my sister." Varvara Alekseyevna Moshkova (by her second marriage); Kuzmin had lived for a short time with his sister and brother-in-law in 1906.

‡". . . that ditty of Dalayrac's." Dalayrac (1753–1809) was born Nicholas d'Alayrac but cautiously dropped the aristocratic "de" after the French Revolution. Dalayrac was the composer of some sixty operas. The line quoted (inaccurately) is from Nina's aria from the opera *Nina* (1786). The correct version of the line quoted by Kuzmin is: "Mais je regarde, mais je regarde, hélas, hélas,/Le bien aimé ne revient pas."

10
EPILOGUE

What's to be done with you, beloved verses?
You come to an end, hardly having begun.
Everyone's happy: betrotheds and suitors,*
The late lamented's pushing up the daisies, having died.

In novels according to the rules all words are clear,
There's a full stop at the end;
It's quite clear who Armand is, who the widow,
Whose daughter Elise† turned out to be.

But in my story's heedless course
There isn't even a hint of order,
It flies above the abyss more unfettered
Than the bound of a gazelle.

The crybaby reader
Will see no tearstains on my face,
No period is furnished by fate at the close,
But just a blot.

---

*"Everyone's happy: betrotheds and suitors . . ." On the biographical plane, the "Story" was "Interrupted" by the marriage of Sergei Sudeikin to Olga Glebova on December 26, 1906.

†But let us leave the last word to Pushkin: "Armand" and "Elise" are the hero and heroine of a "sentimental novel," "classic and old-fashioned," entitled "The Love of Elise and Armand or A Correspondence between Two Families." And who is losing herself in this worthy tome? None other than Natalya Pavlovna, the heroine of "Count Nulin," a poem suggested to Pushkin, if not exactly "inspired" by Shakespeare's "Rape of Lucrece" (what if Lucrece's would-be ravisher were to be given the resounding slap he so richly deserved, what then?).

Mikhail Kuzmin (1872–1936)

THREE POEMS FROM *ALEXANDRIAN SONGS*

[Aleksandriiskie pesni, 1905–1908]

Translated by Michael Green

LOVE

1

When it was I first encountered you
poor memory cannot tell me:
was it morning, or in the afternoon,
evening, perhaps, or late at night?
I remember only the wan cheeks,
the gray eyes beneath dark brows
and the deep-blue collar at the swarthy throat,
and all this seems to come to me from childhood,
although I am older than you, older by many years.

2

Were you apprenticed to a fortune teller?—
My heart lies open to you,
you can divine my every thought,
my deepest meditations are not hidden from you;
but knowing this, you know but little,
few words are needed for the telling of it,
no crystal ball or glowing brazier:
my heart, my thoughts, my deepest meditations
are filled with voices endlessly repeating:
"I love you, and my love shall have no ending!"

3

At noon I must have been conceived,
at noon I must have come into the world,
and from my childhood I have loved
the beaming radiance of the sun.
One day I looked upon your eyes
and I became indifferent to the sun:
why should I adore a single sun
now that two of them are mine?

4

People see gardens and houses
and the sea crimson with the sunset,
people see gulls skimming the waves,
and women on flat roofs,
people see warriors in armor
and pie-sellers in the town square,
people see sun and stars,
brooks and bright rivers,
but I see only
gray eyes beneath dark brows,
the touch of pallor in the swarthy cheeks,
the form of matchless grace—
thus do the eyes of lovers see
no more than the wise heart wills.

5

Leaving my house in the morning,
I look up at the sun and think:
"How like my love
when he bathes in the river,
or gazes at the distant vegetable plots!"
And when in the heat of noon I gaze
at the same burning sun,
again you come into my mind, my dearest one:
"How like my love
when he rides through the crowded streets!"
And when I look upon soft sunsets,
it is to you that memory returns,
drowsing, wan from our caresses,
your drooping eyelids shadowed deep.

6

Not for nothing did we read the theologians
and studied the rhetoricians not in vain,
for every word we have a definition
and can interpret all things seven different ways.
In your body I can locate the four virtues,
and, needless to say, the seven sins;
nor am I backward in tasting these delights;

but of all words one is changeless:
when, gazing deep into your gray eyes,
I say, "I love you"—the cleverest rhetorician
will understand only, "I love you"—nothing more.

7

Were I a general of olden times,
I would subdue the Ethiops and the Persians,
I would dethrone Pharaoh,
I would build myself a pyramid
higher than Cheops',
and I would become
more glorious than any man in Egypt.

Were I a nimble thief,
I would rob the tomb of Menkaure,
I would sell the gems to the Jews of Alexandria,
I would buy up land and mills,
and I would become
richer than any man in Egypt.

Were I a second Antinous,
he who drowned in the sacred Nile—
I would drive all men mad with my beauty,
temples would be raised to me while I yet lived,
and I would become
more powerful than any man in Egypt.

Were I a sage steeped in wisdom,
I would squander all my wealth,
I would shun office and occupation,
I would guard other men's orchards,
and I would become
freer than any man in Egypt.

Were I your lowliest slave,
I would sit in a dungeon
and once a year or once in two years
I would glimpse the golden tracery of your sandals
when you chanced to walk by the prison house,
and I would become
happier than any man in Egypt.

"Once again I beheld the town where I was born"

Once again I beheld the town where I was born
and spent my far-off youth;
I knew
that all my family and friends were gone,
I knew
that even the memory of me had vanished,
but the houses, the winding streets,
the green and distant sea
spoke to me continually
of what was unchanging—
the distant days of my childhood,
the dreams and plans of my youth
and love that had dissolved like smoke.
A stranger utterly,
penniless,
not knowing where to lay my head,
I found myself in a remote quarter of the city
where lights shone through lowered shutters
and singing and the rattle of tambourines
came from the inner rooms.
By a drawn curtain
stood a curled and pretty boy,
and when I slackened my steps, being weary,
he said to me:
"Abba,
you seem like one who has lost his way
and has no friend to turn to.
Enter in:
all things are here
to make a foreigner forget his loneliness.
Here you may find
a gay and sportive mistress,
firm-bodied and with fragrant hair."
I lingered, my mind on other things,
and, smiling, he continued:
"And if such things do not tempt you,
wanderer,
we can offer other joys
not to be despised by a wise and courageous heart."
Crossing the threshold, I cast off my sandals,
lest I should bring into a house of pleasure
the sacred dust of the desert.

Glancing at the doorkeeper,
I saw
that he was all but naked;
together we passed along the corridor
toward the welcoming tambourines.

ANTINOUS*

Three times I saw him face to face.
The first time was in the gardens—
I had been sent to fetch food for my comrades,
and to make the journey shorter
I took the path by the palace wing;
suddenly I caught the tremor of strings,
and, being tall of stature,
I peered through the broad window and saw
him:
he was sitting alone and sad,
his slender fingers idly plucking the strings of a lyre;
a white dog
lay silent at his feet,
and only the fountain's splashing
mingled with the music.
Sensing my gaze,
he put down his lyre
and lifted his lowered face.
Magic to me his beauty
and his silence in the empty room,
in the noontide stillness.
Crossing myself, I ran away in fear,
away from the window . . .
Later, on guard duty at Lochias,
I was standing in the passage
leading to the quarters of the imperial astrologer.
The moon cast a bright square on the floor,
and the copper buckles of my sandals
glinted
as I trod the patch of brightness.

---

*Antinous (ca. 111–130 A.D.) was the beautiful Bithynian youth, lover of Roman Emperor Hadrian. He drowned in the River Nile in Egypt, whether by accident or self-sacrifice to purchase his lover's health. Hadrian deified him and his statues were disseminated throughout the ancient world.

Hearing footsteps,
I halted.
From the inner chamber,
a slave bearing a torch before them,
three men came forth,
he being one.
He was pale,
but it seemed to me
that the room was lit
not by the torch, but by his countenance.
As he passed, he glanced at me
and said, "I've seen you before, my friend,"
and withdrew to the astrologer's quarters.
Long after his white robes were lost to view
and the torch had been swallowed in darkness,
I stood there, not moving, not breathing,
and afterwards in the barracks,
feeling Martius, who slept next to me,
touch my hand in his usual way,
I pretended to be asleep.
And then one evening
we met again.
We were bathing
near the tents of Caesar's camp,
when suddenly a cry went up.
We ran, but it was too late.
Dragged from the water, the body
lay on the sand,
and that same unearthly face,
the face of a magician,
stared with wide-open eyes.
Still far off, the Emperor was hurrying toward us,
shaken by the grievous tidings;
but I stood seeing nothing,
not feeling tears unknown to me since childhood
running down my cheeks.
All night I whispered prayers,
raving of my native Asia, of Nicomedia,
and angel voices sang:
"Hosannah!
A new god
is given unto men!"

MIKHAIL KUZMIN: PAST AND PRESENT

Michael Green

> From the other end of the room, steady as two planets,
> two eyes were moving toward me. The eyes were—here.
> Before me stood—Kuzmin!
>
> Marina Tsvetayeva, "Otherworldly Evening"

O N A RECENT visit to Moscow I was delighted to stumble across a Russian version of Apuleius' *Golden Ass*, the Latin novel from the age of the Antonines. I vaguely recalled some lines from the "Alexandrian Songs" in which Mikhail Kuzmin had sought to persuade his readers that the wisest way to make a graceful exit from this earthly existence is:

> to return from a pleasant stroll/to the house you no longer own,/to eat a leisurely supper,/and, having read the tale of Apuleius through/for the hundred and first time,/to lie in a warm, fragrant bath,/and without hearing a single farewell/to open your veins,/while through the long ceiling window/the scent of stock comes drifting in,/the sunset glitters/and the sound of flutes comes floating from afar.

It occurred to me that, since Kuzmin had made his own translation of this adored classic, the little brown and yellow paperback with its belaureled and betoga-ed donkey was more than likely to be a republication of the Kuzmin *Golden Ass*. No translator's name was to be found on either of the two title pages, but I persevered and, sure enough, discovered, in minuscule italic print: "translated by M. Kuz'min," the name spelled with a Cyrillic "soft sign"—the usual spelling of a name semantically close to "Smith" and not surprisingly among the most frequently encountered Russian family names. "Kuz'min" is a common name, but the Kuzmin (minus "soft sign") family were not commoners, being Old Believer gentry from the Yaroslavl district. The above-mentioned *Golden Ass* was dated 1992 and published by a "Lenizdat" enigmatically located in "Saint Petersburg" —on the Fontanka indeed. All this may very well seem petty, even piffling —but I can think of no more telling way to bring home the obscurity into which a name once famous, not to say *notorious*, had sunk even in a city that its owner had adopted unreservedly as his own.

So who was Mikhail Alekseyevich Kuzmin? "The Russian Oscar Wilde," as he was dubbed, a hangover from the decadent 'nineties, resolutely purveying "scarlet sins"? Certainly *Wings* (1906) is a more thoroughgoing if less epigrammatic "gay novel" (essentially a twentieth-century genre?) than Wilde's *Picture of Dorian Gray* of 1891 had ventured or even wanted to be. Then, again a distinctly 'nineties figure, there is the author of "Concerning Beautiful Clarity" (1910), advocate of a reformed prose of exquisite simplicity.

Most memorably of all there is the famous "manifesto" poem first published in 1907:

> Where shall I find a style to catch a stroll,
> Chablis on ice, a crisply toasted roll,
> The agate succulence of cherries ripe?

A question—asked not exactly in wide-eyed innocence—that serves to introduce a sequence of poems dedicated to a beautiful young army officer. A new style for a new theme? Yes, Kuzmin is indisputably a central figure of Russian *Dekadenstvo*. And it is doubtless from this "Chablis on ice" association that the stereotype of Kuzmin is derived: a *minor* poet of exquisite self-indulgence—and unapologetically homosexual in the bargain.

Let me attempt to convey something of the unique aureole of scandalous celebrity that encircled Mikhail Kuzmin. The future citizen and singer of St. Petersburg was born in 1872 in Yaroslavl, an ancient city some hundred and sixty miles northeast of Moscow. The pall of prudishness that fell over Russia during its Soviet decades still renders difficult the recovery of the unconstricted experimentalism of the generous years that followed the not totally unsuccessful "revolution" (even Soviet historiography graced it with this title) of 1905. This was the era of a youthful Kandinsky and Stravinsky, when abstractionism made its way into painting and new dissonances and new rhythms into music. Nor, with an unprecedented relaxation of an officially imposed censorship, did the sexual conventions go unchallenged— most notably by what was to become a scandalous bestseller: Kuzmin's novella *Wings*, first published in the November 1906 number of *The Scales*, a leading literary magazine of the day. *Wings* is a *roman à thèse* that postulates sexual nonconformism with considerable self-assurance (and let us not forget that André Gide's *Immoralist*, an early example of that twentieth century genre par excellence the "gay novel," had been published in a cautious edition of three hundred only four years previously).

Kuzmin's two poetic cycles included in the present anthology, *A Summer Affair* and *A Story Interrupted*—each inspired by a new lover (see notes to the poems)—likewise made their first appearance in literary journals published in 1906. Such daring brought down upon Kuzmin the outrage of the critical establishment, perhaps best typified by a certain G. S. Novopolin, who, in an opus entitled *The Pornographic Element in Russian Literature* (1909) denounced the "open publicity" given to an "unnatural vice" that was to be encountered in the Caucasus (where "such practices are widespread") as well as "among aristocratic circles in both our capitals." An attempt to organize a literary boycott of Kuzmin met with failure in 1909.

A whisper and tumult of voices, like rye blown in the wind; "He's going to sing. . . . He's going to sing. . . . He's going to sing. . . ."

The last thing I remember—with a final turn of the head—is Kuzmin walking up to the piano.

These two fragments have been chipped from Marina Tsvetayeva's breathless account of her one and only encounter with Mikhail Alekseyevich, which took place in January 1916. Here we catch a glimpse of Kuzmin in another of his roles—the chosen entertainer of the capital's literary set. Music had been Kuzmin's first love, and although personality conflicts had prevented him from completing the seven-year course at the St. Petersburg Conservatory (where he studied from 1891 to 1893, and was in Rimsky-Korsakov's composition class), he became both a competent composer and a resourceful performer of his own songs at the piano. Indeed had he never written a word, Kuzmin would have a secure place in the annals of Russian theatrical history as the composer of the incidental music for Vsevolod Meyerhold's epoch-making production in 1906 of Aleksandr Blok's *Puppet Show* at Vera Komissarzhevskaya's new theatre. His operetta (he wrote words *and* music, needless to say) *Maidens' Pleasure* (with Sudeikin's dazzling oriental sets) was the hit of the season at Suvorin's St. Petersburg Maly Theatre in 1911, in which year—along with Meyerhold, Evreinov, Remizov, and Walter Nouvel—he became a founding member of the "Intimate Theatre Society" that inspired Boris Pronin's "Stray Dog," the most celebrated of all the St. Petersburg/Petrograd cabarets. Kuzmin's old friend Serge Diaghilev was so taken with an evening devoted to the poet's drama at the "Stray Dog" in 1914 that he proposed, in true impresario style, to take the "Dog" troupe on a Paris tour (the First World War made this project impractical, alas). Would that we had more space to devote to an aspect ("the Russian Noel Coward/Cole Porter") of Kuzmin's career that is in itself deserving of a separate study.

Kuzmin greeted the October Revolution with genuine if short-lived enthusiasm, and during the relatively unconstrained pre-Stalinist 'twenties succeeded in publishing two fine collections—*Otherworldly Evenings* in 1921 and *Parabolas* in the following year, as well as his first and only collection of articles, *Conventions*, in 1924. Yet the skies were darkening: in his *Literature and Revolution* of 1923 Leon Trotsky paired Kuzmin with Sologub as writers whose books were "completely and entirely superfluous to modern post-October man, like a glass bead to a soldier on a battlefield," defining them as "internal émigrés." No review appeared under his name in the Soviet press after 1926: no longer able to make a living in journalism, Kuzmin was dependent on literary translation to keep body and soul together, putting nine of Shakespeare's plays—most impressively, *King Lear*—into Russian, and meeting Byron's challenge to the ingenious rhymer in his translation of *Don Juan*. His publication of his last and finest collection, *The Trout Breaks the Ice* (1929) in this season of dearth approaches the miraculous. When Kuzmin died of pneumonia in a Leningrad hospital on March 1, 1936 his death went virtually unmentioned in the Soviet press.

In 1928 Kuzmin had given his last public reading, a curious, scandalous and touching occasion. The students of the Leningrad literary institutes had the idea of inviting virtually the last distinguished writer of his generation who was still alive and living in Leningrad. Kuzmin went, expecting the evening to be poorly attended, imagining himself to be a forgotten versifier. But when he arrived at the hall it was packed. The evening was clearly a rare success; Kuzmin read, among other things, the poem on which he had been working most recently, *The Trout Breaks the Ice*, and the audience grew ever more enthusiastic. But at last what the organizers of the event feared actually came to pass; the ticket system having broken down, there came crowding into the hall a mob of Leningrad homosexuals, many carrying flowers with which they showered the poet during the ovation that followed his reading. Kuzmin's delight equalled the alarm and horror of the affair's organizers; it was only by persuading the authorities that they were not party to the disgraceful events that they escaped serious trouble.

This is a suitable point for a flashback account of the more intimate connections of our poet's life, a survey of the men with whom Kuzmin was sexually involved over the years. Chronologically the first of these loves to be recorded by Kuzmin was the enigmatic "Prince Georges" (his identity has yet to be established), an officer in a cavalry regiment, four years Kuzmin's senior, he first encountered—so we are informed in the "condensed" diary for the years between 1884 and 1894 to be found elsewhere in this collection—in 1893, who died of a heart ailment in Vienna, where he had taken time out to visit an aunt in the course of a grand tour of the Near East undertaken by the lovers in the course of 1894.

The cycle "A Summer Affair" that opens "Part One" of Kuzmin's first collection, *Nets*, and which was first published in the March 1907 number of the leading Symbolist literary magazine *The Scales* (sometimes dubbed "Libra" by the astrologically inclined) bears the dedication "To P. V. Maslov." Pavel Maslov, we are informed in the useful notes to the 1990 Kuzmin collection edited by Shmakov, was a young army officer concerning whom Kuzmin wrote in a letter of June 1906 to Walter Nouvel, ". . . I love him more than I did before, more than I thought I did, more than I have ever loved anybody." Soldier boy Pavel (we are not informed of his patronymic) was much—"Oh lips kissed by so many . . ."—in demand, a fact confirmed by the note of weary resignation typical of this cycle. "A Story Interrupted," so near in date to the previous cycle (it was first published in the Petersburg Almanac "White Nights" in July 1907 that contains a story, "The Cardboard House" in which Kuzmin puts the same material to use) has a different "onlie begetter"—none other than the talented painter Sergei Sudeikin. "My Portrait," the cycle's opening poem, refers to a portrait of Kuzmin (where is it now?) being completed by his lover. The setting for these poems is not the Russian provinces of "A Summer Affair" but the domain of the St. Petersburg theatre with its "chitchat of little actresses" and forbidden pleasures somehow snatched at a party.

Olga Glebova (or Glebova-Sudeikina, as she was generally known after her marriage), celebrated beauty and inseparable friend of Anna Akhmatova, was destined, by an odd twist of fate, to play a deadly role in the life of Mikhail Kuzmin. Now a feted entertainer and an established poet, the mature Kuzmin was to have two great loves, both of whom, curiously enough, also had authorial ambitions (it would seem that Kuzmin, in addition to the sensual and emotional satisfaction customarily sought in a lover, felt the need for some sharing of creative ideals). The first of them, Vsevolod Knyazev, was a minor poet whom Kuzmin seems to have encountered in Riga in 1910; he too was an army officer. Knyazev is the ". . . stripling/With a bullet through his brain" who is to be located among the fauna of the "Second Prologue" to *The Trout Breaks the Ice*. Glebova-Sudeikina, let us note, was on friendly terms with Kuzmin. She was a professional actress, and was to play a part in *The Venetian Madcaps*, a playlet to which Kuzmin had written both words and music, when it was staged at the Nosov mansion in 1914. In the previous year, the bisexual Knyazev, rebuffed by Glebova-Sudeikina, had put an end to his life.

Kuzmin's last grand passion was Yuri Yurkun (the "Mister Dorian" of that same "Second Prologue" referred to above). Only seventeen years old when Kuzmin first took up with him in 1913, Yurkun had the good fortune to preserve his youthful good looks in the manner of Oscar Wilde's Dorian Gray—hence Kuzmin's nickname for him. Nothing could bear more eloquent witness to the passing of the institutionalized prudishness of Soviet days than the appearance in 1995 of what was virtually the complete works of Yuri Yurkun (all of which had appeared in St. Petersburg—or rather Petrograd—before the city had changed its name to Leningrad on Lenin's death in 1924). The collection bears a title taken from a work it includes—*Bad Company*, a novella first published in 1915 and dedicated to, of all people, Sergei Sudeikin.

The book has an odd and somehow touching dustjacket on which a balding, bespectacled but *unmistakable* Kuzmin passes (they are walking in opposite directions) an elegantly beruffed and begloved Yurkun (whose first and longest novel happened to have been called *The Swedish Gloves*). Vasili Kondratyev, the author of the lively introduction, is not in the least troubled by the nature of the relationship between Kuzmin and Yurkun, "his beloved and friend." True, the edition is smallish by Russian standards—a mere fifteen thousand—and the blurb on the bookjacket contrives to misspell Kuzmin's name in a manner heralded in the opening paragraph of this introduction. The volume was, needless to say, published in St. Petersburg.

The final item in the volume is a chatty, cheeky and informative memoir entitled "About Yurochka"—"Yurochka" being the pet name bestowed upon Yuri Yurkun by Olga Nikolayevna Arbenina-Gildebrandt (1897–1980), the woman he married in 1921. Fortunately, this new desertion was by no means as calamitous as Knyazev's had been. Yurkun had soon moved back to the apartment he shared with Kuzmin, and Kuzmin seems to have found peace and contentment in the somewhat bizarre menage of which he now found himself the center: in addition to the two men there was Yurkun's mother (who had never left the apartment) and Arbenina herself, who was not a permanent resident of the apartment but who frequently stayed there. Yurkun was to be the eventual loser. To quote the orange lettering on the rich brown dustjacket on the posthumous edition of his life's work: "In 1938 Yuri Yurkun was arrested and shot in the so-called 'Writers' Affair.' "

So much for the past. What about the present? In 1980 I published a selection of Kuzmin's poetry and prose, in the introduction to which I made the following extravagant assertion:

> He was, as might have been said of Pushkin, a great poet, an outstanding prose writer, and a skilled and original playwright.

Such an appraisal of Kuzmin will perhaps be a mite less startling now, the invocation of Pushkin slightly less of a "sacrilege." In 1980 no Kuzmin collection had appeared in Russia since *The Trout Breaks the Ice*, which was published when its author was still among the living; but *since* 1980 we have had good cause to offer sacrifice to the mysterious deity who foreordained the motions of Russian publishing houses in Soviet days. Two large collections have appeared, one in 1989 (*Verse and Prose*), in an edition of 300,000 copies, the other in 1990 (*Selected Works*), in an edition of 200,000.

And what of Kuzmin today in what used to be called the Soviet Union? I have mentioned two recent selections from Kuzmin's work published in what is now the Russian Federation—the second of them quite astonishingly candid in its treatment of a subject long unmentionable in a Russian/Soviet context. In the same year that this volume appeared in the bookshops (1990) occurred another happy portent of our poet's flourishing future. Between May 17th and May 19th, at the Anna Akhmatova Museum on the Fontanka, in what was then still Leningrad there took place a Conference under the heading: "Mikhail Kuzmin and the Russian Culture of the Twentieth Century." Conference proceedings ("Theses and Materials") were published in the same year, and were dedicated "To the Memory of Gennady Grigoryevich Shmakov": it is indeed to the untiring, courageous, self-sacrificing labors of Gennady Shmakov (1940–1988) that the rediscovery of Mikhail Kuzmin in Russia and beyond its borders is in a great measure due.

The most valuable service of these Proceedings is to present to our readerly mind's eye a completely new Kuzmin: not "the Russian Oscar Wilde"; not "the Russian Noel Coward"; but "the Russian Samuel Pepys." Like Mr. Pepys, Kuzmin was a devoted and diligent diarist (though, unlike Pepys he didn't keep his in a code that delayed its enjoyment for over a century). Kuzmin kept an almost daily record of his activities between August 1905 and December 1931. "The shocking revelations of the diary, if they do not overturn, will certainly to a significant degree disturb settled notions concerning the intimate life and amorous relationships in the epoch of the 'silver' and 'post-silver' age." The author of the report, "Mikhail Kuzmin's Diary: An Archival Pre-History," is roundly condemnatory of the "Soviet mentality" that has led to the systematized intolerance of a country where "homosexuality, to which Kuzmin devotes so much attention, has been and is to this very day qualified as a criminal offense. . . ." S. V. Shumikhin, author of the report, draws an intriguing parallel between Kuzmin's diary and the "Notebook" (still not published in full) of F. F. Vigel' (Wiegel), the buddy whom Pushkin jocularly implored in a famous line to "have mercy on my ass": both could provide much invaluable information concerning the literature, the theatre, the social and political life of their day.

At all events, we are assured that "the diaries of M. A. Kuzmin, long inaccessible to researchers by reason of the extreme intimacy of their contents" will now *definitely* be published, once they have been deciphered and an adequate commentary has been assembled. Let us then rejoice! And let these thoughts be brought to a conclusion with the unfinished sentence that was Kuzmin's last recorded utterance:

Well, that's it, it's all over—and all that's left are the details. . . .

MIKHAIL KUZMIN'S DIARIES—A FORETASTE

Michael Green

THE ADVENTURES and adversities of Mikhail Kuzmin's archives are instructive. This treasure trove (which contained work both published and unpublished in manuscript form together with a multitude of letters in addition to nineteen bound volumes of diary), was sold by Kuzmin in 1933 to the State Literary Museum, under the directorship of a respected activist of the pre-revolutionary period, Vladimir Bonch-Bruyevich, for the considerable sum (then!) of 25,000 roubles. Kuzmin made the stipulation that the diary should be published only after his death "and if in the course of my lifetime, only with my permission." Bonch-Bruyevich soon—the following year—came under attack from an investigative commission of the Party Central Committee for having wasted museum funds on "records for the most part dealing with homosexual topics, which are of no historical or literary value." Bonch-Bruyevich responded that in addition to the homosexual "motifs" to be expected from such a writer as Kuzmin the diary contained a great deal of literary information, and, surely an irrefutable argument from a Marxist-Leninist point of view, it presented a vivid picture of the decay of the bourgeoisie at the end of the last century and, *in particular*, at the beginning of this one. Other actors in this diverting tale are the GPU and its later metamorphosis the NKVD: for the invaluable information it could supply to these Soviet institutions, Kuzmin's diary became a resident of the ill-famed security citadel of the Lubianka for the space of a half-dozen years (in a querulous letter of June 1939 addressed to Lavrentii Beria, People's Commissar for Internal Affairs, Bonch-Bruyevich begs to be informed of the fate of these materials of which it is his duty to keep account and which were confiscated by Beria's department far back in 1934). The Diary was returned in 1940, when Bonch-Bruyevich had already ceased to be Museum Director.

"Histoire édifiante de mes commencements" (Edifying Story of My Beginnings)—such was the inscription that Kuzmin scribbled at the top of some autobiographical notes before folding them in a triangle and tucking them between the pages of a volume of his diary covering events of 1906. The "Histoire," an antedated sketch of the decade from 1884 to 1894, prefaced by some intriguing family data, was intended to take the place of a journal for 1894–96 that had been destroyed by its author—less, one surmises, for reasons of discretion (a virtue of which like all good diarists Kuzmin was blessedly devoid) than for the painful memories it would have aroused of his peregrinations among the ancient cities of Asia Minor in the company of Prince Georges, the lover who had died soon after their conclusion. Certainly, in these reminiscences of more than a decade later the prince—all we are told about him is that he was a cavalry officer four years Kuzmin's senior—remains a remote and abrupt figure. Wisely, perhaps, Kuzmin makes hardly any more effort to "evoke" his lost love than he does to bring before us his instructor in fugue and counterpoint at the St. Petersburg Conservatoire, Nikolai Rimsky-Korsakov. Fortunately, however, in this ultimate decade of a millennium we will be accounted fortunate to survive, the piece finds a practical purpose: to serve as introduction to the diary of more than Pepysian proportions kept diligently by our poet-musician between 1905 and 1931 and sold by him to the Soviet state in 1933. The extract from the "Histoire" presented here— roughly a third of its full length—should convey something of the flavor of the diary itself, the publication of which *in full* is solemnly promised in the near future. This section, with its original dated heading (only a brief passage of musical minutiae has been omitted) will be of special interest as it deals with Kuzmin's first serious love affair (unless we award that title to a high school episode, also recorded here, that would seem to have gone rather beyond the bounds of schoolboy misbehavior). And then there is the curiously lighthearted account (here, surely, we strike a peculiarly *Kuzminian* note) of the diarist's attempted suicide.

A name that crops up with some frequency in these pages is that of "Yusha" Chicherin. Georgii Vasilyevich Chicherin will no doubt be more familiar in the role of people's commissar for foreign affairs (in which he succeeded Leon Trotsky in 1918) than in that of the intimate and confidant of Mikhail Kuzmin. But he was both. The Cicerinis had come to Russia in the retinue of Zoe Palaeologus, niece of the last Byzantine emperor, who had not hesitated to abjure the Catholicism in which she had been raised as a refugee at the papal court in order, in 1472, to become the consort of Ivan III, Grand Prince of Muscovy, whose alliance with the fallen Byzantine dynasty helped greatly to reinforce Moscow's claim to be the "Third Rome." Beginning in 1886, when he had moved from the Tambov region of the Chicherin family estate, Yusha had become Kuzmin's schoolfellow at the Alexandrovsky Lyceum, one of the most stylish St. Petersburg gymnasia, one patronized by families of ancient lineage such as Chicherin's.

"I have revolution and I have Mozart," Chicherin is reported to have said toward the end of his life, and no doubt his closeness to Kuzmin derived largely from his accomplishment as a pianist and his dedication to music in general (a volume of his musings on Mozart was published in 1971). It is hard to overestimate the importance of the Chicherin influence on Kuzmin's formative years. The home of B. N. Chicherin is mentioned as his residence when he was preparing to enter the St. Petersburg Conservatoire. Boris Nikolayevich was perhaps the most formidable of the Chicherins to participate in the ideological struggles of the nineteenth century: finding himself to the left of the "tsar liberator," he had resigned as professor of law at Moscow University in 1868, and no doubt the short duration of his term as governor-general of Moscow (1882–83) was not unconnected with his opposition to the reactionary policies of Alexander III.

But do not trouble yourself, gentle reader, with these weighty concerns and connections if you have no mind or mood to. They are not necessary to the understanding, still less to the enjoyment of this extraordinary auto-biographical fragment. Could a piece so utterly self-accepting, so totally unridden by any kind of guilt, so—in any sense you like—*gay* have possibly been written so close to the turn of the nineteenth rather than the twentieth century?

1884-1894

It was very uncomfortable in St. Petersburg: the little apartment facing onto the yard, Father's illness, his operation, the obligatory round of visits to relatives, my failures at high school, the darkness, the barrel organs trundled from yard to yard—all this filled me with an inexpressible dejection. The first year we lived on the Mokhovaya, then we moved permanently to Vasilyevsky Island. We saw a good deal of the Myasoyedovs—the daughter of the family becoming my one and only girlfriend. I have a poor memory of this period. My father died after moving to a big apartment; just before his death he managed to have a final quarrel with my aunt. I remember his dying. Tired out, Mama had laid herself down for a nap; the maid was sitting at Father's bedside; I was reading a popular magazine where it was told how the Samoyeds swallow medicine intended for external application, and I exploded with laughter. Nastasya said: "What is it, Mishenka?"—"I'm reading something funny."—"But your daddy's at death's door: just you listen to his wheezing; you'd better wake up the mistress."—"He's always wheezing, I'll just finish what I'm reading." Father was indeed breathing heavily and making a wheezing sound. "Mishenka . . ." "What's the matter now?" But suddenly came a sound that was louder and harsher—first one, then another, and everything became quiet. Then Nastasya shrieked: "The master's dead, Ma'am!" I sat down on the sofa, Mama put her arms about me and burst into tears. I didn't cry at all. My aunt, who hadn't visited us once in the course of Father's illness, sobbed loudly, reaching out her hands to grasp a coffin. The Myasoyedovs looked after me for days at a time in order to provide distraction. Things were going badly, and we moved again, this time to a small apartment in the same building. Soon my elder sister arrived from Siberia and gave birth to Seryozha. We were terribly crowded, the baby screaming, and the wet nurse taking pride of place in the household.

I was a poor student but liked going to school, being much taken with the study of languages as well as with my schoolmates. And this was the time I had my first liaison, with a student who was older than I was; he was tall and half-German, with eyes that were almost white, such was their pallor, eyes that were innocent and depraved; he was fair-headed. He was a good dancer and apart from breaks we used to see each other at dancing classes; later I was able to visit him at his own place. My sister, while remaining in town, had moved in by herself, giving lessons, renting out rooms, arranging student parties with beer, sausage, and student sewing songs ("Along the Volga there's a steep . . . ," "Flinging his cloak about him . . ."). I used to visit her and to attend her parties, although they weren't my style at all and I felt bored and heavy of heart. But that was later anyway.

This is a period that coincides with my first access of a religious fervor that was largely focused on fast days, church services, and ritual. Along with it came a passion for the classics; I also began to make up my eyes and brows, though this was something I soon gave up. In the summers we used to stay at Sestroretsk, at that time a wild and overgrown spot that seemed to my imagination a veritable Greece. In fifth grade we were joined by Chicherin, with whom I was soon to establish a close friendship and whose family had an immense influence on me. I was happy to spend my leisure with a large and "respectable" family belonging to the gentry amid the semblances of a well-provided existence. We were united in our adoration of music, together rushing to get tickets for Belyayev's Russian Symphony Concerts, immersing ourselves in Mozart, and adorning the gallery of the local theatre. I began writing music, and the two of us used to perform our compositions at family gatherings [. . . .]One summer I was staying in Revel and, since Yusha imagined himself to be enamoured of the Mya- soyedov girl, I took upon myself the role of enamoured swain of Xenia Podgurskaya—a sixteen-year-old miss who gave herself the airs of the lady of the regiment. Of all our adventures this one was the most childish. My religious mood had evaporated (I had gone as far as contemplating entry into the priesthood, and everyone at school made fun of me, knowing of my unhappy passion for the Capital, of my liaison with Kondratyev of the depraved and innocent eyes as well as the ones I had with my own class- mates after that); I was obsessed with the latest French fads, was intoler- ant, arrogant, rude, and passionate. That summer, while staying with Chicherin's uncle B. N. Chicherin I was busy preparing myself to enter the St. Petersburg Conservatoire. I was rude to everyone, made deliberately shocking remarks and did my best to behave in an ingeniously eccentric manner. Everyone kept trying to persuade me to go to university, but I would give a contemptuous sniff and deliver myself of an epigram. At the conservatoire I had Lyadov for solfège, Solovyov for harmony, Rimsky- Korsakov for counterpoint and fugue. It was at this time that I formed a friendship with Yurkevich, again suffering torments of jealousy and mak- ing many a scene before our final quarrel. In 1893 I met a man I was to become very fond of and with whom I formed what promised to be a dur- able attachment. He was four years older than I and was an officer in a cavalry regiment. It was difficult to find sufficient time to make the trip to see him, to keep our meeting place secret, and so on—but this was one of the happiest times of my life, a time that I wrote a great deal of music, entranced as I was with Massenet and Delibes and Bizet. It was an enchanted time, all the more so as I became the center of a merry circle of friends from my old school, but younger than I was and all of them now university students—Senyavin, Ginze, Repinsky. My way of life did not meet with my mother's particular approval and, strange as it may seem, my attempt to poison myself dates from this period. I don't understand what guided my judgment in this deed: perhaps I hoped that someone would come to my aid. It seems to me that ignorance of life, consideration of my situation as some kind of special case, dissatisfaction with the conservatoire, the impossibility of living in a sufficiently grand style, romanticism and lightmindedness all played their part. I made an admission of my affair with Prince Georges to Chicherin, to Senyavin and to my cousin, army officer Fyodorov, who took a particularly serious view of the matter for some reason. I bought some laurel water drops containing prussic acid and, having written a farewell letter, swallowed the lot. It was a very pleasant sensation, but suddenly I was seized with terror of death and roused Mama. "Misha, why did you do it?"—much running up and down stairs, much banging of doors, tears, the doctor; we took a cab to the hospital—I was like a drunken man, talking loudly in French. At the hospital I was given an emetic as a matter of course (a disgusting experience) and, having been bathed, was deposited on a bed someone had died on that same morning. All night long a sal-ammoniac drinker kept yelling and I was delirious and kept trying to jump out of bed; one orderly said to another: "What a handsome lad they've brought in—can't be Russian though." Mama arrived next morning and I stayed just a few more days before leaving; I wasn't allowed any activities for some time, though, and left the conservatoire. I was more in love than ever; I confessed everything to my mother; she became tenderhearted and open with me and we had long talks during the night or in the evening over picquet. We always spoke French for some reason.

That spring I made a trip to Egypt with Prince Georges. We went to Constantinople, Athens, Smyrna, Alexandria, Cairo, Memphis. It was a fantastic voyage, an enchanting *collage* of the unknown newly discovered. On the return journey my friend had to make a trip to Vienna, where his auntie was, so I came back by myself. In Vienna the prince died of a heart ailment, and I attempted to find oblivion by redoubling my studies. I began taking classes with Basil Kühner, and each new step was sure to get enthusiastic encouragement from Chicherin—this being the honeymoon year of my friendship with him.

Fyodor Sologub (1863–1927)

SELECTIONS FROM *THE PETTY DEMON*

[Melkii bes]

Translated by S. D. Cioran

FYODOR SOLOGUB (1863–1927) was a "decadent" Symbolist writer and poet. He taught school in provincial Russia before he became known as a writer. His novel *Petty Demon* (1907) describes a schoolteacher's sado-masochistic tendencies and his lust for his young male pupils. The present translation was published originally by Ardis (1983) in its complete edition of the novel.

XII

PEREDONOV WENT OFF to vespers in the gymnasium church. There he stood behind the students and kept an attentive eye on how they behaved. Several of them, it seemed to him, were being naughty, poking each other, whispering and laughing. He took note of who they were and tried to memorize their names. There were a lot of them and he was annoyed with himself because he hadn't thought to take some paper and a pencil from home to write it down. He felt sad that the students were behaving themselves poorly and that no one was paying any attention to that although the headmaster and the inspector were both standing right there in the church with their wives and children.

In actual fact the students were standing there in a well-behaved and modest manner. Some were unconsciously making the sign of the cross, others were thinking about something unconnected with the church and yet others were praying assiduously. Very rarely did anyone whisper something to his neighbor, only two or three words without turning his head, and the other would reply just as briefly and quietly, or even with just a quick movement, a glance, a shrugging of shoulders or a smile. But these small movements, which went unnoticed by the senior class prefect, produced an illusion of extreme disorderliness on the anxiety-ridden, but dull sensibilities of Peredonov. Even in a calm state Peredonov, like all vulgar people, was incapable of precisely evaluating minor events. Either he did not notice them, or he exaggerated their significance. But now, when he was upset by expectations and fears, his sensibilities served him even more poorly and little by little before his very eyes all of reality was becoming enshrouded in a mist of repulsive and wicked illusions.

Besides, what had the students meant to Peredonov even earlier? Had they performed any other function than dragging pen and ink across paper and retelling in stilted language what at one time had been said in a human language! In all of his pedagogical activity Peredonov had sincerely not understood or thought about the fact that the students were just like people, just like adults. Only the bearded students at the gymnasium, with their awakening attraction to women, had suddenly become equals in his eyes.

Having stood in the back for a while and accumulated enough melancholy impressions, Peredonov moved forward to the middle rows. There on the right, at the end of one of the rows, stood Sasha Pylnikov. He was praying modestly and frequently knelt down. Peredonov kept glancing at him and it was particularly pleasant for him to see Sasha on his knees, like someone being punished, and gazing directly in front towards the gleaming altar doors with an anxious and pleading expression on his face, with prayerfulness and sorrow in the dark eyes that were overshadowed with long, almost bluish-black lashes. He was swarthy and shapely and this was particularly noticeable when he was on his knees, calm and erect, as though beneath someone's stern and observing eye. With his high and broad chest, as far as Peredonov was concerned, he looked completely like a girl.

Peredonov firmly decided now to pay him a visit at his lodgings that very evening after vespers.

People started to leave the church. They noticed that Peredonov wasn't wearing his ordinary hat, as he always had done before, but rather his official cap with the cockade. Rutilov asked with a laugh:

"What's this, Ardalyon Borisych, now you're showing off in fancy dress with your cockade? That's what it means when a person is aiming for an inspectorship."

"Will soldiers have to salute you now?" Valeriya asked with affected naiveté.

"Come now, what silliness!" Peredonov said angrily.

"You don't understand anything, Valerochka," Darya said. "Soldiers have nothing to do with it! It's only from the gymnasium students that Ardalyon Borisych will get much more respect than before."

Lyudmila laughed. Peredonov hastened to say his farewells to them in order to escape their sarcasm.

It was still early to go to Pylnikov's and he didn't feel like going home. Peredonov walked along the dark streets, trying to think of where he could spend an hour. There were a lot of houses, lights were burning in many of the windows and at times voices could be heard through opened windows. People who were coming from church walked along the streets and there was the sound of gates and doors being opened and closed. People who were alien and hostile to Peredonov lived everywhere and some of them even now might be plotting ill against him. Perhaps someone was already wondering why Peredonov was alone at that late hour and where he was going. It seemed to Peredonov that someone was trailing him and lurking behind him. He felt melancholy. He hurried along without any purpose.

He was thinking that every house contained its deceased. And all the people who had lived in these old houses about fifty years before, they had all died. He could still remember some of the deceased.

"When a person dies, the house should be burned," Peredonov thought with melancholy. "Otherwise it's very frightening."

Olga Vasilyevna Kokovkina, with whom the gymnasium student Sasha Pylnikov lived, was the widow of a treasury official. Her husband had left her a pension and a small house in which she had enough space that she was able to set aside two or three rooms for lodgers. But she preferred gymnasium students. She was lucky in that she was always given the most modest students who studied properly and finished the gymnasium. In other lodgings a significant portion were made up of those students who wandered from one educational institution to the other and ended up as students with a smattering of subjects.

Olga Vasilyevna, a skinny old woman, tall and erect, with a kind face that she nevertheless tried to make appear stern, and Sasha Pylnikov, who had been well-fed and sternly controlled by his aunt, were sitting at tea. It was Sasha's turn today to provide the jam from the country and for that reason he felt like the host and he was ceremoniously serving Olga Vasilyevna and his dark eyes were gleaming.

There was a ring, and following that, Peredonov appeared in the dining room. Kokovkina was amazed at such a late visit.

"I've come to have a look at our student," he said. "To see how he's getting on here."

Kokovkina tried to offer Peredonov some hospitality, but he refused. He wanted them to finish their tea as quickly as possible so that he could be alone with the student. They finished their tea and went to Sasha's room, but Kokovkina wouldn't leave them alone and she kept chattering on endlessly. Peredonov looked sullenly at Sasha, and the latter was bashfully silent.

"Nothing will come of this visit," Peredonov thought with annoyance.

The maid called Kokovkina for something. She left. With a melancholy feeling Sasha watched her leave. His eyes lost their glitter and were partially screened by his eyelashes and it seemed as though these eyelashes, overly long, cast a shadow over his entire face which was swarthy but had suddenly turned pale. He felt awkward in the presence of this sullen person. Peredonov sat down beside him, put his arm clumsily around him and without altering the impassive expression on his face, asked:

"Well, Sashenka, did you pray to God nicely?"

Sasha glanced at Peredonov with shame and fear, then blushed and was silent.

"Well? What about it? Did you?" Peredonov questioned.

"I did," Sasha said finally.

"Goodness, just look at the blush on those cheeks," Peredonov said. "Admit it now, you're really a girl? A girl, you rascal!"

"No I'm not a girl," Sasha said and suddenly, getting angry with himself because of his bashfulness, he asked in a ringing voice: "Why do you say I look like a girl? It's those students of yours at the gymnasium who've thought it up in order to tease me because I'm afraid of bad words. I'm not accustomed to saying them and I won't say them for anything. Besides why should I say such vile things?"

"Will your mama punish you?" Peredonov asked.

"I don't have a mother," Sasha said. "Mama died a long time ago. I have an aunt."

"Well then, will your aunt punish you?"

"Of course she would if I started to say vile things. What's so nice about that?"

"But how will your aunt find out?"

"I don't want to say them myself," Sasha said calmly. "My aunt could hardly find out. Perhaps I would tell on myself."

"Who of your comrades says bad words?" Peredonov asked.

Sasha blushed again and was silent.

"Come now, tell me," Peredonov insisted. "You are obliged to tell me, you mustn't hide it."

"No one says them," Sasha said with embarrassment.

"But you yourself were just complaining."

"I wasn't complaining."

"Why are you denying it?" Peredonov said angrily.

Sasha felt caught in some kind of miserable trap. He said:

"I was just explaining to you why some of my comrades tease me like a girl. But I don't want to tattle on them."

"Now is that really the reason?" Peredonov asked spitefully.

"It's not nice," Sasha said with vexed grin.

"Well I'll tell the headmaster so that they'll make you tell," Peredonov said maliciously.

Sasha looked at Peredonov with angrily blazing eyes.

"No! Please don't tell, Ardalyon Borisych," he begged. And it was audible from the impetuous sound of his voice that he was making an effort to beg and that he wanted instead to shout words that were bold and threatening.

"No, I will tell him. Then you'll see what you get for covering up vile things. You ought to have complained right away. Just you wait, you'll get it."

Sasha stood up and started to twist his belt in his dismay. Kokovkina came.

"A fine one your goody-goody is, what can I say," Peredonov said spitefully.

Kokovkina was frightened. She went hastily up to Sasha, sat down beside him. Her legs always gave way in the midst of excitement. She asked timidly:

"But what is it, Ardalyon Borisych? What has he done?"

"Why don't you ask him," Peredonov replied with sullen spite.

"What is it, Sasha, what did you do wrong?" Kokovkina asked, touching Sasha's elbow.

"I don't know," Sasha said and burst into tears.

"But what is it, what's the matter with you that you're crying?" Kokovkina asked.

She laid her hands on the boy's shoulders, pulled him over towards herself and didn't notice that he felt awkward. He stood up, hunched over and covered his eyes with a handkerchief. Peredonov explained:

"They're teaching him bad words in the gymnasium, but he doesn't want to say who's doing it. He mustn't hide it. Otherwise he'll learn vile things himself and conceal the others."

"Oh, Sashenka, Sashenka, how could you do that! It's not possible! Aren't you ashamed!" Kokovkina said in dismay as she released Sasha.

"I didn't do anything," Sasha said, weeping. "I didn't do anything bad. They tease me because I can't say bad words."

"Who's saying bad words?" Peredonov asked again.

"No one is saying them," Sasha exclaimed desperately.

"You see how he's lying," Peredonov said. "He ought to be properly punished. He should be punished so that he'll reveal who is saying vile things, otherwise our gymnasium will be censured and we won't be able to do anything."

"But you must forgive him, Ardalyon Borisych!" Kokovkina said. "How can he tell on his comrades? They won't leave him in peace afterwards."

"He is obliged to tell," Peredonov said angrily. "It can only do him good. We will take measures to punish them."

"But they'll beat him up!" Kokovkina said uncertainly.

"They won't dare. If he's afraid then let him tell in secret."

"Well, Sashenka, tell him in secret. No one will find out that you did."

Sasha wept in silence. Kokovkina drew him to herself, embraced him and for a long while whispered something in his ear. He shook his head negatively.

"He doesn't want to," said Kokovkina.

"When he's reprimanded with a birch rod then he'll start to talk," Peredonov said fiercely. "Bring me a rod and I'll make him talk."

"Olga Vasilyevna, what for?" Sasha exclaimed.

Kokovkina stood up and embraced him.

"Enough bawling now," she said tenderly and sternly. "No one's going to touch you."

"As you like," Peredonov said. "But in that case I'll have to tell the headmaster. I was thinking it would be better for him to keep it within the family. Perhaps your little Sashenka is the rascal. We still don't know why they tease him like a girl. Perhaps it's for a different reason. Perhaps they're not the ones teaching him but he's the one who is perverting the others."

Peredonov left the room angrily. Kokovkina followed him out. She said reproachfully:

"Ardalyon Borisych, how can you upset the boy so much for goodness knows what! It's a good thing that he still doesn't understand what you're saying."

"Well, goodbye," Peredonov said angrily. "Only I will tell the headmaster. This must be investigated."

He left. Kokovkina went to console Sasha. Sasha was sitting sadly by the window and was looking at the starry sky. His dark eyes were already calm and strangely melancholy. Kokovkina silently caressed him on the head.

"I'm to blame myself," he said. "I let it slip why I was being teased and he kept on at me. He's the most vulgar one. None of the students like him."

XIII

As evening set in Peredonov showed up at the headmaster's—to have a serious discussion.

The headmaster, Nikolai Vlasyevich Khripach, possessed a certain set of rules which applied to life so comfortably that it was not burdensome in the least to adhere to them. At work he calmly fulfilled everything that was required by the laws or the directions of the authorities, as well as the rules of a generally accepted moderate liberalism. For that reason, the authorities, parents and students were all equally satisfied with the headmaster. He was a stranger to dubious circumstances, indecisiveness and vacillations, and who needed them anyway? One could always find support either in a resolution of the pedagogical council or in the instructions of the authorities. He was just as correct and calm in his personal dealings. His external appearance revealed an air of good-naturedness and steadfastness. Of medium height, solid, agile, with energetic eyes and a confident manner of speaking, he seemed to be a person who had found a good position for himself and intended to do even better. A great many books stood on the shelves in his study. He was making excerpts out of them. When the excerpts had piled up to a sufficient degree, he would put them in order and render them in his own words—and thus, a textbook would be composed, printed and sold out. Not the way the books of Ushinsky* or Evtushevsky* were sold out, but nevertheless they did quite well. Sometimes it was from foreign books that he would put together a compendium that was respected and which no one needed and it would be printed in a journal that was also respected and which no one needed as well. He had a lot of children and all of them, both boys and girls, had already manifested embryonic talents of the most diverse nature: one wrote verses, another sketched, yet another was having rapid success in music.

Peredonov said sullenly:

"You're always attacking me, Nikolai Vlasyevich. Perhaps people have been slandering me to you, but I haven't done anything of the sort."

"Excuse me," the headmaster interrupted, "I cannot comprehend what slander you are being so good as to indicate. In the administration of the gymnasium which has been entrusted to me, I am guided by my very own observations and I dare to hope that my official experience is sufficient to enable me to evaluate what I see and hear with the requisite precision, and, moreover, to maintain the attentive attitude to work that I adopt for myself as an invariable rule," Khripach said quickly and distinctly, and his voice had a dry clear ring to it like the crackling sound of zinc bars when they're being bent. "As far as my personal opinion of you is concerned, I still continue to think that distressing flaws are manifesting themselves in your official activity."

"Yes," Peredonov said sullenly, "you have gotten it into your head that I'm not good for anything, yet I am constantly concerned for the gymnasium."

Khripach raised his eyebrows in amazement and gave Peredonov a questioning look.

"You haven't noticed," Peredonov continued, "that a scandal could break out in our gymnasium. No one has noticed, only I have kept an eye out."

"What scandal?" Khripach asked with a dry chuckle and started to pace nimbly around the study. "You intrigue me although I must say frankly that I have little faith in the possibility of a scandal in our gymnasium."

"You see, you don't know whom you've recently accepted," Peredonov said with such malice that Khripach came to a halt and stared attentively at him.

---

*Evtushevsky, Vasiliy Andrianovich (1836–1888). A Russian pedagogue and editor of the journal *Narodnaya shkola* (*Public School*). Developed a methodology for teaching arithmetic and numbers. Author of widely distributed textbooks in the 1870s and 1880s.

Ushinsky, Konstantin Dmitrievich (1824–1870). One of Russia's most famous pedagogues and one of the principal founders of pedagogical methodology in Russia's public school system. Author of numerous texts for beginners. These textbooks were used for many decades by millions of school children.

"All the newly accepted students have been examined," he said drily. "Moreover, the ones accepted into the first form haven't been rejected by another gymnasium, whereas the single student who joined the fifth form came to us with the kind of recommendations that would exclude the possibility of any unflattering suppositions."

"Yes, only he shouldn't have been sent to us, but to another institution," Peredonov muttered sullenly, almost unwillingly.

"Explain yourself, Ardalyon Borisych, I beg you," Khripach said. "I hope that you are not wanting to say that Pylnikov ought to be sent to a colony for juvenile delinquents."

"No, this creature should have been sent to a boarding school where they don't teach classical languages," Peredonov said maliciously, and his eyes glittered with spite.

Khripach, sticking his hands into the pockets of his short smoking jacket, looked at Peredonov with extraordinary amazement.

"What kind of boarding school?" he asked. "Are you aware of what institutions have that kind of name? And if you are aware, then why were you determined to make such an indecent comparison?"

Khripach blushed deeply and his voice had an even drier and more distinct ring. At another time these signs of the headmaster's wrath would have caused Peredonov great dismay. But now he wasn't embarrassed.

"You all think that it's a boy," he said, screwing up his eyes sardonically, "but it's no boy, it's a girl, and some girl she is!"

Khripach gave a dry and brief laugh, almost an affected laugh that was clear and distinct—that was the way he always laughed.

"Ha-ha-ha!" he laughed distinctly, and when he finished laughing he sat down in his armchair and threw back his head as though dying from laughter. "You have astounded me, my respected Ardalyon Borisych! Ha-ha-ha! Be so kind as to tell me what you base your proposition on, if the premises which have led you to this conclusion are not a secret! Ha-ha-ha!"

Peredonov related everything that he had heard from Varvara and at the same time enlarged upon the bad qualities of Kokovkina. Khripach listened, bursting forth into a dry, distant laughter from time to time.

"My dear Ardalyon Borisych, your imagination is playing tricks on you," he said, stood up and clapped Peredonov on the arm. "Many of my esteemed colleagues, as is the case with myself, have their own children, we weren't born yesterday and do you really think that we could take a disguised girl for a boy?"

"If that's going to be your attitude, who'll be to blame if something happens?" Peredonov asked.

"Ha-ha-ha!" Khripach laughed. "What consequences are you afraid of?"

"There'll be depravity starting in the gymnasium," Peredonov said.

Khripach frowned and said:

"You're going too far. Everything that you've told me until now does not give me the least cause to share your suspicions."

* * *

That same evening Peredonov hastily made the rounds of all his colleagues, from the inspector to the class prefects and he told all of them that Pylnikov was a girl in disguise. Everyone laughed and they wouldn't believe him, but after he left they were overcome with doubt. Almost to a person the wives of the teachers believed it at once.

By the following morning many arrived at classes with the thought that perhaps Peredonov was right. They didn't say so openly, but they no longer argued with Peredonov and restricted themselves to indecisive and ambiguous responses. Each was afraid that he would be thought silly if he started to argue and then suddenly it transpired that it had been true. Many wanted to hear what the headmaster would say about it, but the headmaster, contrary to habit, did not leave his apartment at all on that day. He merely passed by, quite late for his one lesson that day in the sixth form, stayed on an extra five minutes there and then left directly for his own quarters without showing himself to anyone.

Finally, before the fourth lesson, the gray-headed teacher of religion and two other teachers went to the headmaster's study under the pretext of some business or other and the old fellow cautiously brought the conversation around to Pylnikov. But the headmaster laughed so confidently and innocently that all three were overwhelmed at once with the assurance that it was nothing but rubbish. Then the headmaster quickly switched to different topics, related the latest town news, complained of an extremely bad headache and said that, apparently, he would have to call the gymnasium doctor, Evgeniy Ivanovich. Then, in a very good-natured tone he told of how the lesson that day had made his headache even worse, because Peredonov had happened to be in the neighboring classroom and the students there for some reason were often laughing unusually loud. Laughing his dry laugh, Khripach said:

"Fate has been unkind to me this year, three times a week I have to sit beside a classroom where Ardalyon Borisych is teaching and just imagine, nothing but laughter and I do mean laughter. It would appear that Ardalyon Borisych is not a humorous person, but he really does seem to provoke constant glee!"

And without giving anyone the opportunity to say something in this regard, Khripach quickly switched to another topic.

In Peredonov's classes people had truly been laughing a great deal lately—and not because he enjoyed it. On the contrary, Peredonov was irritated by children's laughter. But he couldn't restrain himself from saying something superfluous or indecent. First he would tell a silly anecdote, then he would start to mildly tease someone. In a class one could always find those who were happy for the opportunity to create disorder, and they would produce a furious bout of laughter at every trick of Peredonov's.

Towards the end of the lessons Khripach sent for the doctor while he himself took his hat and went off into the garden which lay between the gymnasium and the bank of the river. The garden was extensive and shady. The young students loved it. They could run about without restriction during the recesses. For that reason the class prefects didn't like the garden. They were afraid that something would happen to the boys. But Khripach required the boys to be there during the recesses. He needed it for aesthetic reasons in his reports.

Passing along the corridor, Khripach stopped by the open door leading into the gymnastics room. He stood there for a while, his head lowered, and then entered. Everyone already knew from his cheerless face and slow walk that he had a headache.

The fifth form had gathered there for gymnastics. They were arranged in a single file and the teacher of gymnastics, a lieutenant from the local reserve battalion, was about to give the command for something, but seeing the headmaster, he went up to greet him. The headmaster shook his hand, gave a distracted look at the students and asked:

"Are you satisfied with them? How are they doing, are they trying hard? They're not getting too tired?"

In his heart the lieutenant deeply despised the students who, in his opinion, neither had nor ever could have any military bearing. If they had been cadets, then he would have said outright what he thought of them. But there was no point in telling the person upon whom his lessons depended what he thought of the bumpkins.

And smiling pleasantly with his thin lips and giving the director an amiable and cheerful look, he said:

"Oh, yes, they're fine lads."

The director took several steps along the front, turned towards the exit and suddenly stopped, as though he remembered something.

"What about our new student, are you satisfied with him? How is he doing, is he making an effort? He's not getting too tired?" he asked sluggishly with a frown and put his hand to his forehead.

For the sake of variety and thinking that after all it was a new student from elsewhere, the lieutenant said:

"A little listless and he quickly tires."

But the director wasn't listening to him any more and left the room.

Apparently the air outside did little to refresh Khripach. He returned after half an hour and once again, standing by the door for half a minute, dropped in on the lesson. Exercises were underway on the athletic equipment. Two or three students, who weren't involved for the moment and who didn't notice the headmaster, were standing about leaning on the wall, making use of the fact that the lieutenant wasn't looking at them. Khripach went up to them.

"Ah, Pylnikov," he said. "Why are you leaning against the wall?"

Sasha turned a brilliant crimson, straightened up and was silent.

"If you're so tired, then maybe the gymnastics aren't good for you?" Khripach asked sternly.

"I'm to blame, I'm not tired," Sasha said fearfully.

"Take your choice," Khripach continued. "Either don't attend the gymnastics lessons, or . . . Anyway, drop in to see me after classes."

He quickly left and Sasha stood there, embarrassed and frightened.

"You're in for it!" his comrades said to him. "He'll lecture you till evening."

Khripach liked to deliver extended reprimands and more than anything else the students feared his invitations.

After classes Sasha timidly set out for the headmaster's study. Khripach invited him in immediately. He quickly approached Sasha as though he were rolling up to him on his short legs, leaned closely and said while peering attentively right into his eyes:

"Pylnikov, are the gymnastics lessons tiring you out in fact? You're a healthy enough boy to look at, but 'appearances can be deceiving.' You don't have any illness do you? Perhaps it's harmful for you to do gymnastics?"

"No, Nikolai Vlasyevich, I'm healthy," Sasha replied, blushing with embarrassment.

"Nevertheless," Khripach objected, "Alexei Alexeevich is complaining about your listlessness and about the fact that you quickly tire. I too noticed today at the lesson that you had a tired look. Or perhaps I was mistaken?"

Sasha didn't know where to avert his eyes from Khripach's penetrating gaze. He muttered distractedly:

"Excuse me, I won't do it again, it's just that I was being lazy standing there. I'm really healthy. I'll do my gymnastics diligently."

Suddenly, quite unexpectedly for himself, he started to cry.

"There you see," Khripach said. "Obviously you are tired. You're crying as though I had given you a stern reprimand. Calm down."

He laid a hand on Sasha's shoulder and said:

"I didn't summon you here to lecture you but to clarify. . . . Never mind, just sit down, Pylnikov, I see that you're tired."

Sasha hastily wiped his damp eyes with a handkerchief and said:

"I'm not tired at all."

"Sit down, sit down," Khripach said and pushed a chair up to Sasha.

"Really, I'm not tired, Nikolai Vlasyevich," Sasha tried to assure him.

Khripach took him by the shoulders, sat him down, and then sat down opposite him and said:

"Let's have a calm talk, Pylnikov. You yourself can't know the genuine state of your health. You're a diligent boy and fine in all respects, therefore it's completely understandable to me that you wouldn't want to ask to be dismissed from gymnastics lessons. Incidentally, I have asked Evgeniy Ivanovich to come and see me today because I'm not feeling well. He can have a look at you while he's here. I hope that you don't have anything against it?"

Khripach glanced at his watch and without waiting for a response started to talk to Sasha about how he had spent the summer.

Evgeniy Ivanovich Surovtsev soon appeared. He was the gymnasium doctor, a small man, dark, spritely, who loved conversations on politics and the news. He didn't possess a great deal of expertise but he exercised an attentive attitude towards his patients, preferring diet and hygiene to medications and for that reason he was successful in his treatments.

Sasha was ordered to undress. Surovtsev examined him carefully and found no defect, but Khripach had been convinced that Sasha wasn't a girl. Even though he had been certain of that earlier, nevertheless he considered it useful so that if he had to respond to inquiries from the district authorities, the gymnasium doctor as a consequence would have the opportunity to certify the fact without any further examinations.

Dismissing Sasha, Khripach said to him affectionately:

"Now that we know that you're healthy, I'll tell Alexei Alexeevich that he's not to spare you."

* * *

Peredonov had no doubt that the discovery of a girl in one of the gymnasium students would bring the attention of the authorities to him and that, in addition to promotion, he would be given a medal. That encouraged him to keep a vigilant eye on the behavior of the students. Moreover, for a few days in a row the weather had been cloudy and cold and few people gathered for billiards. All that was left to do was to walk about the town and visit the students who were in lodgings as well as those who were living with their parents.

Peredonov selected parents who were less worldly. He would arrive, complain about the boy, he would be whipped—and Peredonov would be satisfied. That was how he complained most of all about Iosif Kramarenko to his father who owned a beer factory in the town. He said that Iosif was being naughty in church. The father believed him and punished his son. Subsequently the very same fate befell several more students. Peredonov didn't go to the ones who might have interceded on behalf of their sons— they might complain to the district authorities.

Every day he visited at least one student in his lodgings. There he acted in an authoritative fashion: he administered scoldings, gave orders and made threats. But the students who were in lodgings felt more independent and at times they teased Peredonov. However, Flavitskaya, an energetic woman who was tall and clear-voiced, painfully whipped her little lodger, Vladimir Bultyakov, at the request of Peredonov.

Peredonov told about his feats the following day in class. He didn't mention the names, but the victims gave themselves away with their embarrassment.

Vyacheslav Ivanov (1866–1949)

TWO POEMS

Translated by Vitaly Chernetsky

VYACHESLAV IVANOV (1866–1949) was one of the leading poets of the Russian Symbolist movement, recognized both for his poetry and his theoretical and critical essays. Ivanov's home in St. Petersburg in the years after the revolution of 1905, known as "the Tower," hosted Russia's main literary salon of the time. Ivanov emigrated to Italy in 1924.

Ivanov was bisexual, as was his second wife, Lidiya Zinov'eva-Annibal (1866–1907), author of the lesbian novel, *Thirty-Three Freaks* (1907). Their circle of friends included many gay writers and artists, most importantly Mikhail Kuzmin, who boarded at the Tower for several years (see photos pp. 14, 68). In 1906 Ivanov experienced the greatest same-sex attraction of his life, to the poet Sergei Gorodetsky, his protégé and eighteen years his junior. While Ivanov's feelings contained a strong physical element, their relationship apparently remained unconsummated: Gorodetsky resisted Ivanov's advances, saying his own love for Ivanov was strictly platonic. This relationship inspired several of Ivanov's poems, published in the collection *Eros* (1907). Two of these poems are translated below.

CALLING OUT FOR BACCHUS

I practiced sorcery and wizardry,
Inviting Bacchus the god
To the river rapids,
Into the dark forests and tar bogs,
To abundant and starving lands,
And to the seashore boulders.

I practiced sorcery and wizardry,
Inviting Bacchus the god
To the crossing of all roads,
In the spellbound hour of Hecate,
At noon, begotten through witchcraft:
The god was close by invisible.

Again I called and implored,
Addressing Bacchus the god,
"You, invisible, are here with me!
Why then you hide your daytime face?
Why disturb my heart with mystery?
Why do you hide your night-time face?

Take pity on my bitter grief,
Appear in any incarnation,
In streaming water or in fire;
Or, like a late-time young visitor
Turn your calling and tired eyes
In this night to me.

Am I not waiting for you
And, loving, won't I recognize
The flute of your wine-colored eyes?
Won't I greet you at the door
And daringly answer your call
Rushing into the drunken night? . . ."

A slender appearance at the doorstep . . .
Sweet anxiety in my heart . . .
No breathing . . . No light . . .
Half a youth, and half a bird . . .
Under his eyebrows lightning in clouds
Flashes through dim darkness . . .

Evil demon or guest from heavens,
He now shares my abode,
Pecking with his beak at my breast
And throwing away the bloody flesh . . .
My heart melts and resurrects,
And the scarlet spring keeps pouring out . . .

INCANTATION

When magical Midnight, key-holder of the deepest depths
Fans dusk onto the flame of quiet but fervent candles,
Granting to parched lips the drunkenness of delightful dew,
The guiding sovereign of inescapable encounters,
Deliverer of the Sun's spells—Mother Night,
The deaf-mute daughter of the blind prisoner Chaos:

Come, lie down with me for feasts of languor,
You alone, and share my black and fiery cup!
The pupils of my eyes are empty, my dark wells are dry:
Come, you of midnight, and quench my torrid noon!
Come, my son, my brother! One wife awaits the two of us—
Night; magical Mother—secluded, quiet, drunken, avid . . .

Vasily Rozanov (1856–1919)

SELECTIONS FROM *PEOPLE OF THE MOONLIGHT*

[Liudi lunnogo sveta, 1913]

Translated by Spencer E. Roberts

VASILY ROZANOV (1856–1919) was a literary critic and philosopher. As Simon Karlinsky points out, his ideas about homosexuality have more to do with abstract theory than with any real knowledge of actual gay life, yet they were widely disseminated. In *People of the Moonlight* (1913), he advances the idea that homosexuality in the guise of celibacy lies at the heart of all Christian spirituality. The present translation appeared originally in *Four Faces of Rozanov* (Philosophical Library, NY, 1978). This selection has been abridged, with deleted text indicated by [. . .].

THE THIRD SEX

SEX AS A PROGRESSION OF
DECREASING AND INCREASING QUANTITIES

IN ALL THE FACTS we cited, both Christian and pre-Christian, we have as the heart of the matter an organic, insuperable, innate (one's own, not inspired from without) aversion to copulation, i.e. to the joining of one's genitals to the genitals of the opposite sex, which complement them. "I don't want to! I simply don't want to!"—it is like a cry of nature itself, and it is the basis of all those seemingly antinatural religious phenomena we referred to earlier. [. . .]

Sex would be a completely clear, or a fairly clear, phenomenon if it merely consisted in the periodic coupling of a male and a female in order to produce a new person: in that case it would be the same as the elements oxygen and hydrogen forming "in combination" a third and "new being" —water. But oxygen and hydrogen do not know "counterflows": and if suddenly we saw not a particle of oxygen combining eagerly (as always in chemical affinity) with a particle of hydrogen to produce a drop of water but, on the contrary, a particle of hydrogen—some exceptional one— suddenly starting, also "with eagerness," to climb on a particle of hydrogen similar to itself, avoiding with disgust the particle of oxygen complementing it, we would say: "It is a miracle! It is alive! It is individually different! It is a person!!" The individual began where it was suddenly said to the law of nature: "Stop! I won't let you function here." And the one who refused to let it function was also the first "spirit"—*not* "nature,"

142

not "mechanics." And so the "individual" appeared in the world in that place where for the first time there was a violation of the law—a violation of it as uniformity and constancy, as the norm and the "ordinary," as the "natural" and the "generally-expected." [. . .]

The assumption that sex is a constant and not in the least "flowing" gave rise to the expectation that every male will want a female and that every female will want a male—an expectation so universal that it even turned into a demand: "every male *will* want his own female" and "every female *will* want her own male" . . . Of course, "be fruitful and multiply" includes all this. But it will always remain a mystery why, considering the universal commandment to be fruitful and multiply, given to all nature, one person, Adam, was created entirely alone. Our amazement will increase even more if we note that Eve, the "mother of life" (in Hebrew—the "mother of lives," egg-bearing, viviparous *"ad infinitum"*), later emerged from Adam: i.e. Eve was concealed in Adam's essence, and it was she who set him dreaming about a "life's companion" . . . Adam, "created in the image and likeness of God," was, in his concealed completeness, Adam-Eve, both male and (*in potenta*) female; the two then divided, and this was the creation of Eve, with whom, as we know, the creation of new creatures came to an end. "There will be nothing more that is new." Eve was the last innovation in the world, the very last.

Only because of the general expectation that "every male will want a female," and so on, did the expectation also arise that the very pairing of males and females will flow with the regularity of the rotation of the sun and the moon, or according to the model of oxygen uniting with hydrogen, *without exception*. But everything that lives, beginning with the grammar of languages, has "exceptions": and sex, i.e. the principle of *life*, would simply not be *alive* if it did not have "exceptions"—and, of course, all the more so the more alive, vital, viable, and life-giving it is. . . . Not everyone knows that one meets in the animal kingdom all, or almost all, the "deviations" that one meets in man—but less frequently. [. . .]

* * *

What is "one's own" with each person manifests itself first and foremost in strength, in intensity. We have here a series of degrees that can easily be expressed by a series of natural numbers:

$$\ldots +7 +6 +5 +4 +3 +2 +1 \pm 0 -1 -2 -3 -4 -5 -6 -7 \ldots$$

The greatest intensity so far as the possibility of giving satisfaction and the constant desire for receiving satisfaction are concerned denotes the highest degree of sexuality—of the male in satisfying the female lying opposite him and of the female the male opposite her. The most "male" male is the one who copulates with a woman most often, most willingly, and most vigorously, while the most "female" female is the one who submits to the male the most languidly, tenderly, and submissively. [. . .]

One must only keep this numeration in mind:

$$\ldots +8+7+6+5+4+3+2+1\pm0-1-2-3-4-5-6-7-8\ldots$$

The "sainte prostituée" is the $+8+7+6\ldots$ And the closer we come to the lower numbers, to the $+3+2+1$, the harsher is the timbre of the voice, the sterner the look, the cruder the manners, the greater the "brazenness," as seminarians would say. There appear those typical "priests' daughters," who enter into marriage with a sack filled with a fixed dowry, and who all their lives are happy merely putting together "a dowry to add to their own dowry"—not a very pleasant life for the priest and the deacon, but it is "not bad," "one can put up with it." And finally there comes the "±0." Note both the "$+$" and "$-$" signs. Such women are not dead, although they absolutely never "have the desire." There is something of the "$+$" in them: but it is bound up with something of the "$-$." Thus, there is no *unilinear* attraction in them to the "male": it is as if there were two arrows here, their tips pointing in different directions: the one toward the "male" and the other. . . ? The law of progression, as well as the fact that everything here takes place between two sexes only, shows that the second arrow can be pointed toward nothing but the female. The female seeks a female; consequently, in this type of female, there simultaneously exists the male. [. . .]

And finally everything passes over to the purely minus quantities: "she" is agitated in the presence of those of her own sex, she casts passionate glances, she gets excited, she feels hot all over in the presence of women and girls. Their braids, their hands, their necks . . . and, alas, their invisible breasts, and, alas, alas, their completely hidden parts, the whole of a woman's "secret"—everything, inexplicably excites them, makes them yearn, the more so, to the point of torment and suffering, because all this is to be hidden from them forever, hidden precisely from *them*, and revealed only to a man, to a husband. The torments of Tantalus: it is so close, it is always around, it can even be seen if a woman is careless when undressing or when bathing; but one cannot get a good look at it without dying then and there of shame. There is a universal barrier in the very arrangement of things, in the plan of the world. "So near, and yet so far!" The torments of Tantalus: the realization of one's desires being put off endlessly; it is impossible, it will never be!

Tears, depression, dreams. Daydreams. Poetry, much poetry. Philosophy—lengthy philosophy! And, by the way, she has a certain talent for it. This "drill sergeant in a skirt" easily masters both Marx and Kuno Fischer—and, in general, she is superior to the "weaker sex" mentally, spiritually, ideologically, verbally, and even in so far as a capacity for work is concerned.

This law can, of course, be applied to the male as well. How does it manifest itself here?

Whereas women like this often have a slight moustache, the men often have a sparse beard. All this has to do not with things physical, but mainly with those relating to the spirit, disposition, manners and morals, the heart, but partly to things physical as well.

The northern Normans, as described by Ilovaisky, probably provide us best of all with a vivid picture of the primordial male—the "+ 8 + 7" of the male progression: "In time of peace, when at war with no one, they would ride out to the fields; closing their eyes tightly, they would rush forward and slash the air with their swords, as if striking down their enemies. And in battle they would throw themselves fearlessly into the very slaughter; they would slash at the enemy, inflict wounds, and would perish themselves, expecting after death to cross over to Valhalla, which they also imagined to be filled with heroes, fighting eternally." An indomitable energy—as with the Turks, who astounded Europe with their bravery and their wars. Probably the early wars of the Romans and the everlasting "internecine struggle" of the early Hellenes are also based on this very same type of male who, because of his burning ardor, does not know what to do with himself—so he rushes here and there, into battles, adventures, travels (Odysseus and the period of Henry the Navigator). All this is the primordial, crude upturning of the stones of culture. A volcano upturns the earth, seemingly disfiguring it, splitting it open, breaking it up: but, as a matter of fact, this is already the *beginning* of culture. A small island is more "cultural" than a continent; a "tiny land" always receives God's first ray. And the breaking up, the smashing of something or other in general, is the first step toward culture.

But it is one thing to break up an inert mass and another to start to polish the pieces. Breaking up and polishing are different phases of a single process, and they require quite different qualities.

And it is here, in the universal need for *polishing*, that the role of "+ 2 + 1 ± 0" and the "− 1 − 2 and so on" of sex comes to the fore.

The beard begins to be shorter and sparser, the ardor to decrease, and the disposition, up to now harsh, crude, and unbearable to one's neighbor, begins to acquire a gentleness that makes proximity to it comfortable and even pleasant. "Neighbors" appear both in the territorial and the moral sense; "kinship" appears, in the spiritual and figurative sense, not only in the consanguineous one. All this is in proportion as the male shifts from the higher degrees—the "+ 8 and + 7"—to the middle and very low ones— the "+ 3 + 2 + 1." In these middle stages, marriage occurs because of the attachment of the one to the *other*, the satisfaction of the one by the other. And finally there appears the mysterious "± 0," the complete lack of desire for sex, the lack of "I want to" . . . There is no desire for it at all. The peace and quiet of existence are not disturbed. Such a man will never challenge another to a duel, he will never take offense—and least of all will he give offense. Socrates, who said that it was easier for him to suffer an insult than to inflict one on someone else, falls into this category. So does

the conciliatory: "Father, forgive them, for they know not what they do."
In general, there comes to the fore the principle of forgiveness, meekness,
the conciliatory "nonresistance to evil." Platon Karatayev, in Tolstoy's
War and Peace, is here too, right along with Socrates; so is Spinoza, peacefully writing his treatises and observing the life of spiders. They all are
spokesmen of the conciliatory "I don't want to," "I don't feel like it" . . .
There is in these people an extremely great increase in contemplation, there
is an extremely great decrease in energy, almost to the point where it no
longer exists (Amiel, Marcus Aurelius). There are long periods of daydreaming, endless daydreaming. The whole of existence here is lacy and
weblike; it is as if the sun never played here, as if all this had barely been
born and existed in some dark and unilluminated corner of the world. The
mystery of the world. . . . In the character of these people, there is much
that is lunar, tender, and pensive; much that is useless for life, for action.
But there is much that is surprisingly fruitful for culture, for civilization.
It is precisely a cobweb, it is precisely lace, with long threads running from
it and attaching themselves to everything else. In the nature of these people, there is also something melancholic, despite all the serenity and calm
of their appearance and life; moreover, it is a melancholy that is unconscious and without cause. "World sorrow," "Weltschmerz," has its roots
here in this mysterious "I don't want to" of the organism. Here the sciences
and philosophy blossom. And finally the "± 0," breaks down into the
"$+0$" and "-0": the former dies away—after all, there was nothing in
it anyway. And there remains the "-0," which quickly changes to "-1,"
"-2," "-3," and so on.

In the lower, primary degrees, the "-0," "-1," we observe this in the
form of those well-known dual friendships—not in the form of a noisy
comradeship of many friends, who go in for all sorts of amusements and
"undertakings," but always in the form of a quiet, noiseless friendship of
just *two*. If you look closely, you will see that they are always opposites—so
far as their spirit, way of life, character, and even physical characteristics
are concerned: and the one seems to complement the other. There is mutual
"complementation," and from this comes the harmony and union of their
lives. One might say that life is crammed with these wandering and station-
ary dyads (a linking of two), who, in general, always make a pretty picture,
attracting the attention of everybody by their silence, their modest behavior, by the fact that they disturb no one and are obviously pleased with
their quiet contentment, pleased with their life. Gogol was the first to give
us such a dyad in those two well-known neighbors, Ivan Ivanovich and
Ivan Nikiforovich.* But spiteful Gogol made them quarrel: usually, however, they do not quarrel, and the one buries the other. Why *should* they
quarrel? One sees this also in the works of Turgenev: he has portrayed a

---

*In "How Ivan Ivanovich Quarrelled with Ivan Nikiforovich." [Tr.]

whole series of such dyads— "Khor and Kalinych," "Chertopkhanov and Nedopyuskin," to a certain extent Rudin and Lezhnyov (fire and water) in *Rudin*—and, I think, several more, many more. Most often the one is the protector, the other, the protected; the one is harsh, cruel, coarse, brusque, the other gentle, mild, complaisant. They are like a man and wife, a man and a woman. But this is nothing yet. In Dostoevsky, we find all this expressed in the idyll "An Honest Thief," where a weak, spineless, and, moreover, a hard-drinking man is taken under the protection of a sober, quiet, and amiable tailor. Rephrasing the observation of the early Christians, according to which "the very virtues of the pagans are but beautiful *vices*," we can say that "the very *vices* of these dyads are somehow innocent." With other people, their thievery would reveal all their greed and dishonesty, and others would respond with a thrashing. But with these men, even theft is virtuous: "An Honest Thief." And, as a matter of fact, he *is* "honest"—so meek it would never occur to anyone to scold, let alone to beat him up. Moreover, he is so amiable and virtuous that a single quiet reprimand is enough to make him hang himself. In truth, "of such is the Kingdom of Heaven" . . . If they do something, it is good for them, and if they do nothing, that too is good. If they do not steal, that is good, and if they have stolen, that too is good. It is all somehow harmless, without "consequences." And if they "commit adultery," that too is good. But they almost never "commit adultery." "They don't feel like it." We could never imagine Khor, Kalinych, Chertopkhanov, Nedopyuskin, or the "Superfluous Man" (in Turgenev's "Diary of a Superfluous Man") with a woman or even around a girl. These dyads, or passive loners, are to such an extent incipient "righteous men," lines of incipient Christian righteousness, so special, so typical, what with their gentle eyes, their limp arms, their quiet gaze, distant and pensive, that one can have no doubt that long before Christianity ever appeared on earth, it already existed in them; or that the Gospel, itself being of this same category of phenomena, upon coming into contact with this tendency, merged with it, "embraced" it, and their combined stream produced what we call "the history of Christianity," "the history of Christian civilization," "the history of the Church." I said that the Gospel is also of this category. And, as a matter of fact, that is its explicit word. The "immaculate conception"—that is what it begins with— the demand that we acknowledge that idea. That is the miracle, the "ineffable," which "does not fit into reason," which never happens, which is beyond all belief, which makes someone hearing about it for the first time burst out laughing. For it is the "$2 \times 2 = 5$" of sex: and yet unless you agree to this "miracle" and "nonsense," you are no Christian. But as soon as you do accept it and submit to it, as soon as you do come to believe in this sexual "$2 \times 2 = 5$," you are a "Christian," one of the "sons of salvation," one of the "Kingdom of God." [. . .]

THE SELF-DENIAL OF SEX.
SPIRITUAL HOMOSEXUALITY AND ASCETICISM

As a matter of fact, this is a rare but quite natural phenomenon in "flow-ing" sex, this phenomenon of the " ± " of sexual desire. It is like a tiny mustard seed from which grew a tree that has shaded the whole earth with its branches and from the fruits of which all nations are spiritually nourished.

If envoys of the Pope, proselytes of the faith, potential martyrs, rush off to the distant lands of newly-discovered America or ancient China, you can rest assured that they are virgins. They will never marry.

If a strict judge rushes off to a seminary to rid himself of his excessive worldly-mindedness, his excessive interest in things of the world, his exces-sive passion for knowledge instead of holiness, you can rest assured without even asking, that this is a man who has never "defiled" himself by con-tact with a woman!

Who composed all the wonderful invocations to God? People like this!

Who worked out all our rituals with such marvelous taste? They did!

Who wove the whole of that vast fabric of our religiosity? They did!

"Special spiritual powers!" . . .

"Special help!"

The " ± " of sex is also that candle about whose light it was said that "darkness will never envelop it." The darkness of what? "Of sin," "lust," "desire for a woman," "filth."

This name "filth," as soon as it rang out anywhere, B.C. or A.D., in Hellas or in Germany, in a secular book or in a sacred one, expressed the sense of smell of the female/male, the sense of taste of the female/male, the notions of female/male, the imagination of him/her. And this alone sets the watershed between the " + " of sex and its " ± "—between repro-duction and homosexuality. And nothing else! It is the main thing, almost all!

All this "it is to my taste" and "it is not to my taste" penetrates the man to the marrow of his bones, right down to his last gut, to his very smallest artery; it takes possession of his mind, his sight, his hearing, his sense of smell. With the spiritual homosexual, all this is different from what you find in the person who reproduces, in the one who has many children.

The gaze of the homosexual is different!

His handshake is different!

His smile is completely different! His habits, manners, everything, ab-solutely everything, is new!

If you wish, he is a third person around Adam and Eve, as a matter of fact, the "Adam" from whom Eve has not yet emerged—the first complete Adam. He is older than the "first man who began to reproduce." He looks at the world with an older eye; he has in his nature older tales of the world, older songs of the earth. In the cosmological and religious sequence, he precedes reproduction. Reproduction came later, it came later and covered him over, just as the present-day layers of the earth have covered over the Devonian or Jurassic formations. He is the Devonian formation, reproduction is that of the present day.

From these "older tales" and "older songs" which he has in his nature and which he remembers and yet does not remember, which he has forgotten and yet has not completely forgotten, his whole being is in a way patient, resistant, persevering, invincible. "And he will not be swallowed by the darkness" (of reproduction). No matter how few of them there have been on earth since the beginning of time—so few that even by "doomsday," according to revelation, they will number no more than 144,000—what they have created, beginning with those two sages of Greece, Socrates and Plato, is immeasurably great, and not only is it lasting, it is absolutely eternal. "The Devonian formation in mankind has begun to speak." They are almost always conservatives ("the Devonian formation"), they dislike the new, or, more precisely, the brand new, the "modern." They are always drawn to the past, to the depths of the centuries. This is that ancient song manifesting itself in them, that ancient song, summoning them to it. Their "paradise" is metaphysical, their "paradise" is in their bones, in their blood, in their sense of taste. If a person like this becomes a composer, his music will be special; if he becomes a painter, his painting will be special. That their philosophy was special is shown by the works of Socrates and Plato, the former that unsuccessful husband of Xanthippe, the latter that eternal virgin, that "monk-starets" of the ancient world. Before him, philosophy had only sextons and deacons: but then from the groves of Academe there came, as if carrying a three-branched candlestick and dressed in full regalia, the great "bishop" of metaphysics. And all grew still, bowed low, and rejoiced.

FEMALE-MALES AND THEIR TEACHING

A person with a " + 1 + 2 + 3," and so on, attraction to sex, of course, feels that the sex act is 1) healthy 2) moral 3) useful 4) noble 5) beautiful. And mothers and fathers of the purest girls are furious when they find their daughter has married a sexually inadequate man; they demand the dissolution of such a "foul and loathsome" marriage so that the girl can marry again, this time a man who is sexually adequate, one who will be able to deflower and impregnate her. And as I have noticed on two occasions, when the daughter has her first child, the grandfathers very touchingly carry photographs of the baby around with them (in one case the child was photographed naked). Spiritual homosexuals, on the other hand, cannot even imagine the sex act as anything but shameful, silly, obscene, dirty, and, on a religious plane, sinful, disagreeable to God, and immoral. The obdurate tone with which complete physical homosexuals say "I am a girl" when physicians and judges call them by the male name given them at baptism is identical with the obduracy that manifests itself in semi-homosexuals in their feeling that the sex act is vile and their complete confidence that the whole world is in sympathy with them, that all people feel the same as they. And that is understandable. All the aversion that a normal person (with a " + 1" of sex) feels for so-called perverted sexual relations, imagined or real—a man with a man or a woman with a woman—all this same horror and mystical fear is felt by a person with a " ± " attraction to sex when he thinks of natural sexual relations, i.e. the usual method of coitus and of marriage in general: "You can't imagine anyone not loathing it," "you can't believe that anyone would do it without a feeling of sin!" No one can jump over his own blood: and what is a homosexual act for us is a normal one for them. Homosexuality is a "perversion" to us: but conversely, "our way" is a perversion to the homosexual. In countless pieces of writing, both secular and philosophical, but mainly religious, they try to convince us, they assure us, they swear that it is "vile," although everyone else says that it is "good"; they assure us that "no one feels that it is *good*," that "everyone is ashamed of it," when, of course, no one is ashamed of it (the open family status, the open way in which daughters are given in marriage, the open way in which parents find wives for their sons). And then too they say over and over that God forbade it, that He "does not want it," even though "be fruitful and multiply" is on the very first page of the Bible. "We think of ourselves as virgins," say these fellows with long, girlish hair; and there is not a single voice, at least in sacred literature, that tends to destroy this harmony, this unanimity—from which one can conclude that all sacred literature flows from this source, that it owes its origin to it alone, and, in a word, that the "essence of spiritual" is at the same time the "essence of the homosexual." I am not saying that all writers of sacred literature are sincere in asserting this, since they reproduce just as we, and, generally speaking, the clergy *cannot* belong to this rare category: but even if one of them does not inwardly agree with this homosexual taste, he is obliged by law and tradition to repeat it anyway: "decency demands" that the spiritual homosexual not be betrayed, that not a single word be said in favor of the biblical, natural, and universal method of copulation and the sensation of that copulation. "*We too* dislike it," say archpriests with ten children and deacons with eight. "We too are ashamed—we feel how unnatural and sinful it is," says the dean of a cathedral, searching quickly and eagerly for a husband for his daughter.

Nikolai Klyuev (1887–1937)

TWO POEMS

Translated by Simon Karlinsky

NIKOLAI KLYUEV (1887–1937) was the most talented of the peasant poets. He composed songs for various peasant religious sects. Karlinsky tells of his love affairs with peasant painters, writers, and poets. He pursued Esenin relentlessly, though his attentions may not have been wanted. Under the Soviets, Klyuev got into trouble with the authorities, was branded a reactionary, and exiled to Siberia, where he eventually died. His unpublished poems and correspondence were preserved by his ex-lover Nikolai Arkhipov, but were lost forever when Arkhipov himself was arrested.

That fellow with the green eyes
Smells of ginger and mint.
What Pripyat and what Euphrates
Might be flowing in the blood in his veins?
Isn't there a desert sunset in his earlobes,
Leopards at their water hole?
In the tart buds of aspen trees
There's the biblical vinegar of sultry Chaldea.
The shouts of a Russian carpenters' guild
Are an echo of an Arab encampment.
In a Lapland snowstorm you discern
An African's coral-hued dance.
Corals and Russia leather—
Such things cause poetry's spring floods.
In an Orthodox chapel, an arabesque-clad mufti
Is in tears over an ancient liturgy book.
This is an encounter, amidst our native furrows,
Of grain and earthy nipples.
In the fellow's eye sockets, starlike,
Is a green nocturnal flame,
As if amidst bamboo thickets
Tiger cubs slink in their mother's wake,
As if on pussy willows, biliously,
Ginger and Chilean mint have sprouted.

(1924)

151

When you push fifty, roses are headier,
Flax is drowsier, violets bluer,
The mignonette spicier, more earthy,
As if the turf by the old pond had been ploughed up
By my merry nephew for the spring sowing;
As if mama had come back in a rickety cart
From her cemetery for a visit to our house
Under the elder trees.
                              Sunlight sleeps
Like a red calf upon the path. A smell of grapes
Comes from the swollen, slimy brittle-willows.
I keep imagining the hoofbeats over slabs
Of flint, from which there's no returning.
From the Babel of cities memories come back
Plinking like a bumblebee zither amidst flowers.
I've gone beyond earthly boundaries
And broken time's padlock like one breaks
A churchdoor latch. And now I feel
Like a priest's daughter, newlywed, as I enter
The promised, secret tower chamber
Where my intended shepherd boy
Will hide his soul in my wicker basket
To make the stars smell of mignonette,
My poems of spring floods, rafts,
Tempestuous spawning fish, spring auguries
Of maidens among the beehives.
Is it to be odd or even? Is he my darling or my slave?
And now that youth, my merry nephew,
Is rooting up the turf by the old pond
With his own lovely, merry spade,
As he sings and rubs his hands in glee
Preparing for the heather and the flax
Their fiftieth springtime!

                                        (1932–33)

Sergei Esenin (1895–1925)

FOUR POEMS

Translated by Vitaly Chernetsky

SERGEI ALEKSANDROVICH ESENIN (1895–1925) is a Russian poet who gained high popular acclaim, and has achieved almost a cult status among many Russian poetry lovers. His poetry, which sounds melodious and simple in the original Russian, effectively bridged the gap between high and low culture. Born in a small village in central Russia, Esenin started out his literary career in 1912 as a member of the group known as the "peasant poets." The leader of the group, Nikolai Klyuev, became Esenin's mentor and lover, although there has been speculation whether Esenin's motives in this relationship were romantic or merely pragmatic. Their breakup coincided with the 1917 revolution. From 1919 on, Esenin was associated with the Russian Imagist movement, which included gay poet, Ryurik Ivnev (1891–1981), as well as Anatoly Mariengof (1897–1962), with whom, according to the biographers, Esenin had a "legendary passionate friendship" that lasted for about three years. Esenin's turbulent personal life included several marriages to women, among them Isadora Duncan, but his strong emotional attachments were almost exclusively with men. Increasingly at odds with the Soviet regime and generally feeling lonely and alienated, Esenin killed himself in 1925; soon after that, several of his fans killed themselves at his grave. Of the poems translated here, the first three poems were written to Nikolai Klyuev, the third of them after their breakup. The fourth poem was written to Anatoly Mariengof, on the occasion of Esenin's departure from Russia for a year of travels with Isadora Duncan.

Yesterday's rain hasn't dried away yet,
Green water soaks the grass . . .
The forsaken fields are filled with melancholy,
And orache plants are drooping.

I wander in the streets, over puddles,
The autumn day is both timid and wild.
And in every man I meet on my way
I want to discern your dear face.

You are ever more mysterious and beautiful,
Gazing into the unclear horizon.
For you there's only our happiness
And my faithful comradeship.

And if death, following God's will
Were to close your eyes with its hand,
I swear that like a shadow in an open field
I would follow death and you.

(1916)

Springtime doesn't always resemble joy,
And the sand is yellow not because of the sunlight.
Your weather-beaten skin exuded
The rays of buckwheat-colored fuzz.

Near the sky-blue watering hole
Over the fields of prickly orache
We swore that we shall be two
And will never ever part.

Darkness puffed smoke, and the scrawny evening
Was curling up in fiery fretwork.
I walked with you until the grove
Where stood your parents' cabin.

And for a long, long time in a hazy daydream
I could not turn my face away
When you were waving your hat from the porch
With a tender smile.

(1916)

To Klyuev

Now my love is not what it used to be.
Oh, I know, you are grieving, you are grieving
That the broom of the moon
Didn't splash around the puddles of verses.

Feeling sad and rejoicing at the star
That falls down onto your eyebrows
You have given the cabin a heart through song,
But you didn't build a home inside your heart.

And the man for whom you waited in the night
Again passed by the hospitable cover.
Oh my friend, for whom did you gild your keys
With the signing word?

You will not sing about the sun
And you won't see heaven through a window.
This is how a windmill, waving its wing,
Still cannot fly away from the earth.

(1918)

Sergei Esenin (left, aged 21) with Nikolai Klyuev (aged 29), ca. 1916.

A FAREWELL TO MARIENGOF

[Proshchanie s Mariengofom]

There's crazy happiness in friendship,
And the convulsion of wild passions—
The fire melts the body down
As if it were a stearine candle.

Oh my beloved! give me your hands—
I'm not used to doing it any other way—
I want to wash them at this time of parting
With the yellow foam of my hair.

Ah, Tolya, Tolya, is it you, is it you,
For one more moment, one more time—
The circles of unmoving eyes
Have grown still again like milk.

Farewell, farewell. In the moonlit fires
Will I wait until the joyful day?
Of all the praised and all the young
You were the very best for me.

At a certain time, in a certain year
Perhaps we shall meet yet again . . .
I am frightened—for the soul passes
Away, just like our youth and love.

Another man will extinguish me inside you.
Isn't this why—in unison to the speeches—
My ears, which are also sobbing
Now touch the shoulders, like the oars touch water?

Farewell, farewell. In the moonlit fires
I will not see the joyful day,
But still of all the tender and all the young
You were the very best for me.

(1922)

III

HIDDEN FROM VIEW UNDER THE SOVIETS: UNDERGROUND AND EMIGRE LITERATURE (1920–1980)

Yevgeny Kharitonov (1941–1981), the foremost Russian gay writer after Kuzmin, was persecuted during the Soviet regime. (See his work on pp. 196–225). Photo from 1970s, courtesy of Glagol.

Ryurik Ivnev (1891–1981)

SELECTIONS FROM IVNEV'S *DIARIES*

Translated by Michael Molnar

RYURIK IVNEV (Mikhail Aleksandrovich Kovalev, 1891–1981), a poet and a novelist, was born in Tiflis (now Tbilisi, Georgia) in a military family and graduated from Moscow University in 1912 with a law degree. Soon afterwards, he published his first collection of poetry, *Self-Immolation* (1913), that shocked the reading public by its prevalent theme of homoerotic pyromasochism, with some religious overtones, that continued in his other pre-revolutionary collections. He also became an active participant in bohemian literary circles. After the revolution, in 1918, Ivnev became secretary to the People's Commissar of Enlightenment (i.e. minister of culture and education) Alexander Lunacharsky, which is probably the main reason why he was spared in the years of Stalinist purges. In 1919–1921 he participated in the Imagist movement, together with such poets as Sergei Esenin and Anatoly Mariengof, and also traveled widely across the front lines in the Caucasus. In the 1920s, he published several novels, primarily devoted to the bohemian life of the cultural circles of Tiflis and Baku, which were an important haven for many writers and artists in the years of the revolution and the civil war. He continued publishing works in all possible genres through the rest of his life, most of them of questionable quality; but this enabled him to survive under the Soviet regime. His unorthodox pre-revolutionary poetry was not reprinted, he entered a marriage of convenience, and kept a low public profile. However, the daily struggle involved in living such a life is reflected in his diary, excerpts from which are included here. Like the diary of Mikhail Kuzmin, this is an important human document of a gay man's survival under the Soviet regime, as well as an informative chronicle of literary life. Perhaps the publication in the future of the entire diary and of his more explicitly homoerotic poetry would bring about a reevaluation of Ivnev's place in Russian literature.

The present text of diaries and poem is printed with permission of Ivnev's current Russian agent Glagol (Moscow). The *Diaries* appeared first in English in *Index on Censorship I*, 1995.

13 September 1930   Returned to Moscow at 10 a.m. today. These two days have worn me out and brought me nothing good in return, apart from a small financial gain (2 lectures). I was satisfied with my second lecture (at the builders' club), but not so much with the first.

I remember an official at the club (Makarov, the club storekeeper) asking me: "Is Kamchatka Soviet territory?" Kolya promised to visit me in Moscow. He was very sweet when we parted.

Evening. At home. Felt worse again. Tried a home cure once again. Apple tea is boiling up on the kerosene cooker. I'll stuff myself with aspirins and go to bed.

Luckily I met Anatoly during the afternoon and took him home with me, otherwise I wouldn't have held it out at home, despite feeling ill, and would have fled to Michel or to the Okunevs.[1]

I feel an increasing need for human company. Can this be a sign that youth is fading?

Today Inna Pavlovna (TsBK)[2] showed herself up again. During the tea break one of the members complained of ill health. "What's wrong?" they asked him. Slightly embarrassed, he answered: "You know, it's my stomach." Then IP blurted out (she had just come back from holiday): "Well, my stomach has been working absolutely marvelously this summer!" . . .

23 September   Today I'm going to Serpukhov—I have two lectures there. Kolya's in Kashira now. I saw him off a few days ago and will visit him for the day on the 28th. Kashira is drowning in apple orchards, but provincial to the bone. Even so, how I would love to be going, not to Serpukhov today, which without Kolya has lost all its charm, but to Kashira.

29 September   Kashira. Arrived here yesterday evening. Kolya met me at the arranged place. I think he was glad of my arrival. He shook my hand firmly in his hot hand and held it for a long time, not letting go . . .

Today I wandered around Kashira, sat in some park or other, it was a dull morning, but brightened up around one o'clock. It was so pleasant to look at the yellow branches of the trees and watch the leaves fall like yellow snowflakes. I lay on a bench and gazed at the blue sky veiled with torn clouds.

Between 10 and 20 Oct., I will lecture here (on Kamchatka again). I remember how hostile Kozyrev[3] was towards my poem "The Steel Boat" (about the party congress), which was published in the last number of *Kras-*

---

[1]Okunev, Yakov Markovich (real name Okun), 1882–1932, writer.
[2]Central Library distribution center.
[3]Kozyrev, Mikhail Yakovlevich, 1892–1941, writer.

naya Niva. "You're beginning to sing the praises of 16 galoshes," he said, and Sven echoed him.[4]

Recently Klychkov said to Kirillov[5] in my presence: "Yesenin slandered me to everyone, tried to turn everyone against me, including you. Remember what he told you about me not long before his death"; this is, of course, true, alas.

Not long ago I read (or rather, reread) Beletsky's memoirs of Rasputin.[6] I thought: if I hadn't met in real life such people as Klyuev, Yesenin and Shergin, I would be psychologically incapable of imagining anything even approximately like Rasputin's type. But since I know these three well, or even very well, I can see Rasputin as if he were alive. That does not mean that they are like Rasputin. That is not the case. But all three are undoubtedly people of the same type, the same inner fire . . .

I remembered approaching Kashira yesterday evening. Darkness, lights, the roar of the train and a bridge. Bridges at night always have a sort of disturbing effect on me, as if I were crossing from one period of my life to another.

3 October   It is a long time since I last experienced such an emotional upheaval. I never thought I was so firmly and profoundly attached to Anatoly. Yesterday I saw him off at the station; he went to visit his mother in Novocherkassk, he left seriously ill, with a temperature of 38.7, dressed only in the jacket that I got for him from dear old Vl T Kirillov. Until then he had been going around just in his blue shirt. Although I told Anatoly off for the carelessness that has landed him in this complete penury, when I saw him outside in the autumn chill I nevertheless trembled all over in pity, and at the same time in anger at him (for he had been working all winter, was paid more than 100 roubles a month—he could have bought himself something). Above all I was tormented by the fact that I could not help him in any way, except by buying his ticket, I have no possessions; I have given everything away and the way I now look makes me turn aside when I meet very well dressed people. And above all there is nowhere to buy anything, and coupons are so much trouble, and often useless trouble, so that I have given up on them.

I arrived at the station at 10 o'clock. Tosik was waiting for me in the restaurant. He was extremely touching, extremely human, good and profound, and spoke so simply and at the same time so marvelously, in the sort of simple language that the heroes of the greatest literary masters use. I marvelled at him as never before and felt awful about his poor health,

---

[4]Sven, Ilya Lvovich, real name, Kremlev, 1897–1943, poet.

[5]Apparently, Vladimir Timofeevich Kirilov, 1890–1943, poet.

[6]S. P. Beletsky, *Grigorii Rasputin (From My Notes)*, Byloe, Petrograd, 1923; Stepan Petrovich Beletsky, 1873–1918, senator, director of the Police Department. Knew Rasputin personally.

about the journey ahead and the uncertainty whether he would get there in that state or whether his sickness would get worse. Despite all my efforts of will to preserve, outwardly, a "decent appearance," I failed. Tears gushed from my eyes and flowed wildly and uncontrollably down my cheeks. Tosik tilted his cap over his forehead so as not to show that he was weeping.

When we found his carriage and sat down, our emotion overstepped all bounds. Even now I cannot recollect it calmly and weep exactly as I wept as a child when I read Dostoevsky's *Poor Folk*. Whoever has not been moved by that book will never understand my pain. Tosik kept remembering how a few years ago when his mother saw him off to Moscow she was so upset that she was unable to speak a single word and could only stuff the sausage she'd prepared for the journey into his pocket. "I felt like that now," he said, "I want to tell you lots of things and can't say anything." But it only seemed to him that he couldn't tell me anything, in actual fact he spoke a lot, and his words were amazingly touching and profound. When the last bell rang he embraced me passionately and whispered: "You know that you're the only one I've ever loved," and I felt pain and shame at not having prized his deep love enough, and how often, how often I have wronged Tosik.

I ran after the train as long as I could and followed his lovely eyes that watched me through the dusty pane.

5 October   Yesterday I sent a telegram to Anatoly and have not yet received a reply, I am terribly worried.

6 October   At last I received a telegram: "Healthy, Send *papirosy* [Russian cigarettes: editor's note]." That took a load off my mind. All day I was walking on air. The telegram came early in the morning. When there was a knock at the door I immediately thought: that must be a telegram, and too impatient to dress I leapt to the door in my shirt. That note "send *papirosy*" is particularly reassuring and set my mind at rest. If he is thinking about *papirosy*, it means he must really have recovered. Even so I will not be entirely at peace until I have received a letter.

15 October   Received a letter from Tosik. He is healthy, feels well, recently gave a reading of his long poem. As I expected, he wants to come back to Moscow. I am very glad of that.

Kolya returned from Kashira a few days ago. He lived with me for those days. The day before yesterday he went to Serpukhov. He has given up technical college, wants to work in a factory. There was much that was good about these few days—I experienced intense pleasure, but even so it was not "real." We had one conversation that showed me we would never ultimately understand one another.

31 October   Midnight. Received a marvelous letter from Tosik, such a direct, picturesque one. Warm, good feelings. Such happiness fills my heart when I think of him.

Recently the arts club on Pimenovsky staged a writers' and dramatists' evening. Awful impression. The only witty performance was Aduev (*feuilleton* in verse).[7] He himself is very unpleasant, like a puffed-up, petty, provincial actor, but nevertheless he is talented. Vera Inber is phenomenally affected, her affectation makes you feel sick. However, even that was bearable, but when, towards the end, they allowed some youth or other on (Vilensky, it seems), the audience could no longer restrain itself and guffawed. Seriously (and with feeling) he declaimed some unimaginable tripe. His verse included the line: "And we'll come to a stop" which was greeted with Homeric laughter by the auditorium. The author was astonished at the audience's laughter . . .

1 November   Yesterday I didn't manage to finish—Kolya came (he arrived from Serpukhov yesterday and could not find me anywhere). I was very glad of his arrival. We went to bed and whispered together for a long time. Today he has gone to Kashira for a day to get his documents and will, incidentally, discuss my lecture there.

24 November, night of 25th . . .   Visited MA Kuzmin.[8] He looks much older, but is still as pleasant, witty and charming. Usually, however well-inclined he is towards his friends, he can't resist having a dig at them, but today he was quiet and docile. Yurochka Yurkun[9] showed his collection of diaries of unknown people. (This is his new hobby.) And his collection of old photo cards. MA read out extracts from these diaries, i.e. actually from one: the diary of a rollicking student whose jolly likeness was pasted to the diary. In one of the diaries in the "collection" there was something about some acquaintances of the diary writer whom MA and Yurochka also know. There are scandalous details about a (nowadays) much respected lady, from the time of her youth. To crown it all, it appears that this lady lives in the same block as them, on Spasskaya Street, on a floor below!

This diary story is just like the theme of a novel. Incidentally, to finish with the subject of diaries.

When I visited MA and Yurkun, Yurochka met me with the words: "Today I was reading about you in Mikhail Alekseevich's diary for 1914" (when I paid a visit on MA at Pavlovsk). I can imagine what he described.

---

[7]Aduev, Nikolai Alfredovich (real name, Rabinovich), 1895–1940, writer, poet, playwright.

[8]Kuzmin, Mikhail Alekseevich, 1872–1936, poet, translator, prose writer.

[9]Yurkun, Yury Ivanovich, 1895–1938, lover of Kuzmin, author of the novel *Swedish Gloves*, written under his influence.

For all his virtues, MA loves making caustic remarks, even lovingly. It gives him pleasure and I am convinced that his diary is, in spite of himself, steeped in malicious gossip.

From MA I learned that poor dear Evdokiya Apollonovna Nagrod-skaya[10] died this spring in Paris. I so well remember an evening at EA's on the Moika (when MA was living there), especially one dress ball, when I was in a red domino (having read Andrei Bely's "Petersburg"), and how I mystified Tyrkov, changing my voice and playing the part of a woman who was trying to pretend to be a man. And then returning home late at night when the icy wind blew in my face and tore at the red silk under my coat.

EA was always nice to me. I shall never forget how she visited me when I was living with the Pavlovs on Simeonovskaya Street[11] and how she hinted that she would like to "sin" with me. And how I didn't understand her hints and how she went away disappointed and dissatisfied. But this did not affect our relationship and she continued treating me with exceptional warmth.

1931

24 January   Yesterday I went to see Kolya at Shabolovka. He said he would be home but wasn't. I waited a bit and then went for a walk. It was an amazing evening. I particularly remember the shadow of trees on the lilac snow, just like a Japanese aquarelle. Unwittingly some lines of poetry sprang to my lips (the sequel: "Beneath the gold and azure vault, as if desiring to bereave, the lanterns of a steamer fixed their gaze on me").[12] Strolling along the road to the bus, I noticed a young girl coming from the bus and being met by a young fellow. Their meeting was so touching and affectionate that I found myself involuntarily envying them (not a bad kind of envy but a good one—for envy like a medal has two sides). Evidently he knew the time of her arrival and had gone to meet her, and evidently this happened every day—so it seemed to me. I thought: this is a patch of human happiness. This patch of happiness was like a young sapling or a lilac bush that has not yet bloomed. They met in a particular way, there was a particular grace in all their movements. And I thought that in my life there had been a few such "patches." Only a few, but they had given

---

[10]Nagrodskaya, Evdokiya Apollonovna, 1866–1930, writer.
[11]Ivnev went to school with Pavel Pavlov in the Corps of Pages. Pavlov's father bought a library on Semenovskaya Street, Petrograd which belonged to the family of the poet Vladimir Piast. There was a three-roomed flat at the library. In one of the rooms lived a female relative of the Pavlovs. When she left, the Pavlovs invited Ivnev to stay there.
[12]The poem "On the Open Sea" ("Beneath a vault of gold and blue . . .") was written in 1927 on the Pacific Ocean.

me enough faith and courage for a whole lifetime. Now that I was going through a hard, bitter period of my life, the reflection of these "suns" warmed me and saved me from the mortal cold of solitude.

With Kolya everything is confused and unexplained. There are some gleams of hope of something larger and better, but only gleams. And these are illusory. It is a long time since I have felt such pain. The pain is increased because of the fact that I have experienced amazing joy, thanks to Kolya. If it had not been for that joy, then it would probably be easier for me. To lose joy is far more painful than never to have had it. My head is spinning!

3 February   Dull, heavy pain! The break with K. How unbearably painful. I could not have expected another outcome—yet even so this is an unexpected blow for me. How stupid and absurd: in Leningrad Anatoly is waiting for me—who loves me with eternal devotion and whom I love so much—and I am seeking out suffering for myself here, stalking it like a hunter after game—savagely and unremittingly, I desire the unattainable, I torment myself, torture myself, I want to break down someone who, by their character and inner structure, is totally unsuitable!

Yesterday I had a look at old diaries, I chanced on 1923. Surely that was almost yesterday, yet seven years have sped past since then! It is terrible to think how time speeds furiously by! I found Emelyanov's note in my diary: "I loved you because you killed in me the small desire to live." I thought: now fate has its revenge on me. In relation to Emelyanov I was a criminal. My only justification is that I did not love him. But—sometimes fortunately, sometimes unfortunately—that justification is too broad. In the same diary I read an entry about Medvezhonok, read a copy of my letters to him (it was a good thing I copied those letters into my diary), I remembered that great passion—that has now turned to ashes, and I thought: this present pain of mine will also pass! Despite all the "rationality" of these thoughts—pain remains pain, and until time has healed the wounds, consolation remains mere paper.

A wonderful meeting, straight out of the pages of Dostoevsky, took place on my last trip to Leningrad. I shall never forget it, but in order to remember it later in all its clarity and color, I shall sketch it here. (It would take too long to describe all the details.) 2 a.m.: the corner of Kamennoostrovsky Boulevard and Pesochnaya Street. I am returning home. Three fellows. I am smoking a *papirosa*. One of them: "You're a visitor." "Yes." I look at him: the driver type, with a cap. Good face, but with something gangsterish about it. "Maybe you've got nowhere to stay?" I answer: "No, I have somewhere to stay." I indicate a house on the corner of Vologodskaya Street. "Maybe you'd like to come to my place?" "What would we do at your place?" "Warm up the stove and have a chat." I decide to go to his place. The depths of Pesochnaya Street. Further on is the house where EG Guro[13] once lived and where I read out my first novel *The Sad Angel* for the first time. A gateway. In the distance a park. No houses are visible. I'm carrying a wallet with money (a fairly large sum), my documents. (Before this his phrase too. To my question: "What will we chat about?" "Brother, surely two people can find something to talk about. I'll tell you my life, you'll tell me yours. Now, for instance, I left my wife, or, why tell a lie, she left. . . . I'll tell you everything and you'll tell me about yourself . . .")

He says: "Carry straight on." The path is covered in thick snow. We are walking literally up to our knees in snow. Finally a hut. He opens the door. A kitchen. Nobody there. The light is on. Suddenly: "Hands up." I smile distractedly. It turns out he is joking. We go into his room. Icy cold. He has not heated it for several days. He begins warming up the stove. I'm trembling from the cold. He warms my legs with his hands. He tells me about himself. Then he asks me about my life. Under the influence of the troubles I have been through I tell him a great deal.

Tears spring to his eyes. "My God," he exclaims, "my suffering is nothing compared to yours." He bent over and kissed my hand.

Night. The stove has warmed up. We went to bed. He is affectionate. In the morning he arranged a time for us to meet. I did not go, nor did I visit him, neither the following nor the next day, but I wrote him a letter from Moscow thanking him for the good, human feeling.

He is a worker—Ivan Dmitriev.

8 February   Made it up with Kolya. I can breathe freely. From 28 January (the day we split up) until now I have been a living corpse. I moved around mechanically—inside I was totally dead. Today it is as if I had been raised from the dead. When Kolya and I were on the bus (having already made it up), a little boy about 4–5 years old was sitting next to me, and I, usually fairly indifferent towards children, suddenly felt unusual affection toward him. And all the faces in the bus seemed to me sweet, kind and good.

Now I remember that when I wrote about my pain (on 3 February), I was staring at the following and still blank pages of the notebook with avid, tormented curiosity, trying to guess whether letters spelling out our reconciliation would appear there, or would it be fatal, gravestone words. Oh, how I wish Kolya understood me completely and felt how dear he is to me!

20 March   He [Klyuev] recently read his poem "Beyond the Lakes" at Mariya Ignatevna's house. On 22nd he will read his poem "Scorched

---

[13]Guro, Ekaterina Genrikhovna, sister of the writer Elena Genrikhovna Guro, 1877-1913.

Earth" there.[14]

I went to MI's with Kolya. After dinner Kolya came home with me and stayed the night. He was very sweet and affectionate. When I sleep with Kolya I imagine myself to be the happiest person in the world.

22 April . . .

The day before yesterday Kolya and I went to see *Sensation*[15] at the Vakhtangov theatre. Afterwards we paid a visit to the Sytins. They were extremely kind, really and truly glad of our arrival. We sat there until one in the morning. Then we went home to my place. Kolya's affection touched me. This night I was happier than I have been for a long time.

6 May   On 1 May I moved to Pudovkin's flat for three months.[16] AN Pudovkin has gone to Berlin and left me his beautiful room on Sadovaya Triumfalnaya Square. Kolya went to Serpukhov for the May Day holidays. He returned on the 4th. I called on him at the factory and we went to my place. I read the poem I wrote him when he was in Serpukhov:

I long to float with you on a wide estuary . . .

He liked it very much. We went to bed late; although both of us were tired—*emar ba* [*sic*: a coded expression. Translator's note]. It was beautiful morning. We drank coffee at home, then strolled in the town. Lunched at the Herzen House. At 3 p.m. Kolya went to the factory for the second shift . . .

9 April [Erroneous. Should be 9 May. Publisher's note].   Unexpected and final break with Kolya. My heart is like a burnt-out wilderness. Because it was unexpected I have not yet had time to gauge the degree of pain. But I only feel one thing: a mortal blow is "easier to bear" than cuts and scratches. The consciousness that this is the final break helps me to bear all this pain. It was a house built on sand. So it is better to free oneself finally and forever from such illusions.

13 April [As above. Should be 13 May. Publisher's note]   Yesterday I met Kolya again to part from him for good. Yesterday he drank a lot, then we went by taxi together with Pavel Vasilev to somewhere around the Paveletsk station, to some "gypsy women" at Malaya Tamarskaya, but they

---

[14]The poem "Beyond the Lakes" was written in 1927. Published in *Koster*, a collection of poetry by the Leningrad Union of Poets, Leningrad, 1937. The poem "Scorched Earth" was written in 1928, and published in *Novyi mir*, No. 7, 1987.

[15]A play by Ben Hecht and Charles MacArthur, translated by E. Zamyatin, directed by R. N. Simonov, produced by I. M. Rapoport. Premiere 29 May 1930 in the Vakhtangov Theatre.

[16]Pudovkin, Vsevolod Illarionovich, 1893–1953, director.

turned out not to be at home (it was Pavel Vasilev's idea).[17] Then we went to Malvina. We stayed there until one in the morning. Pavel went home, and Kolya came to spend the night at my place. We had a talk. We decided to part peaceably. Even so, some sort of resentment remains. I remembered (involuntarily) our former friendship and thought how "everything flows and everything passes." I yearn for something impossible . . .

16 May   Yesterday returned home around 3 p.m. Anat Dmitr Golovnya[18] (former cameraman for Pudovkin) said to me: "Some fellow with thick, bushy eyebrows called on you." My heart thudded. I immediately understood that it was Kolya. To make absolutely sure I showed An Dm a photo of Kolya, whom he recognized straight away. So there is no doubt. Kolya came. Intense annoyance that I was not at home gripped me. I had dinner and lay on the divan, not sleeping, lay there and thought. At six in the evening the telephone rang. I lifted the receiver. Kolya's voice: "Ryurik, is that you?" "Yes." "This is Kolya. Are you home? Can I visit you?" "Come round. Where are you calling from?" "From Mariya Ignatevna.[19] I'll be round in 40 minutes." In 40–50 minutes the doorbell. I open. Kolya is facing me. He clasps my hand, smiles. I preserve a neutral air. After 10 minutes he says: "Looking at you in the mirror, it seems to me you're displeased I've come." I understood that this was a challenge to have a talk and began speaking. A noisy explanation followed, completely frank, nakedly sincere.

Kolya told me a great deal and questioned me a lot about my past. He was particularly interested in Leonid, forced me to show him his photo and asked who I loved more, him or Leonid. "For Leonid you went to Kamchatka, but for me you only went to Serpukhov and Kashira, that means you loved him more." We spoke about Anatoly. "Everybody should envy you," he told me, "each of your friends is better than the other." "Anatoly is more handsome than me," he added. We spoke until late into the night, went to bed and carried on talking on the divan. Today he is coming round at 10 this evening, and tomorrow is off to Serpukhov for two weeks.

He told me too: "We are parting, but I know there is nobody better than you and that nobody has loved me as you did. We will no longer have a relationship but we will remain friends." "I am your friend forever, I don't know how you will relate to me," he asked. I answered that I would relate calmly to him, as the countryside is calm after a storm. During these disturbed days I wrote two lovely poems. They are written in blood. Only that sort deserve to be called poems.

---

[17]Vasilev, Pavel Nikolaevich, 1910–1937, a poet discovered by Ryurik Ivnev.
[18]Golovnya, Anatoly Dmitrievich, 1900–1982, film camerman.
[19]Sytina.

25 May   Saw Anatoly off to Leningrad. These few days that he has spent in Moscow have been beautiful, spiritually soothing days. After all the storms and baptisms of fire over love and friendship everything has settled into such a wonderful pattern. I think all the time—how wonderful it would be if my future relationship with Nikolai would settle into such a pattern. That would be the best thing fate could grant me. No trouble or jealousy or torment—a calm, profound feeling of friendship.

Anatoly remains businesslike: he has successfully carried out a difficult commission imposed upon his department (he dispatched some wagons of bricks to a factory etc.). And above all he is emotionally involved in his work. There is no trace of his previous slovenliness. I venture to attribute this change to my influence, i.e. to the endless "moralizing" I subjected him to when we were together.

Ryurik Ivnev (1891–1981)

POEM

Translated by Vitaly Chernetsky

Who will comprehend these feelings?
The sunrise, like a ghost, is behind the window.
Next to me is a friend who is younger
Than me by ten years.

I am looking through sleep, through eyelashes
At the one who is next to me,
And the pages of my life are rustling,
Tainted with yellow.

I know, it's impossible to put up with it,
No matter how much you console yourself.
You've got one kind of soul at twenty, and at thirty—
An altogether different one.

Who will comprehend these feelings?
The sunrise, like a ghost, is behind the window.
Next to me is a friend who is younger
Than me by ten years.

(1926)

Anatoly Steiger (1907–1944)

TEN POEMS (1926–1939)

Translated by Paul Schmidt

ANATOLY STEIGER (1907–1944) emigrated to Paris via Constantinople after the Bolshevik Revolution. There he became close friends with, among others, Georgy Ivanov. Steiger's verse, restrained and precise, is the essence of the Parisian school of Russian émigré poetry, and several of his poems address gay themes. These poems appeared originally in _The Bitter Air of Exile_, edited by Simon Karlinsky, University of California Press, 1977.

1

Until the sun sinks into a green
Smoke and twilight starts to spread
We speak of nothing but summer.

Yet autumn will soon tell us
The truth, in a cold voice.

2

We believe in books, in music and poems,
We believe in the dreams we dream,
We believe in words (even words
Spoken to console us
From the window of a railway car) . . .

3

The dull rattle of shutters being lowered
So the cottage looks like someone blind,
And then, like a shot point-blank—
The roar of a motor in the garden out in front.

. . . And an endlessly accompanying glance:
Hopeless, melancholy, spaniel-eyed.

4

It must be an eternal arrangement:
Some people dissemble and lie,
While others help them do it
(Always seeing through it)—
And it's called love . . .

5
FRIENDSHIP

I   Where is he now, I wonder?
    And what's his life like?
    Don't let me sit by the door
    Expecting a sudden knock:
    He will never come back.

    Was it to hurt me, or himself?
    (Or maybe he was lucky.)

II One dream remains—the thought of peace.
    —Don't need friendship, all words are empty,
    And that word's the emptiest of all.

    (For friendship you need to have two.
    I was one, the other was air: you.)

6

. . . Not an epilogue, but everything coming to an end.
We'll meet. I'll grow very pale.
Your arrogant face will flicker
With annoyance: "What a silly idea!"

At my arrival—a meaningless arrival,
Because I can't behave like all the rest—
What is this constant wanderlust?

Suppose, a variant: (The thought drives me wild)
A clumsy hug?

7

How do we break the habit of big words:
What does "pride" mean? What's "humiliation"?
(When you know perfectly well I'm ready
to respond to the first sign, the first call,
the first slight gesture.) . . .

8

How can I shout, to be heard in that prison,
Beyond those ramparts, through those walls,
That not everyone has betrayed him,
That he is not abandoned, alone in the world?

I dreamed that I broke in to see you,
Sat on your bed and held you in my arms.
(Though he's long lost the habit, surely,
Of tenderness and soft, familiar words.)

Yet friendship exists, it really exists,
And tenderness of male for male as well . . .
It is not obligation, but particular nobility
To say so, with unwavering eyes.

9

Nobody waits at the foot of the stairs any more
Or takes our hand crossing a street, the way they did
When we were young. Nobody tells us about the mean
Ant and the Grasshopper. Or teaches us to believe in God.

Nowadays nobody thinks of us at all—
They all have enough just thinking of themselves,
So we have to live as they do—but alone . . .
(Impotent, dishonest, and inept.)

10

They will not ask us: have you sinned?
They'll ask us only: did you love?
With heads hanging,
Bitterly, we'll say: yes . . . Oh, yes,
We loved . . . Again and again . . .

Georgy Ivanov (1894–1958)

SELECTIONS FROM *THE THIRD ROME*

[Tretii Rim, 1929–30]

Translated by Vitaly Chernetsky

GEORGY VLADIMIROVICH IVANOV (1894–1958) is best known as one of the leading poets of the Russian émigré literature that grew out of the exodus of hundreds of thousands of people from Russia after the 1917 revolution. Ivanov's literary career took an early start: he published his first collection of poetry in 1912, and by then he was already an important participant in the St. Petersburg literary scene. His early poetry was influenced by Kuzmin, but later he became most closely associated with the Acmeist movement and a close friend of its leader, Nikolai Gumilev. In 1921 he married the poet Irina Odoevtseva and in 1923 the couple left Russia, eventually settling in Paris where Ivanov remained for the rest of his life (Odoevtseva returned to Russia shortly before her death in the 1980s). While Ivanov was justly considered a comparatively minor poet in Russia, his talent matured in emigration, where he produced some intensely personal lyric poetry born of much suffering that has been described as "proto-existentialist" and earned him comparison to the *poètes maudits* tradition. He was associated with the "Parisian Note" movement, another prominent member of which was the gay poet Anatoly Steiger. Ivanov's best and most famous collections of poetry are *Roses* (1931) and the posthumous *Poems 1943–1958* (1958). However, Ivanov's somewhat controversial reputation is due to his prose and criticism. An active participant in the St. Petersburg bohemian art scene until his emigration, he described it in his book of reminiscences *St. Petersburg Winters* (1928) which freely mixed fact and fiction and antagonized many of the fellow writers both in Russia and in the émigré community. The controversy was exacerbated by the strong opinions he voiced in many of his critical essays. However, with the literary wars of the 1920s and 1930s receding into the past, Ivanov has finally earned undisputed recognition as a major Russian writer.

Ivanov conceived *The Third Rome* as a novel of epic proportions about St. Petersburg in the 1917 revolution. The project began as a spinoff from *St. Petersburg Winters*, but with a much larger scope; however, while greeted more warmly by the critics than *St. Petersburg Winters*, it remained unfinished. This first part of the novel was published in 1929, the three chapters of the second part in 1930. The excerpt translated here is the opening chapter of the second part. In the first part, set in the fall of 1916, we are introduced to several members of St. Petersburg society; among them

173

Yuriev, a young man of much ambition but no definite occupation and little intelligence who finds himself in a complicated situation through the debts incurred by his girlfriend; prince Velsky, an imposing aristocrat engaged in secret separate negotiations with the Germans, who helps Yuriev in hopes to use him as a pawn in his political intrigues; Adam Adamovich, Velsky's personal secretary of humble appearance whose successful secret long-going project was to turn a patriotic aristocrat, Velsky, into a German sympathizer; and Snetkov, Velsky's right hand and an acquaintance of Yuriev who introduced the two to each other. The sexual orientation of the gay characters is not revealed in the first part. In the published chapters of the second part, set immediately after the February 1917 revolution that brought down the monarchy and established the briefly-existing democratic republic in Russia, we see the transformations that had befallen respectively prince Velsky, Adam Adamovich and Yuriev; thus in a sense it can be seen as a coda or an epilogue for the first part, bringing the narrative to a kind of conclusion. While Ivanov wasn't gay himself, he had many gay friends and acquaintances, and the text translated here is valuable as a perspective on gay life in St. Petersburg around the time of the revolution.

VELSKY WOKE UP exactly at nine, as always. As always, the butler brought the tea. Steam was rising, same as always, from the fragrant water in the bathtub, and roses were still standing on the coffee table. Velsky pulled away the curtain above the bathtub at the level of his head: behind the window was the usual sky, the usual Fontanka River, the usual St. Petersburg morning. But all of this was merely a shadow. The shadow of familiar objects, the shadow of the habits once formed, the shadow of the former life. Waking up, Velsky first of all recalled (with indifference—over the course of a few weeks he had already gotten used to it) that everything, or almost everything in his life had been crossed out, finished and would never repeat again.

Recognizing this made everything that was now surrounding him seem astonishing—astonishing precisely in its ordinariness. Everything was as usual. The butler, hearing the bell, brought the tea, and the bell rang, of course, because the button, pressed by a finger (the same one as always, the polished, slightly gouty index finger of the right hand of His Highness Prince Ippolit Stepanovich Velsky, with its pinkish filed nail)—that button closed, connected something out there, and a spark traveled down the circuit. . . . But everything—the finger, the tea, the bell, as in a dream, were devoid of real foundation—the bell rang, and the butler brought tea, but the touch of the bell could as well have started music, or produced an explosion, or instead of the carefully stepping old, silly, devoted butler, a steam locomotive would enter the room, or that very black hound who, escaping from the rope that tied it, snatched away from the table the butter that was prepared for breakfast, together with the butter dish.

That, the butter incident, happened long ago, a very long time ago—some forty years ago, in the Tver province, in the summer.

In essence, of everything that surrounded him this feeling of unreality was the most reliable—more reliable, anyway, than the tea, the finger and the Fontanka there, behind the window. In essence, everything was always unreliable. But before he did not understand that, and now, finally, he did. That's all. Yes, this was how it had always been: forty years ago, yesterday, a year ago. The glass butter dish sparkled in the grass, licked clean by the greedy dog tongue, Frey arrived from Germany, Rasputin was killed, His Highness Prince Velsky, lowering his slightly crooked legs, clutched a bed sheet and thought that everything was unreliable, even these legs, naked, sparsely covered with hair and the drops of fragrant water, all of this taken together was only an appearance, it was nonsense, a thin film through which a soulless cold void could be seen, each day with ever more clarity.

This void did not frighten; on the contrary, it rather consoled. The recognition that everything was unimportant, everything was uniformly devoid of value, softened the intensity of other thoughts, for example, the thought that Adam Adamovich had left the house nobody knew why and where to, that he had left and had not come back since then.

That Adam Adamovich had disappeared was most bizarre, but the circumstances surrounding his departure were even more bizarre. From questioning the servants it became clear that for a very long time, perhaps until that very morning, he was in the study: the light there was on all through the night. A heap of ash was found in the fireplace: Adam Adamovich burned some papers. Actually, it was absolutely clear to Velsky which papers these were: the secret compartment that used to contain everything related to negotiations with Frey was empty. Well, to burn was the right thing to do: these papers were of no use anymore, except for sending His Highness Prince Velsky to jail, if he were to fall into the right hands. Yes, of course, this was what had to be done—to burn them. But how Adam Adamovich decided to do it, on his own, was impossible to understand. And why did he decide to do it? Why, having destroyed the papers, the next day, in such a hurry, without warning anyone, did he run away from the house? The yardkeeper from the house next door saw Adam Adamovich running in the direction of the Inzhenerny Castle. His hat was not on straight, and on the whole he looked dishevelled and unusual. Extremely surprised, the yardkeeper went to find out what it was that had happened at the prince's mansion—burglary? fire? But there was no burglary and no fire, everything was quiet, nobody even called on the phone. And Adam Adamovich must have used the back door: nobody saw him leave.

As always, Velsky, rubbing himself slowly with a large Turkish towel, covering his cheeks with lather or pouring golden lotion that smelled of rum over his head, reflected upon, weighed and recalled various things related to the war, to politics, to the events that had taken place and were continuing: was it a riot or a revolution? (Velsky still had difficulty choosing one definition out of the two. The coup was undertaken by the Duma; at its head were the pro-census liberals, professors, prominent public figures, people with big names that were known even in Europe; the talk about the lawfulness of the revolution was repeated everywhere; on the other hand, all of this taken together smelled of peasant riots.) But, thinking about the situation at the front or going, smiling, through the strange and contradictory orders of the new democratic minister in his memory, he was doing it all almost mechanically, more out of habit of thinking like this, alone, with a fresh head, about everything one would not have the time to think during the rest of the busy day, than because the war, the Duma and the revolution truly were of interest to him. Yes, the situation at the front was menacing. Yes, it was rather a riot. . . . And who are we to talk about prestige in such a situation, to such people! . . . All of this, one after the other, passed through Prince Velsky's head, while he was combing his part or carefully, as always, tying his necktie—and all of this was equally uninteresting. The uniformly cold void, the uniform boring unreliability seeped through all of this as well.

However, something new started mixing in with these morning thoughts, and this new thing was not part of this surrounding indifference and emptiness. Today Prince Velsky with a particular clarity felt the presence of this new "something." The sensation was still instinctive, one still could not even approximately say what it consisted in, but one thing was clear—it was there, it existed, it grew, and it was precisely this new vague undefinable "it" that contained the most important part of life, its very essence.

The most important part of life, its very essence (today he had a particularly sharp sensation of this) was somewhere right here, very close, nearby. One had only to make one final effort, perhaps a very small, trifling one, to catch it. It was here. Velsky closed his eyes and felt—like warmth or light—its presence. He wandered about through the rooms, counting his steps, and it seemed to him that once he counted up to a certain number, he would suddenly understand everything. He peered deep into the pattern of the rug and somewhere in there, among countless little curls, he imagined a shining hair, a little thread of silk tangled up among thousands of others, that would explain everything once one found it. And at night he dreamt that he glanced at the clock or opened a desk drawer and suddenly came to understand everything.

All of this began recently; Velsky knew exactly when. Suddenly the tingling cold of seltzer water splashed into his face, and Velsky closed his eyes from surprise and shame. The water was still running down his face, under the shirt and onto the suit, and the bubbles of gas tingled the skin and produced a barely audible crackling sound, still keeping on bursting on his face and neck—when he opened them again. Everything was the same as it had been. The red armchairs of the study were still standing in their places, the chandelier under the ceiling was shining, from behind the wall one could still hear the muffled cheerful music. And the hand that splashed water into his face was still holding an empty, unbearably shiny glass. The glass, the hand and the sleeve up to the elbow stood out with particular clarity—the rest was like in a fog. "Farewell, Prince," said Yuriev's voice out of the fog; it was ordinary and not in the least excited. "Farewell!" echoed Velsky.

Yes, "this" began precisely at that moment. It was extremely cold, the sleigh ran swiftly through empty streets, and it seemed to Velsky that it was not the frost biting his face, but the damned bubbles of seltzer water still bursting and crackling. He took out his handkerchief and carefully wiped his forehead, cheeks, neck and behind the collar. The sleigh ran on ice across the Neva (Velsky ordered the coachman to drive where he knew); the river banks seemed black and steep, the sky was all covered with stars. The clock at the fortress tower played its doleful music behind them: the sleigh turned onto Kamennoostrovsky Avenue. Velsky wiped his face again, but one could not wipe away anything. . . . The sleigh was now running across some new bridge, all black and covered with snowdrifts. "It was here, Your Highness, that they found Grigory Efimovich,"[1] said the coachman and took off his hat.

The evening was quiet and warm, and there were few passers-by. Since the first days of the coup the center of Nevsky Avenue had changed. The closer to Liteiny Avenue, the livelier it was, but already near the City Hall the crowd grew noticeably thinner, and here, at the intersection that used to be filled with people so recently, it was completely deserted.

"Everyone must have gathered at Snetkov's by now—it's almost eleven. Perhaps I shouldn't go after all," the troubling thought crossed (for the umpteenth time that day) Velsky's mind. "Perhaps, after all . . ." He slowed his steps and stopped, hesitant, in front of the shopwindow of the Chiefs of Staff publishing house. The shopwindow was not lit, only an edge of it was hit by street light, and one could see a study picture inside. "The large axe, driveable," Velsky read the inscription. "The small axe, portable." The axes themselves were pictured there as well: the driveable was in a cart, driven by a horse that had the eyes of Circassian women on illustrations to Lermontov; the portable one, as it should be, was carried by a dashing sapper.

"Driveable, portable . . . what nonsense, bureaucratese," thought Vel-

---

[1]Rasputin.

sky. "Perhaps I shouldn't go to Snetkov's after all? *To-por*,"[2] he read syllable by syllable, absent-mindedly but attentively, as if weighing each letter separately. And suddenly, for a second, these "t," "o," "p," and "r," intended since time immemorial to induce by their combination the habitual image of an axe, as it were, somehow switched, and shuddered with some other hidden, muffled, threatening meaning. Right to left the same letters suddenly produced "*ropot*,"[3] and Velsky suddenly imagined some bearded men, the glitter of iron and humming voices. "Peasants are coming, carrying axes . . ." he suddenly remembered. "who was it that prophesied this? Here, it's coming true . . ."

"Yes, it would be more reasonable not to go. . . . What is there, in essence, that I haven't seen? But then it would be awkward, Snetkov is waiting, and after all, this is entertainment. Let's see if he is truly good— Snetkov is crazy about him, but for him the uniform alone is enough. And truly, what a wonderful uniform—anyone would be beautiful in it. Maria Lvovna, even she would be all right." Velsky smiled, imagining Palitsyna in a sailor's jacket and hat with ribbons.[4]

He turned onto the square. A car with a red flag passed him, going at a crazy speed towards Millionnaya Street, signalling hoarsely to some figure that briefly appeared in its lights. The black mass of the palace looked higher and more solemn than during the day. "There is something fake in the splendour of the Russian palace," Velsky recalled the words of one foreigner who was a connoisseur of both splendour and palaces. "Well, perhaps this is why everything came down, all at the same time. . . . Fake might, fake power. . . . His Majesty signed the abdication like a restaurant bill and is asking to be let to go to the Crimea to grow roses. . . . Poor His Majesty! . . ." Velsky sighed. "Yes, window dressing. This sailor who will be at Snetkov's is of more importance and of greater interest to me than the fate of Russia," he suddenly thought. "Isn't that right? The sailor more important than Russia?"

This thought appeared clearly, suddenly and unexpectedly, and it seemed to Velsky that a bright and deadly light suddenly and unexpectedly shone on everything around. He felt disgusted and frightened.

This light flashed and died down, like magnesium, and everything suddenly got mixed up. The heart was beating fast and anxiously, the head was spinning, and one could not understand anything anymore: from left to right one read "*topor*," from right to left "*ropot*," from left to right was Russia, from right to left the sailor. The icy fear of death enveloped everything.

---

[2] I.e., "axe."

[3] "Grumble, unrest."

[4] The traditional Russian sailor's hat is white with two black ribbons hanging in the back.

Then, as if on a screen, appeared the contours of a pale desired face with earrings and slightly impudent eyes, and everything—the sailor, Russia, His Majesty growing roses faded, retreated into the background, dissolved in the feeling of complete hopelessness which was cool, resembling the moonlight, and actually pleasing. The pale desired face with earrings looked at Velsky, smiled to him and, like the background of a portrait—the cool moonlit background—behind it one discerned the futility of everything: life and desires, disappointments and hopes. And here, so close, physically perceptible, was flowing the key, the most important thing in life, its very essence. . . . Velsky was standing on a bridge looking into dark water—now he would understand everything, everything! Actually, he has already understood, but he is too scared to confess that to himself, it is sweet and scary, as it is before one jumps into water from high above, into precisely this kind of water, from this height. Perhaps to jump, with one's eyes closed, into this dark water—perhaps this is the final movement one must make?

"If I indeed . . ." something began taking shape in his mind, but Velsky, making an effort, stopped that thought. "Tra-la-la-la," he started hammering with his fingers on the bridge's railing, repeating aloud the first things that came in order to chase away, to not let some impossible, unthinkable word take shape. "Tra-la-la-la," he hammered. "La donna mobile. The Tigris and the Euphrates. The Tigris and the Euphrates. Among the emerald waves that kiss the shores of Taurida I saw a water nymph at sunrise . . ."

The water nymph smiled to him and splashed with its scaly tail, creating circles on the water. Velsky looked attentively at them growing wider, sparkling, and disappearing. This was pleasing and comforting.

"Leshy, hold the ropes!" the lazy voice cried out comfortingly out of the darkness. A tugboat passed under the bridge, the green lantern waving comfortingly on its stern.

Dropping the extinguished cigarette, Velsky walked on. "Neurasthenia," he thought.

Snetkov's apartment was on the third floor. Removing their coats, as was customary in St. Petersburg, at the doorman's, the guests went up the staircase covered with a red carpet; there was no elevator: this was a very old house. Taking off Velsky's coat and receiving his walking stick and bowler-hat, the doorman, recognizing by the clothes that this was a "real" aristocrat (he did not know Velsky's face), said somehow mysteriously, "It will be without a number, I'll take it back to my room, to make sure it doesn't get substituted," and Velsky, already going up, suddenly turned red, understanding the meaning of what the doorman had said. Apparently the company where he was going was such that one's coat could get substituted or one's wallet pulled out; apparently, there had already been instances of this kind, and the doorman was saying this out of experience. He also probably knew why solid and well-dressed people like him, Velsky, frequent this company, and knowing this he now probably looked at him with indifferent plebeian condemnation. Of course it was of no importance what the doorman was thinking, but still Velsky grew a little uneasy: no matter what, there was something dirty about all this, and now going up to Snetkov he partook of this dirt.

This was the first time Velsky was going to this kind of party at Snetkov's. These parties started long ago, already before the war, and, of course, Velsky knew in detail what was happening there and knew many of the people who frequented them. He listened with interest to reports about these gatherings the following day, smiling about amusing or cynical details, advising to organize this and that, invite so-and-so, chatting about all this in the intimate circle of the people who shared his tastes. But to go there himself? Truly Snetkov had proved himself to be an excellent organizer—over the whole course of these parties' existence, there was never a serious scandal, never any blackmail or anything of that nature; truly, other people of the same age as Velsky and from similar circles of society had visited these parties and safely came out clean; but Velsky was too careful, he cherished his peace and his reputation too much to allow himself before the revolution the perhaps improbable but still possible risk of it becoming known that he, His Highness Prince Velsky, habitually visited the gatherings of St. Petersburg homosexuals.

In addition to these considerations of caution, another thing stopped Velsky. For example, he was not sure whether having found himself in a large heterogeneous company (usually something like fifty or sixty people gathered at Snetkov's), the company of people united only by one specific feature, he would be able to carry himself the right way. And several times he felt lost at the thought that he would suddenly find himself in a heterogeneous and unfamiliar crowd, different from any other crowd due to the fact that everyone there, thanks only to his, Velsky's, presence there, would know in advance about something most intimate, the most carefully cherished part of him, and, knowing that, would have some claims on him, on his soul, on the most intimate and carefully cherished part of it, some claims that resemble those of friendship or of being part of the family.

The latter aspect (in theory) had a high share of probability. There was the exciting image of simplicity, fraternal closeness of the people who found beautiful and natural that which the others—the huge hostile majority—found repulsive and shameful; the exciting image of freedom, at least for a few hours, to be what he was, not to pretend or to play a part, finally, the hope for the blindingly bright and blissful meeting that God had put in every person's soul and that—equally unrealizable for everyone— in the imagination of a blind person, a prisoner, or a homosexual grows as many times in its unrealizability, as many times their loneliness in this world is wider and scarier than the loneliness of ordinary people.

Velsky knew, of course, that nowhere else did the reality differ from imagination as sharply as in this area. Of course, these "spiritual brothers" of his (both at Snetkov's parties and everywhere else) were what they were. . . . Giggly, lisping, sensitive, all of them stingily calculating, all of them superficially gifted in arts (especially music), incapable of anything serious, but receptive to everything in a petty womanly fashion, all of them stupid, all of them extremely cunning, shy (and somewhat mean), hiding beneath excessive, syrupy politeness an incredibly developed harsh icy egoism—"half-human" or "quarter-human"—all of them, with rare exceptions, were the same.

Velsky generally did not like people, did not trust them, scorned them, but clearly saw that if one were to compare, then simply people, the crowd, the human dust still would be winning in comparison with those (a scream resembling a woman's resounded above, then came the sound of a door slammed) who were now there, at Snetkov's apartment, slamming doors and screaming. And at the same time . . . And at the same time there existed between him, prince Velsky, and those people a blood relation. A blood relation, unbreakable, insurmountable—and this relation (Velsky clearly saw that) went much deeper than the circumstance that in him, like in them, a sailor or a cavalry guard soldier encountered on the street inspired the same feelings that arise in an ordinary man at an encounter with a pretty woman. Oh no! This tie went much deeper, and there, in that depth where it led (Velsky firmly knew that), at that depth where there were neither cavalry guard soldiers nor women nor a distinction between those, there remained, like there previously were, a difference between the entire world and these people, between the entire world and prince Velsky, brilliant, generous, intelligent, magnanimous, completely, it would seem, unlike them, and still ultimately in something that could not be defined by words, but most important—the same as them, pitiful and funny, sensitive and heartless, lightheaded, stingy, all powdered up, lisping—half-human or quarter-human . . .

A scream resembling a woman's resounded above. The door slammed, and then came the squeaky sounds of a two-step. Velsky suddenly sensed weakness, shame, uncertainty, joy—a desire to run away and simultaneously a desire to mix as soon as possible with the crowd of these people (lightheaded, funny, and the same as him, the same as him) who were there, at Snetkov's apartment, dancing to the gramophone, making passes at soldiers, screaming and acting like buffoons. He started going faster up the staircase, feeling unusual pleasure from the lightness of his walk, his elegance, the freshness of his silk underwear and the smartness of his suit, from the recognition that he was not old yet, and had just taken a fragrant bath, and that there where he would now enter, he was expected as the desired, dear guest. "Just like Kitty going to the ball," he thought briefly. "How rightly did Tolstoy note everything, how true!"

The door opened immediately; bright lights, music and the crowd surrounded Velsky. "Prince, darling!" said Snetkov in a mosquito-like high voice, rushing towards him. Snetkov was wearing a sparkling dress with fake breasts and a wig. Somebody threw confetti into Velsky's face, somebody gave him a glass and, pouring champagne, spilled it on his hand and sleeve. Whispering some nonsense into his ear, Snetkov, his breath smelling of wine, dragged Velsky through the crowd to the corner next to the piano where, all surrounded by people, sat the young sailor, "the star of the party," who was already half-drunk but still had not completely lost an embarrassed expression; he truly was very beautiful. At the piano a famous poet, accompanying himself, sang,[5]

> Between a woman and a young man
> I do not find much difference—
> It's all just trifles, all just trifles . . .

burring, lisping and casting after each phrase a glance filled with edifying tenderness into the blue, slightly Finnish eyes of the sailor.

---

[5] A clear reference to Kuzmin.

Valery Pereleshin [pseud.] (1913–1992)

SELECTED POEMS

Translated by Simon Karlinsky and Vitaly Chernetsky

VALERY PERELESHIN (1913–1992) is the pen-name of Valery Salatko-Petryshche. Born in Irkutsk, he escaped to China with his family after the Bolshevik Revolution. In 1920 his mother brought him to Harbin, China where he graduated from high school and later studied law and theology. In 1932 he joined the literary journal *Rubezh* (The Frontier). From 1939 to 1943 he studied Chinese in Peking and subsequently became an Orthodox monk for a while. Later he moved to Shanghai and then Tientsin, and in 1953 arrived in Rio de Janeiro, Brazil where he spent the rest of his life.

After many years he returned to literature in 1967, publishing in *La Renaissance*, *The New Review*, *Novoye Russkoye Slovo*, *La Pensée Russe*, *The Contemporary* and elsewhere. His book *Ariel* (1976) comprises 169 classical sonnets, an epistolary romance with a married man in Moscow, Zhenya Vitkovsky. The collection is a technical tour de force, incorporating word games and classical form with frank treatment of homoerotic desire. Pereleshin also wrote a verse narrative "Poem without an object": 8400 lines of the Onegin stanza, where he addresses his love affairs.

"My chronicle will not be to the taste of uncles and aunts—for half a century we haven't gotten on, the breeders and I." Pereleshin in *Sovremennik* 42, 1979.

"During the period 1977–1991 I met him many times in Brazil and found him an engaging, if eccentric, man, fully open to the joys of gay love but retaining many of the formalities of his generation. He generously gave me permission to publish excellent translations of some of his work in *Gay Sunshine*, and, when I informed him of my plans for the present anthology, gave me *carte blanche* to publish translations of any of his poems from *Ariel* or other sources. The poem "To One Who Confessed" was written by Pereleshin specially for *Gay Sunshine* in 1977. The poet also worked closely with Professor Simon Karlinsky, and the present writer is grateful for his assistance when preparing this Pereleshin section. Of the poems printed here, the three Sonnets from *Ariel* appeared originally in *Christopher Street*, Dec. 1977. The poems "To One Who Confessed," "Straight from the Shoulder," "Admiration" and "A Declaration of Love" appeared in the book anthology *Now the Volcano* (Gay Sunshine Press, 1979). The publication of these poems here is dedicated to the memory of Valery Pereleshin."

—Winston Leyland

THREE POEMS

Translated by Simon Karlinsky

TO ONE WHO CONFESSED

To D. S. F.

The fertile Chinese hold a firm conviction
—I heard it often from their very mouths—
That those immoral creatures called jack rabbits
Can do without the females of their kind,

But manage still to propagate their species;
While in the village taverns in Brazil
Mustachioed *caboclos* will assure you
That deer's the animal that shuns its hinds.

They should at least consult a dictionary:
Stag starts with *ve*, a fellow starts with *vi*,
But they pronounce *veado* and *viado*
In dialects where it sounds the same to me.

Alumnus of religious seminaries
(Acaracu, then in Aracati),
You've been inscribed among those odious creatures
Whom any one may crucify at will.

Those very ones, who in a dormitory
Would clasp you passionately, one and all,
Tormented by desires they could not master
They'd plead with you: "Please let me, dear boy!"

Those very ones—but now they are the fathers
Of children no one dreamed of in those days,
Avoid you and are making you feel guilty
Because *their* lust was stronger than their shame.

"A deer, a deer!"—that's all you ever hear there.
They've branded you and everyone's been told.
But we are friends and I would like to give you
New freedom, which we'll share fraternally.

Just have a look: *Lefthanded Light*, a journal
With drawings, articles and interviews;
And here's *Orgasms of Light*, a book of poems:
I'll lend you both and you can take them home.
We're not alone. Believe me, there are millions
Who'll follow Leyland in the righteous fight
For our equality, for decent legislation
And for the right to live and be ourselves.

(ca. 1977)

POET'S NOTE: In China, "jack rabbit" is a swearword, as in the expression "Ni chê-kè t'u-tzy, nan-nü fen pu ch'u-lai!" ("Why, you jack rabbit, you can't even tell a male from a female!") It is believed in China that jack rabbits are able to breed by means that are called "contrary to nature."

Caboclo is a Brazilian term for a person who is half white and half Indian. Acaracu and Aracati are small towns in the north of Brazil.

TRANSLATOR'S NOTE: This metrical version has omitted an important aspect of the poem: its playful and sparkling rhymes, the English equivalents of which would be somewhere halfway between the Byron of "Don Juan" and Cole Porter. Pereleshin's rendition of *Gay Sunshine* into Russian as "Lefthanded Light" (preserved in the translation) refers to his theory of spiritual lefthandedness, which consists of emancipating oneself from the imperatives of the species and family, and is a prerequisite for admitting one's gayness to oneself and others. The poem is addressed to a Brazilian friend of the poet's, whose biography and consciousness the poem reflects.

Veado (deer) is the Brazilian slang word for homosexual, comparable to the term "queer" in this country. *Orgasms of Light* is the anthology of poems and short stories edited by Winston Leyland and published by Gay Sunshine Press in 1977.

STRAIGHT FROM THE SHOULDER

To Paulo Carlos Peixoto Cruz

If you were someone I invented in a dream
You would be soft as wax between my fingers
And would grow up a pampered adolescent,
A graft that fortunately took to me.

I would believe that in some distant land,
Having matured, you soar in flattened skies
Or are a horse-guard, prancing at parades
And spend your holidays upon the moon.

If you were . . . But in Rio de Janeiro
I met an ordinary *brasileiro*
And fell in love with him, straight from the shoulder.

After I woke, I fashioned from my dream
No fortune's darling and no wealthy heir,
No smartypants, not even a heartbreaker!

(January 28, 1977)

ADMIRATION

"You are so handsome! Why, with such a model
I could have sculpted a crown prince in marble
Disguised as a discobolus and found
Distinguished, wealthy patrons for my art.

And you'd be celebrated and admired,
Whole schools of art arising from your form
To dazzle—such are the vagaries of fate—
Rome, the infallible Eternal City.

At an exhibit under Roman pines
Art lovers would imbibe your lovely lines,
Their mouths atremble, gulping avidly . . ."

But as I think all this, the hostile punk
Feeling my steady gaze upon his body
Calls out: "Go to hell, you cocksucker!"

(August 11, 1977)

THREE SONNETS FROM *ARIEL*

Translated by Simon Karlinsky

WITHOUT A MASK

You willed it so—and you've become my fate.
About the twilight of the waning world,
About the flame of Plato and of Shakespeare,
About myself I now converse with you.

My friends (they—almost every one of them—
Are caustic scoffers, cavillers, fault-finders,
Their trump cards mockery and biting satire)
Are dying to know everything about you.

So I betray you in smoke-filled cafés
Amidst the talk of sports and Leonard Bernstein,
But even at such times we are alone.

Only at night, without a screen or mask,
I blend with care the colors for these sonnets
And am tormented that you are not here.

(November 14, 1972)

Translator's Note: In the original, all the sonnets in *Ariel* are written in lines of precisely rhymed iambic pentameter. The rhyme scheme for "Without a Mask" and "A Declaration of Love" is abba abba ccd eed. The virtuosic "Not for Publication" has only two sets of rhymes throughout, rhyming abba abba bba bab.

NOT FOR PUBLICATION

I am resigned (though inwardly I scream).
You, too, must now endure the hurt of failure.
Try to snatch but a half an hour from your jailer.
Don't be ashamed of self-abasing gestures,

Or else, he will snuff out on the spot
All of our dreams and hopes for an encounter,
And, victim of a modern immolation,
They'll dump you at the foot of Lenin's tomb.

A living dog's more blessed than dead lions.
You'd better lie. Humiliate yourself.
For cover, use some shreds of a red banner.

God doesn't ask you for insane bravado.
He knows that when you trample on the icons
You still have not betrayed your inner self.

(September 10, 1973)

A DECLARATION OF LOVE

That's quite a sweet confession that I got:
You write you love me for my verbal powers
Though I am not renowned among the poets
And other masters have a greater fame.

Well, why turn down the lesser good that comes our way?
I, too, love Sergio because on Sundays
He gives me rides in his three-seat sedan.
I love Antonio as a splendid house painter.

Among the barbers, I love the black barber Nilo.
Among the soaps, it's cocoa butter soap.
No salt but Morton's will for pickles do.

There's Dennis Weaver—I just love him as an actor.
Bald-domed Anselmo—him I love as tram conductor.
And you—I only love the translator in you.

(November 6, 1974)

TWELVE SONNETS FROM *ARIEL*

Translated by Vitaly Chernetsky

TWO

You must have been a Siamese twin of mine
In one of your past earthly incarnations:
You didn't call me father or old man;
Evgeny was a brother to Valery.

We were more trusting and more humble then,
And, tied together not by chains or rings,
But through our joint beginning and joint end,
We shared the pain and happiness of dreams.

And now I watch your highest blooming days
Across the seven seas and three decades,
And I'm not whole but merely a half.

But, to bring back at least a smaller tie,
I wish I could caress you like a son,
The way that now you are caressing yours.

(20 July 1972)

THE SPEECH OF ARISTOPHANES

A long time ago, in an era that's long gone,
The earthly beings were of three sexes:
There was double "he," and double "she," and then
There also was the lecherous "he/she."

That breed of people was of unusual strength,
It was rounded in shape, and slightly funny.
They lived without giving gods their due,
And for that wrongdoing they got split in two!

Since then Ajax is weeping for his Ajax,
And Sappho sings of the maids of Mytilene,
While the third sex has flooded marriage chapels,

Anticipating enticing adulteries;
It conquers concubines in raids, and then
Bears children and sings praises to itself.

(30 September 1972)

THE CRYSTAL BALL

My crystal ball called jealousy—it conjures
The plausible endings: here in front of me
Walks on an Antinous that once worked
In a Russian steam bath, with its standard fare.

And then, a self-absorbed and gout-struck old man
That mutters, toothless, quarrels with his wife—
While he's the Bosie that in his playful youth
Was indiscreetly chasing after Icarus.

Here are Rimbaud and Maximine that now
Are smarter: they count months by passing name days,
And four-year intervals they count by new towels.

And he, my dreamy sly little Ganymede,
He counts time by whining newborn babies
And the meager news of penny-worth achievements!

(4 October 1972)

AUTOBIOGRAPHY

A curly-haired teenager, like Narcissus, I
Was pensive, of few words, full of myself.
Then, virgin Daphnis, I caressed Chloe,
And then, like Paris, did same with Helena.

Scores of eccentric actresses and ballerinas
Amused themselves by playing games with me
Until the *Domostroi* acquired as dressing
Symposium and *Satiricon*, and *Songs of Bilitis*.

The anchorless Argo, not seeking meaty goals,
I turned a dreamer, Ariel, a poet,
A fasting holy man. . . . And now, my hair's grey.

I flee Petronius and Shakespeare, and
The light *Wings* now for me resemble water:
Is this the rancorous world's revenge on me?

(12 October 1972)

ZHENYA

Was it the Evgeny coming out of legends
And out of Januaries that had charmed me? No,
It was the gentle Zhenya that had sent
My poor head spinning ever so strongly.

I'm thinking now: wouldn't it be truly smart
To flee both jealousy and humiliation?
Can one succeed in hiding safely from them
Beyond seven hundred lakes and seventy seas?

But even there, excited and disturbed,
In spite of all the scheming customs vultures,
You'd lovingly appear with singing strings.

Both your wife's husband and a maiden-man.
Let us be loved and let's be listened to by
The Gent of geniuses and the snowy gentle Geneva!

(7 November 1972)

ALCIBIADES

We are lying down, and the roomy overcoat
Is like a tent over our two naked bodies.
Kiss me, and make me worthy of getting close,
And scornfully reject the human shyness.

I'll open all of myself to your caresses
And I'll extinguish then this lamp of gold,
And, getting drunk with all my manly beauty,
You'll tell me all about androgynous love.

Sweet youth, did you decide to gain the honor
Of knowledge in exchange for perishable dust?
Your calculations truly are amusing;

But Alcibiades is neither laughable nor blind
For having chosen as his cherished lover
Nobody else but the pug-nosed balding faun.

(8 December 1972)

IMMORTALITY

The fate of males is to get prolific wives,
Then sons and daughters, and afterwards grandchildren,
So that through them to learn your ABC's,
To huff and puff, and mix the verbal tenses.

But will a man of prayer, a scientist, an ascetic,
Or then a poet whose secret pain's enveloped
In sounds and pauses, suddenly embark
Onto the path of scattering his seed?

By fate and by God's mercy they are spared
Of virgin maids as well as of match-makers—
Both Lermontov, and Marlowe, and Verlaine.

Deprived of home, they lead their chariots
Along the closing walls that are winter-proof—
The rebels, eunuchs and defrocked monks.

(25 December 1972)

TWO IN ONE

Don't go! Consumed by fire and by cold,
I'm dizzy from all these conjoining fevers,
And I don't even feel repulsed that I
Would, loving, sting you and would make you bleed,

That, pulling about your hair and your fingers,
I'd see the rainbows rising through your pain.
But then I, too, would fall right to the ground
To humbly ask you to please pay me back.

I'd put myself at the mercy of your will
And drink not the equal but a greater share of pain,
And you would then revive your cries in mine,

Repay your shame by me fulfilling orders.
Don't go! Light up with a double flame, be both
Marquis de Sade and Herr von Sacher-Masoch!

(27 August 1973)

TOWARDS THE EVENING

For all the long day I live in a rush.
My angry eyes tell clock hands to go faster,
I long to move from the wrong place to the right one,
Into the dream, where I will see the real you.

You're on a river I shall swim along,
You're going dancing—I'm with you at the party.
You're with a girl—I'll look, jealous, through a crack,
And walk away, I will not spoil your luck.

In vain there are moats dug to divide us.
And laughing, we have paved them over with dreams,
And killed off separation with embrace.

What are three decades? Moments, and not years!
What are five seas? Not deeper than a ditch!
What home and duty are compared to love and freedom?

(20 March 1974)

UPON REREADING GUMILEV

I   It is more than praiseworthy to have children,
Said Death right after tasting some fresh meat,
And Griboedov made it clear, yawning,
That for this you don't need to have much brain.

Those who are willing are pushed by Life itself
To join the ranks of fathers and grandfathers
(A few Ganymedes making the exception)
And to make grow the maternity wards.

But since my youth Hecuba's thirsty lips
Were pushed away from mine which didn't seek hers,
I fled their bliss and inventive endeavors.

A cleaner, less poor life was possible for me
But I'm already proud that, old and final,
I've never begotten children from a woman.*

(5 August 1974)

II *And I have never called a man a brother,*
Although I have loved no less than two hundred;
And seeking out the beauty of the south,
I have been most tender towards the mulattoes.

I did not visit either poets or prelates
In search of pathos and of mental heights:
For me, a caught spy with a guilty look
Was infinitely more appealing.

The treatises of Frank and Lossky made me yawn,
And forced to run away into the carnival crowd
And breathe in deep the throng, the heat, the music.

And after midnight, in a cheap old tavern
I spoke to the random Antinous
About death and spleen of our lives.

(19 August 1974)

---

*This line and the succeeding one are quoted by Pereleshin from Gumilev's 1910 sonnet "Don Juan."

DE PROFUNDIS

We have been told to stay away from sin,
To separate ourselves by miles and years,
And here in Brasil a page is written
"From the abyss," that is, from Reading Gaol.

The pattern of life of a dissipated dreamer
Is being conjured out of flame and darkness,
While you're in Moscow. And you have settled down
And cooled the heat with winter snowdrifts.

But still, my dear Lord Alfred, my sweet Bosie,
You haven't yet fully mellowed down to prose,
The branded poet isn't silent yet in you.

While I'm alive, you will be spared trouble,
But when I'm dead the time will come to pay
Your old debt through repentance and through pain.

(26 June 1974)

FIDELITY IN INFIDELITY

Not morgue, but mind. And you inside my mind
Are separated into parts and pieces,
In which I barely recognize the signs
Of my invention, child of my own passion.

Palladio has put your silver rings
On his own fingers delicate like petals,
But how far removed is his touch
From your true Komsomolian hand shaking!

Through ardent sparks in Sergio's lively eyes
I recognize the eyes belonging to you,
Just as I see your curly-haired head
In that of Tullio's, over his black torso.

Through loving what I know in all their bodies,
Out of this mash I'm recreating you!

(26 June 1975)

Yevgeny Kharitonov (1941-1981)

Four Stories:
THE OVEN; ONE BOY'S STORY: HOW I GOT LIKE THAT;
ALYOSHA-SERYOZHA; THE LEAFLET

Translated by Kevin Moss

YEVGENY KHARITONOV (1941-1981), who was never published by the official Soviet press, is the major figure in gay Russian literature in the sixty
years since Kuzmin. He was a modern renaissance man in the world of culture, teaching acting and pantomime at VGIK, the state film institute;
directing at the Theater for the Deaf—among other works, his own play,
"Enchanted Island"; choreographing the rock group "Last Chance"; and
studying speech defects at Moscow State University. Meanwhile, he wrote
unpublishable prose, poetry and drama. When Kharitonov died of a heart
attack in June of 1981, the pages of his just-completed manuscript blew
away down Pushkin Street. He had called his volume *Pod domashnim
arestom—Under House Arrest*. As an underground writer and a gay man,
Kharitonov was under double pressure from the KGB and the police. In
1979 he was suspected in the murder of a gay friend and interrogated. It
may have been this added pressure that led to his premature death.

There are those who say that Kharitonov's greatest work was himself.
The accounts of Kharitonov's life provided by his acquaintances are often
mutually contradictory, making it hard to separate truth from legend. Was
his anti-Semitism real (see his "Leaflet" here), or was it a pose to shock
his Jewish writer friends? And what of his relation to his sexuality? Many
of his heterosexual colleagues want to wish his sexuality away, claiming he
felt it was a cross to bear, a sin he wanted to redeem—some even go so far
as to claim his homosexuality was itself merely a pose! But there is no evidence whatsoever for such an interpretation in his writings, which are as
out and proud and in your face as any in the West. Not only does Kharitonov show a healthy appreciation for his sexual orientation, he even claims
that it is a kind of divine gift directly related to his genius as a writer.

THE OVEN

[Dukhovka]

O N TUESDAY evening on my way to the village for bread, I see him on
the hill from behind, I even commented to Lyonya, "there's a boy
waiting for somebody"; that is, his figure struck me right away, the guitar
on a string around his neck, how he put his foot out. And unexpectedly,
we're on our way back, he still hasn't left, I see him here head on. I asked
for a light, he didn't answer, came towards me, I didn't understand why
he was coming without answering, or it was his street etiquette; he was
simply coming to offer a match and asked for a smoke himself. Now, I
think, we'll go our separate ways, I'll never see him again. I thought again,
asked him to play the guitar. He began right away. His voice has just matured, songs like they sing in the yards. He sang his whole repertoire, nothing left for me to keep him with. I walked home somehow, but left alone
with nobody to talk to, I think, I'll go to the Rainbow, just at least to walk
and not sit in one spot; walked through half the village and meet him.
Amazing, wanted to see him and I saw him, though, since he turned up not
far away, why shouldn't he live here too. I was like walking around with
nothing to do and think I'll join him, it's obvious he's just standing around.
He nodded, I like want to watch how he plays, where to press the strings.
We walk around like that for a long time, not much conversation; found
out he's in school, he'll be in the last grade, and he goes to a math school
for only a few people from the whole region; not just a street boy: caste.
He was standing on the hill waiting for his friend Seryozha, a sambo champion, who was supposed to come back from the city. While we were like
hanging around for no reason along the plywood shacks, girls of his age
come up, talk to him about something, I'm off to the side. I don't inter-
fere. It got dark, he says, —Want to go see the athletes? —Let's go; Of
course I don't say I don't know the athletes, don't know anyone here.
Problems with conversation, when it's about cars or a song they all know.
He has a rating in swimming. This was when I remembered that when I saw
a boy walking along the dacha street with an aqualung and flippers under
his arm, his friends were walking with him, girls, or children, I was struck
then how handsome he was, and his look was callous, from his beauty, I
saw him only a moment, they had just walked by—now I realize this was
him. It's dark, we're sitting on the bench by a house, all the time he's running his fingers over the strings, singing in his street voice these songs, prison songs, pitiful ones about love. From inside the house a woman asked
him not to sing. We went over to the open porch of the cafeteria, there's
a light on all the time in the middle not too high up, a dim light with big
shadows; an old woman standing watch with a cigarette and two little girls
and a boy; and the little girls came over, and the boy too, asked Misha, no

chicks? and Misha laughed; Misha gave him the guitar, this Tolya started
to sing with his Ukrainian accent in a funny way, with feeling, every other
word an obscenity, not like Misha. Tolya sent the girls for cards, I thought,
that's good, there are four of them and I'm extra, they won't find out I
don't play; these girls live in a house nearby, maybe the daughters of the
cafeteria manager; when they came back, Tolya was involved with his singing, they sat down with the old woman in the corner across the way to play
solitaire, and Misha and I listened to Tolya and laughed, already united
by our listening to his singing; Tolya's songs were like this: a homeless boy
tries to steal a ticket and gets arrested, he says, —Citizens, how cruel you
are, citizens, you have no heart, you have forgotten I'm homeless, why do
you offend me? or in a den of thieves a ragamuffin kills a sailor over a girl,
he bends over the body, recognizes his brother, and kills her too; or school
songs about love, with fine phrases, and he sang them so seriously and sincerely they get to you. The singing ended, we went to walk Tolik to the
tents. He unabashedly started to tell us right away about his escapades, how
he had already popped three cherries, and how other people want to marry
a virgin all their lives and can't find one, and how they'd get attached to
him. He was talking mostly to me, Misha was busy with the guitar, maybe
Misha had gotten used to the stories, and I was a good listener. Misha and
I went on farther, he told me about the murder, since I had to go through
the woods; a few days ago a guy was killed here with motorcycle chains.
Farther on our paths split, —Well, see you later. —See you later; and he
says it himself, it's a formality, but even so—we'll see each other tomorrow. After our meeting on the hill I had thought simple acquaintance was
impossible, but it turned out to be possible, we had been together so long,
talking, he lives here, now he knows my name, I know he's Misha, and
we'll see each other tomorrow.

The next day, on Wednesday, on the way to the village and the tents in
the morning, I see Tolik, the Ukrainian, alone on the cliff, —Hi —Hi
—Have you seen Misha? —No, I haven't. Good, I think, when he passes
by here I'll happen to be on his way, he won't see that I was looking for
him, and I'm even with Tolik, like I met Tolik too, and it won't just be a
lonely figure stalking him. The athletes lie down nearby to play cards, their
leader or coach came over with vitamins, they gave me some. I see him
coming, —Hi —Hi; —We're going to the river, Tolya the Ukrainian didn't
go, he had something to do; and on the way he told an anecdote: he's sitting in the dorm, the math school's in the country and he's been living in
the dorm a year, he stuck his leg between the desk and the wall; suddenly
he feels a pain below his knee, the pain gets stronger, he figured out what
it was: on the other side of the wall a drill's humming, they're drilling a hole
from the other side right where his knee is, he can't pull his leg out, the
drill's already in it, and his leg is right between the table and the wall, and
he's in a position where he can't move the table; he yelled into the wall,

only then did they stop, a workman came in, Misha pulled his leg off, the drill had already entered the bone. As a mathematician Misha himself said that the probability of hitting his knee was practically zero. We got to their swimming place, he had on a brown bathing suit with yellow stripes on the sides. He showed me the scar from the drill. He doesn't realize his beauty, maybe girls have told him, but if he looks at himself in the mirror he won't understand, and his friends don't understand it, of course he's just a friend for them, that's all. He suggested we swim to the island, I'll barely be able to swim there and back. I didn't let on, we sat there a bit, he wanted to come back right away, I suggested we dry off, the last few meters were hard for me, we got out, have to catch my breath, further conversation wasn't bad—there's the guitar, and I want to learn how to play and learn some songs. He showed me strumming and some chords. His sister sings in the Zhdanov club at the institute before showings; or else he mentioned his sister yesterday. Tolya the Ukrainian came, learning strumming together— the eight, the seven—such names; Tolya suggested learning them by flicking my head, he says like that you remember them better. They want to swim some more, I say —I'll just get some sun; I was so exhausted. Here's another example: Tolya came from lunch; so when it's time for Misha to go to lunch, Tolya won't go with him; for me to go with Misha and for it to look unpremeditated I say beforehand, —Well, I have to go to lunch soon; that way when Misha wants to go I can go with him; and it won't be like he got up and I tagged along, without setting it up beforehand. Together all the way to his turn, I ask, don't even really ask, like —coming swimming again; —Uhuh. Now I'll know where to find him, and in about an hour; and during lunch he gives me the guitar to practice. At home Vanya's come to visit; and I wanted to tell him about the poems too, and he'll see Misha now, I wonder if he'll be able to appreciate it when he sees a boy who's one in ten thousand. We went to the river, Misha came in half an hour. Here you have the convenient situation of somebody from your circle to talk to. With just Misha a lively and interesting conversation won't work out, but through Vanya Misha will listen too, laugh, be drawn in, get some insight into me. And it's important that I not seem alone to Misha, that I have friends too. We spent about three hours like that, Vanya wants to go into town, I went to walk him to the bus. Misha asks, —Coming back? It's a formality, but still; we already know each other, we can walk around the village together, on Tuesday after the meeting on the hill I wouldn't have dreamed. Conversation with Vanya on the way—a man of passions different from my own confirmed everything about Misha. I was tired, the island, and I'd walked so much that day, I decided not to go there again. And it's good not to show up too often, let him think I have my life too, and not like I'm all alone and stalking him all the time. Here the guitar was useful, all my interest was in the guitar and the songs. That first night he said he was coming to Moscow this summer to apply to the university; and in the winter he was coming to Moscow for the holidays; I think I'll give him my address.

Wake up on Thursday, good thing, I think, didn't wear out my welcome yesterday; though I won't make that mistake; still it's good to keep in mind. The whole long way, kilometer and a half to the cafeteria, same to his swimming place, don't see him. Want to go to his house, he said thirty-two yesterday, and coming from lunch with Vanya I even yelled "Misha"; I thought then he was at the river, but it turned out he just didn't hear; but since I yelled then and mostly since I didn't go last night, but was planning to; I think, now it's OK. See his grandmother with the dishes, and picked out the house by the flippers and aqualung by the door before I saw the number. —Is Misha at the river? I ask. —He's asleep, I'm just fixing breakfast; no particular cordiality, always suspicious of the children's acquaintances, and the man who dropped by was older than Misha. Then I saw through the open door the end of a cot with legs sticking over the edge under a sheet. I go meanwhile to the river to sleep an hour in the meadow, so the time passes quickly, where I lay the morning before, so he'd run into me himself when he passed by. An hour passed, maybe half an hour seemed like an hour, I couldn't wait, went to the house, and you keep feeling that somebody in the neighboring houses is getting suspicious. Finally he comes out, shirt in a knot on his stomach. —I've come to see you, I say, —let's go to the river; I made a point of saying I'd dropped by once, his grandmother had surely told him; so it didn't look like I didn't want to admit it for some reason. He takes the guitar from across the street, he lent it yesterday, halfway there he's called by Seryozha, ugly and strong in a striped army shirt, the one he was waiting for from town that first evening, as I thought; it's inappropriate to make introductions, that's right, we're only river companions for two days, Sergei and I will get acquainted on our own if need be; we don't need formalities. But Misha and I had agreed he would ask Sergei for the notebook with the songs. Later we're all three at the river, they swam to the island; no, Sergei didn't change, he sat in his clothes. Misha learned guitar from him. Sergei can make fun of him, for example, of how he plays; though he himself is just so-so, only to have the guitar around like everyone else. There's some roughhousing between them when Sergei can embrace or press against him in fun. That day or the day before I asked, do I have a lot of time to practice; he said he was leaving the twentieth; and that was the eighth. They have their own slang: "traveling" means good; "wife" 's a girl you've slept with; "skin" 's jacket; you can't give in to the temptation to ask Misha with the affectionate smile of an older man, your arm around his shoulder, what "wife" or "rub" means—right away you'd be a man from a different circle, like this you're an equal, with all the advantages of friendship on an equal footing. By Sergei's house, where they sat on an upturned boat, even before they got there, Misha asked Sergei for the notebook; it's not that he remembers and that's nice, but that he remembers and my walks with him have an explanation. Sergei brought out the notebook with mistakes in it, I ask for it till evening, but again excessive politeness is out of place, it would just push him away, and I have a sense of moderation, not to ingratiate myself and not to stand out too much. Copied it, quickly went back to them, when I was leaving they invited me, —We'll be there, come. Again the whole way to their swimming place, he's not there; on my way back, see him coming far away; I show him the notebook so he can see why I've come, —here, I say, I copied it and forgot where Sergei lives. We went to his house, called him with a whistle, all sat on the boat like we were all bored together. He kept at the guitar, —I've got a headache from your music, you can't play for shit. I sat down on the grass to see better. When it was time for me to go Misha said, —we'll be at the campfire, where the athletes are. And for the third time I came toward night, found him by his guitar in the house by the cafeteria, where the girls had gone the first night for cards; in the windows were the same two girls and Misha and Sergei. Still, I think, maybe I shouldn't, since they are two and two, but still it's obvious they're just sitting there; they opened the door, —you found me by the guitar? —by the guitar; Misha and I sit together on a cot with no mattress, he keeps playing and singing. The mother of the girls or of one of them comes and asks us plainly to go home. We went to the campfire, the athletes were slightly drunk, one of them called, —Hey, come here, sing something; and this is just like him, he simply started to sing for them right away, and he sings badly as anyone sensible can tell, he wants to sound like Tolya the Ukrainian yesterday, he liked his accent. When it's time for us to go he says, —probably I'll go into town tomorrow; are you going? he asks me; —yes, I say, I should; we agreed to go together. The three of us walked back, deep night; how lucky: Sergei lives in the middle, further on it's just us two; here I told him about the murder: on Tuesday Misha himself told me they killed him with chains, then on Wednesday Lyonya told me they hung him with chains, and now I pass on what Lyonya said, he laughs, —different stories from different people; and we agreed that tomorrow morning he'll stop by for me, since he has to go by my place on the way to the bus; and he gave me the guitar, —want it for now? he says. I walk on, learning his strumming on the way, tomorrow we go into town together.

The next day Friday woke up about seven, he'll come a little after nine, I'm sitting meanwhile on the porch with the guitar. He comes in a white shirt, he says, —heard your guitar from a ways. I brought my translations, of course, they don't mean a thing to him, no conversation along the way, on the bus he strums the guitar slightly, first we're both standing, then I sit, he stands, he didn't want to sit in an empty seat. He goes further on a different bus. He says he'll go back maybe tonight, maybe tomorrow morning; and he was going to the math school; I think he wants to brag about what he's learned; but maybe I guess wrong. But now we can't agree to call each other when we're ready to go back, he heard me yell when I was leaving the dacha that I'd be back at four; when he calls, let's say, it'll look to him like I waited for him on purpose for no real reason. Maybe he didn't even hear when I said I'd be back, or forgot; but it's already impossible, it'll seem planned. And I was counting on coming back together since last night. Friday, dance day, Friday, Saturday, Sunday. I got back to the village and went straight to Sergei's. Here the plan was to be closer to him, so when I go around with them Misha wouldn't get it into his head too soon, Sergei either, and Sergei could point out to Misha that I was going around with them because of Misha. It's cool, Sergei's in his bathing suit, and everybody strolling around is dressed, they're all looking at him, I ask, aren't you cold, he laughs, —I'm an athlete. Little conversation, I fill the silences by whistling; he's strong, not much to look at next to Misha, but I noticed that on Wednesday. Awkwardness in conversation when it's about badminton or tennis; this time I didn't have a suit on, a good reason not to get in the water; but I had come to get him myself to ask him to the river, I'm walking and thinking, I'll have to swim. He even took the flippers, if you want, he says, you can try the flippers. Before we get to the swimming place, we see a drunk athlete loudly hitting a stick against a pine tree, hey you, he orders, step on the end, but there are two of us, Sergei's built like a boxer; when I passed by without saying anything the athlete didn't pick on me, farther on we hear a bicycle fall, he stuck the stick out on a boy of fifteen, he fell, picked up the bike, without picking a fight, knowing what would happen, and the athlete's having fun. But when we ran down the big steep hill, Sergei said, —why didn't you take your sandals off? you'll get water in them; I took note of my blunders; I should also go in, after all, I invited him, he was sitting home with a book, and now I'm not going, I say, —I'll just sit; though we went to swim in the flippers, and there's only one pair, so him, then me. He invited me to the island, but the memory was fresh of how tired I got then; and then I was up, but now it's cold; he thinks I'm as good a swimmer as he is. He swam to the island and back, then I should go in, and I don't know what to do, go in or not: first I wash the sand off my feet, so as not to get his flippers dirty; in the process I see it's ridiculous, I'm going in the water after all, but he might not have noticed or might have taken it for a habit, and he's only seventeen, and I'm a man from the capital, maybe that's the way one should do it. It's hard to go in the water in flippers; and before this it's funny, Sergei said people drown even more in flippers, he says you have to go backwards. Sergei took another dip, we went back by the low way, under the cliff; and when I came to get him it was with the message that Misha would be back tonight, or most likely, tomorrow morning. We're going along the low path, he told how last year in weather like this—he also commented when we were going there over the cliff that the water was up, or no, down, by the edge of the island across the way—in weather like this two girls invited a sailor on purpose, they knew he couldn't swim and wanted to have a laugh; the sailor didn't go in, the girls went in and drowned; when the water's up it forms whirlpools. He also told how, when the young pioneers had parents' day, he and the boys were out in a boat and one would dive on purpose like he was looking for something, and the other would yell, —Well? and he'd answer —Nothing, so they'd ask from one shore —What are you looking for? and they'd answer —Some pioneer drowned. There were two camps here, and the next day they'd be saying in each one that some pioneer in the other drowned. And we came back to the murder again; to keep the conversation up I started to talk about it; not only, I say, did they kill him with chains, but they hung him with chains; that's what I heard from the neighbor boy Lyonya, but Lyonya said two kilometers from here and at night, and Sergei says in daytime, and in the middle of the village. I like a fool asked What for? —What do you mean "What for?" as usual, for no reason, they were drunk, and Sergei knows who. Two boys from the city, and they killed a city boy of seventeen. The police won't find them. We got to his place —see you; he asked if I was coming to the dance, we agreed on ten o'clock. First we had agreed, on the way to the river, I'd come by for Sergei; can't remember if I said I don't know, where's the dance? now he wanted to explain, I say I know, it's all right, so he doesn't get the idea a guy lives here and doesn't know where the dances are; and I do know in my head, from the music. In the evening I went just to show my face; it was nice at home, pies getting done in the oven. I arrived at the dance floor at the peak; and see Misha's come; in a gray sweater he wears when it's cold, —Oh, you've come, when? —Yeah, and when did you (me) get here —Today. Sergei said he thought I wouldn't come. Everybody's excited. All around there are scary youths, looking for somebody to beat up. You have to joke with the girls. Misha and Sergei do this. It's sad because of the music, and because they're all having fun, and you have no life, they're dancing, you're not, and there's murder in your head. His cousin's there, a girl of fourteen in a leather jacket, and with her a wife, a girl he slept with; maybe he's making it up, though a year in the dorm. Sergei prods me, —go dance, you're freezing, show how it's done in Moscow. Talk about looking for girls for them or not. Boys jumping around with boys, Misha calls me —No, I say, Misha, I'll just stand here. Cut off from them, and sadness from the music. We pretend to be interested in how they dance or how Misha plays; and a suitable excuse, a certain Olga came with a young man, and I realized it was his sister, like I found something to keep me busy, want to listen. They surrounded her, the girls, the waitress Lyusya, Misha's at home, and I understand he needs a friend like Seryozha, he's better off with him. But what a family! Misha, his sister, and the cousin in the leather jacket, his sister's a singer and very beautiful, though she doesn't have Misha's face, and they surrounded her immediately, her husband's a handsome Jew, though not so handsome.

But the girls and the brother! the younger one, the cousin, first I thought she was a sister, I hardly looked at her, but Olya and Misha! I realized she was his sister at once when she started singing so confidently. Now Misha asks the one I think is her husband —what's your name? not to get to know him, but to ask him for something, he gave his name, Slava, and later it turns out, Sergei said he wasn't her husband. Her husband went away to a meet. Sergei pointed out two criminal-looking youths—one of them's the murderer, the one they're looking for but won't find. Maybe not, but what a picture—and these princes of the blood here feel comfortable, the king's children amid thieves don't know who they are themselves. How Misha danced: of course he's not good, but he's not shy, the same way he sang for the athletes yesterday. His sister and her lover were getting ready to leave, I think, are they going to sleep at home with the grandmother there? Misha and Sergei aren't looking for anyone, they were just saying it. The three of us, Misha, Seryozha, and me, went through the woods, lots of people, embracing, in the bushes. One old man, not even an old man, told me, forty seven, lively, he goes with everyone to listen and get warm with the young people. He helps, he sent the guys for wood, laughs at himself about his age, and he goes there with everyone, and they laugh at him without malice. But he's nineteen years older than me, an old man among them, and that's the way he acts, and I'm also twelve years older than Misha. The bonfire's good, it's warm, the ground's damp, I'm tired of standing, found a log, Misha and his friend aren't tired, they stand. I end up at Misha's feet. Misha gave me his guitar until tomorrow, somebody else here has a guitar, the old man's having fun, and it's all right that the old man wants to be with young folks like them. One singer sang with a high, almost a child's plaintive voice, he himself looked like a boy with a small face, tender voice, sang straining at the top end and with modulations, and the song's long, whenever it seems it'll end, he starts again. When others sang with him a bit differently, he had a syncopation in the verse, he was impossible to throw off, he was so sure of his singing. They took the guitar away from him. Misha and Seryozha were ready to go. And during the singing I glanced at Misha and laughed, how good the singer was singing, and my opinion passed to Misha; and then, this was the next day, when I was praising Misha's sister to him, and said the singer was unlike any other, Misha later said the same thing about him in my words. They left and invited me, and I go the opposite direction, and if I had left with them, I'd be following Misha again, and if I got up to go home it would have looked like I was sitting there only while Misha was there, I said, —I'll watch a little longer. Once they were away, I left too.

Saturday, want to go to the village for cigarettes, I'm also thinking of stocking up, they're closed Monday and Tuesday; forgot tomorrow's Sunday, thought today was Sunday. Don't see him there. I see Olga, the singer-sister, with the younger cousin in the leather jacket yesterday; they appeared in the trees by the fence. Again this path to swimming, no; maybe he's asleep. And I know what I want: I want to get money to drink with the guys. Everything'll be more lively, and actions are easier, and any slip will be written off as drunkenness. About time I tried something to somehow win him over. They took the white bag away, I asked Anya for money. First I wanted to drink with them, but they sell it on tap, so I'll be a little tipsy and they'll happen on me. Got some wine, a fresh cucumber to cover the taste, and sat on the steps to watch and see if he'd come by; no. Finished, leaving, ah, that's where I saw Olga behind me with her cousin by the fence; because I kept turning around. Intending to go to Anya and ask for more money; when I get drunk from this it'll be just a little, I feel. Anya is preparation, I talk, I want to get myself talking, and went like that to the cafeteria; half an hour till the break. That Slava's by the cafeteria, the lover, we nod. And then while I drink standing on the porch walking around, there's almost nobody, glass in one hand, cucumber in the other, it's nice like this walking, then I see him riding on his bike —want some wine? I ask, he refuses, did I stay long yesterday, he asks, here's where I remembered the singer using my expression; and he wants to go study chemistry for an hour, he didn't pass it, there was a one day break between chemistry and the preceding exam, many people didn't take it; It's true, things had gotten easier, I could already say, —well, it's Saturday, relax on Saturday, he says even so I have to, I promised. I got mixed up, this was during the first glass, I sat at Anya's half an hour and half an hour for the walk, because during that hour he was studying chemistry; and after the second glass I hope to meet him on the street or at the river and I ask Sergei to join me. Two glasses, it's true, between them an hour break, didn't affect me much; and I've only got enough money for a glass each for me and Sergei. But they brought beer; I got in line behind Slava the lover, he's fashionable and unshaven on purpose, remembers, of course, that I sat with them at the dance, when Olga sang and I listened carefully. And here I'm in boots, and my body feels completely different. Slava, that's what Misha called him, we haven't been introduced, looks about my age, and by his manner I can see his circle's closer to mine than Sergei's, relatively. Slava began with someone else from the line to unload the cases of beer, I also helped, Sergei too, the saleswoman closed the window in our face to count —I'll let you boys have some, she says; and behind me a man asks for some for him too, I gave Slava a ruble to get some for me and went over meanwhile to ask Lyusya for glasses, it's also new for me to use the familiar address with her, like all the clients do so easily with the waitresses and cashiers, she's sitting at the register. I took the bottles from Slava and see Misha on the street; I pointed to Seryozha —Seryozha's here, come with us. He doesn't want beer, doesn't like it, he says, it's bitter. Seryozha and I drank, and Misha finished the bottle. The boy feels completely at home, even when he refuses he said, there's no glass, it doesn't matter, we can share, possibly he didn't even realize he said it wrong. He didn't study chemistry that hour, he was busy with the bike, he'll go study now. We try to talk him out of it, it seems he 's decided not to study, but he has to go home for something, then he'll find us. Then Sergei and I are behind the fence about thirty steps from Misha's, you can't see through the bushes. Sergei climbed up a sour cherry, said there are also wild raspberries here; I lie on the ground, not far beyond the bushes there was a drunk lying a long time, and a woman passed, asked if it was our friend. Since I'm in the grass, he must be our friend. Soon the agreed-on whistle, Misha. When Misha was coming, he only saw Seryozha in the tree, asked him about me. Three of us together not for long, then I can't remember how we part company; we are still heading for the swimming place, where the ping-pong table is by the tents, there they'll play up to a high score in Sergei's favor, and on the way I remembered about Olga, his sister, I have to tell Misha through her how beautiful he is. They're playing ping-pong, I'll like lie on the grass, don't understand anything, and thoughts about Misha are coursing; I only hear them talking, the score's 21 to 3, then a shutout for Sergei. I collected some dented balls that were lying in the grass, I can't remember, Sergei or Misha asked, what, are you going to burn them? They like to burn them, Misha sat down and lit them, and they burned well. I can't remember how we part company; as usual, we're all three walking, Sergei turned off his way, and Misha and I go further to our fork; but here: we went to the ping-pong table, the athletes are there, and the one Misha left his guitar with yesterday, now they were going to get the guitar, but the athlete wasn't there. Sergei also told, while we were all together, how once last year they had nothing to smoke, and he and Misha see a carton of cigarettes here in a window. Misha pushed, the glass broke, and it was in daylight, I also asked, won't your hand get injured that way, they said, no, how you have to push, they pulled out the shards, Misha's thin, squeezed through, Sergei standing guard hears Misha laughing in the house, turns out they opened the boxes and all of them have nails in them. Also when just Misha and I are walking, he said he had a sister who died before he was born, I say, that's good, otherwise your parents wouldn't have taken the trouble to make you, and I'm in the same situation. So the game, burning the balls, these stories, how we part company I don't remember, there's a gap here and a blank after. At home our folks had come, this is where I put the boots on, I asked them to bring them: but as far as it being nice to walk around there on the porch with wine in one hand and a cucumber in the other and sitting at the empty table, all that's so. There is no blank, because we really did walk to the fork with Misha, in parting I said, well, we'll meet at the dance, and he says, come before. So, I'm walking, it's a long way till the dance, still light, on the way to the ping-pong table, don't see him, go back, the field where the volleyball court is, here's where fate was decided. I still thought it's better for the guys to find me here, but they're not here, went to Sergei's next to the field, he's in just a shirt, no jacket, we meet Misha, or we go to his place, or Sergei whistles for him; we go in, once it was like this, we were going in together, I went in, Sergei stood next to me, Misha with his guitar, we walked a bit, he said I'll go leave the guitar, Sergei was trying to talk him out of it, but he went, then Misha caught up with us, Sergei's in my jacket down to his knees, and he asked Misha how he liked the jacket; early to go to the dance, still we went, soon it'll start. And the dance was completely different, how little it takes, and already I'm one of them. We got there, no one was there, and for those who came, we were the first; and on the way their talk about how whenever they go to the dance they're met with the same record, and to-day there was another, they laugh—they didn't recognize Sergei in my jacket. We sit, people come up, and Olga and that Slava and some other friend and the fourteen year old cousin come up, it's all familiar, and the sister sits with me, clearly I interest her, we have nothing to smoke, and that Slava finds cigarettes for us, Olga, after smoking a while, shares her cigarettes with me every time, and after dancing, sits down next to me; and it's obvious she found out about me and Misha. I asked her to sing, she sings, looking into my eyes; then young people's conversations, Slava and the friend, throwing out the names of books out of place, but still it's a familiar circle of people. And these boots with support for the foot, and I've had a look at how they dance here—Olga and I went to dance. She was just waiting for me to ask her. I also told her —when they start playing in rhythm, and I got my confidence back, before this when just three of us were standing, Sergei and Misha and I, I was freezing without my jacket, and to hold back the shivers, more from excitement, I remembered you have to tense up, and the blood will come quicker—so Misha was just mov-ing his knees to the music, I started too, for lack of anything better to do, and Sergei, he kept asking me to show how they dance in Moscow, because he was always expecting something from me, noticed right away and even said —look, Misha, how good; I had distinctly caught his rhythm out of excitement; and it just stayed in my legs, and I kept it with me all the time, and in my shoulder; I said to Olga —when something starts in rhythm we'll go; true, I couldn't tell if it was the right thing or not they were starting, they give slow introductions, then shift to a shake; and while I'm think-ing about it, Olga's already being asked to dance. During one introduction Olga holds a cigarette out towards me, I thought to smoke, but she wants to throw it away and she's reaching out to ask me to dance; I also called the cigarette butt a *chinarik*, they didn't understand —what? and they look in amazement, laughing; they say *bychok*; but they liked it, a man from the capital, and he has different words. Olga and I dance and I'm free, and when we were doing a slow dance before this, when you just step from one foot to the other, I told her that she should give up everything and go to Moscow to sing. She, it's true, said —what kind of singer am I, but she's wrong, and it didn't fit with her confidence and her fervor. In the right circumstances she could be a star, and she'd be surrounded immediately with boy admirers and other girls, little girls, and they'd look with delight on her crazy whims and her verve. And Slava, possibly, isn't even her lover, she needs a tested circle around her to create an effect, Seryozha and Misha, of course, didn't catch this. It was Misha who said to Sergei that Slava was her lover, and Sergei laughed—no sooner than her husband left for the competition. Lover or not, she needs first of all friends who can admire her, and through them it will be transferred to others who don't know her. Then Olga, that Slava, the second friend, and the little cousin want to leave, Olga asks me —will you see us home? and on the way she embraces now Slava the Jew, now the friend, it's play, for the cousin too, and a glance at me so I don't lag behind, but without wine I won't cross the boundary. Now she takes me by the hand, afraid she'll trip, now she runs to the Jew Slava, kisses him, or asks the friend to kiss her. And the young men responded like this: the friend, his name was Shurik, asks the little cousin to kiss him, and shows how sweet it is, then Olga kisses him, and he spits after her on purpose, and they all laugh. We got to the tents, Lyusya was walking with us, the one who works the register at the cafeteria, and she and I danced the waltz, and she said very seriously —hold me tighter, when we're spinning, I'll let go; this Lyusya was crying at the beginning of the evening, and Olga took her aside, said something to her like a girl, and it was clear Olga liked that role. We got to the tents, to a small two-man tent where, it turns out, Slava the Jew and this Shurik were living, and Olga's going to her grandmother's and that's it. Olga's concert continued at the tent. She sang a lot from "The Queen of Spades," all the heroes and the orchestra; and you could see they're all children of well-off families. And this Shurik, the friend, says lying in Olga's lap —Olga, when did such-and-such a girl find out that I was like that? My god, I understand it all. And his voice is like that. But Slava the Jew doesn't look it. A completely different picture, compared to yesterday's. Olga keeps getting called, let's go home, it's late, this is Lyusya, and without waiting for her she went home through the woods, nobody got up to see her off. Olga and the little cousin also got up to go, and are you going, Olga asked me using the formal address—I was sitting next to her, didn't embrace her once, didn't take her hand, even on the way home. In parting she invited me tomorrow to the tent. From her place I went to check on the friends and got lost, call loudly —Slava, they can't hear, and I see, the tent, the second time they called back, but the first time I was calling two feet away; when we were saying goodbye to them, when I went with Olga and the cousin, Slava said happily, Shurik and I also have to go to sleep, we'll love each other; maybe he said it in jest—I thought they still hadn't gone to bed, I'd sit, listen to them talk, they were respectful, interested how things were in Moscow; but I found them, and Slava says from the tent —but we're already asleep, can you find the way? —Ah, you're asleep? yes, of course; and so I left.

On Sunday rain since morning the first time all this time. Won't find the tent again, and don't want to yell loud; went to the house, they opened the door, grandmother's baking cookies, Misha took me into the room, smoky, they're all four sitting there. Olga and the two young men are playing cards, the sister's in bed. I was already making plans the night before how Olga would go to Moscow to get a job and I'd talk Misha into it, of course we'd agree to spend the holidays in winter. The little sister comes; a lot of Misha in her, she'll be beautiful, her teeth are rotten from candy; Olga started kissing her and repeating how she loves her brothers and sisters, aren't they beautiful? she says. Now Slava the Jew also asks me if he should apply to school in Moscow. Yesterday, when I was walking Olga home, she said Slava's a journalist and Sasha's studying to be a doctor. Slava, then, isn't studying to be a journalist, so, he's pounding the pavement for a newspaper; but I also see he's seven years younger than me; though he looks my age. But he's a real journalist, knows about everything happening in the world, a smattering of everything. Misha started showing me books, talking about their merits, chemistry, a scholarly book about water tension. And here's a new twist. Olga mentioned their last name, and how small the world is; it's their father who's the professor, and how close everything became, they had been children I didn't know, I told their grandmother loudly beyond the curtain, so you see, we know each other through the parents, so she would be more approving of our relationship when I come for Misha. And their father is Lev Moiseevich; I ask Misha —how is it then you talk about Jews as if from outside, and Misha explained, —no, father's not a Jew, he's Russian, only one fourth Jewish, but it makes no difference, I don't make a distinction between Jews and Russians. So their mother's Russian, and their father, I later learned, is half Russian, but half Jewish. They're planning to go into the city, Misha too. Misha wants to go for three days to do his chemistry, and I'll go with them. Olga's husband's at home, we'll get together at one of the friends, at Sasha the med student's. From behind the curtain the grandmother tells Misha not to go, well, it backfires. On the way he'll even say something cruel —I'm fed up with grandfather and grandmother, hope they die soon. I suggested making a little detour on the way to the bus by my place, I want a snack, because here they refused, when the grandmother had offered. And at home, when I seated them at tea and I had no place to sit, Slava or Sasha wanted to clear the cups off a chair, I refused, and sat on the floor, and Misha said —let him, he likes it better; and to me —I've noticed you like to sit that way; and sat down himself exactly the same way. On the way they changed their minds about getting together today. Slava then suggested, maybe I should go back, and come tomorrow for their gathering. I said no, I'll go, I have things to do in the city, and I walk now with Olga, now with

Misha after all, since her friends are embracing her, and it's far to walk, we saw the forty-six leave, we went for the twenty-six. At the last stop there was a big puddle, a stump in the middle. I got over to the stump, Misha stood at the edge of the puddle, the rest went to the bench. I should go over to them, it's obvious Misha won't stand at the edge of the puddle long, and then I'd sit next to him; but then Misha went to the bench and sat with them, and it's already too late for me to go over, they'd notice I came for Misha. So I sat like that apart till the bus came. There were lots of people on the bus, and I managed it so there was no place to sit with Olga, she was with the two friends, and Misha and I sat in front together. Suddenly he got worried, he left his bag, the bus hadn't started yet, and in the bag was a rare translated Chemistry book. He started working his way to the exit, I'm saving his place, scared somebody might take it, and the bus hasn't started, his cousin yells from behind some passengers —Misha, I've found your bag; Misha came back, and we set off. I suggested —Let's go back to the window, so we don't have to give up our seats, and Misha says —I can't, I always give it up; I didn't hear him —don't give it up? He says, —no, I do; and I say —Well, of course, you're right to. And I made the suggestion thinking he'd like it. But there weren't any elderly people near us. Closer to the city there were fewer people in the aisle, I occasionally glanced at Olga, so she wouldn't feel that I was sitting with Misha and didn't need anything. We arrived, the three of us get off, Olga, Misha, and I, the friends are going farther. Misha asked me before we got off —are you going farther? it's better for me to go farther, I said —no, I'll get off with you and walk. Possibly Misha thought I did it because of Olga. The three of us got off and I don't know how to talk with her, she keeps expecting something from me, she won't understand anything; well, today's gathering was put off, and, I think, she'll attribute my silence to the fact that she's going to her husband, she was embracing her friends on the way, and that made me gloomy. So we walked in painful silence to their stop, I'm off, I say; tomorrow morning I'll go to the village, I'll be back for the gathering by evening; though, I think, I shouldn't come back, that would be better than coming to see them and remaining silent. But when we were on the way to the bus in the village, Olga said: I'll call you in the city, and I told her my number, she repeated it, and Sasha the med student, where we're getting together, drew his number for me on the road, showed me how to remember it, symmetrical numbers at both ends—anyway now we were saying goodbye she couldn't remember my number. I decided to call her drunk from home, so she'd know I'd been drinking, and without wine I didn't know what to say. I called. Olga, let's see each other today; she says, we can't, I have Arkasha (the husband) at home, see you tomorrow. I called about four more times and either nobody answered, or another voice said she wasn't there, or you got the wrong number; after I asked for Misha directly, as if I wanted to reach Olga through him, that's what both he and Olga could have thought.

On the next day, Monday, I came to the village late for having to go back to the city. It's obvious they won't take Misha with them. To Olga he's a younger brother, and much younger than for me. And I see the weather's changed for good, for the first time all season, and with no end in sight. I get ready to go to Misha's house for the guitar, I asked him for it yesterday for two or three days to practice while he's in the city, he didn't take it with him so it wouldn't stop him from studying. And suddenly I see his back in the gray sweater, he's going into the back from the house, so he's returned, but at the same time I saw him I was already asking at the open door —can I come in? His grandfather answered —yes, Arkady? thought it was Olga's husband; sees me —what's up? I'm looking for Misha, I say; I already see where Misha is, but it's too late, I'd already asked: Misha, he says, is packing the car and they're leaving now. I catch up with Misha, he just happens to be carrying the guitar out now with the other things— that's it, I say, I know, and I came like I said to take the guitar. The car is blue behind the fence and their father's there; and for the first time for the father I'm a friend of his children; I say hello, he answers drily — hello—and turns to the trunk. He always used to greet me with a friendly smile. He goes to the house, Misha says they're taking all the things and leaving, because the weather's changed like this, he also asks me aren't I cold? it's raining, though just at this moment not hard. I say —so that's it? He says —no, maybe we'll come back; but it's logical, the weather's changed completely, it should have long ago, and it was preparing all these days, and yesterday's rain was the beginning. And it's also logical, as it was earlier, but now it's apparent, that Misha's still a kid, he doesn't decide anything, they're grown up, that's how the father talks with Misha, for the father there is no Antinous, one boy in a hundred thousand, but just his sixteen year old son he has to be strict with. I say to Misha —how drily his father said hello to me; and Misha says, He's just in a hurry; I see myself he's in a hurry, but no, it's not my imagination. I don't know, the grandmother and grandfather told him that Olga spent these two days with young people and came back at two in the morning, and that I was there yesterday, I gave my name, and the grandmother connected it with me, and maybe yesterday's phone calls, maybe he heard that someone was calling Olga and Misha too, and insistently, four times, of course he doesn't know who, but I turned up among those young people Olga spent her time with, the grandmother told him that, she knows me now, and that now I'd come to see Misha, a fine sixteen year old friend he's found himself; maybe there was only half this much, but still it seemed to me all this was in his "hello." While Misha and I stand there the father takes things out to the fence from the house, asks Misha to take some sort of tub, a few times, and each time I seem to want to help, but Misha beats me to it; it's not that I seem to want to, but it looks like I seem to. And here's something else: I tell Misha I'm here because I wanted to take the guitar, so he doesn't feel like I'm seeing him off—so he offers me the guitar, —here—so I can play while they're packing. Mishenka. Then, for example, the grandmother came out, and it turned out that I didn't manage to say hello, she's at a distance, for her to hear, I'd have to yell, and it would look ridiculous; but it seems she's not looking my way on purpose, and she's treating me different, maybe after she told the father about Olga, and though she was talking to me yesterday, today's another matter, she and the father now have a new relation. Of course, they're in a hurry, but still; then I'm alone with the little sister whose teeth are rotten from candy, they've all gone to get things, I smiled at her, so as to say something, asked about some medal and read the writing "Budni-Radosti" [Workdays-Joys]; it turns out it's "Budni-Raduga" [Workdays-Rainbow]; even so it doesn't make sense; she says she's a champion here, children's competitions, running maybe; I don't understand a thing, smile at her, Misha comes with things —you see, he says, she's already our champion. Yes, I already know.—Bragging—he looked at her. —No, it was me who asked her where she got the medal; and I stay with Misha a while; or else that was before this, since the grandmother had gone; he asks —you know my phone number? I say —yes; Misha, I say, better you should call me, got a pencil? —There's paper, but no pencil. —Well, you can look it up in the book; he's a mathematician, I should have told him, he'd have remembered. Also think I should say I called yesterday, he was surely home and heard all the calls; maybe he didn't hear, but even so it would come out, so, I say, —I called you yesterday, only I was drunk, asked for Olga, then you. —Drunk? He asked that probably because he knows about the calls, and this explained the absurdity of four or five calls in a row; or maybe he just asked. They get in, the father says —goodbye, but not looking my way; I say goodbye, very politely, and stand and watch them go. Misha's in the front seat with his father, the car takes a long time turning around, I think I'm wrong to go home, they'll pass on their way, this figure in the rain, obviously I'm going home and only came to see Misha, I shouldn't, it'll be very sad, but it's too late to turn, and it would have been good if I went the other way from the car, as if I was going to have lunch, but the car, I see, turns around to go back behind the fence, along the dacha road, so they won't see me. And when they had left I also went along their road to the bus, again I saw the forty-six drive by, and like yesterday I went to the far bus stop for the twenty-six. The meeting that evening was canceled, I called Sasha, he said Olga wasn't coming, so, because of her husband; and I just asked where and when to meet, without planning to go.

We didn't see each other for a week. He, of course, didn't call, I, while I was studying, also tried not to call, so as not to change anything that had happened; and another thing, I thought I could call only after I finished everything and writing would be a delay and a way of keeping myself from excess haste. I called twice in that period, but once, it seems, there was nobody home, and once they said Misha wasn't home, can I take a message? I said —no, thank you, I'll call back. When she hung up I realized it was Olga, and she recognized my voice, that's why she asked after a pause —can I take a message; so as to continue the conversation. But I didn't catch it and didn't continue the conversation, now it was too late. But I didn't understand—I called in the morning, I thought she was at work then. But by writing I kept myself from doing anything for a week, now I call and ask for Misha and a woman's voice, not Olga, not an old voice, not the grandmother, the mother, I think, answered, I thought—a minute; she went to call Misha and then someone hung up. In my impatience I didn't care and called back. Again the mother answered and said —Misha's not home, like I said; who's calling? I gave my name, explained I didn't hear her the first time, and I thought you had gone to call him. No, she says, that's what I said, that he's not home. I did the right thing calling back, or else I would have thought they hung up on purpose, and maybe he even asked them to himself. And this was Friday, the day of the dance, and the weather's good, I think, he's in the village. I rush there, to the house—all closed, shades down, only an empty tea jar on the windowsill on the other side, and old boots by the door, and a brush with a long handle. Everything's as it was when they left. In the last three days I had come here once and seen this picture, so, he still hadn't come. And the next day Saturday Misha didn't come, and Sunday he didn't come either. On Monday early in the morning I'm of course in the city and call him, I waited for ten. Before that he may be asleep, later he'll leave. First time nobody answered. Second time he answered himself, I think, he heard the first rings in his sleep and, maybe, put together that I was calling, but even so. When are you going to the village? I say. —Well, tomorrow, or more likely day after, Wednesday. I say —I'm going to be in your neighborhood, I have something to do, come outside if you're not planning to do anything. All right, he says, I'll be in the yard, explained which building, gave the address and how to recognize it. I say I'll be there in about forty minutes on my way back. On the way there I looked into his yard, it would be good, I think, to take him along on my errand, that way it would be more apparent that I have something to do in his neighborhood. But he's not there, I went and got the keys, back to his place, he whistles at me from the second floor. And all that week, exactly a week we hadn't seen each other, when I closed my eyes, I couldn't precisely imagine him, my image of him suddenly started to fade, and now I saw him like after a long separation. He comes out and says —did you see Arkady? he was walking right behind you; Olga's husband. No, I say, and secretly I was sorry I didn't notice, it'd be interesting to see what Olga's husband's like. Shall we go to a movie he asks. Yes, I say, but let's go downtown; so how's the chemistry, I ask, have you learned it? that is, is he free or not; no, he says, I haven't sat down to it yet, yesterday we went to Olga and Arkady's dacha, it's a lot more fun there than at ours, it's boring in the village; there are a hundred dachas in our village, while where he was there are a thousand. What was a life crowded with people for me was a remote backwater for him. He started to recall what films were showing in town, this one he's seen, it seems, "Rash Marriage," we would go. No conversation on the bus, we get off, let's go, I say, to my place. You go, he says, I'll wait. They like to be seen on the street, their whole lives are spent on the street out of their parents' sight, that's why they want so much to go away to a dorm or to Moscow to study. Still we went to my place, looked at the schedule in the paper, and basically there are only things he's seen, and what he hasn't seen is inconvenient, two hours till it starts, I'm afraid he'll change his mind, and when we went out he said the paper was Sunday's, and they change the program on Monday, though I'm almost positive the new program was there too and he read it. All's going well, only he calls on the way from a pay phone to let them know, neither of us had any change, and he wanted to call without money, suggested I go into the booth to watch how he does it; pity the phone didn't work, and I didn't hear how and with whom he'd speak at home; when we got change, going into a working booth with him was now inappropriate. He also told on the way, how Arkady, Olga's husband, has a cross the size of a hand on a chain to his waist of pure gold, he got it from his grandmother, she has a lot of valuables and lives alone in a big apartment, no one, he says, thinks to rob her; and there's gold in our apartment too, a man drowned with a backpack of gold, an old woman has gold reserves in bottles, and he wanted to rob her. So Arkady could interest him with such a rare object. And an hour before the movie, and after, when we were walking around downtown, it's obvious I've got nothing to interest him with, I don't know anything and there's nothing at all to support our friendship. He had no reason to call me, he has lots of pleasures, but what can I offer him. He and a friend were riding a "Yava," turned over into a ditch, because the asphalt road suddenly turned to sand, and lots of people were flipping over like that, before them somebody even died in a crash. I can't offer him a ride on a "Yava." On Wednesday or even on Tuesday he said he'd come to the village, and I didn't do what I'd been thinking about all week, write down for him my Moscow address, and I didn't have a pencil and paper, and if I'd asked him, he wouldn't have had them either, he was without a jacket, and the invitation would have hung in the air, I would have had to repeat it another time. And you have to do it once, nonchalantly. I remembered coming out of the house in the morning that I didn't have a pencil, but I thought if I got one in anticipation I'd be punished for my calculation and wouldn't reach him on the phone. It's all like the first day—a complete stranger, a boy of rare beauty standing on the hill playing the guitar, and for him I'm just a passerby, and he has no use for our acquaintance, there's nothing for him in my actions and conversations, no matter how I might adapt myself.

On Tuesday I go to the village, he said he was coming on Tuesday or Wednesday. Now if only I can give him my address, or else the thread is lost forever. In the house, as before, the curtains are down, the tea jar there on the other side, the brush with the long handle and the old shoes by the entrance. I came by at seven in the evening, then came by again, there was still Wednesday. On Wednesday I came in the morning, and in the afternoon, and about eight in the evening, I went to Sergei's, he looked out all excited, says, I'm eating, a friend of mine came, now we're going to the field to play badminton; seems like he was even upset that I came and he couldn't keep me company on my walk. I went back under the cliff, so Sergei couldn't see that I was going home and had only come to see him, Wednesday had gone by, Misha won't come any more. And the next day just in case I went to look in at Misha's house. And from the fence I see his black window, and it had been white because of the curtain, I didn't even believe my eyes, went closer—the brush, the boots, the tea jar, all were gone, my heart started pounding, I thought, he's come, he's still asleep, or some of the relatives are in the house and he's out for a walk, I looked into the window—nobody there, they've all left for good, the season's over, the house is empty, and you can see everything from one window to the other. So yesterday, when I was too lazy to come late at night, he was here, maybe they left this morning, with his father in the car, since the curtains and mattresses were gone, he didn't carry them off. So, they've left for good, and I won't be able to write my address, can't ask him to call, it would all have the opposite effect. And I had three days left before leaving, and they won't come here. And of course again it was pouring, like when we said goodbye then after the sunny days, as if on purpose for melancholy—after that time we said goodbye all the days were sunny, on Monday, when we went to the movies, it was hot, and now rain and I'm standing alone, there's no one in the village, they aren't even hidden, they've gone away for good. When Misha and I walked here before, there was one empty house, I always looked at myself in the glass, and when Misha and I walked by, he also stopped to have a look, I thought, in such a dark mirror the twelve years' difference between us is not so visible. In such a dark mirror thirteen years' difference wouldn't be so visible. So now I thought that house was a portent. They're all lived in only till fall, they'll all be empty in turn, and now the turn of Misha's house has come. I walked again along the whole dacha street, all the way to their swimming place, even hope for a while maybe he's here. Yesterday I was almost indifferent, but today, because I missed him so foolishly, walked and walked, and when he came I missed him, today it's like it was then again. And that evening in town another reminder: a young man called to his friend from a balcony using exactly the same whistle as Misha and Sergei, a signal from some Western song they know.

ONE BOY'S STORY: "HOW I GOT LIKE THAT"

[Rasskaz odnogo mal'chika: kak ia stal takim]

"So for the Eighth of March I went to Moscow (from Izh-sk). And that's where I found out. No, before that there was the story with that people's artist. He came to visit our school, asked me to come to his place to pose. Well and then he started talking on those themes, but it was all so tactful, and the main thing was the relations between teacher and pupil, he showed me so much about art, he said this should be the most important thing for me, that all those distractions are a swamp, that first I had to study, to become an artist. Almost everything was clean with him, and it would have been repulsive, he's 60, I only respected him as a person. He taught me a lot of good things. But in bed we mostly just lay there, he just liked to stroke me, he went into raptures over me, over my figure, said that I was everything in his life, son, and wife, and friend, and pupil. He himself had a family, a wife and a daughter. Then he sent me to Moscow for the holidays (Eighth of March) to look at the museums, the exhibits, gave me the address of his friend, he's married and not like that. Well and in Moscow I found out: at Bykovo airport I went into the toilet, there it's all written, look into such and such a hole, and there one guy beckoned me with his finger, gave me a blow job through the hole."

—And how did you find out they meet Downtown?—

"Well this guy told me and offered to meet me. I didn't meet him, but over the next few days I did meet others, and that's how I found all this out. Well, all I had to do was appear, they'd all come right up, I won't go with this one, won't go with that one, I look for someone I like."

—Well, and before, when you were a boy, something like that happened, probably, with some school chum, like kids do?—

"Yes, there was one friend, we used to jerk each other off."

—Often?—

"Just as soon as there was nobody around, we'd jerk off. But we just jerked off, nothing else."

—And you also had girls?—

"What do you mean? Of course."

—And how come no steady girlfriend?—

"Well, they're like stupid, all of them, and I never had a steady girlfriend, but well, just to go out with her, take her places and talk about God knows what, that's not interesting. They don't want to sleep with you, what they need more is just love and an escort. Well, there were some isolated cases, yes, I liked them a lot. At the collective farm with one, I checked the clock, I was plowing her an hour and ten minutes, for an experiment, I was controlling things, I'd feel the end soon and hold back, she was already pouring streams."

—Well, do you like it better with girls or with boys?—

"Of course with girls, everything inside her there wraps around you, it's nice and wet all the time."

But gradually he told more about those days in Moscow, and about all his liaisons.

"In general, to be honest, it didn't all begin in Moscow, in Bykovo; or with the artist. But once when I was passing through Kirov I went into the toilet, and there was some graffiti: go to another toilet on such and such a street. I went there."

—And you weren't scared? weren't turned off?—

"Well, nobody in the city knew me and I didn't know anyone. And I was leaving that evening. And there was one guy standing there, scary, though it's true he was young, with glasses, and thick lips. And he suggested we go into the stall, two different stalls next to each other, and from there he beckoned me with his finger and went down on me. O! And there it was even better than in a pussy, even wetter. And his mouth was so big, he didn't scratch with his teeth, it was all so soft. I was just in ecstasy. And he was so delighted, he says, you have such a big one! let's meet again! I say, no, I can't, I'm leaving today. He says, when you come back let's see each other, I'll wait for you. But he was so scary, those thick lips, such a big mouth. So when I came to Izh-sk I started to look for people like that."

—And where did you find them?—

"Well, also in the same places, at the station. But they're all so awful, there are no cute young ones at all, they all laugh at each other, they all have nicknames, that one's Juliet, that one's some kind of Jacqueline, one they called Nun, she used to work in a church, she corrupted everyone there. So, with the people's artist. When he came to visit our school, I already knew all this. And I immediately knew what he was up to when he invited me to his place. He, when I was posing, immediately started conversations on these themes. He'd touch me lightly, Oh, he'd say, what equipment you've got there. This was in his studio. Then he went into the other room, there next to a sofa was a table with drinks. Then he asked me to lie down on the sofa with him, he touched my member, said all the women would go crazy, caressed me. But of course I found him unpleasant in bed, he was old, but as a person, that was something else, he gave me a lot, we had more of a friendship. Of course, I respected him. He would say, Ah, I would gladly give myself to you, but my hole is narrow, it won't go in. He blew me, but mostly just to make me happy; he'd take a little, he couldn't do like that guy with the lips. And he used to say, never in your life tell anyone that you come to see me, and don't say you posed. He made a present of my portrait, also asked me not to show it to anybody, then, he says, someday, when you finish school and become an artist, then you can show it, I'll say myself, this is my pupil, but now you can't, then I'd have to commit suicide, I'd be driven out of everywhere, I have so many enemies! For the Eighth of March I decided to go to Moscow for the first time, he told me to go see the museums, gave me an address where I could stay, and so I got downtown, and here the main thing was meeting people; this guy named Misha came up to me the last night, pleasant-looking with a little mustache, I liked him best right away, and we went to his place. He lived at home with his sister and her husband, they weren't home. We went into his bathroom, there he greased me from behind and fucked me. And I liked him so much, this is the only case when I even wanted to blow him myself. But I didn't! I really didn't want to say goodbye to him. It was such an unusual situation, that night his sister and her husband didn't come home and I slept with him all night. And the next day I had to catch the plane, I couldn't part with him until the last minute! Somehow I made the plane. I couldn't think about anything else, my mind was on him only. Spring had begun there in our city, I walked around town looking for somebody who might look like him, but there was no one. We wrote each other. I was waiting for May Day, so I could go to Moscow again. I told my teacher all about him, but he said that it was very bad, that I should study and think only about school, and these adventures were a swamp, they would pull me in. He talked me out of it, didn't let me go to Moscow. And I wrote Misha that I wasn't coming. Since then I haven't gotten any letters from him. And I also wrote a letter to that friend of mine Sasha, the one I jerked off all through school, we should see each other, I'll tell you something! something good! how I went to Moscow, it'll take your breath away, for God's sake come, I can't describe it all. So instead of going to Moscow for May Day to see Misha, I listened to the artist and went home to the village and saw Sasha, this school friend of mine. He listened and even moaned, then he heated the bath and said, do to me everything they did to you in Moscow! And I got blown there, and what, was I supposed to do that to him too? I had gotten tired of that sort of bent cock of his with the blue head when we were kids. Well, I figured, so be it, went down on him and almost threw up. That was the only time, never again, for anybody! He's sort of delicate, sits at home all the time, likes to read about history, all about medieval Russia, doesn't accept anything Western, such a patriot, and listens only to classical music, doesn't like all these rock groups and pop singers, only recently began to listen to it just a little. And what kind of friend is he, you know who your friends are in times of trouble, but with him it's only when something interests him, but if not . . . so we went, for example, once back in high school, went to a dance, all the girls there were asking me to dance one after the other, and their boyfriends threatened me, so I'd go away. Well I didn't want to look like a coward, kept on dancing. And they called me off to the side and broke my lip. So Sasha also started saying let's go, didn't stay with me, got scared. That's what kind of friend he is.''

For the November holidays I went to Izhevsk myself and saw them all, both the people's artist and Sasha, a bit later. We agreed with Seryozha ("How I Got Like That") that he would invite Sasha when I came. The people's artist is not at all an old man, as he appeared from Seryozha's story. Just of the post-war school. And his studio isn't a basement, as I imagined too out of habit. A big clean room in a new building, not a spot of dust. Pictures like in the Palace of Culture. And the people's artist was very quiet, polite, careful that his name shouldn't get into the story. And it wouldn't be bad if some new gangster coming to take his place were to publicly defame him among their directors, write to *Krokodil*, break everything he has, and send him out into the world. Then maybe he would turn into a people's artist.

And Sasha came for the holiday. Here they are: Seryozha and Sasha next to each other. Seryozha "How I Got Like That" has a pleasant playful breeze in his head, he's a dancer, and his dorm-mates sense that somehow he's not like they are, and like him for it, unconsciously they even flirt. And Sasha has already gotten so used to sitting there at home reading about medieval Russia and the Church that he'll just keep doing it. Until something falls into his lap. Like when he knew for sure someone was coming from Moscow to visit Seryozha, then he came too. And was waiting to see what would come of it. But things don't start by themselves. I think his heart was sinking. But he didn't let on. In bed, though, he was so willing, so gentle. So skinny, warm, young. He found everything that was done to him sweet. He touched my cock with a tentative hand. Again, only if I put his hand there myself. But he wouldn't have done it on his own, just in case.

And I would predict for him the following path. He really should go into the Church. There all his lines would meet. He couldn't even pass his favorite subject, history, at the institute, because he more or less knew only medieval Russia. Such a wonderful narrowness. What a gift to love one thing and not look to the right or the left. And his mind set is humble, not creative. He'll remember what happened when, what people's names were, what rank. But so much the better! And somehow surprisingly pleasant. Therefore he won't become a heretic-theologian, a Florensky in the pride of his mind. He'll just be a good, obedient holy father. Seryozha says, what do you mean, how can he go against his father and mother (his father's a party organizer at the collective farm, his mother a schoolteacher); it would be a shame for them. Oh no, Seryozha. Sasha only has to work up his patience, explain things to his parents like he should. Anti-religious propaganda notwithstanding, he'll say, even so the Church has its honor from the Soviet point of view, it also has ranks and opportunities for advancement. Before the holidays, he'll say, Brezhnev gave medals to the patriarch and the metropolitans. And the old ladies in their village long ago started a rumor that Sasha would be a priest, that he collects old books and crosses. And being a priest would suit him so well. He has such expressive eyes, long black eyebrows, bright lips; the beard will look good. He'll have to apply himself, go to Zagorsk. That's where his happiness lies. Among the seminarians, of course, sodomy flourishes, as it does in the church in general, to say nothing of the monastic life. Yes, if a boy hides from the other boys in a corner, doesn't play their war games, if a boy occupies himself with dreams not of war, not of cars, but of ummarried saints dressed up in holy robes, this boy, as Rozanov said, is a boy-girl. He recognizes in their unwarrishness his own and is glad that there is a morality that places it so high.

But Sasha has another, non-church path as well.

Seryozha told the people's artist about Sasha, like he told me. And the people's artist also started quizzing him, he'd say, when's Sasha coming? you have to bring him to see me, he'd say, I'll get him into the history department, I have connections. And Sasha himself also lectured Seryozha, why don't you value the people's artist, he has such connections, he'll help you in life. In other words, Sasha would be a find for the people's artist. The artist wanted so much to have a discreet, steady, non-partying boy. And Sasha would have been content to be faithful to the old man. But Sasha would have become a historian; then would come social sciences, the party membership; the artist would have married him off to cover their affair, and everything would have been in its place according to the mousey tastes of the people's artist. Seryozha shouldn't introduce them! Let him go into the Church. And we'll put a cross on the map of the USSR where a young priest we know serves.

ALYOSHA-SERYOZHA

[Alesha-Serezha]

IN OUR COMPANY he took his shirt off torso like a schoolboy's and flew to me lost his support, noticed I didn't take my eyes off him. He'll easily lure leave a boy who loves to love and to be loved, plays on you very well and you understand he'll play the same way when he sees a new man—with a smile and a light caress, dancing from you to another. Alyosha knows his worth, turns everyone's heads, have to give presents take him visiting in the best clothes, he wears whatever and he'll simply get attached love who loves him, he'll start to care about you himself. And if you want love with him in more than words and to move him in with you, you also need talent, know-how style improvisation calculation, and one or the other: either talent for life, or live on words of love no money spending your life on working out confessions for him and he's tired of being a model for your designs for you to look your fill at and leave it for a whole day alone becoming absorbed in your art. You don't compare to him in looks or behavior and that's why you're attracted to him dying of love to kiss kiss kiss not letting go like the miserly knight having gotten for yourself not giving to others taking in kisses all that is leaving you, with the years it can't be replaced and seems it never was there such arms legs torso eyes he aims them with a smirk when he goes out in society. And in the daylight when his arms legs aren't yours you make up for the unsightliness of your looks with your behavior, that is, your soul. But if you want to succeed in love in words, your soul will not reach him, your confessions won't penetrate his youth and unenlightenedness. If only you could dump them at the market as rare goods and get the recognition of the very highest society and the position of a star of the first magnitude, achieve the needed look in clothes friends situation in exchange for your love in words and then in your own way compare to him—but you're hopeless. And you wanted simply love happiness to move him in with you—then make up for your looks with your soul in life, with presents trips happy earnings. We trade with Western countries. In the stores, if you look, there are excellent goods. But don't expose yourself to him in words. You know very well yourself—he's such that you couldn't think of anything better for you. But you are not at all what he should be dreaming of. You got someone you could only dream about, but he's been cheated. But don't reveal this to him and don't reveal that you love who you would like to be and can't possibly be, that you would like to be him and envy his looks, that he doesn't have to waste his efforts in love, he'll clearly see you're telling the truth and that you are simply not as good as him and you can't even imagine in a way that power that even he would want impossibly to be dying of love to kiss kiss kiss taking in kisses all that he himself doesn't have and never will have. You want the words to say everything openly just the way it is, and it seems you even love the fact that at last you can stand before the one you love as you are without fear of being disarmed. But these tears and weakness that you so want in moments of love are exactly what kills his love for you. You, in your own words, have fewer virtues than he, otherwise you wouldn't love him so much, and you're right to simply be afraid of losing him and you have come to the final confession that this is inevitable. And for him, like for you and for anybody, it's also best to lean on someone who can't compare to him himself and confess to him that he is nothing himself before him, because he also loves to love for that: only in love can one become so weak and bow down in admiration. Therefore, if you want love and happiness in life, don't make any confessions about yourself, you only need them because you're a man of the word, and if you want love and talent in life and not in words, you don't need them either. When you love to have a cry and repent to the one you love you get weak and lose what he needs to see in you, your success with everyone.

And here's a suitable situation, Seryozha calls and asks to come see me. Alyosha will see this. Seryozha will rush here to see me and Alyosha will see how much I'm loved. I used to love Seryozha myself, but he fought it in himself, disappeared, then couldn't hold out after half a year, said he only came to test himself, now he could see finally that he's not attracted—in the usual relaxation after we'd slept together hoped to see his conclusive disinclination and hurried to leave as quickly as possible, having convinced himself of this. The first few days I loved Seryozha, but afterwards I was only interested in how he would call in a year, thinking I'd invite him right away, but I, since he was restraining himself, took my time on purpose, waiting with interest for him to ask to come himself. But he wasn't so much restraining himself as wanting by restraint to maximally raise the price of the moment when at last he could throw himself into it like into a whirlpool. A young man with a spark, he didn't want his arrivals to become a habit. And I was interested in acting differently from what he expected—so as not to deceive his expectations at the very end, because he needed to have what he was attracted to slip away from him, so he could desire it more strongly and the desire would never end. And now Seryozha was coming to throw himself on me, and Alyosha would see this. And Seryozha held himself back a year, couldn't hold back longer and came, and suddenly he'd see that his arrival doesn't mean anything to me, even without him I have Alyosha and he can't compare to Alyosha, Alyosha arms and legs in all directions like an adolescent, the delight of a millionaire on in years, with the ways of a star, and he loves me devotedly. I even asked Alyosha to dress up, to busy himself with the household chores and then in front of Seryozha to sit down and sew up my fur coat.

Everything acts on Seryozha as I wanted. When it was time to get ready for bed, Alyosha made his bed like a meticulous servant, Alyosha and I got in bed and I even asked Alyosha to go in to Seryozha's room and kiss him good night from me. If I had gone up to Seryozha graciously myself and kissed him, possibly he wouldn't have missed the chance to turn things around and take the high ground—like I love him again, and he doesn't need it. But I am not kissing you myself, my friend, it's enough to do it through my messenger; and you see how Alyosha obeys me, everything I say; and I don't begrudge parting with it, giving you the kiss of such an Alyosha. The game is going perfectly, Seryozha's driven mad, himself trembling couldn't take it came over to us like he wanted to ask for an extra blanket, thought I might invite him we might invite him to join us as a third. Then I thought up something else, agreed with Alyosha that he would go as a present from me to Seryozha, for two hours. So I would be his complete master in Seryozha's eyes. I calmly went to sleep for two hours, and when I called Alyosha back, no answer, I went into their room and saw they were lying without breathing, Alyosha clinging to Seryozha not at all like he does with me. Even so Alyosha obediently followed me, and Ser-yozha said why did I give him Alyosha for two hours, it would have been better not to give him at all. Then I got the idea to turn it around as if I had been testing Alyosha from the very beginning. I said to Alyosha: I thought to give you your freedom in the guise of a game—so I wasn't wrong to think I was giving you freedom, since I saw you didn't have it with me. But you didn't understand the test, were happy to do, finally, what you wanted to. Now I don't love you in life, since for this love you'd have to love me no less. Leave. Let me not have daily happiness and every-thing will go back to normal, you'll leave, take the talisman that your mother brought to you in the boarding school when you were little from God knows where and you take it with you, when you move in with a new man and put it in a prominent place in your new corner. A man in a hat with an accordion riding on a big frog, the frog's on a turtle, one of the turtle's feet is broken off it doesn't balance and this painted piece of wood is like a living being to me like Alyosha himself and if it were broken fell under the wheels as if Alyosha himself had been hit and died. Let Alyosha leave and everything will be like before him, like before I love to be alone, like always, the one who loves is the only one who loves, and the one he loves never loves him like that, even when it seems he loves him. If we sub-tract your love from my love only mine will remain. It was no mistake that I alone loved to confess my love, and Alyosha said nothing. If he had decided to confess before the end, he would have had to confess that he didn't love, and love in life would have ended earlier. But he understood that by not speaking out, by keeping it unclear, he was after all holding on to love, and he acted wisely, behind the lack of clarity you can't see if he has love or not, and he can be deceived that he has. But if you talk through to complete clarity, then it will be clear that there isn't any love. And as soon as he had confessed that there wasn't any it would have been impos-sible to be deceived anymore and it really would have ceased to exist. But this way it could still be possible, it would have been played into deception without confessing that it was deception, it would have developed for him out of the lack of clarity. It was I who hastened his confession, as is my habit I brought it on myself, so that love and happiness in life would end for me. My happiness in confessions and habit of confessing are hindered by even happiness in life. In life love and happiness I still have a ways to go to success, but in my love in words I already have success, and if I try, I'll be loved like a singer when she sings about love and everyone's in love with her for the way she sings, and she only loves to sing. That is she doesn't love in life like Alyosha doesn't love, but she smiles at you, and you are impossibly attracted to her.

LEAFLET

[Listovka]

WE ARE BARREN fatal flowers. And like flowers we should be gathered and put in a vase for our beauty.

Our question is in some respects like the Jewish question.

Just as, for example, their genius, according to the common anti-Semitic opinion, flourishes most often in commerce, in mimicry, in the feuilleton, in art without pathos, in worldly tact, in the art of survival, and as there are, one may say, certain spheres of activity created intentionally by them and for them—even so has our genius flourished, for example, in the emptiest and most pretentious of the arts—ballet. It is obvious that it was created by us. Whether it is literally a dance or any pop song, or any other art with sensual pleasure as its basis. Just as Judaic people have to be ridiculed in anecdote and as the image of the sparrow-Jew has to be held firm in the consciousness of all non-Jewish humanity so that Judeophobia is not extinguished—otherwise what would prevent the Jews from occupying all positions in the world? (and there is a belief that exactly this would be the end of the world)—even so our lightweight floral species with its pollen flying who knows where has to be ridiculed and turned by the crude straight common sense of the simple people into a curse word. So that foolish young boys, their masculine aspirations not yet firmly established, shouldn't take it into their heads to indulge the weakness of falling in love with themselves. For of course, and of this there can be no doubt (for us), but the thought is extremely dangerous and should not be sent openly into the world (so as not to bring closer the end of the world, on the other hand), but it is so: you are all frustrated homosexuals; and you are right, you have once and for all to imagine this pursuit as pitiful and vile and generally not imagine it at all.

And that all of you are us is clear as day.

Otherwise tell me why you like yourselves, that is a person of your own sex in the mirror? why are adolescents platonically in love with the leader of their courtyard gang? why do people no longer young look at times with a sigh at the young, seeing in them themselves as they can no longer be? why do you exhibit the beautiful and the young for the adoration of the whole world at the Olympics? Of course in your straight eyes all this has no romantic meaning! And it shouldn't! Otherwise the world would become distinctly polarized, the passions of the sexes would close in on themselves, and Sodom and Gomorrah would come.

We as the chosen and the predestined ones have to be encircled by a hostile boundary, so our example doesn't infect others.

Our chosenness and predestination are in living by love alone (insatiable and infinite).

While you, having found yourself at a young age a friend for life (a girl-friend), even if you look at other people, even if you break up, and then take up with another, still you basically live in the warmth of the family and are free from the daily search for love, free to do something with your mind, to take up a trade, or even to get drunk. But we, the Flowers, have ephemeral unions, tied neither by fruits nor by responsibilities. Living every hour in expectation of a new meeting, we, the shallowest people, to our graves play records with songs of love and look around with nervous eyes in expectation of ever newer young people like you.

But the best flower of our shallow people is called like no other to dance the dance of impossible love and to sing of it sweetly.

We secretly control the tastes of the world. What you find beautiful is in part established by us, but you don't always guess this (as Rozanov did). Avoiding in life much that arouses you, we at various times and in various ages have expressed ourselves in our own signs, and you have taken them for an expression of ascetic heights or the beauty of decadence which seemed to have a universal meaning. To say nothing of the fact that we often dictate fashion in clothes, we also present for your admiration women—such women as you might not have chosen in your straight desire. If it weren't for us, you would tend more strongly in your tastes to the direct, the carnal, the bloody. With a backwards glance at us, though not always realizing it, you have placed a high significance on the playful and the impractical. And it is also clear as day that everything fragile, decep-tive, all the fallen angels, all that is in beads, paper flowers and tears, all this God keeps in his bosom; all shall have the first place in paradise and a divine kiss. The best of our young perished creatures he will seat closest to himself. And everything pious, normal, bearded, everything that is presented as a model on earth, though the Lord assures all this of his love, secretly in his heart he does not love it very much.

Western law allows our flowers open meetings, a direct showing of us in art, clubs, gatherings, and declarations of rights—but what rights? and rights to what?

The stagnant morality of our Russian Soviet Fatherland has its purpose! It pretends we don't exist, but its Criminal Code sees in our floral existence a violation of the Law; because the more visible we are, the closer the End of the World.

Gennady Trifonov (b. 1945)

FOUR POEMS

Translated by Simon Karlinsky

GENNADY TRIFONOV was born in Leningrad in 1945. At the age of 20, when he was drafted into the army for two years, the KGB tried to force him to work for them. He attempted suicide as a result. After leaving the army he worked as a literary translator to the well-known Soviet writer Vera Panova and her husband David Dar in Leningrad. This position shielded him from KGB provocation. But after Panova died in 1973 he was defenseless, and he was arrested after the Soviet Secret Police became aware that he had been writing a series of unpublished articles on "unofficial" Soviet poetry, and had circulated privately a series of masterfully written poems about his love for another man. In November 1976 he was tried and sentenced in a closed trial to four years in Siberia.

In early 1978 Trifonov sent to his friends a poem/letter from prison. To support Trifonov, several western gay periodicals, including *Gay Sunshine* (San Francisco), agreed to publish this poem simultaneously, along with an article about Trifonov by David Dar. This prison poem is reprinted here, along with three poems from *Tbilisi by Candlelight* (*Gay Sunshine Journal* 32, 1977)—all in translations by Simon Karlinsky, who helped to publicize Trifonov's case in the West.

Trifonov currently lives in St. Petersburg. Selections from his recent novella, *Two Ballets by George Balanchine*, are printed in the "New Russia" section of the present anthology (see page 346). All Trifonov material in this book is published with permission of the author's agent, Glagol.

Gennady Trifonov, St. Petersburg, 1995.

LETTER FROM PRISON

I get your letters, telling me
that I'm a poet, which is dazzling,
that this is why my lofty star
is not extinguished in the dark.

All of you write me that my voice
has been absorbed by wintry groves
which are obedient to my hand,
obedient like my own handwriting.

All of you tell me: I alone
sang—as no one's allowed to sing—
of how we love without response
him who's our sole necessity,

Him who gives shape to all our lives
the way the branches form a garden
when God will kiss us on the lips
the way the snowfall kisses earth;

The one for whom I shout at night,
for whom I call, a wounded bird;
One who no longer haunts my dreams,
One about whom my verse is silent.

You write, responding in advance.
You plead with me: "Do not give up,
Endure it all and stay alive."
And I live on. And there's no life.

February 1978
North Urals

THREE POEMS FROM *TBILISI BY CANDLELIGHT*

To Ghivi Kanteladze*

April in Tbilisi is like a boy—
whimsical, brusque and enamored.
He quietly weeps in Georgian
While my resurrected hand
dandles him in Russian.

What does he fear? I am the one
who's most affectionate of all,
who falls to the ground from the heights
without breaking his neck or windpipe,
who opens his mouth wide to rhymes.

I'm music. Take me. Play me.
I am the reed flute of the steppes.
I know all there's to know of this life,
both when I laugh and when I moan
and that is my entire truth.

So take your time and play me. Search for
the meaning of your own Pan's flute.
God is no help in what we're doing,
not in this April, nor the next.
Pull all the stops out!
Play me! Don't stay silent!

---

*Ghivi Kanteladze, to whom this cycle of poems is addressed, was a male ballet dancer in Tbilisi, Georgia, and a close friend of the renowned Soviet theatrical and ballet director, Vakhtang Chabukiani.

* * *

Those sleepless nights of Tbilisi . . .
I would like the sky of Georgia
to reinvent me, affectionate and naked.
Like the merging Georgian rivers—
the Kura and Aragvi—believe me,
I would master the only heroics: the truth
of eternal successes and losses.
I am kissing you now (it's permitted!)
in the cleft of your suntanned face.
And I feel with my skin as I kiss you
how dissimilar you and I are.
Your need is for insolence mainly,
for games played with candles blown out,
while I—like just now—all my life
must keep still from the scream that is tearing me.

* * *

What's the use of this joy,
this nightingale whistling
which enfolds in one sweep
both you and me?

What's the point of this freedom,
insolence and trembling?
It is funny, it hurts
that you resemble another.

I no longer remember him,
but it rhymes, so I've said it.
I myself must resemble
someone else in your past.

Yes, I know: we could spend
an eternity here
kissing roses of Georgia
in the warm Georgian wind.

Gennady Trifonov (b. 1945)

OPEN LETTER TO *LITERATURNAYA GAZETA*

Translated by Kevin Moss

Angelo Pezzana, an Italian human and gay rights activist, visited Moscow in 1977 and staged a one-man demonstration for the rights of homosexuals. Pezzana also enlisted the support of the head of the Venice Biennale exhibit, di Meane. *Literaturnaya gazeta*, a weekly newspaper read by most intellectuals, published a mocking account of Pezzana's action, writing it off as mere stupidity and hinting that no international organization would come to the defense of sexual perversion. Trifonov, from his prison in the Urals, wrote an open letter to *Literaturnaya gazeta* defending the human rights of homosexuals, but it was not published. The text was smuggled to the West at the time and appeared in translation there. The present abridged version has been translated especially for this anthology.

T HE STYLE AND methods of the criminal justice system of the USSR in regard to homosexuals (even without addressing the question of their criminality) is fraught for them with unprecedented insults and degradation of their human dignity. These methods bring about the following results: a trampling of elementary human rights, a base and intolerable interference by the state in the sphere of intimate relations between people and one more possibility to slander and defame any person, if such a person becomes for concrete reasons unpleasant to the governing regime. Such is the reality, and turning away from it means not valuing and not understanding life and not respecting people. . . .

I am deeply convinced that if influential international legal and social organizations and institutions were to have at their disposal complete information, the conscience of many honest and civilized people in the modern world would be significantly troubled, and perhaps people in the Soviet Union would listen to the voice of such people beyond its borders with the attention appropriate to put an end to the criminal persecution of homosexuals in the USSR. This question has never been raised by anyone here, since through someone's malicious and cruel whim the very term "homosexuality" is forbidden in the Soviet press, literature, even science. But if we distance ourselves from these stupid prejudices, from this tradition that has distorted our ideas of Good and Evil, we would have something to think about and see the need for a deep and open discussion about people's moral and physical health. And here's why: based on the information I possess, the Soviet courts have since January, 1970 sentenced sixty

230

thousand people to various terms for homosexuality. . . .

Let's imagine (since this is perfectly easy) that instead of the piddling anti-Soviet Gennady Trifonov, the Soviet courts have used articles 210, 120, and 121 of the Criminal Code of the Russian Federation to sentence to 8 years of prison the brilliant Russian composer Tchaikovsky together with [the actor who played him in the film] Innokenty Smoktunovsky (NB: I have included the film star here only as my contemporary, nothing more!). Or rather, why such a harsh sentence, let it only be 4 years. And (you may crucify me if I'm lying!) in only three months both of these prisoners (how can they avoid it?) will definitely be subjected to the cruelest physical treatment by the "non-homosexual" convicts with the naturally silent agreement of the administration of the prisons. In three more months our prisoners will be neurasthenic and dystrophic, but they will work (with the aim of firmly setting out on the road to improvement) with the inhuman load of 10–15 hours a day from the first day of their incarceration (how can they avoid it?), working for themselves and for the guys who [screw them]. In three months they will contract some serious infectious disease, in three more they will think about suicide and worse. In three more . . . But one gets used to everything, especially our Soviet man. And our Soviet homosexual literally gets used to everything!

I have experienced all these horrors and nightmares, and it is impossible to get used to them. Now that my name is well known in the West, I am treated less barbarically. But for a year and a half I have observed what it is to be a convicted homosexual in a Soviet correctional facility. His position is child's play compared to the situation of those like him in the death camps of the Third Reich. They had a clear future—the gas chamber; we have a semi-animal existence, doomed to a hungry death while dreaming of some serious illness to get a few days of rest on a hospital cot in the camp clinic. I know people who have either completely forgotten about the end of their sentence or have physically not made it to the day of their release. Their corpses were removed from the electric fences or were found where they had hanged themselves in the prison cells, tortured to death by enraged criminals or beaten by a convoy gang gone mad. I know their names, I have written testimony of eye witnesses! The administration of the prisons, basing its reasoning on the state conception of "relations" to homosexuals, pays no attention to their protests and complaints, allowing other convicts to torment us unpunished. The overwhelming majority of homosexuals (unless they are young and attractive or naturally scum) are forced to eat food others throw in the garbage; they are forbidden to approach the common tables in camp cafeterias, in prisons they generally starve. For example, during the three months of the pre-trial investigation while I was moved from cell to cell, where I was cruelly beaten by the convicts and slept only a half an hour a day on the cement floor, I had no hot food at all for a month and a half. Food packages in prison were taken from me by my cellmates. The administration of the prison—one of the largest investigative prisons in the USSR—of the Leningrad Office of Internal Affairs, headed by Colonel Smirnov—did not react at all to my protests, and set the other prisoners against me. My investigators—iron men in all respects —informed me that I was a malicious slanderer trying to defame the agents of the Ministry of Internal Affairs and the public prosecutors of the USSR.

Food packages in camp—this rare joy of the Soviet prisoner!—are taken away from homosexuals, and additionally their kidneys are beaten or some other severe bodily damage is caused. Many incarcerated homosexuals are deprived of a place to sleep altogether, required at all seasons to be outside the living barracks and to be cruelly punished for this by the administration. As a rule we are denied medical care. The situation of the homosexual is truly tragic if, in the opinion of the other prisoners, such a person cannot be used for the satisfaction of their base desires. This concerns those who are elderly or invalids. . . .

I would consider my mission successful if *Literaturnaya gazeta* would remember the appeal for real humanism and humanity in the treatment of homosexuals in the USSR made by the Nobel prize-winning French writer André Gide and show its good will, thereby putting an end to the renaissance of normal fascism in regard to people whose sexual exceptionality has given the world the genius of Michelangelo, Oscar Wilde, Pier Paolo Pasolini, Shakespeare, Socrates, Thomas Mann, Sappho, Mikhail Kuzmin . . .

As a poet and a citizen, as a human being and a journalist, I will devote all my strength to the defense of these people who, the very symbols of Sorrow and Suffering, are in my country the tragic victims of crime without punishment—of stupidity, falsehood, cruelty, and cynicism. This I see as a manifestation of common decency natural for every intelligent and honest person, and such is the meaning of my current and future life and work.

Gennady Trifonov
Western Urals, 7 Dec. 1977

IV

GAY LIFE REBORN IN THE NEW RUSSIA
(1990–   )

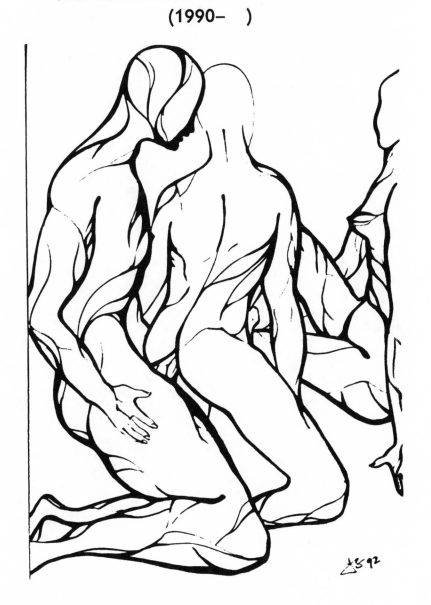

Photo by Vitaly Lazarenko.

[Anonymous]

LETTERS TO THE EDITOR OF *TEMA* AND *1/10*

Translated by Kevin Moss

ROMAN KALININ, who established *Tema*, the first gay newspaper in Russia in 1991, was also one of the first radical gay activists. Among other controversial acts, he submitted his name as a candidate for President of Russia. These first letters (mostly anonymous) were published in the pages of *Tema* in 1991/92; they are followed by letters to another Moscow gay lib paper, *1/10* and its editor Dima Lytchev.

Hello, Roman!

I'm feeling really bad and I don't know who I should turn to. I'm writing you because I trust you, I trust you and hope you can help.

Just now on the street three guys beat me up because I'm gay. These bastards found out about it from a guy I used to love (now I'm surprised myself that I could love such a piece of garbage!). These scum demanded that I let them fuck me. I refused, and the result was a bloody face. One of the guys demanded that I bring him 50 rubles tomorrow. Earlier he shook me down for a hundred. But tomorrow I won't give him anything. I know after that he'll beat me up, but I still won't take him anything!!! Sooner a cock in his throat, but no money!

Roman, you understand I can't go to the police. First of all I'm afraid everyone would find out, and second if they don't get me their friends will. God, how I want to get out of this stinking little town where everybody knows everybody else!

There's so much I want to write, but I don't know how. I'm afraid my letter won't make much sense, but you have to understand I'm in a horrible state both physically and morally!

. . . My God, how I loved that bastard who betrayed me! I did everything he wanted, called him every day, wrote letters to him in the army. . . . And then this low trick! You know, it's like an unexpected stab in the back. . . . Everything was fine, then suddenly. . .

Now he's in the army, but when he comes home how will he have the courage to look me in the eyes?

Roman, I'm writing you because I don't know who I can share this with. We used to have a few boys here, but they've almost all gone into the army, and the ones who are left are shit! They'd betray anyone for a kopeck. . .

You know, lately I've been needing something (or maybe someone?!) really bad. I so much want real, true, eternal Love! I want Him (so far I don't know who this is) always to understand me, respect me, love me. But

235

where is he, where?!

Why doesn't anyone understand me?! Even my parents!

. . . Once again I'm alone, lying and crying in my snow-white bed . . . my little five-year-old brother sleeping soundly next to me. God grant he doesn't have such trials as I've endured!

. . . I don't want to live like this any more. I'm sick to death of these beatings and money-collecting. I'm young, I want to live, but I can't live like this. I feel like I'll break soon. And I'm sorry for my mother, my brother, my father! I'm sorry for my friends! Sorry for everybody!!! I'm sorry because practically everybody has to live in shit like this.

But before I do something to myself I'll crush all that scum. Bastards, they've ruined my youth! How I'd like to erase them from my life!

I still have one tiny shred of hope. . . . I'm not asking for anything, I'm just hoping. For what? I don't know myself. . .

I'm tired of catching curious stares and of pushing hands off my ass on crowded buses.

I hope my letter won't be a cry in the wilderness. . . . I'll be waiting!!!

* * *

Something happened to me recently. I was walking in the park. It was raining. I went over to a flowerbed and was looking at a flower. And since I had an umbrella, I didn't notice when a boy came up to me. He handed me a flower. At first I didn't understand, I got flustered, but we looked each other in the eye and I understood I couldn't wait any longer. We walked together in the rain. We talked for a long time, and when we stopped he embraced me and started kissing me. I just melted in his embrace. In all my life I've never been so happy.

* * *

Because of its stupidity and its narrow-mindedness so-called society will never be able to accept one thing: that a boy can love a boy and a girl a girl. In my opinion it's not at all worse than what we not so long ago used to see on our TVs: our General Secretary Leonid Brezhnev tenderly and voluptuously kissing his whole team of voluptuous old fools, the leaders of the Central Committee of the Communist Youth Organization. I know this firsthand, because in my day I often visited the Central Committee of the Communist Youth Organization, I was present at a few intimate gatherings, and what took place there is simply impossible to describe: both homosexual and other relations between the members of our youth groups. And I can guarantee the reliability of this claim because I myself was a participant in such amusing "youth" weekends.

* * *

One warm May evening I'm sitting in the shadow of the great Pushkin after work waiting for something to come up. Out of the corner of my eye I notice floating out of the underground passageway a young, innocent creature, one of those sexless creations of the Lord straight folks shy away from thinking they're typical fags, and our people shun because they can't imagine how one could have sex with this (it has no sex!).

Meanwhile It, gazing over those present with its bedroom eyes, sashays back and forth, fixes its skirt, and with a theatrical sigh sits down next to me.

Without much thought I ask a direct question:

"So is this the new cruising area?"

It widens its eyes in amazement and asks,

"Meaning?"

"You know perfectly well what I mean."

There follows a short pause. It is visibly trying to think. Then it asks,

"What, are you gay?"

"No, green! [Russian for "gay" is "blue."]

"I'm not gay!!!"

And pursing its lips, it lights a cigarette.

"I'm sorry!" (this was me)

I get out another cigarette and continue to warm myself in the heavenly sun, waiting for the Sun of my life. Time passes . . . with a flamboyant flip I throw my Camel stub in the ashtray and raise my exhausted body to have a look at the gay press in the passageway.

Suddenly I hear behind me a light cough and a shy question:

"You're already leaving?"

This was my friend innocently reminding me of his presence.

"Of course I'm leaving, I'm not interested, after all you're not gay."

My answer clearly hurts him and he makes one more uncertain attempt to rehabilitate himself in my eyes:

"In general I have done it . . . but I don't get any pleasure out of it."

I sit down next to him.

"And how often?"

"10 or 15 times a day, but that's for money, and when men fuck me I don't get a hard-on."

"When you do, then come back."

And with a clear conscience I set off for the passageway.

From this encounter I've made the following remarkable conclusion: if you're being fucked and don't get a hard-on it means you're not gay.

Mytischi

* * *

Last summer I found out by accident where Minsk homosexuals meet: strangely enough it's on the trolleybuses, line 2 along Lenin Prospect (near the rear door). I'm a student at the university, and that's the bus I take to class, but I'd always walked before. I was in shock when they suddenly started feeling me up without so much as a by-your-leave. . . . And then I too started trying to touch men I found attractive. Once I was on my way to the university and one man and I felt each other up, I liked him, and I almost drove him crazy (as he told me later). My stop came, I had an exam to go to, and he gets off after me and says, "Where can we go?" I almost had a stroke I got so scared, I knew you weren't supposed to meet people on public transportation. I told him we were going different directions and we split up.

In the fall on the same "number 2" I got picked up by a hot man, this time I wanted to make contact, gave him my number, though I was afraid of blackmail and of being compromised. I was on my way home still aroused and what do you think? I see on the "number 2" the same man I met that summer. This time, encouraged by my recent acquaintance, I decided to make contact. For people to begin to understand each other you have to have at least 6 hours of conversation, not just a sexual attraction. So for three days in a row we just talked, and then we went to bed. I can't imagine a more gentle and pleasant partner, one who first of all thinks about the other, then of himself. Since then we've been together.

L., Minsk

* * *

Dear everyone!

Wow! How great that you exist! And your newspaper (God grant you a rich sponsor) and the work you do. Now it is not without pride that I point out my homosexuality, and when I buy your newspaper I add, "Oh, I love men! I just can't stand it! I think soon it'll even be fashionable to be gay or lesbian, and everybody will start adding the honorific title to their names, digging up something that happened in their distant childhood with friend Vanya or girlfriend Manya. But I'll be outside the competition because all my adult life I've loved only Him, and when I committed the act of sodomy (article 121 of the Criminal Code) I couldn't understand what was a crime and what was punishment. Whoever thought up that article had their brains in their ass. And those homophobes have no business standing by our beds with a candle. Enough!

I don't know how to express in words the feeling of joy I have because people are not indifferent to my fate, the feeling of freedom that inspires hope. And if there is hope, it will continue to live.

Igor, Moscow

* * *

. . . I'm 23, I'm gay, and I'm not at all repentant. I've found what I want and I like living like that. And I've been living like that since the 10th grade. I had a boyfriend, I loved him very much and he loved me. It was wonderful. But as they say, all good things come to an end. My friend was drafted into the army and sent to Afghanistan, and when he had 2 months left till demobilization he was killed. I thought, "Life's over," even took poison, but as you see I was saved and I suppose it's for the best.

After that I had another boyfriend, but he betrayed me badly, and I thought to myself, "Life's a deception, everyone lives for himself." For the last three years I've been hustling; I like it and they even pay bucks. God gave me good looks, I have everything. But sometimes I think youth isn't forever. And then what can I expect—life in the gutter, public toilets? I'm afraid of that most of all. A man with no future? But maybe I can still find love?

Igor, Murmansk

* * *

Dear thoroughly dis-respected editors of the newspaper *Tema*!

Probably the end of the world has finally come. All around savage morals reign, cynicism, filth, vice! What are you writing about, what are you appealing for! Are you aware in the slightest? I think not!

I am a teacher, now retired. All my life I have taught children in school. I taught them to respect and obey their elders, to conscientiously expand their knowledge and not to be lazy. And was it all for nothing? Perhaps because of my devoted service to a noble cause I have never had a personal life.

It hurts me to see what is happening to our young people. And all this thanks to people of your sort. I am horrified to think things have gone so far. Already boys are not ashamed to exchange caresses and act affected the way girls do. Various obscene newsrags are published and sold openly, filthy reading! We should burn this infection with white-hot iron! This is the very real putrid influence of the decaying bourgeois countries.

I look at it this way: democracy is playing with the world of capital and it will lead to no good. We need order in the country, even if it takes some harsh measures. It's all right, the cure is not always painless. Otherwise we'll reach a point where people will fulfill their physiological needs in broad daylight like animals; men will go to the altar with men, women with women; all our young people will be depraved in the extreme and the last remnants of spiritual values will be trampled in the mud. I am very upset that the government makes indulgences for people of your sort. If I had my way, I'd gather you all and send you off to Siberia to cut trees. There you'd have no time to indulge your vice! And I wouldn't be sorry in the least.

I beg of you, think about your life before it's too late.

After quickly leafing through a copy of your little paper I accidentally picked up, I washed my hands for a long time.

Galina Alexeevna, Moscow

* * *

Galina Alexeevna, Hello!

I don't want to offend you and say unpleasant things about you, but . . . You yourself write that you are retired, and that means your ideals are Stalin, Brezhnev, Communism and its shining future. But dear, where is your shining future? Of course it would be hard to change your mind, but time reveals all. As far as cutting trees is concerned, that's stupid. I got back from there six months ago and it's not so bad. I would like to inform you, dear Galina Alexeevna, that people are people everywhere. . . . Cutting trees is hard, exhausting labor. And usually the camps are located far from populated areas. And you always have in front of you barbed wire, soldiers, dogs, mean faces, tired people. And you want a little happiness.

I was in prison for Article 121, my sentence was printed in *Tema*. So first of all I was afraid. And then it all went away. For all those 4 years I never lifted anything heavier than a pen in my hands. Who's going to indulge the men, relieve their stress if not me and those like me? Everywhere I was warmly and kindly received, and if you take care of yourself, keep yourself clean and neat, you can get into any circle. They'll always give you tea (that's the currency in the camps), feed you, give you something to drink. There were only a few of us there, and not one was offended or beaten. Since they stood up for us, valued us for a good "blowjob," etc.

Of course you don't know all the joys of sex, of orgasm, of the flight of the soul after passionate nights. Of course this is your trouble and your misery. I forgive you for your rude letter. It's understandable—you were not loved.

* * *

I often hear or read in the papers about somebody sentenced under Article 121 hanging himself in prison. This is sad, and the problem is that the article still hangs over us like a sword. But if you should find yourself suddenly in that situation you don't have to kill yourself, and climbing into the noose is stupid: you only live once, after all. The most important thing is to weigh all the pros and cons. Don't talk to the investigating policeman until the lawyer comes—this should be your first condition. And all talks should be conducted in the presence of the lawyer. Second, every prison has cells for the "girls," they're called "the humiliated." You should ask politely to be placed with them. The most important thing is not to scream or be rude, or they can put you in the press-room, where you'll be beaten and raped all night.

When you get to the cell with the "girls" don't open up too much. Remember that every casual word will be reported to the administration. Basically you yourself should ask about life behind bars. Try to find a friend among the "girls"—if he's well dressed and looks good. If you look good, are young, can handle the situation, you're saved. You'll have protectors. But if you panic, if you're dressed badly, if there's fear in your eyes, you're doomed. Don't be afraid to flirt, don't let rags and washing floors demean you. It's better to wash the floor 10 times than to be fucked 20. If you're obliging, the brigade leaders and the inmate officers will protect you. Try not to look like a victim. Always be careful in your discussions of somebody. Your best listener should be your pillow. Rarely does one find friends behind bars—everything and everyone there is for sale.

Try to avoid the administration and don't go there too often for chats. You might be misunderstood.

* * *

. . . I did my service with an artillery unit. Our regiment was stationed in Czechoslovakia. Relations with my fellow servicemen were very difficult. Though I didn't flaunt my "gayness," the way I acted must have allowed my brothers in arms to guess my sexual proclivities. This was all expressed in hints; they told me they dreamed they had sex with me and offered to make the dream a reality. But since not one of them appealed to me, I got off with a joke.

Speculation that I was gay reached the company commander, Lieutenant Borisenko. That's when I felt all the "joys" of service and learned from personal experience what homophobia is. There wasn't any kind of dirty or hard labor I wasn't assigned. It reached the point of idiocy. For example, in the winter of 1980 we were participating in the joint exercises called "Friendship 80." Before the exercises we were all issued felt boots, but by the personal order of the lieutenant, none were issued to me. I was afraid to complain, since I already knew how professionally our commander could beat people.

So I endured all the "trials and deprivations of army service." I even participated in an amateur evening, since I read poetry rather well. And on the 20th of February, 1980 I was transferred to the district command, to the town of Mlada Boleslav to participate in a concert for Soviet Army Day on February 23. Two musicians were sent there with me. One of them, Borya Khramov, I liked right away.

On arrival we were quartered with a musicians' platoon. The commission saw our act and decided to keep us there for the May 9 Victory Day concert.

The housing for the platoon was cramped, and we had to sleep two to a bed.

Relations with the guys were more or less OK. It was the usual rehearsal workday. Of course the way I acted didn't fit the usual manly stereotype here either.

The 28th of March I had my birthday and treated the guys to good wine.

We had a good time and went to bed. As I already said, we were sleeping two to a bed. The day before had been bath day, and I ended up with no underwear, and therefore I had to sleep in my birthday suit. When everyone went to sleep, Borya (and I ended up sleeping with him) started kissing me and stroking me. And then . . . I didn't even put up a fight, since I'd wanted this myself for a long time. And Borya finished his business and got up from the bed, woke up the whole platoon and told them a "faggot" had wormed his way in and that he (that is me) fucks like a cat, and so on and so forth.

Lord! How they beat me! Ten enraged men against one! The results of this "conversation" were lamentable for me. My jaw and one rib were broken. And then when they got tired of beating me they put me on all fours and each had a go. . . . Then they beat me again, then raped me again. . . . In the morning my own mother wouldn't have recognized me. According to regulations I was taken to the infirmary in the morning. There I was patched up, and I had to invent some story about some strangers who asked me for a light. There was no way I could have told the truth then. My fellow servicemen and "lovers" came after taps to the infirmary, took me without anyone's saying a word to the basement and beat me again. Finally they wanted to hang me, but I convinced them to put the execution off until the next day. When I got back to the ward I drank a vial of carbolic acid and passed out.

Naturally news of my poisoning myself with carbolic acid reached the public prosecutor's office. I was taken to a central (TsGV) hospital, and after they brought me back to consciousness in intensive care, they put me in an isolated psychiatric ward. The investigating detective turned up immediately. At first I tried to deny it, making something up about the reasons for my attempted suicide. Finally the detective got tired of my stories and gave me a tape of the interrogation of my "lovers" who sincerely repented everything. There was nothing for me to do but confess my "gayness" and tell him everything.

Then there was a psychiatric exam. I was held in the psych ward a month. The whole exam consisted of huge doses of sulphazine, aminazine, and soul-saving chats with the department head on the subject of "How could you?! tsk, tsk, tsk!"

Just before the trial I was transferred to a KGB solitary cell for interrogation. There I was surprised to learn that only Borya and I were on the docket, the rest got off light and were acting only as witnesses.

Then came the comedy of the trial. At the judge's bench sat a colonel, next to him two jurymen-sergeants. Since it wasn't deemed necessary to familiarize me with the materials of the case before the trial, it was only from the indictment of the prosecutor that I learned what a disgusting person I was and how my "deviant" personality had contributed to the disruption of the valorous Soviet Army. And it turns out the ones who beat me up were practically the foremost fighters for protecting the military preparedness of the army. My attempts to be upset at such an interpretation of events and tell about the insults of these "champions of morality" were decisively cut off by the presiding judge, since they "had nothing to do with the case."

After a thorough "examination" of the case the court pronounced sentence: ". . . for the satisfaction of sexual passion in deviant form to sentence:

—me to 4 years deprivation of freedom in a camp of common regime
—Boris to one and a half years of common regime. . ."

Of course I was not let out to "chemistry." When my two weeks were up I was called to the head of the operative section, Captain Ch. He chatted for a long time on the subject of "tsk, tsk, tsk," then "imperceptibly" shifted to the topic of my sexual preferences. He asked for a long time about what I feel during sex. And he ended the conversation by expressing the desire to "try" me. He was young and damned handsome. And I didn't want to refuse him. After this I spent a wonderful half hour on his work desk. True, that evening I was again put away in the psych ward for "offending the head of the operative section." I was put into solitary. The next day I announced a hunger strike and demanded that they call the head of operations. He came, locked himself in his office with me, and said, "don't fight it, it has to be like this." After that I went down on him. And in three days I was transferred as a "vicious disrupter of discipline" to the PKT, and after two months there to another camp. That camp and the relations in it were exactly the same as the previous one. The only difference was that I soon became the lover of one of the inspectors. I can't remember his name anymore, but in the camps he was called "Vanka with the accordion."

* * *

Photo by Vitaly Lazarenko.

Hello!

I would like very much to learn more about female homosexuality. Only don't imagine that I practice this, I'd simply like to find out for myself. I await your reply.

Vova [a man], Donetsk

* * *

Please explain to me what is the name of the kind of homosexuality I practice—I really love to lick my wife's clitoris. Please respond. I am 50 years old.

Nizhny Novgorod

LETTERS TO THE EDITOR OF *1/10*

My grandfather was an archpriest. When I turned 14, the deacon Fr. Vladimir was transferred to our parish. He was 21 then. . . . I didn't know what was happening to me, I avoided him, but whenever he left on business I would almost start crying. He began to show an interest in me. In the summer we moved to the hayloft to sleep, and once I somehow got up the courage to stroke his butt. It was soft and hairy and he wasn't asleep. I found that out when I started trying to take his underpants off. He helped me, turned to face me, and embraced me, whispering in my ear that he now understood everything, the way I'd been acting towards him. Then he was ordained a priest and left for another parish, but I went with him and served as an altar boy. In 1983 he suddenly died of heart failure. I thought I'd go crazy. After his funeral I walked in the woods all day long and thought about leaving the world for Holy Orders.

* * *

Amazing things happen here in Bryansk. Imagine, even in the baths by the showers the bath attendants check for gays and hand them over to the cops. They spy on who takes a long time in the shower, and then yell "Faggot! Catch him!" They handed over two while I was there. Later I met them in town, they said they'd been beaten at the police and had to pay a 2,000 ruble fine for "disorderly conduct in public." At the train station young cops in civilian clothes set up "homos." Meanwhile they themselves fuck you, but then you'd better either pay up or be prepared to be exposed. It's wild to see a broad running and yelling till she's blue in the face "Police, fag here!" It makes my soul disgusted and empty.

* * *

. . . For a long time, ever since my childhood, I've been oppressed and tormented by the subject of your newspaper. I had snowballs and rocks thrown at me, to say nothing of the mocking epithets. . . . I thought I would grow out of it. But IT is for life. I work in the theater. Behind my back there are whispers, sideways glances. Indirect gossip is always the most hardy. If somebody says to me, "Read this book, look at this film," I know it's about gays. And I have to admit the image is pretty disgusting. But I can't fight it. I'm not attracted to women. Sometimes I like to day-dream, to imagine a fairy or a sylph, but all I have to do is see a woman in the flesh, and I run for my life. The faster the better. Sometimes literally. Funny, right? Nature gave me a pretty face and curly hair: "the shaggier the beast, the more the ladies are enraptured." I sincerely tried to be with a woman. It was so lousy! I despise myself for being weak. I hated her and myself. And we were such good friends! We used to touch a lot. I could make her crazy, I can do that. But she had to have intimacy. She got it. She drove me to it. "You're a man, after all!" And that was it. As soon as I got out of her embrace I told her I'd never come see her again. I almost committed suicide. How bad I felt! . . . Now even the name "Anna" makes me wince. She still lives nearby.

We started kissing and "feeling up" at 8–9. I don't judge childhood by years. We kissed like children, carefully touching each other. Probably everyone goes through this. At about 12 I fell madly in love. I had no idea it was forbidden, that you couldn't talk about it. Lyosha suffered, a beautiful boy. In short it was like this: "Debase myself in love! I don't want to and I won't. I'll forget you. You bring me misfortune. You drive me crazy . . . only how can I leave if you don't go?" He amused himself with my feelings at will and didn't let me go. "That's all. . . . I separate you from me. That's all. And I'll teach myself to forget you! Forget your arms. Your lips. Your eyes . . . forget misfortune, and torment. Enough!" He tortured me. He wouldn't let me near him and wouldn't let me go. He was already experienced, already flirted with all the girls. And not only; an early bloomer . . . He wanted variety. I moved to another city, otherwise my heart couldn't tear itself from him. I saw and knew everything. Even his marriage wasn't news, though it was painful. Then I befriended, or rather commiserated with a friend from the university. He was a closeted gay. Tried to fight it horribly. It even came to blows. He beat my face, my arms. I didn't give up; it was a risk, of course. I believed in myself. And Sergei finally backed off. I remember the night he told me I didn't repulse him and he wasn't indifferent to me, that my caresses disturbed him, only he was afraid to admit it right away. For the first time he allowed me to caress him, telling me where and how he liked it. I taught him to kiss. I remember our first kisses in the frost, minty lips, the park covered in snow, the streetlamps. . . . Nobody cared. Night, not a soul. We only instinctively sensed the danger, without realizing it completely. That was passion. We couldn't live without each other. Often we argued violently. Then I would have said, "I'm leaving you; I say farewell in parting. I'm leaving, but you'll find no peace. You will run after me in despair, with no hope of finding me again. . . . Some evening your friends will get together. Someone will embrace you and whisper words of love. You'll be cold and indifferent to him; for I at that moment will embrace you unseen. There'll be no point in seducing you and luring you; even if you wanted you couldn't betray me. I have left, dissolved like ice in the shimmering sand; I will you to remain in tears and anguish. To struggle alone, shivering like grass in the night. This is my curse. . . . May these words be fulfilled!" I was the last person to wish misery on Sergei, but these words say it all. Though I understand perfectly well I have no right to Sergei. None at all. And I have pangs of conscience that perhaps I changed Sergei's "normal" orientation, and if it weren't for me he'd be married and happy, rather than oppressed. Sergei after all likes girls, he's attracted to them. But gay practices over many years will not pass in vain. I wanted to let him go, but you can't even always let a bird go free, and this was a man. When I ask him if he regrets it, he avoids answering. He says he loves me. And me? We have a lot in common. College years, we've been through a lot . . . but he's already started talking about marriage. He needs a woman, I can feel it. Even psychologically. How can it be that a handsome, healthy young man doesn't date girls? This pressures Sergei. And what can I do? I can go crazy again. I'm not bragging, but there was a time when Sergei wanted to commit suicide because of me. Good thing it turned out OK.

I had another acquaintance, Anton. What a guy! "I follow her with my eyes and there's nothing there, but I keep looking. . ." That's the way it was here. A face like Alexander Malinin,* only not so blond. Green eyes, reddish-brown hair, charm. The girls stuck to him, and I was drawn too. Wit, irony, experience in life. An addict; so what? I adored him and don't regret it one bit. Thin, but what a guy! We were fast friends. He understood everything, I held myself back. It hurts to acknowledge one's own hopelessness, to sweetly surrender to the insanity of love in vain. I gave him money. Anton loved taxis. His hobby was riding around in taxis. And for drugs. He showed me great books that gave me a lot. I worked with Anton in a theater, a different one than I work in now. I held myself back, but once when, as luck would have it, we ended up together in bed, I lost control. . . . I remember his shock. I only managed to steal one kiss. I lost my mind. Anton pressed my head to his chest, "Quiet, quiet, calm down!" He talked to me like a sick man; that's how he took it. We talked all night. Anton couldn't overcome his contempt for me. We grew farther and farther apart, then separated. I can't sleep with a guy in bed and just sleep. I'd rather not sleep at all. My feelings for Anton are "Fate preserve

---

*A Russian rock star.

you. . .'' He's married, and God grant him happiness! There was another little friend, a boy, a bambino. He looked like Raphael in his youth. He surrendered to me; he said, "I'm melting." I was even cruel. Who in my shoes wouldn't have been drunk with his tenderness? The bambino was scared of this. He got married really quick, practically to the first one who came along. Just to get married. At 18! Why? You know, as many married men as I've met, not one bragged about it, they all complain. I asked him, "So who do you like it better with, her or me? I've never been with a woman, tell me." He said nothing. We knew each other for a short time. Well, I thought, he'll end it. We had everything: jealousy, tenderness, passion . . . all in the space of a few days. Is that freedom—living with a woman you don't love? But he's afraid of his parents. He stifled his own feelings to please society. I have no right to judge. If that's better for him, let it be like that . . .

Recently I had a bad case of lovesickness. The guy's name was Mikhail. Looks like a page-boy, reminded me of Patricia Kaas. I can't describe his character. I was afraid to touch him. "Do not say 'farewell.' I hate that word. I won't offend you, grazing your arm by accident. My fate hangs by a hair. I've built my castle in the sand . . .'' I remember my trembling like a schoolboy when I first touched him. He was sitting like a prince, his heart thumping. I embraced his legs, kissed his knees. His soul is so pure. I regret I couldn't hold myself back. He told me, "My head is spinning from your words. Don't speak to me like that. I don't want to fall in love with your words. Don't do that." Mikhail reminded me of a fairytale. A few words are enough to describe him: "the charm of sadness." He was tormented by not being able to respond to my love. I wanted to relieve him of his guilt complex. "His eyes were caressed sadly by snow in summer." Snow fell in a mad spring. And roses. . . . And we were in light raincoats. His name is his alone forever, no matter who else might have it. He too married. Apparently for love. It's been over a year since I've heard anything about him. I don't have a photo. I destroyed everything that could have reminded me of him. But I will never forget him. Like I did all those girls and women who offered themselves to me. How often I used to come across the name "Mikhail," and it didn't mean anything. I remember his every touch. His hair like silk, black, rustling, and his face, his grey starry eyes. I'm incapable of falling out of love. They say dark eyes like mine absorb light, and light ones like Mikhail's radiate light. I don't know his body, didn't see him naked . . . but I can't forget him. What is this brand on me? I loved each one. They say one can love only once. But love was different each time.

There was another episode in my childhood, little Igor. Now he's mad at me. Once he said in anger, "Why did you show me what girls are like? Now I can't even speak to those cows." Now I'm getting to the reason I began this long letter. I'm an actor, an actor by vocation. I've worked in

the theater a long time. I love the world, music, painting, poetry, literature, and psychology. I love nature, stars, contemplation and participation,
ballet, expressions . . . there's a long list. In other words, I love life. But
the fact that I'm gay puts a barrier between me and other people. It's true.
I've conducted an experiment. As an actor I can enter into any situation
you suggest. In other words, enter an image. People are willing to be
friends with a murderer, a junkie, a thief . . . a religious believer, a
gypsy . . . but with a gay man?! And that's just what I am. There's this
guy, I wouldn't have expected it from him. "Could you have a junkie for
a friend?" He smiles, "I have one!" He tells me about a junkie girlfriend.
"And with a gay man?" He screwed up his face and said in an indescribable tone, "Well they're people, after all!" So! Well, thanks a lot! This
bothers me.

Everybody in my family's "normal." Kids, aunts, uncles, nephews,
nieces. But me? But another thing bothers me even more. I'm affectionate. Painfully affectionate since I was a child. There are two types of gays.
Those who give and those who receive. It used to be fifty-fifty. But somewhere along the way I met a man. What I wrote about above had long since
passed. Now it's harder and more painful. This man was with me the whole
time. It was senseless for me to try to leave. He was strong, and he bound
me hand and foot with his passion. In a death-grip. You know, there's no
slavery stronger than voluntary slavery. Whoever I was with, I always came
back to him. His power over me was insane, beyond all measure. He poi-
soned me with kindness, addicted me to him like a drug. If I know anything
about erotica and sex, he was my teacher. His hands. . . . He just radiates
power. I can never refuse his call. No matter what happens. He was the first
to kiss me like an adult. I was going after Lyosha, but stayed with Gena.
His name's Gena. He's well known in the city, an important position. Married. He can torment me incredibly through intimacy, it's sweet torture.
You know, when it's slow, awfully slow. I bite my hands not to scream.
And I get dizzy from his kisses. When he strokes my legs I go mad, just get
drunk. Such weakness right away from his touch. Gena doesn't rush. But
sometimes he can be sharp, abrupt. Then I really go crazy. I feel like I'm
his toy. You know, I change from a person to a thing. My body takes control over me. And my heart as well. Gena tried to attach me to himself
spiritually. He's a musician: smart, erudite, witty, and cold-blooded on the
outside. He can control himself, he's a Leo, almost condescending, strict,
cold, terse.

I become a toy, and a living toy at that. I lose my will. My self-defense
is destroyed and the brakes fail. I've begun to notice that even accidental
touching disturbs me. And if somebody on a public bus touches my leg or
my thigh I forget where I'm going. . .

You see, I'm becoming a slut. There was one time I was caught, I was
fighting them off, I can fight, though I'm no black belt. But they kissed

me, and I melted. Into the car and to the house. And there . . . a gang-bang . . . but it wasn't rape! That is, my soul resisted, but not my body. It's torture. When you want to resist but you can't. Though you try. I pushed their hands away, and they kissed me, and it's all over. I can't control myself. And they had me, the animals, four of them, one after the other. Laughing and egging each other on, the scum.

Gena's jealous of me with everyone. But he's the one who made me like this. He made me sensitive to a glance, with a weakness for affection. . . . I'm not asking for advice. How could you help? I only wanted to get it all out.

You know, Gena and I had a night . . . when I felt with all my insides it was the last. I almost died: my heart, my blood-pressure. Then Gena said, "Forgive me, Valera, please forgive me!" And it was unbearably sweet, such a high that it didn't matter what would happen after. I couldn't stop him, I hadn't the strength. The deadliest thing is that his caresses are so slow, like a noose tightening around the neck, slowly stopping the air. Even if he simply teases my nipples I can't catch my breath. He has a way of stopping my objections by running his hands over my whole body. You can't refuse him with his sense of rhythm. When he strokes my back, you just can't touch the small of the back, it's like bare nerves. Probably you know the joke that if the rape is inevitable, just lie back and enjoy it. I am his servant, his slave, his dog.

What do you think, can gay people love? Or is it just impure passion? I'm becoming a slut. I'm drawn to men, very strongly. They say it'll pass, but it doesn't. For a prostitute it makes sense: anyone who pays has every right. But I don't need money. I get off on it myself. Sergei used to say, "Valera, your legs start at your neck." He used to say, "Your moans turn me on." I don't even hear my moans. Would I like to be a woman? I don't even know. It seems to me if I became a woman, I'd be a lesbian. Funny, right? My body. It demands what it wants. I don't know, maybe it's like that with other people. I've never once spoken with gay people, only with bisexuals. They gossip behind my back and tease me by calling me "Valerie!" It's not the words that hurt, it's the tone. "Many of his friends have had him." It would have been better if they'd hit me. Had him! They ask for it themselves, then they spit on me. Strange people, right? In your newspaper you write "gay life" as if it was so easy. But I'm a black sheep! Three times I've moved to a different city, but what's the point? There's no horse you can ride to take you away from yourself.

I still meet with Sergei. Sergei knows that he can't tear me away from Gena, he tried. Sergei doesn't know that I wouldn't be myself without Gena. Sergei and I have a love-friendship. I remember a train ride with Sergei. We were lucky, the two of us in one compartment. We closed the door and the window. Kisses in the pitch dark, the speed of the train, words can't express it. We were both going crazy. In the morning I was hoarse and my lips were like ripe cherries.

I remember the first time I "took it" from Sergei. He didn't want to. He thought it would demean me. I insisted. Imperceptibly, while we were caressing. When I touched it with my lips he cried out. And then he kept kissing and kissing me on the lips, pressed to me. That was the sweetest thing; grateful hugs. In the morning he kneeled down and suddenly kissed my bare feet. I was surprised. I kissed Gena's feet, but only in the throes of passion. But Sergei! In broad daylight. Sergei loves me and forgives me Gena. He's jealous, but silently. He used to wait for me at the university. My friends used to joke, "your dog's waiting for you there." Lyosha's words, by the way, my first love's. We wanted to rent an apartment and live together. But . . . Gena won't let me go. Gena has an impeccable reputation. The wife of Caesar is above suspicion. Once his wife and daughter were on vacation. I lived at his place a whole month. We went to bed at 9:00, and this was in the summer, when it's still light. We were so greedy for each other we didn't sleep all night. When we got up late, Gena would be surprised "Is it really already morning?" I get more worn out with Sergei. Sergei doesn't know about all my adventures. He doesn't know that I'm an "honest slut." What can I do? Maybe kill myself, period? So far my appearance still lets me conceal my internal fire. Appearance? The eyes of the beholder. My colleagues at the theater, especially of the weaker sex, call me "monkey" for my agility, limberness, "dog's" eyes. But at this rate my looks will pass quickly. Plus the makeup; actors' faces age quickly. A woman would get married, but I'm not a woman. . . . Somewhere I heard that gay men have 100 partners a year. I haven't kept count, but . . . I'm drawn, pulled incredibly. When I say "no" it doesn't sound like "no," but like "yes." And there are diseases too. So far God's been kind. But AIDS? I'm terrified of AIDS as long as I'm alone. But give me a good partner, and I'm willing. Willing to die in pain only to feel it again and again. Stupid? Do they treat gays? Can it really be cured?

But you're young. You've shaken me up. Good! AIDS . . . we're all mortal. Just nobody knows when. What's the big deal? Makes no difference: you have to die sometime. Isn't love worth dying for?

Vladivostok

*　*　*

I didn't know Igor very well. We met in strange circumstances: we got stuck in an elevator. The two hours we spent together brought us closer. Recently I ran into him on a bus. It was 11 p.m. Igor suggested we take a night walk through the quiet city. We walked in silence for a while, not wanting to speak. The snow was crunching beneath our feet, a full moon shining. Suddenly he asked a question, "Do gays fall in love?" His question was a direct hit at my heart. I used to ask myself this question often, and always to answer in the affirmative.

"Want me to tell you about myself?" asked Igor, and he began without listening to my answer.

. . . When Igor was 12 his parents died in an automobile accident. The tragedy left its mark on his little child's heart. Igor closed in on himself, became quiet. He was raised by his grandmother. But the years passed, and his granny quietly left for the other world. At 16 Igor was left alone, all alone in the world, unprotected, unneeded. He kept waiting for someone. . . . He dreamed of getting out of this city, but he couldn't: he couldn't because his nearest and dearest ones lay here. On quiet rainy nights he watched the dark sky. Old people say that our relatives watch over us at night from the heavens. Igor looked at the sky but saw nothing. Tears choked him, his heart ached. The sound of the rain increased his sadness. On winter evenings he sat on the sofa in the dark, remembering his mama, his papa, his granny. Remembering his carefree childhood. Remembering the holidays, the workdays. Remembering the sound of slamming doors, the voices, the laughter. He took tranquilizers by the handful to forget everything for a while. He'd wake up and everything would be back to normal. The same empty apartment, ticking clock, and silence. Last summer Igor was coming back from the cemetery. He was sitting at a cafe, and a guy sat down with him to have some ice cream. They started talking. They stayed until closing. Sergei, that was the guy's name, offered to walk Igor home. They chatted at the front door till late at night. They agreed to meet the next day. For the first time in nine years Igor felt happy. Sergei and Igor spent day and night together. They went to the beach for the summer. The nights they spent together seemed magical. It lasted a year. Then it stopped suddenly: Sergei didn't appear for several days.

Igor decided to go see Sergei himself.

"It would have been better for me not to go," he told me, "better if I had waited and waited all my life. If only I didn't know he'd left me." Sergei's parents had exchanged their apartment and moved to another city. Sergei left without telling Igor anything.

For half a year Igor was alone. He kept waiting for Sergei, waiting for him to call.

"I don't know, was that love?" I remember his words.

We walked till morning. We agreed I'd call him that evening. We exchanged phone numbers and addresses. But I couldn't reach him that evening or the next day. Never. That morning he hung himself in his quiet, empty apartment. The clock was ticking. His mouth was frozen in a smirk or a smile. Maybe he was glad he had tricked life that had treated him so cruelly. Or that he would at last see his parents and his grandmother. He missed them so much.

There were a few people at the funeral. They took him to the cemetery, buried him. No one lamented. No one remembered him. Only the old lady from next door cried over his coffin all night. And she's still lighting candles for him.

Igor was a handsome boy. He would have been 24 in January. He died two days short of his birthday. If I could only bring him back. But you often think of people and remember them when they're already gone.

Sergei, I think Igor's death won't be a shock to you. You forgot your promise not to leave him alone. I searched for your address for a long time. I'll make you read this! Though you probably won't understand anything! You've lost every ounce of brain not to understand what you've done.

Lord! Igor, why did you live? To suffer and die for love?! I know you were unhappy in this cruel world. You paid for your first and only love with your life!

On a winter day I walk in the cemetery. The snow crunches beneath my feet. I turn to your grave.

"Hi! I've brought you black roses. You love them! You're probably happy?!"

No one remembers you on this Earth except the old lady neighbor and me. Our conversation lasts for hours.

It gets dark, I head home. A snowstorm comes up.

"Do gays fall in love?" I ask myself. And answer in the affirmative.

P.S. I can't understand why Igor left this world after our conversation. Probably he didn't want to go to a better world with a heavy heart full of tears, misery, and offense. Someday I will definitely see you and ask you! Life is not eternal . . .

    Marat P. Laskari

*   *   *

I am a young poet-psychologist, Alexander Voronin. Lately much literature and many publications have appeared about homosexuals. Only I have never once in my life had the opportunity to see them with my own eyes, touch them, find out what kind of people they are. And how is it possible—aside from usual friendship and friendly relations to transgress the bounds of reason and subject oneself to spiritual torment in the eyes of the majority of normal people, if they suddenly want sexual satisfaction. It's stupid and absurd. In satisfying their flesh, they destroy their spiritual principle, their spiritual nature, their reason, their spirit, their intellect, their fate, their life, their health—everything.

They have to be treated, to find any methods of treatment, immediate help in changing their psychosexual orientation. Here in Nizhny Novgorod we have a specialist who can treat even transsexuals without operations or injections. By means of psychic influence and holotropic breathing.

These people are unfortunate; in my opinion they are the weakest and have been degraded by fate.

Can one really encourage such a life that you call "gay"? What nonsense!

Your newspaper should sound the alarm and seek doctors and psychologists to immediately and methodically treat and cure such people, so they can live like everyone else.

Apparently you yourself are unfortunate.

I would really like to receive one of your newspapers about the so-called "gays." I would like to know what they say. Maybe it's just nonsense and it's all thought up in the days of glasnost to tickle people's nerves, to create a sensation. In all my 37 years I had no idea that there were people in real life with a hypertrophic sexual attraction and a perverted sexual orientation. Everything is going fine, the boys go with the girls, young men love and court young women, and men can't live without chicks.

But for a guy to get into some other guy's pants—that's something weird and irrational. Maybe it only happens there in Moscow out of boredom and luxury?

     Sincerely, A. Voronin
     Nizhny Novgorod region

* * *

This is what happened to a friend of mine, Seryozha. Last spring he was walking downtown. The weather was sunny, but cool. Seryozha was in a long raincoat, a hat, smoked sunglasses. Not long before that he had gotten himself a perm with curls. Not a boy, but a picture, in his own words.

Suddenly a smartly dressed man comes up to him, a foreigner by the look of him. When Seryozha talked to him it turned out he was an Italian. He spoke Russian badly, it was even funny. He acts freely, uninhibited. They talked and talked about the weather, and suddenly this Italian asked him to give him a blow job. He asked, then he was a little embarrassed. Seryozha smiled and agreed. Neither one could wait, so they went to some archway. . .

. . . The Italian, his name was Mario, was quite happy. You might say he was high, he even offered money. They were going to leave, and Mario says, "Wait, I want to touch you." Seryozha smiled nicely, go ahead, why should I care. . . . Mario groped for his breasts, found nothing there, and asked in horror, "You're a boy?" Seryozha laughed, "What, you only just found out?"

. . . In my opinion this incident proves decisively that it's not who you sleep with that matters, girls or boys. The main thing is what you tell yourself while you're doing it.

     Alex, Moscow

* * *

I'm 20 years old, my name's Sergei. I'm writing you because there's no one else to write. I'm still alive, though I don't know why, and I don't know what will happen to me tomorrow. I have lost the closest person to me in all the world. Two years ago I went to Moscow—thank God it's not far, only a two hour ride—to walk around and take a look at this wonderful city. I "had to go" and went into the toilet near the University metro stop. When I was about to leave, a guy about my age came up to me. He started talking to me, invited me to his apartment, and promised to show me around Moscow. I agreed. I think there's no need for me to describe his apartment. In just one night with the help of his amazing talent for attaching people to him he turned a guy who before didn't know anything and couldn't do anything into the happiest person, or rather, he made me into a gay. After that night I understood that I'd been born for this. Then I was drafted into the army, and for some reason he wasn't taken, and he stayed home. First he wrote often, then less and less, and the last half year I didn't receive a single letter from him. When I got back I went to see him and saw at once that it was all over, he already had someone else. Sometimes it seems it would have been better for me to have been born ugly, rather than good looking, then he wouldn't have come up to me and I would have lived peacefully, without ever knowing about this. When I got home to my empty apartment after that last visit I couldn't eat or sleep for a long time. I walked around the room and yelled, "Sasha! Sasha! What have you done to me? Why?" I decided to die. As fast as possible. I heard a song of Alla Pugacheva's,* I don't even remember which one, I paid no attention to the words. Only it seemed like she was saying to me, "Live, you have to live, have to be strong, everything will work out." It seemed like I was losing my mind. I took out all the Pugacheva cassettes I had at home and started listening to them. "Hope, live, fight." As if she took me by the hand, strong, grave, understanding everything, and started to console me, crying along with me, shouting at me, whispering words of consolation. As if something broke inside me. I managed to go out on the street, to look around. I could live. Thanks to her! I don't know if it will last for long. I'm still alone and I live alone. Though even so I don't want to live. But I put on Alla Pugacheva's cassettes, and the day is mine. What's next I don't know. Letters, letters. . . . To be honest I don't know why I'm writing a letter to strangers. Probably I want to share my pain with someone, you have to share it, but the problem is—with whom? It's hard for me now, for some reason I'm not lucky, I have trouble meeting people. But I believe Pugacheva's prediction: everything will be all right.

Sincerely, Sergei

---

*A pop singer very popular with gay men; the Russian Bette Midler.

* * *

I want to tell you how I became a homo. By the way, I don't regret it at all, I'm even grateful to that man.

It happened when I was in the 6th grade, I was just a little over 12. For some misunderstanding, I don't remember now what, four 8th graders and two from the 10th decided to "humiliate" me. They took me into the changing room of the gym. No, they didn't beat me, they tore off my pants together with the underpants and laid me on the mats. It was so unexpected I didn't have time to realize what was happening when I felt a sharp, strong, bursting pain from the rear. It turned out this was Zhenya from the 10th grade, and as I later learned, he has the biggest cock. Everything went black, I almost threw up. When the others fucked me I no longer fought it and didn't feel any pain.

But I felt bad about it later. Shame, fear they'd find out in school. I wanted the earth to swallow me up.

Two weeks later Zhenya came up to me with another boy, Oleg. I was on duty, cleaning up the classroom. They locked the door.

Then it started. Almost every day they led me home to Zhenya's. Zhenya started putting me under his 14-year-old brother. . .

I wanted to transfer to another school, but I couldn't explain the reason to my parents. Time passed, and it turned out I was wrong to worry. The guys in my class didn't change towards me. What surprised me was that the 8th graders who had slept with me started acting even nicer, becoming more friendly. I was surprised at this and couldn't understand it.

Later I found out from Zhenya's brother that Zhenya had strictly ordered everyone to be quiet. I understood that I wasn't just a bed for him. He held his feelings in check, though there was such warmth in his eyes. Fool that I was, I didn't completely understand this. Did I love him? Yes, I did, but I didn't know it right away. Zhenya remains in my memory as the brightest and most beautiful thing in my life.

Now I'm alone and very lonely. It's 4 years now since Zhenya got married, his brother moved in with his parents. Oleg met with tragedy: he was sentenced under article 117 [heterosexual rape].

Why am I writing all this? Don't believe all those homos who curse their fate and seek to be rid of this supposed vice. They're not homos, they're rubbish. A real homo is incapable of suicide. The only problem is how to find a friend.

How to meet people, how to identify that one and only one? how to let him know about you, get the attention of the one you need? and the one who needs you.

　　　　Albert, 21, Kazan

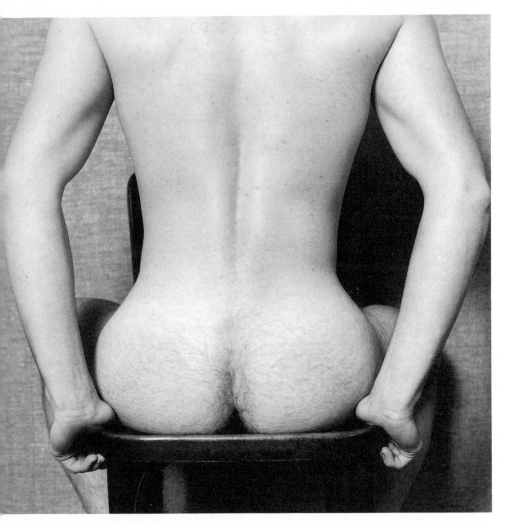

Photo by Alexei Sedov.

V.K. and Nikolai Serov

LETTERS ABOUT PRISON LIFE

[Pis'ma iz zony]

Translated by Dan Healey

THESE LETTERS on Russian prison conditions and the place of homosexual relations behind bars make depressing reading. It is not only that the fate of those convicted under the anti-sodomy statute was harrowing, but it's even more disturbing that the lives of male prisoners in Russia continue to be ruled by a culture of sexual humiliation. The extreme brutality and the imbedded sexism of the practice of male rape as a tool of group discipline and group definition is of course not unique to Russia's penal system. Nevertheless, it should not be assumed that because Russian legislators have taken sodomy off the books, abuses such as the ones catalogued in these letters no longer take place. If anything, with the decline in Russian public institutions, the opposite may be true.

These two letters by prisoners describe how prison life is for "queers," as gays are known in the Russian penal institutions and describe current attitudes. They were published in the Russian gay journal *Kristofer* in 1992.

Letter No. 1: by V.K. (Detention Establishment No. 42, Arkhangelsk in Northern Russia)

IN PLACES OF detention a group of people exists which is totally outcast from the chief mass of prisoners. These are the so-called "humiliated" or "insulted" ones, or more simply—"queers."

Of all prisoners only they have no right to their own opinions and lack the right to be heard. Only other queers may associate with them and they eat strictly from their own dishes. These unfortunates sit and sleep in places specially set aside for them. Their condition: a complete lack of rights and absolute defenselessness. The queer may not return insults in kind, nor give as good as he gets if someone beats him.

In penal camps, queer [*petukh*] is a synonym for homosexual [*pederast*], although the words are not very similar in Russian. The word *pederast* is in lively use in the camps, as a rule, and is pronounced with scorn and hatred as *pidar* or *pidor*.

The queers are used for sexual intercourse and other forms of sexual gratification. This is the primary reason why they are in such a degrading position. More simply put, queers are those who one way or another become the passive sexual partner. The absolute majority of queers become that way after being in penal colonies for minors or soon after they find themselves in the adult camps for the first time. For many queers, the investigation cells are the start of their new condition.

That is because "it" is as a rule linked with rape, and these cells are the most suitable places for this. A man behaves "incorrectly," his actions go against the generally accepted norms. He might steal something from his cellmates, lose at cards without having the means to pay up. He might turn out to be a stooge and be discovered. Prisoners also hate those who have been convicted of raping minors and will "humiliate" them.

Someone finding themselves in this situation may accept it and live without paying much attention. He works, with nowhere to slink off to. If necessity arises, he may himself proposition someone. In the camps it is well-known that queers are paid for their work. Basically they are given a pack of cigarettes or a pot of tea. Thus for some it becomes a fair way to earn money—in the "zones" as a rule most do not have a surplus of tea or smokes. However, not all of the "humiliated" choose this path. Some do not engage in "it" at all.

The chief category of prisoners who use the queers are of course, younger. Older people are generally indifferent to them. And naturally the younger ones and the nicer lads enjoy the most success as queers.

It is easier for young prisoners to end up as outcasts: they do not know how to behave in a given situation. If in a youth or adult camp, whether soft or strict regime, it is usually by force that a person is "humiliated," then in strictest regime colonies there are often cases where this is done peacefully.

I don't speak about this off the top of my head, but as someone who has seen all of this life. They often give the queers women's names, calling them perhaps Juliia, Shurochka, Eleonora—or, for example, a "neutral" nickname like *Pushok* [bit of fluff], *Oduvanchik* [dandelion] or something else of that type. Of course, those who practiced homosexuality on the outside are strictly distinguished from their colleagues in the "zone." Approaches and principles are completely different. In the camp a queer can make a proposition not because he really wants to do "it," but because he doesn't have any tobacco. But somehow or other the "humiliated" in the camps will feel attraction for someone. A queer will keep coming back to you, if you don't insult him or yell at him. If, in a word, you treat him humanely.

It's not true that all queers work for the prison administration. Many live their lives, some might "help" in some fashion in the administration. It depends on the man himself, and there are many prisoners not belonging to this low category who work for the warden's office. The attitude of the administration toward the insulted ones is not bad. If someone goes to the guard for help, because someone has beaten them or something like that, they will usually not turn him away. Practically all the administration in the investigation detention centers and the penal colonies know full well what is going on and are understanding about it.

Letter No. 2: by Nikolai Serov

IN NOT ONE of the transit camps have I encountered any clear discrimination on the part of the prisoners. And I have a little joke on the guards in every prison; they ask me: "Are you an amateur?" To this joke I unfailingly reply, "No, you are the amateurs, and I am the professional!" In every prison they find my reply impossible to accept calmly, and they put me in the *strogach* [isolation cell] or the "special regime" cell. In the cell I immediately advise everyone that I'm gay and that I'm inside for Article 121 [sodomy], and no one touches me or proposes that we share a bunk.

Attitude toward the *grebni* ("queers, fags"): Since I have become familiar with various regimes, I can judge their attitude towards us. Although we are all queers, among ourselves there is a caste system. Pure homosexuals belong to the highest caste—that is those who can give themselves willingly, and don't have to because they are guilty of theft or of other sins. I was part of this social estate. I never experienced the horrors which it is now fashionable to write about in the papers. I was never forced to eat from "drilled" plates; I had the right to go anywhere I liked, and not to be confined to the limits of the "stall." The single limitation was that I didn't have the right to drink with the *muzhiki* from the same glass. But that is understandable. It's not every straight who would kiss a woman if she performs fellatio, even if it's on him. But even this reluctance is only displayed in public (I call this the herd instinct). One-on-one, even with a lover in the "authorities" there were no limitations.

Nevertheless, there were only two such homosexuals "of blue blood" [pun on *goluboi*] in this whole "zone."

The next caste down consists of 50% of the queers. These are the "humiliated" and the "insulted." They are not inclined to passive homosexual sex and do not lead a passive sex life. They were first "insulted" most often in the investigation cells. There are three methods of "humiliating": thump your dick on their lips, force them to perform fellatio or coitus per anus [sic]. Usually it's thieves, stooges, losers at cards. And among these I've never met one who was raped, as such. Humiliation happens very simply: the guilty party is given a choice—either a blade in the gut, or your ass. I've never heard of anyone choosing the knife. And then they send him away to live in the "stall."

Sometimes they "humiliate" a boy they like the looks of, someone in for a short stretch. He's not guilty of anything, but considers himself a victim of the criminal justice system; and most of all, he's damned sexually attractive. So to sleep with him, they suggest they all play cards for fun. The boy loses, of course, and then they explain to him that playing for fun means playing for his butt, since in the camp they fuck you in the ass for fun. Before the boy figures out what's what, they work him over and send him to live in the "stall."

In this case there are also some who have just been thrown in with the "humiliated," who have nothing at all to do with homosexuality. These are people who suffer from mental illnesses and the like.

The third caste is the *pidory* ["fags," another slang variant of *pederast*] or "prostitutes," who give themselves to anyone for a ration of bread, sugar, a pot of tea (a half-liter). They do it with disgust, clumsily, and they don't get any satisfaction whatsoever. The rest of the "humiliated" fall into this category.

These two castes are recognized only by the queers, while to the rest of the *zeks* they are all just fags. In general regime camps their lives are hell. They always walk at the end of the line. In the canteen, the auditorium, they have their stall. They can't go anywhere ahead of a *muzhik*. They don't have the right to shake hands with *muzhiks* and so on. . . . Even at the latrine they have their own toilet. They do not have the right to refuse a *muzhik* when ordered to wash his underwear, socks or when they send him to stand watch for the guards. I don't have to mention that the most filthy, heavy, unattractive work is the privilege of the fags.

How many queers are there? In the zone I was in, in every detachment there were 10–20 queers. There were 14 detachments in all. There were about 150–200 queers in a total zone population of 1600–1700 men. About 50% of all prisoners actively used the sexual services of the queers. These were basically guys up to 35 years of age. The other half used the services of the queers sporadically. And a very small percentage (in my detachment of 120 men there were only 8) do not pursue homosexual contacts. Queer-prostitutes could serve up to 20 men a night (oh, yes!—in a row!). The genuine homosexuals did it only when they themselves wanted to, and only for love.

There's one other category of homosexuals in the camps. About this category I've never seen anything in any of the publications on the prison theme. I'm speaking of the "secret ones," who in the criminal "Table of Ranks" number among the "authorities." Yes, they do exist. They proclaim their disgust for the fags loudest of all, expressing their scorn in every possible way. But they simultaneously secretly lead a homosexual life and support and defend their brothers-in-spirit, inasmuch as it is possible in zone conditions. I myself was the lover (the *active* partner, not the passive one) of one of the "authorities." Almost everyone considered me his "female" lover, but I wisely held my tongue. An attempt to reveal the truth in such cases threatens the truth-teller with a blade in the gut and would not lower the "authority's" prestige one bit.

Photo by Vitaly Lazarenko, Moscow, 1995.

Vladimir Makanin (b. 1937)

THE PRISONER OF THE CAUCASUS

[Kavkazskii plennyi]

Translated by Anatoly Vishevsky and Michael Biggins

VLADIMIR MAKANIN (b. 1937 in Orsk, Russia) ranks among Russia's most prominent writers of prose fiction. A mathematician by training, in the late 1960s Makanin left his position as an instructor at Moscow University to devote himself full-time to writing. Makanin's work is chiefly concerned with examining the psychological development of ordinary, sometimes inarticulate people who find themselves in extraordinary situations. His short novel *Baize-covered Table with Decanter*, which deals with the old Soviet methods of bureaucratic investigation and demeaning interrogations, was published in English in 1995 (tr. by Arch Tait, Readers International). For readers familiar with Russian literary tradition, the story presented here, which is set in the ongoing war in Chechnya, will seem as timeless as it is timely. Since the early nineteenth century numerous major works of Russian literature have taken Chechnya and the centuries-old conflict between Russians and the indigenous peoples of the Caucasus as their setting. Makanin builds on this tradition, but his Prisoner of the Caucasus (the title itself is almost identical to that of a story by Tolstoy) introduced a new element, rarely explored in Russian literature until now. This story appeared originally in *Novyi mir* (Moscow, April 1995).

1

THE SOLDIERS MOST likely didn't know that beauty would save the world, but they did both have some idea what beauty was, in general terms. They sensed the beauty of the mountains (the beauty of place) too well, and it was frightening. A spring suddenly leaping forth in a mountain gorge. Even more alarming for both was an open meadow, which the sun had painted a blinding yellow. Rubakhin led the way as the more experienced of the two.

Where had the mountains suddenly gone? The sun-drenched space reminded Rubakhin of the happy childhood he never had. Off to the side there were proud southern trees looming up over the grass (he didn't know their names). But most of all it was the tall grass stirring in the breeze that moved his flatland soul.

"Hold up, Vovka. Take it easy," Rubakhin warns him softly.

Being out in a strange open space is as good as being in someone else's sights. Before he steps out of the dense brush, Vovka the sniper unshoulders his rifle and aims it from right to left with a studied deliberateness, using its telescopic sights as binoculars. He holds his breath. He surveys the space flooded in sunlight. He notices a small transistor radio beside a hillock.

"Aha," Vovka the sniper exclaims in a whisper. (The hillock is dry. The glass of the radio had glinted in the sun.) In a series of short dashes both of the soldiers in camouflage fatigues reach a half-dug (and long since abandoned) gasline trench, and, from there, the hill, which is drenched in flaming autumn red. They examine the radio which they have already recognized. When he was drunk, Corporal Boyarkov liked to steal away and lie in the grass hugging this old radio. They part the tall grass, looking for the body. They find it close by. Boyarkov's body has been pinned down with two stones. He had met his death. (Shot at close range. It looked like he had barely managed to open his drunken eyes. Sunken cheeks. In the squad they had assumed he was AWOL.) No papers of any kind. Have to report. Why didn't the rebels take the radio? Because it's evidence? No. Because it's too old and scratchy. Not worth it. The irreversible nature of what had happened (death being one of the clearest instances of irreversibility) hurries, whips them on against their will. It makes both of them agitated. Laboring with flat stones as shovels, they bury the dead man energetically, quickly. Just as quickly they shape a mound of earth over him (a recognizable, man-made mound), and then they move on.

And again, just as they leave the gorge, there is tall grass that hasn't dried up. It rustles softly. In the sky (above the trees, above both of the soldiers) birds joyously call to each other. Maybe in this sense beauty does save the world. Suddenly, out of nowhere, it appears as a sign, and keeps a person from going astray (walking beside him, watching him). By forcing him to stay alert, beauty makes him remember.

But this time the sunny, open space proves familiar and safe. The mountains part. From here on the path is level. A little farther and there is a fork in the road worn dusty by many vehicles. Then, the army base. The soldiers instinctively quicken their pace.

But Lieutenant Colonel Gurov isn't on the base. He's at home. They will have to go there. Without a minute's rest, the soldiers foot it to the lieutenant colonel's, who is omnipotent in this and all the surrounding (beautiful and equally sunny) places of the earth.

He and his wife live in a nice country house with a terrace for relaxing, overgrown with grape vines. The property includes a garden and some livestock. It is noon and hot. On the terrace Lieutenant Colonel Gurov and his guest, Alibekov, pliant after a large meal, doze off in light wicker chairs as they wait for tea. Rubakhin makes his report. Haltingly and somewhat timidly. Gurov drowsily looks at the two of them, covered in dust and unbidden, and what's also not in their favor, totally unfamiliar faces. For an instant Gurov becomes young. He raises his voice, shouting that there will be no help, no matter who for. What help, goddamn you? He finds it ludicrous even to hear about sending his soldiers to pull out trucks that by their own stupidity have gotten stuck in the gorge. What's more, he's not going to let them go. Angrily, he orders both soldiers to get to work spreading sand. Let them do honest work, get something done around the house. About face . . . march! and make sure that mountain of sand gets spread at the entrance. And spread that sand on all the paths leading up to the house and the garden, too. Otherwise it's nothing but fucking mud, you can't get anywhere. The lieutenant colonel's wife, like all wives everywhere, was glad to have the extra hands around for free. Anna Fedorovna, with her sleeves rolled up, and wearing a pair of muddy, worn-out men's boots, immediately appears in the garden, joyously exclaiming yes, yes, and they can help in the vegetable garden, too.

The soldiers move the sand around in wheelbarrows. With shovels they fling it around, sowing the paths with it. It's hot. But the sand is damp, probably hauled up from the river.

Vovka has planted the dead corporal's radio on a mound of sand and has found some music with a beat that keeps his spirits up. (But not loud, for his own good, so as not to bother Gurov and Alibekov while they talk on the terrace. Alibekov, judging by the unctuous words that reach this far, is bargaining for weapons, serious business.)

The radio sitting on its sandy hillock reminds Rubakhin what a beautiful place Boyarkov chose to die. Drunken dummy, he was afraid to sleep in the woods so he came out into the meadow. And on top of a hillock, at that. When the rebels rushed him, Boyarkov shoved his radio aside (his loyal friend), causing it to slide down into the grass. He was afraid they'd take it away. As though he figured he'd manage somehow, but never give up the radio. Not likely. He fell asleep drunk and the radio simply fell out of his hands, and after sliding a bit, it rolled down the slope.

They shot him point blank. They were young, probably the kind anxious to make their first kill and develop an appetite for it. Even if it's asleep. Now the radio was sitting on the mound of sand, and Rubakhin could see that hillock blazing red in the sun, with the two bushes clinging to its northern slope. The beauty of the place overwhelmed him, and Rubakhin—in memory—refuses to leave (in fact, continues to absorb in himself) the hillside where Boyarkov fell asleep, that hillock, the grass, the golden foliage of the bushes, and with all this yet another irreplaceable lesson in survival.

Beauty is unflagging in its effort to save. It calls to man in his memory. Reminds him.

At first they sped the wheelbarrows over the tacky ground, and then it occurred to them to throw some planks over the paths. Vovka takes the lead. Nimbly wheeling his barrow. Behind him, Rubakhin pushes his huge, overloaded cart. Bare to the waist, his powerful, sweaty body glistens in the sun.

2

"You can have ten AK-47s and five boxes of ammunition. Do you hear me, Alibek? Not three boxes, five."

"I hear you."

"But make sure you get the provisions to us by the first."

"Petrovich, I'm a little drowsy after dinner. You, too, I believe. Has Anna Fedorovna forgotten about our tea?"

"She hasn't forgotten. Don't worry about the tea."

"How can I not worry," the guest laughs. "Tea isn't like war, you know. Tea gets cold."

Gurov and Alibekov gradually take up their never-ending dialogue. But the languor of their words (just like a certain laziness in the argument) is deceptive. Alibekov is here for weapons. And Gurov, his officers and soldiers desperately need provisions (quite simply, food). The medium of exchange is of course weapons, sometimes gasoline.

"Food by the first, and none of your stupid mountain ambushes. Wine is optional. But there has to be some vodka."

"There isn't any vodka."

"Find some, Alibek. I'm finding ammunition for you."

The lieutenant colonel calls to his wife, how's the tea coming? Oh, what excellent, strong tea we'll have here in a minute. Anya, what do you mean? You called to us from the garden that it was brewing already.

In anticipation of the tea, both of them slowly, lazily light up after-dinner cigarettes. The smoke just as lazily crawls across the cool terrace onto the grape vines and drifts in layers toward the garden.

Making a sign to Rubakhin that he'll try to get them something to drink (seeing they were stuck here anyway), the sniper approaches the wicker fence step by step. (Vovka always uses clever signs and gestures.) A young woman and child are on the other side of the fence, and Vovka the sniper immediately starts flirting. He leaps over the fence and starts a conversation with her. Good for him. Rubakhin keeps on shoving his barrow of sand. To each his own. Vovka is one of those fast-moving soldiers who can't stand sluggish work (or any other kind of work, for that matter).

Just look at them, they've found each other. It's amazing how readily this young woman responds to him, as though she'd been waiting all along for a soldier to talk nicely to her. But then, Vovka is friendly and smiles a lot, and wherever he dawdles for a second he puts out roots.

Vovka grabs her and she slaps his hands. The usual business. They're in plain view, and Vovka realizes that he needs to lure her inside the house. He pleads with her, tries to lead her off by force, but the woman resists. "I don't have any," she laughs. But step by step they move toward the house, toward the door left open on account of the heat. And finally they're there. A child sitting not far from the door continues playing with a cat.

Rubakhin meanwhile has stayed with his wheelbarrow. Wherever it was impossible to get through, he picked the boards up from their previous places and set them down in a line. He guided the wheel over them carefully, keeping the heavy load of sand balanced. Lieutenant Colonel Gurov continues his leisurely negotiations with Alibekov. His wife (she has washed her hands and put on her red blouse) serves each of them tea in separate, exquisite Oriental teapots.

"She brews a good tea, she does," Alibekov praises her.

Gurov: "Why are you being so stubborn, Alibek? If you look at this one way, you're a prisoner. Don't forget where you are, after all. You're on my turf."

"And just how is this your turf?"

"Because we control the valleys."

"You control the valleys. We control the mountains." Alibekov laughs. "You're joking, Petrovich. Me, a prisoner? You're the prisoner here." He laughs and points at Rubakhin, who is fanatically pushing the wheelbarrow. "He's a prisoner. You're a prisoner. And every one of your soldiers is a prisoner." He laughs. "I'm hardly a prisoner." And with that, he's back at his earlier offer. "Twelve AK-47s and seven boxes of ammunition."

Now it's Gurov's turn to laugh.

"Twelve. You're joking. What kind of a figure is that? Twelve. Where do you get these numbers? I could understand ten, or a regular number like that. It's easy to remember. So, ten barrels. Agreed."

"Twelve."

"Ten."

Alibekov sighs rapturously. "What an evening this is going to be."

"Evening's still a long way off."

They drink their tea slowly. The unhurried conversation of two people who have known and respected each other for a long time. (Rubakhin wheels along his next barrowful. He tips it. He pours out the sand. He scatters the sand around and evens it out with his shovel.)

"Do you know what our elders say, Petrovich? Our towns and auls are full of wise old men."

"What do they say, then?"

"They say it's time to move on Europe. That it's time to go back there."

"Oh, come on now, Alibek. Europe!"

"What of it? Europe is Europe. Our elders say it isn't that far. Our elders are unhappy. Our elders say that wherever the Russians go, we go, too. And why are we shooting at each other?"

"You go ask your friends why," Gurov shouts angrily.

"Oh, now you're offended. We drink tea, we warm our souls. . . ."

They are silent for a while. Alibekov then begins to reason, slowly pouring tea into his cup.

". . . It's not that far. We have to move on Europe from time to time. The elders say we will have peace then. And life will be as it should be."

"We should live so long."

"The tea is excellent, Anna Fedorovna, brew us some more. Be so kind."

Gurov sighs.

"This is going to be a wonderful evening. There you're right."

"Oh, but I'm always right, Petrovich. All right, ten AK-47s, it's a deal. But seven boxes of ammunition."

"Back at it again. Where do you get these numbers, there is no such number: seven."

The lady of the house brings out (in two white dishes) leftovers from dinner to feed the soldiers.

Rubakhin responds quickly, "Yes, how could a soldier refuse?"

"And where's the other one?" Rubakhin stutters and resorts to some heavy lying, saying that the other one got the runs. He thinks for a minute and then adds more convincingly, "He's pretty bad off."

"Maybe he ate too many green apples?" the lieutenant colonel's wife asks sympathetically.

The soup is good, with hard boiled egg and chunks of sausage. Rubakhin bends over one of the dishes. His spoon collides loudly with the sides of the dish. It rattles. As a sign.

Vovka the sniper hears (and of course understands) the sound of the rattling spoon. But eating is not on his mind now. The young woman in turn also hears (and understands) the hysterical meowing coming from the yard, following by the wailing of her child who has just been scratched. "Mom!" Apparently he pushed the cat too far. But the woman, who is starved for touch, has become wholly absorbed in her passion. She clings to the soldier, joyously, greedily, unwilling to let this happy moment slip away. There's nothing much to be said about the sniper. Soldiers will be soldiers. Then there is the child's willful whine from the yard again.

The woman flies off the bed, sticks her head out the door, shushes the child and then shuts the door more tightly. She pads barefoot back over to her soldier and it's as if she takes fire all over again. "You are hot! You're really something," Vovka is enraptured. She holds her hand over his mouth, "Shhh." In a whisper Vovka sets forth simple soldier's instructions to her. He asks the young woman to go to the village store and buy their cheap red wine. They won't sell it to a soldier in uniform, but it would be no problem for her. He shares his main concern with her. They don't need a bottle, they need a whole case of red wine now.

"What for?"

"As payment. They've blocked the road."

"So if you need wine, why have you come to see the lieutenant colonel?"

"Because we're idiots, that's why."

The young woman bursts into tears. She tells how she recently lost her way and was raped. Vovka the sniper whistles in surprise: what do you know. He makes some expression of sympathy and then asks (with curiosity) how many were there?—there were four of them, she sobs, wiping her eyes with the corner of the bedsheet. He wants to get details. But she would rather be silent. She nuzzles his chest with her head, with her mouth. She needs words of consolation, a simple feeling.

They talk: yes, of course she would buy him a bottle of red wine, but only if the sniper goes with her to the store. She would hand the bottle over to him as soon as she buys it. She can't carry a bottle home. After what happened to her—people know, what would they think? . . .

In the other dish is also a lot of food. Groats and a piece of meat from a can. Rubakhin packs it all away. He eats slowly, not greedily. He washes it down with two cups of cold water. The water makes him shiver a little, and he puts on his tunic.

"Let's have a little rest," he tells himself and goes back to the fence.

He lies down, falling into a light slumber. Through the open window of the house next door, into which Vovka vanished, comes the sound of quiet bargaining.

Vovka: . . . I'll buy you a present. A pretty kerchief. Or I'll find you a shawl.

She: But you'll go away.—She cries.

Vovka: So I'll send it to you if I leave. How can you doubt?

Vovka begged her for a long time to bend over. Vovka, who was not particularly tall (he never tried to hide that and readily told the other soldiers about it) liked to embrace big women from behind. How could she not understand? It's so nice when the woman is big. . . . She tries to wiggle out of it, makes excuses. Rubakhin falls asleep to their drawn-out, heated whispering (the words had become indistinguishable).

Outside the store, Vovka had scarcely taken the bottle of wine out of her hands and shoved it into the deep, safe pocket of his army trousers, when he raced back to where he had left Rubakhin. The young woman had done so much for him, and now she shouts, straining her voice with some trepidation out in the street. She shouts after him in rebuke. But Vovka can't be bothered with her anymore. That's it, time to go. He runs down the narrow street. He runs between the wicker fences, taking a short-cut to Lieutenant Colonel Gurov's house. There's news (and what news!). The sniper stood looking over his shoulder outside their crummy little store (waiting for a bottle), and heard about it from some soldiers passing by.

Jumping over the fence, he finds Rubakhin asleep and shakes him awake.

"Rubakha, listen. This is a sure thing: Lieutenant Savkin is headed into the woods for a disarmament operation.

"What?" Rubakhin looks at him sleepily.

The words tumble out of Vovka's mouth; he hurries Rubakhin.

"It's a disarmament operation. We should go with them. We'll grab us a wog. Wouldn't that be great? You said it yourself. . . ."

Rubakhin is fully awake now. Yes, he understood. Yes. That would be just great. Well, yeah, we'll probably get lucky there, we've got to go. The soldiers surreptitiously make their way out of the lieutenant colonel's estate. Cautiously they collect their packs and weapons left standing at the well, they climb over the fence and leave by the neighbor's gate, so that the two men on the terrace don't catch sight of them. And call them back.

They didn't notice them and didn't call them back. They sit.

It's hot. It's quiet. Alibekov sings not too loudly and in a clear voice:

> ". . . If you only kneeeww . . . , how much I looove
> These quiet Moscow nights."

It's quiet.

"People don't change, Alibek."

"You think they don't?"

"They just get old."

"Hm. Like you and me." Alibekov pours a thin stream of tea into his cup. He's tired of bargaining. He feels sad. What's more, he's already said all the words, and now the rights words (according to their own unhurried logic) will reach his old friend Gurov of their own accord. There's no need even to say them aloud.

"Now the good tea's all gone."

"So what."

"Tea's getting more expensive. Food's getting more expensive. But the times aren't changing," Alibekov says in a lazy drawl.

Just then the lieutenant colonel's wife brings two teapots out to replace the empty ones. Tea is getting expensive, there you're right. "Changing times or not, you're bringing me food, my friend," Gurov thinks, also keeping the words to himself for now.

Gurov knows that Alibekov is wiser and more clever than he is. By contrast, the few thoughts Gurov has are solid ones, thought through to crystal clarity over the years, and becoming more like parts of his body—arms, legs—than thoughts.

At one time (in the old days), whenever there were supply line disruptions or even just delays with the soldiers' rations, Gurov would immediately put on his parade dress uniform. He would fasten his decoration and medals to his chest. He would race in an army GAZ-69 jeep (what dust! what wind!) over winding mountain roads to the regional center, finally reaching the colonnaded building he knew so well; and he would walk into it just as briskly (and without even a glance at the visitors and petitioners

man running. "Aha, so Gesha covered me. Two on two."

He didn't grab or try to wrestle the rebel down when he caught up with him (while he dealt with the one that was down, the first one would be sure to get away). With a strong left punch he knocked him into a ditch, into some brittle brush, and he shouted to Gesha, "One of them's in the ditch. Get him," and he dashed after the first one with long hair.

Rubakhin was already going at top speed, but the other was a runner, too. Just as Rubakhin started to catch up with him, he also speeded up. Now they were running at the same speed, twenty-five to thirty feet apart. The fugitive turned around, raised a pistol and fired. Rubakhin saw that he was very young. He fired again (and lost speed). If he hadn't fired, he would have gotten away. He was firing over his left shoulder. The bullets didn't even come close, so Rubakhin stopped ducking each time the rebel aimed his pistol. But he didn't fire all of his bullets, clever guy. He was starting to get away, Rubakhin realized. Without a second's hesitation Rubakhin flung his rifle at his legs. This did the job.

The fugitive howled in pain, jerked, and began to fall. Rubakhin caught up with him in a single leap, pinned him down and grabbed the wrist with his right hand. There was no pistol. He had dropped it when he fell; what a soldier. Rubakhin yanked his hands behind his back, then jerked his arm up, causing pain, of course. The other yelped and went limp. On the same impulse Rubakhin pulled a strap out of his pocket, tied his hands together and sat him down beneath a tree, pushing his weak body up against the trunk—"Sit there." Only now did he straighten up and start roaming around the path, catching his breath and searching for something in the grass with a careful eye—his rifle and the pistol that the fugitive had dropped.

He heard the stomping of feet again. Rubakhin jumped off the path toward the gnarled oak where his captive was sitting. "Quiet," Rubakhin ordered. In a moment several swift, lucky rebels darted past them. Soldiers ran behind them, swearing. Rubakhin stayed out of it. He'd done his job. He glanced at his captive, whose face surprised him. By its youth, to start with, even though such boys of sixteen or seventeen weren't so rare among the rebels. Nice features, soft skin. There was something else about this face that struck him, but what was it. He didn't have time to figure it out.

"Let's go," Rubakhin said, helping him get up since his hands were tied behind his back.

As they were walking, he warned him, "No running away. Don't even think about it. I won't shoot you. But I'll beat you up badly, understand?"

The young prisoner limped. Rubakhin's rifle when he threw it had hurt his leg. Or is he faking it? Captives usually try to evoke sympathy for themselves. They limp. Or they cough a lot.

4

There were lots of disarmed captives, twenty-two altogether. And this is probably why Rubakhin was able to keep his prisoner without much trouble. "This one's mine," Rubakhin said over and over amidst the general commotion, keeping a hand on his shoulder throughout that last-minute confusion when prisoners are being assembled for the march into camp. There was no break in the tension. The prisoners crowded together, afraid of being separated. They clutched onto each other, shouting back and forth in their language. Some of them didn't even have their hands tied. "What do you mean, yours? Look how many of them there are. They're all ours." But Rubakhin shook his head, as if to say those are ours, but this one is mine. Vovka the sniper appeared, as always in the nick of time and when he was needed most. Far more skillfully than Rubakhin, he knew how to tell the truth and blow smoke, both at the same time. "Top priority. Leave it. Got a note from Gurov. For a prisoner exchange," he lied with inspiration. "Fine, but clear it with the lieutenant." "Already done, all clear," Vovka continued breathlessly, telling them that the lieu-tenant colonel was at home drinking tea now (which was true), that the two of them had just come from there (also true), and that Gurov himself had written the note for them. Right, the note was there, back at headquarters.

Vovka looked visibly worn down. Rubakhin cast a baffled glance in his direction: after all, he was the one who ran through the brush after their long-haired captive, he was the one who tackled and bound him, he was the one who had sweated. But it was Vovka who looked worn down.

The captives (once assembled) were taken to the trucks. The soldiers car-ried the weapons separately, and someone kept a tally out loud: seventeen AK-47s, seven pistols, a dozen grenades. Two killed in the chase, two wounded; on our side one wounded and Korotkov killed. The canvas-top trucks pulled out to form a column, and under escort of two armored per-sonnel carriers (one at the head, one at the rear) they gunned their engines, picked up speed and set out for camp. In the vehicles the soldiers, holler-ing excitedly, exchanged stories. They were all hungry.

On their arrival Rubakhin and Vovka the sniper had barely gotten out of the truck with their captive when they strayed from the group. Nobody stopped them. What were they going to do with the prisoners, anyway? The young ones would be released, the seasoned fighters would be held in the guardhouse for a few months, as if in prison. And if some of them try to run, they'll have fun picking them off—this is war. It's possible that these same rebels shot Boyarkov in his sleep (or just as he was opening his eyes). There hadn't been a single scratch on his face. And there were ants. At first Rubakhin and Vovka started to brush the ants off, but when they turned him over they saw a hole gaping in Boyarkov's back. They had shot him point blank, so the bullets didn't disperse and struck his chest in a cluster.

After breaking through the ribs, the bullets forced out all of his guts—on the ground (in the ground) lay fragments of ribs, with the liver, kidneys and rings of intestines on top of them, all of it in a big pool of curdling blood. Several bullets had been caught in the intestines, which were still steaming. Boyarkov lay face down and with a huge hole in his back, and his guts lay in the ground together with the bullets.

Vovka turned towards the mess hall.

". . . taking this one to exchange. The lieutenant colonel gave his permission," Vovka hastened to explain, heading off queries from members of Orlikov's platoon as they passed them.

Stuffed from their meal, they shouted to him to convey their best regards. They asked who'd been captured and who he was being traded for.

"For an exchange," Vovka the sniper kept repeating.

Vanya Bravchenko laughed.

"Hard currency."

Sergeant Khodzhaev shouted, "Good going, nice catch! That's the kind they like. Their leader," and he jerked his head toward the mountains, "their leader really likes them like this."

To elucidate, Khodzhaev laughed, showing his strong, white soldier's teeth.

"You can get back two, three, even five of ours for one like this," he shouted. "They like them the same as girls." And when he met up with them he winked at Rubakhin.

Rubakhin snickered. He suddenly realized what had been bothering him about his captive rebel. The boy was very beautiful.

The prisoner didn't speak Russian particularly well, but of course he understood everything. In spiteful, guttural squeals he yelled something back at Khodzhaev. His cheekbones and face flashed red, making it even more obvious how beautiful he was—his long hair curved down to his shoulders in an almost perfect oval. The line of his lips. The fine definition of his nose. The dark brown eyes forced you to linger on them especially—big, angular, and just barely slanting.

Vovka made a quick deal with the cook. They had to have a good meal before setting out. It was noisy and stuffy around the long plank table. And hot. They sat down at one end, and Vovka instantly extracted the half-empty bottle of wine from his pack. Secretly he shoved it under the table into Rubakhin's hands, so that he could prop it between his knees in the classic maneuver and finish it off unnoticed. "I've left you exactly half, to the drop. Remember who's good to you, Rubakha."

He set a plate down in front of the prisoner: "I don't vant," he answered abruptly. He turned away, shaking his dark locks.

Vovka moved the plate closer to him: "At least sling back some meat. We've got a long way to go."

The prisoner said nothing. Vovka started to worry that he might shove the plate with his elbow, and the extra portion of groats and meat so painstakingly finagled from the cook would wind up on the floor.

He quickly divided the third portion between his and Rubakhin's plates. They ate. It was time to go.

5

At a stream they took turns dipping a plastic cup in the water and drinking from it. The prisoner was obviously dying of thirst. Lurching forward, he fell to his knees in what could pass for collapse, crunching the pebbles. He didn't wait for them to untie his hands or hold the cup to his lips. On his knees, bending his face down to the rushing water, he drank for a long time. His arms, tied behind his back and bruised at the wrists, inclined upward, as if he were praying in some unusual way.

Then he sat on the sand. His face was wet. Pressing his cheek to his shoulder and without the use of his hands, he tried to shake off the drops of water that clung here and there to his face. Rubakhin approached him.

"We would have let you drink. We would have untied your hands, too. What's your hurry?"

He didn't answer. Rubakhin looked at him and with the palm of his hand brushed the water off his chin. His skin was so soft that Rubakhin's hand trembled. He hadn't expected it. But it was true, just like a girl's, he thought.

Their eyes met, and Rubakhin immediately turned away, embarrassed suddenly at his fleeting and not quite decent thoughts.

For an instant the wind rushing through the bushes startled him. Could it be footsteps? His embarrassment subsided (but it only hid, it wasn't completely gone). Rubakhin was a simple soldier—he wasn't immune to human beauty as such. And here again, almost unawares, a new and unknown feeling was stealing up on him. And of course he remembered perfectly how Sergeant Khodzhaev had shouted and winked at him earlier. Now they would have to come face to face. The prisoner couldn't cross the stream on his own. The pebbles were large and the current was strong; but he was barefoot and his foot was so badly swollen at the ankle that he had taken off his sneakers at the very beginning of their trek (for the time being they were in Rubakhin's pack). If he falls once or twice while they cross the stream, he could become totally useless. The current would drag him downstream. There is no choice. And it was natural that Rubakhin—who else?—should carry him across the water. Wasn't he the one who injured his foot by throwing his rifle when they captured him?

A sense of compassion helped Rubakhin; this compassion was very well-timed and came to him from somewhere above, from the sky (but his embarrassment was now rushing back from there, too, together with a new understanding of this dangerous beauty). Rubakhin was confused only for an instant. He picked the boy up in his arms and started carrying him across the stream. The boy recoiled, but Rubakhin's arms were strong and powerful.

"Come on, now, don't kick," he said, and those were roughly the same gruff words he would have said to a woman in a similar situation.

As he carried him he could hear his breathing. The boy intentionally turned his face away from Rubakhin, and yet his hands (untied for the duration of the crossing) were tenaciously clinging to Rubakhin—after all, he didn't want to fall onto the rocks in the water. Like anyone who carries a person in his arms, Rubakhin could see nothing beneath his feet and stepped cautiously. From the corner of his eye he could only see the racing water of the stream in the distance, and against a background of leaping water, the boy's profile, tender, clean, with an unexpectedly pouting lower lip jutting capriciously like a young girl's.

It was here, by the stream, that they made their first stop. To be safe, they got off the path and headed a short distance downstream. Rubakhin held his rifle in his lap with the safety off. They weren't hungry yet, but they drank water several times. Lying on his side, Vovka tuned the radio, which almost inaudibly whistled, bubbled, meowed and burst in an unfamiliar language. As always, Vovka depended on Rubakhin's tested ability to hear a stone under a stranger's foot a mile away.

"Rubakha, I'm gonna sleep. Hear me? I'm going to sleep," he straightforwardly warned, falling into an instantaneous soldier's slumber.

When the vigilant lieutenant had eliminated him from among the candidates for the disarmament operation, Vovka for lack of anything else to do had returned to the house where the young woman lived. (The little house next to the lieutenant colonel's. But Vovka was careful.) Naturally, she scolded and reproached the soldier who had so abruptly abandoned her at the store. But within a minute they were face to face once again, and a minute after that they were in bed. As a result, Vovka was pleasantly exhausted now. He could manage the hike, but during the breaks he instantly pitched into sleep.

Rubakhin found it easier to talk while walking fast.

". . . if you really think about it, are we really enemies? We understand each other. After all, we were friends, weren't we?" Rubakhin argued heatedly and even seemed to insist, hiding the feelings that bothered him in familiar (Soviet) words. And his feet kept marching.

Vovka the sniper snorted.

"Long live the unshakable friendship of peoples!"

Rubakhin of course got the irony, but he said with restraint:

"Vov, I'm not talking to you."

Vovka fell silent, to be on the safe side. But the boy was silent, too.

"I'm the same kind of person as you. And you're the same as me. Why should we fight?'' Rubakhin continued saying words familiar to everyone, but they missed their mark; it turned out that he was pronouncing these trite words to himself and the brush around him. And also the path that led from the stream directly up into the mountains. Rubakhin wanted the boy to object in some way. He wanted to hear his voice. Let him say something. (Rubakhin felt more and more ill at ease.)

As they walked Vovka the sniper flicked a finger and the radio in his pack came to life, began chirping. Vovka flicked his finger again and found a marching song. Rubakhin kept talking. At last he grew tired and quit.

It isn't easy to walk with hands tied (and with a bad foot) when the incline is steep. The captive rebel kept stumbling, walking with difficulty. On one of the inclines he suddenly fell. Somehow he got up, without complaining; yet Rubakhin noticed his crying.

Rubakhin said somewhat rashly, ''I'll untie your hands if you won't run. Give me your word.''

Vovka the sniper heard this (over the music from his radio) and exclaimed, ''Rubakha, are you crazy?''

Vovka was walking in the lead. He swore at such a dumb move. The radio kept playing at high volume.

''Vov, knock it off. I've got to hear.''

''Okay.''

The music stopped.

Rubakhin untied the prisoner's hands—how could he escape from him, from Rubakhin, with a foot like that?

They were moving fairly fast.

The prisoner went first. Vovka, half sleeping, walked next to him. And just behind, silent and all instincts, Rubakhin.

It's gratifying to untie even just a person's hands, even if only for part of the journey. He swallowed, discerning just a hint of something sweet in his throat. It was a rare moment. But this hint aside, he kept alert. The path was getting steeper. Off to one side they passed the mound where they had buried Boyarkov, the drunk. A wonderful place, awash in the light of the evening sun.

When they made camp for the night Rubakhin gave him his woolen socks. This left him with just his boots on his feet. Lights out. (And just the smallest campfire.) Rubakhin took the radio away from Vovka (not a peep at night). The rifle lay, as always, in his lap. He sat with the prisoner to his side and his back to a tree, the hunter's pose he had favored since long ago (vigilant, but permitting him to doze off a bit). Night fell. He half slept. Parallel to his slumber he could hear the prisoner sitting next to him, he could hear and feel him enough so that if the other made even the slightest unorthodox move he would be able to react immediately. But the prisoner didn't even think of flight. He was downhearted (Rubakhin was delving into another soul.) And here both of them dropped off (trusting each other), and then Rubakhin could sense low spirits overcoming the boy again. By day he had tried to act the proud warrior, but now he was obviously succumbing to anguish. What precisely was he so sad about? That day Rubakhin had given him unmistakable indications that they weren't taking him to a military prison or for some other shady purpose, but to return him to his people in exchange for the right to pass. As simple as that: to return him to his people. Seated next to Rubakhin he could feel at ease. He may not know about the trucks and roadblock up ahead, but at least he knows (can sense) that he has nothing to fear. What's more, he can of course sense that Rubakhin likes him. . . . Suddenly Rubakhin felt embarrassed again. Rubakhin stole a sideward glance. The boy was downcast. Even through the darkness the prisoner's face was as beautiful as before and so sad. "Now, now," Rubakhin said amicably, trying to lift his spirits.

And he slowly stretched his arm out. Afraid to disturb the half-profile of his face and the remarkable beauty of his steady gaze, Rubakhin barely brushed the fine cheekbone with his fingers, as if to smooth a long lock of hair that was hanging down over his cheek. The boy didn't jerk his face away. He was quiet. And as it seemed—but it could have just seemed this way—his cheek almost imperceptibly responded to Rubakhin's touch.

As soon as he closed his eyes Vovka the sniper began to relive the sweet, fleeting minutes that had raced past so swiftly in that village house. Moment by moment, the minute and so short-lived joy of a woman's closeness. He slept sitting down, standing up, and while walking. Small wonder that he fell so soundly asleep this night (even though it was his watch) and didn't notice an animal (possibly a wild boar) running past. This shook everyone. It took an overlong time for the snapping of branches in the underbrush to subside. "Do you want them to shoot us in our sleep, too?" Rubakhin gently pulled at the soldier's ear. He got up and listened. It was quiet.

Rubakhin threw some brush on the fire, circled the camp several times, stood looking over the ravine and came back. He sat next to the prisoner, who was still tense after their scare. His shoulders were hunched and he was slumping. The beautiful face had completely vanished in the night. "How are you doing?" he asked straightforwardly. In this instance a question served first and foremost as a way of keeping tabs on the prisoner. Was his sleeping a trick? Has he laid hands on a knife? Has he planned to escape into the night while they sleep (stupidly, because Rubakhin would catch him instantly).

"Fine," he answered curtly. Neither of them said anything for a while.

As it happened, Rubakhin remained sitting next to him after asking his question (why should he change places by the fire every minute?).

Rubakhin patted him on the shoulder. "Don't be afraid. I told you, as soon as we get you there, we're going to give you back to your people. Do you understand?"

He nodded. Yes, he understood. Rubakhin gave a funny snort, "You really are beautiful."

They were silent a while.

"How's the foot?"

"Fine."

"Okay. Got to sleep. We don't have much time. We've got to get some more shut-eye, it'll be morning before you know it."

At this, as if in agreement that it was time to sleep, the captive boy slowly inclined his head to the right onto Rubakhin's shoulder. It was nothing out of the ordinary—this is how soldiers draw out their night's rest, leaning against each other. Then the warmth of his body, together with a current of sensuality (both in distinct waves) began to penetrate in wave after rushing wave from the boy's pressing shoulder into Rubakhin's.

But no. The boy is asleep. The boy is simply asleep, Rubakhin thought, chasing the delusion away. But he immediately tensed and went wooden, as such an overpowering charge of warmth and unexpected tenderness penetrated his shoulder and muffled soul. Rubakhin froze. The boy, either hearing or guessing his guardedness, also cautiously froze. Another minute, and their touch lost all sensuality. They simply sat next to each other.

"Right, so let's get some sleep," Rubakhin said to no one without taking his eyes off the fire's small, red flames.

The prisoner shifted, positioning his head more comfortably on his shoulder. Almost immediately he again began to feel the current of submissive and enticing warmth. This time Rubakhin could make out the boy's quiet trembling, how can that be? . . . what's that?, he wondered in perplexity. Again he withdrew completely, restraining himself (afraid that his response in kind would give him away). But trembling is only that, and you can survive it. Most of all Rubakhin was afraid that the boy would quietly turn his head toward him (all his movements were quiet, palpably ingratiating and devoid of significance at the same time—the person moved a little in his sleep, so what?), that he would turn to face him, almost touching, after which he would inescapably feel his young breath and the closeness of his lips. The moment drew to its climax. Rubakhin also experienced a moment of weakness. His stomach, first among a bundle of organs, could no longer withstand such an unaccustomed sensual overload. A spasm seized at him, and his seasoned soldier's abdominal muscles went rigid as a washboard. Then he was suddenly short of breath. In an instant Rubakhin launched into a coughing fit, and the frightened boy removed his head from his shoulder.

Vovka the sniper awoke.

"You're booming like a cannon. Have you lost your mind? You can hear that half a mile away."

Easy-going Vovka fell right back asleep and started to snore, as if in response, and with such a loud whistle, to boot.

Rubakhin laughed. Some comrade in arms I've got, sleeping non-stop. By day, by night.

The prisoner said slowly and with a smile, "I think he had a woman. Yesterday."

Rubakhin was startled: really? And as he reflected, conceded he was right. "Looks like it."

"I think it was yesterday afternoon."

"That's exactly right."

Both of them laughed, as happens among men in these situations.

But then (very carefully) the young captive asked, "And you, is it long since you had a woman?"

Rubakhin shrugged his shoulders. "Long. A year or so."

"She was very ugly? A dog? I think she was not very pretty. Soldiers never have pretty women."

There was a long, uncomfortable pause. Rubakhin could feel a rock descending on his neck (and pressing, pressing).

By early morning the fire was completely extinguished. To keep from freezing, Vovka had joined them, pressing his face and shoulders against Rubakhin's back. From the other side the prisoner huddled close to Rubakhin, luring the soldier all night long by his tempting warmth. In this way, keeping each other warm, the three of them made it through till morning.

They put a pot with water on the fire.

"Let's treat ourselves to some tea," Rubakhin said with some sense of guilt for the disturbing events of the night before.

Now, since waking up, he had stopped hiding that guilt, though he still wasn't sure what it meant: all at once Rubakhin started looking after the boy. (This concerned him. He would never have expected this of himself.) His hands started to fidget, as though from some affliction. He steeped two glasses of tea for him. He threw in some sugar cubes, stirred it with a clattery spoon and handed it to him. He let him keep his socks, for good it seemed—don't take them off, you'll need them—this is the kind of concern that emerged.

Rubakhin began to fuss over him; he kept stoking the fire so he would be warmer.

The prisoner drank his tea. He sat on his haunches, watching Rubakhin's hands as they moved.

"The socks are warm. Good ones," he praised them, shifting his gaze to his feet.

"My mother knitted them."

"Ahh."

"Don't take them off. I told you you'll need them. I'll wrap something around my feet.''

The boy pulled a comb out of his pocket and attended to his hair: he spent a long time combing it. From time to time he would proudly shake his head, then, in long, measured strokes, comb his hair down to the shoulders again. A sense of his own beauty was as natural to him as breathing.

In the thick, warm woolen socks the boy walked with greater assurance. All around he was behaving with more confidence. The sadness was gone from his eyes. He undoubtedly noticed that Rubakhin was uncomfortable with the direction their relations had taken. He may even have enjoyed this. He stole glances at Rubakhin, at his hands, his rifle, and he smiled fleetingly to himself at the effortless victory he had won over this huge, powerful, timid man.

When they reached a stream he didn't remove his socks. He stood waiting for Rubakhin to pick him up. This time the boy's hand didn't clutch onto his collar; unashamedly he put his soft arms around Rubakhin's neck as he carried him over the stream. Sometimes, depending on their pace, he would move his hand under the other's tunic, seeking the most comfortable hold.

Rubakhin took Vovka the sniper's radio away from him again and signaled him to keep quiet: he was in charge, and as the path widened and became more traveled here, he trusted no one (as far as the white cliff itself). But at the same time it was safer because of the way the two narrow paths diverged (or converged, depending on how you viewed them).

The cliff (in soldier's parlance) was called the Nose. Its big, white, triangular stone prominence approached them like the bow of a ship, looming larger and larger.

They had already started to climb up the mountain's base, directly under the cliff, working their way through the tangled brush. *This can't be!* it flashed through the soldier's mind when he heard the danger approaching up above (from both the right and the left). People were descending on both sides of the cliff. Foreign, firm, yet quick and undisciplined footsteps. *Bastards.*

That two separate enemy formations should come together at exactly the same minute and take up both of the paths—that *just can't be!* The cliff's great advantage was that it allowed you to hear and switch paths in time.

Now they wouldn't be able to move forward in either direction. Nor could they dash back from beneath the cliff across the open space behind them into the forest. There were three of them, and one of them was a prisoner. They would spot them in no time and either shoot them or drive them back into the forest and corner them. *This can't be!* The same thought squeaked plaintively for the third time, refusing to die (and then left, vanished, abandoned him). Now he was all instinct. He drew the cold air in through his nostrils. Not just their footsteps. In the almost total stillness of the air he could hear the grass slowly rising in their wake.

"Shhh."

He pressed a finger to his lips. Vovka understood, and he nodded toward the prisoner, what about him? Rubakhin glanced at his face: the boy also instantly understood (he understood that these were his people coming, his forehead and cheeks were slowly filling with color—a sign of unpredictable behavior).

"Aw, so be it," Rubakhin said to himself as he readied his rifle for combat. He patted his spare ammunition cartridges. But the thought of combat (like every thought in a moment of danger) also receded (abandoned him), unwilling to assume the burden of responsibility.

Instinct commanded vigilance. And patience. He drew the cold air in deeply through his nostrils. The grass rustled with quiet foreboding. The footsteps were getting closer. *No.* There were lots of them. Too many. Rubakhin looked again, reading the prisoner's face and trying to guess—how would he. . . what would he. . . . Would he lie low and keep quiet for fear of being killed (that would be nice), or would he dash out to meet them, with joy and stupidity in his huge, half-crazed eyes (and, most importantly, shouting).

Without taking his eyes off the rebels walking down the left-hand path (this group was already very close and would walk past them first), Rubakhin reached his arm back and carefully touched the prisoner's body. The boy was trembling slightly, like a woman trembles in anticipation of an embrace. Rubakhin touched his neck and felt his way to the face, and with a gentle touch put his palm and fingers over the beautiful lips, over the mouth (which had to be quiet); the lips were trembling slightly.

Slowly, Rubakhin pulled the boy closer to him (not taking his eyes off the left-hand path, off the column of rebels as those in the rear caught up with the others). Vovka kept track of the column on the right: they could already hear footsteps and falling stones from that one, too. One of the soldiers, his rifle slung over his shoulder, kept banging it against the gun of the rebel behind him.

The boy didn't resist Rubakhin. Taking him by the shoulder, Rubakhin turned the boy toward himself—the boy (who was shorter) was already straining toward him, pressing close to him, nuzzling the area of the carotid artery just below his unshaven chin with his lips. Confused, the boy was shaking. "N-n," he exhaled faintly, just like a woman, articulating his no, not as refusal, but as timidity, while Rubakhin observed him and waited (guarding against a shriek). And how his eyes widened as they tried to circumvent Rubakhin's and penetrate air and sky to catch sight of his own people. He opened his mouth, but not to scream. Perhaps he only wanted to breathe in more deeply. But Rubakhin's other hand set the rifle down on the ground and then pressed down over the half-opened mouth with its beautiful lips and the slightly quivering nose. "N-ne," the captive youth tried to finish saying something, but couldn't. His body lurched forward, his legs strained, but there was no support left beneath them. Rubakhin had lifted him off the ground. He held the boy in his embrace, not letting his legs touch the tell-tale bushes or stones that would roll noisily down the slope. With the same arm that embraced him, Rubakhin reached around to get his neck in a stranglehold. Then he squeezed. Beauty was unable to save him. A few convulsions, and that was it.

Beneath the cliff where the paths met, guttural exclamations could be heard. The columns had discovered each other. There followed greetings, questions—how? what? where are you heading? (the most likely questions), they slapped each other on the shoulders. They laughed. One of the rebels decided to use the break to urinate. He ran up to the cliff face, where it would be more convenient. He didn't know he was in someone's sights. He stood only a few yards away from the bushes that sheltered the three— two of them alive, lying in hiding, the third dead. He finished urinating, hiccuped, hiked up his trousers and ran off.

After the columns had moved past and their voices and footsteps, receding into the lowlands, had faded completely, the two soldiers with their rifles brought the dead body out of the bushes. They carried it into a sparse wood, not far down the path to the left, where Rubakhin recalled a dry, bare open area with soft, loamy ground. They dug a ditch, scooping the sand out with flat stones. Vovka the sniper asked if Rubakhin planned to take back his socks. Rubakhin shook his head. And not a word about the person to whom they had already grown accustomed. For half a minute they sat silently beside the grave. How could they sit any longer? This was war.

6

Nothing has changed. The two trucks—Rubakhin can see them from afar—are standing in the same place.

The road abruptly squeezes through a passage between high cliffs, but the narrow canyon is guarded by rebels. The trucks have been shot at, but randomly. If they moved forward even an inch, the rebels would turn them into Swiss cheese. The trucks have been standing here for three days. The rebels want weapons—then they'll let them pass.

". . . but we're not carrying any rifles. We don't have any weapons," come shouts from the direction of the trucks. Someone fires a shot from the cliff in reply, or a hail of shots, a whole burst. Followed by laughter— ha, ha, ha!—such boisterous, forceful, childishly triumphant laughter rolling down from the heights.

The soldiers escorting the trucks and the drivers (altogether six men) had retreated amid bushes at the side of the road, behind the cover of the trucks. Their nomadic life is simple—cooking food on a fire and sleeping.

As Rubakhin and Vovka the sniper draw closer, Rubakhin notices a fire on the cliff where the ambushers are, a pale, daytime fire—the rebels were also fixing their dinner. It was a sluggish war. Why not eat your fill and drink some hot tea as long as you've got the chance?

As Rubakhin and Vovka approach, they are, of course, noticed from the cliff. The rebels have sharp eyes. And even though they can see that these are the same two that had left before (without bringing back anything visible), they shoot at them from the cliff, just in case. A burst of fire. And another.

Rubakhin and Vovka the sniper had already joined up with their side.

The sergeant-major thrust his paunch forward. He asks Rubakhin, "Well, are we getting help?"

"Not shit."

Rubakhin didn't bother to explain.

"And you didn't manage to catch yourselves a prisoner?"

"Uh-uh."

Rubakhin asked for water. He took a long drink from a bucket, spilling the water onto his tunic and chest. Then he groggily stepped to one side and, without choosing a place, collapsed amid the bushes to sleep. The grass hadn't yet sprung back from when he slept in this same place two days ago, when they poked him in the side and sent him to get help (and with Vovka as company). He sank up to his ears into the trampled grass, without hearing the sergeant-major, who was bawling him out. He didn't give a damn. He was too tired.

Vovka sat beneath the shade of a tree, stretched out his legs, and pushed his cap down over his eyes. To make fun of the drivers, he asked, "And how about you, didn't find the detour? . . . you don't say!"

"There is no detour," they answered.

The drivers lay in the tall grass. One of these numskulls was skillfully rolling himself a cigarette out of a piece of newspaper.

Sergeant-Major Beregovoy, exasperated with the failure of the mission, was trying to open negotiations again.

"Hey!" he shouted. "Listen to me. Hey!" he shouted in what he believed was a trustworthy voice. "I swear to you, there's nothing at all in the trucks. Not weapons, not food. We're empty-handed. Let your person come down here and see for himself. We'll show him everything. We won't shoot. Hey, do you hear?"

They sent gunfire in reply. And rollicking laughter.

"Your mothers!" the sergeant-major swore.

The rebels were firing helter skelter. They were firing for so long and so senselessly that the sergeant-major swore again and called out, "Vov, come over here."

Both of the drivers lying in the grass came to life. "Vov, Vov, come here. Show these mountain men how to shoot."

Vovka the sniper yawned and lazily tore himself from the tree. (Since he had been leaning against it he had been so comfortable.)

But once he took up his rifle, he began to aim it with dispatch. He stretched himself out comfortably in the grass, propped up his rifle, and one after the other began to capture in his telescopic sights the figures cavorting on the cliff looming over the left side of the road. There were lots of them. They were all nicely visible. He could probably hit them even without his scope.

Just then one of them standing at the edge of the cliff began to make jeering ululations.

"Vov, care to hit him?" one of the drivers asked.

"What the hell do I need him for?" Vovka snorted.

He paused, and added, "I like taking aim and pulling the trigger. I know when I've scored even without a bullet."

The impossibility of the situation was clear to everyone: if he were to kill one of the rebels, the trucks would go nowhere.

"That one up there shouting you can imagine I've knocked off." Vovka pulled the trigger of his unloaded rifle. He was having fun.

He aimed, dashingly pulled the trigger and the rifle clicked again. "And imagine I've popped that one off, too. Now this one—I can rip half of this guy's ass off. Can't kill him, because he's behind a tree, but rip his ass off, no problem."

Now and then, catching sight of some object in the possession of one of the rebels as it glinted in the sun—a bottle of vodka or (and this happened one morning) an excellent Chinese thermos, Vovka would take careful aim and blow the object to pieces. But this time he couldn't find anything appealing.

Meanwhile, Rubakhin slept fitfully. He was continually being visited by one and the same unsettling, bad dream (or perhaps, having burrowed into the grass, Rubakhin called it on himself): the beautiful face of the captive boy.

"Vovka. Give me a smoke (and what kind of fun can it be to hunt people in your crosshairs)?"

"Just a second." Vovka kept aiming. Hooked on his game, he ran his crosshairs along the outline of the cliff: along the edge of a rock . . . along a mountain shrub . . . along the trunk of a tree. Aha. He noticed an emaciated rebel; standing next to a tree he was chopping away at his long hair with a pair of scissors. A haircut is a very personal thing. His mirror flashed, giving a signal. In an instant Vovka loaded and caught it in his sights. He pulled the trigger and the silvery puddle affixed to the trunk flew into tiny pieces. In reply there came curses, as always, and the usual scattershot. And it was just as though cranes were calling beyond the overhang of the cliff. "Gulyal—kilyal—lyal—kilyal—sniper!" The figures on the cliff started scurrying around—they shouted, howled, and whooped. But then—apparently by command—they fell silent. For some time they stopped showing themselves (and just in general behaved more modestly). And, naturally, they thought they were out of range. Vovka the sniper saw not just their hiding heads and Adam's apples, their bellies—he could see even the buttons on their shirts, and for fun he trained his sights on one after the other of them.

"Vovka, as you were!" the sergeant-major pulled him down.

"Okay, all done," the sniper responded, picking his rifle up and heading toward the tall grass (with the same simple infantryman's thought—to sleep).

Rubakhin was losing: the boy's face refused to stay long before his eyes. The face would disintegrate as soon as it appeared. It would get blurry, losing its essence and leaving only some indistinct and uninteresting handsomeness behind. Anyone's face. Forgotten. The image melted. As if in farewell (bidding farewell and possibly forgiving him), the boy once again acquired more or less distinct features (and how it flared). His face. But not just his face, there was the boy himself. It looked as though he was about to say something. He stepped closer and threw his arms around Rubakhin's neck (as Rubakhin had done back at the cliff). But his slender hands proved as soft as a young woman's—impetuous, but gentle. And Rubakhin (who was on his guard) realized in time that he risked embarrassing himself in his sleep. He ground his teeth, driving the specter away with a great effort, and immediately awoke to an aching weight in his crotch.

"Sure be good to have a smoke," he said hoarsely when he woke up. He heard gunfire.

It may have been the gunshots that woke him up. The thin stream of a rifle burst—chink, chink, chink, chink, chink—sent small stones flying and churned up swirls of dust beside the frozen trucks. The trucks stood there. (Small concern for Rubakhin.) Eventually they would have to let them pass.

Not far away Vovka the sniper slept in the grass, holding his rifle. Vovka had some strong cigarettes now (he had bought them in the village store at the same time as the red wine). The cigarettes were visible, sticking out of his shirt pocket. Rubakhin took one of them. Vovka was quietly snuffling in his sleep.

Rubakhin smoked, inhaling slowly. He lay on his back, looking at the sky: to the right and left, impinging on his peripheral vision, clustered the same mountains that had surrounded him here and wouldn't let him go. Rubakhin has done his duty. Each time he was ready to send everything and everybody to bloody hell (and go home once and for all, back to the steppes beyond the Don), he would hastily pack his battered suitcase and . . . and stay. "And what's so special about this place, anyway? The mountains?" he said out loud, in anger, not at anyone else, but at himself. What can be interesting about a frigid army barrack? For that matter, what was so interesting about these mountains themselves?'' he thought vexatiously. He was about to add, for how many years now? But instead he said for how many centuries? It was as if he had misspoken. The words jumped out of the shadows, and the astonished soldier began to contemplate this subtle thought that had lain in the depths of his consciousness. Gray, mossy canyons. The mountain dwellers' poor, squalid shacks stuck together like birds' nests. But then, the mountains!? Here and there peaks, yellow in the sunlight, crowded together. Mountains. Mountains. Mountains. For how many years now had their majesty, their silent solemnity haunted his heart? But just what was it their beauty was trying to tell him? Why did it call him?

Vassily Aksyonov (b. 1932)

AROUND DUPONT

[V raione ploshchadi Dupont]

Translated by Alla Zbinovsky

VASSILY AKSYONOV was born into an intellectual Muscovite family in 1932. He is known as a typical "man of the 60s," since his early stories embody the youthful idealism of the post-Stalin generation. In 1979 he was involved in the attempt to publish *Metropol,* a collection of official and underground writers. For this he was exiled from the Soviet Union in 1980 and has since lived and worked in the United States. He currently lives with his wife in Washington, D.C. His works include such novels as *Ticket to the Stars, The Island of Crimea, The Burn,* and a new trilogy, *Moskovskaya saga,* partially translated into English as *Generations of Winter.* The story "Around Dupont" appeared originally in *The New Yorker* (Nov. 20, 1995).

ZHENYA KATZNELSON had vanished. In America he went by the name Gene Katzen. He was a freelancer at the editorial offices of a journal, and his colleagues hadn't noticed his absence right away. Generally speaking, the journal was not quite a journal, but more a kind of society—an association, if you will, that monitored democratic and tyrannical systems. There was, of course, a large Russian division, and Zhenya showed up there every day, although he really didn't need to. Perhaps he felt that it was his duty to put in a daily appearance, or perhaps he was motivated by some sort of unconscious shrewdness: turn up every day, get them used to your being there, and then they'll take you on full-time. The situation was fairly typical. Russian freelancers in other Washington establishments similar to this one tended to sway with the wind, to use a worn-out philosophical metaphor, like "thinking reeds."

This metaphor, I should note, was quite appropriate in Zhenya's case. Zhenya had always swayed slightly with some sort of internal storm. If you happened to drop by the offices of *Constitution*—that was the name of the journal—then suddenly, in the midst of all the exaggerated efficiency, a distinct Moscow type would teeter toward you from the wall. A good-looking man with large deer eyes, forty-something. Well, the eyes looked about forty, but he had the physique of a much younger man. He always wore a short jacket and jeans, tennis shoes—you know, that youthful style popular everywhere, Dupont Circle being no exception.

I still remembered him from Moscow, or at least I thought I remembered him. I wouldn't rule out the possibility that we found ourselves on numerous occasions around the same table with some boisterous artistic types. At any rate, he constantly reminisced about different people from Moscow, quite often celebrities. Had I heard how Oleg was doing, or Galka, or a certain Justinas? We would go out for a smoke—there was already a fierce campaign at the journal for the eradication of nicotine in the workplace— and, standing on the stairwell, we would swap five-year-old Moscow gossip. Zhenya's eyes would then begin to shine with a certain boldness, and his shakiness would subside. It was obvious that those old Moscow days had not been the worst in his life.

Once, he gave me his curriculum vitae, asking me to put in some good words from him around town. The vita reflected the not untypical fate of an artistic Russian boy: graduated from an architectural institute, published a book of poems, played in a jazz-rock band called Weapons Warehouse, lectured on ancient architecture at the Knowledge Society, appeared in a film, put on a play, and . . . emigrated.

Now, many of us émigrés tend to overly dramatize or even heroicize our deed. Such rebellious angels of socialism! "We voted against Soviet power with our feet!" However, once you voted with your feet, you had to give the old bitch a kick up the ass at least once, didn't you? You left, so you left; why go on and on about who voted with what against the old lady, and behave smugly to those left behind to boot?

Zhenya Katznelson was not one of those types whose "deed" filled them with self-importance. He obviously yearned for his previous existence— the songs of Okudzhava, Galich, Vysotsky, Veronika Dolina, and everything connected with that stirring Moscow life, things beyond the comprehension of the journal *Constitution*. He had been a resident in America since the mid-seventies—in other words, for more than ten years before he vanished. To put it mildly, he hadn't really made it as an artist. At *Constitution* he worked primarily at sorting out the Soviet press, producing a digest for the directors, and doing some translations. Somehow, money trickled in fairly steadily, which eventually allowed him to take out a loan from the bank to buy an apartment. I remember that he was extremely excited, and proud of this state of affairs. Imagine, I'll get my own house! You know, I'll get a dog! We'll live together, my setter and I. What a poor thing, I thought then, rather strangely. What a poor thing he really is, I thought for some unknown reason in some nineteenth-century Lermontovian manner.

It seems I never came across Zhenya outside the *Constitution* offices, and definitely never at "Russiantonian" or at purely "Washingtonian" parties, or at mixed gatherings. Someone somewhere said that Katznelson was extremely shy. Someone else guffawed like a soldier: "Friends, I don't like those quiet ones!" No, I beg your pardon, that's not right. Once, my wife invited him to a noisy party. He stood there with a drink in his hand, so pale, not himself, that in Russia they'd say he was "out of his plate," if that could be said about a party where there wasn't one real plate, only paper ones: he was an émigré version of the "superfluous man." It seems we then exchanged a few sentences about the schism in the Moscow Art Theatre, or maybe it wasn't then at our place but at the place where he and I usually met, on the smoking stairwell at *Constitution*.

Anyway, he disappeared. The Bulgarian philosopher Valerian Avelianov informed me of this by telephone. It seemed that Zhenya hadn't turned up at the journal for two weeks. At least two weeks, if not three. Perhaps even a month. Finally, they decided to call me, since they considered me to be on friendly terms with Katznelson. It was a curious thing: if our relationship was considered a friendship, I wonder what they considered to be mere fellowship in that international agency for the study of tyranny.

My wife started to call all our friends and acquaintances. Nobody even knew where Zhenya lived, where that exciting condominium he had bought was situated. Someone remembered seeing him once at Dupont Circle, quite a while before his disappearance, with a young Irish setter, called Mikhail, on a leash. Or maybe the dog's name was Kuzma? One woman presumed that a particular group of New Yorkers would certainly know where Katznelson had gone, because he definitely hung out with that crowd. This was news to me. He had never mentioned anything about the company he kept in New York. Nobody in Washington knew any names, and everyone made helpless gestures—they certainly couldn't call the entire Manhattan émigré community.

As a result of the alarm raised by the babbling Russians, *Constitution* made an official police inquiry. The police didn't have anything on Gene Katzen. Then someone surmised that he could have returned to Moscow; the climate was different there now, the Communists were behaving more decently. At the journal, someone remembered that he had recently got into some trouble because of Moscow. People from this organization couldn't go to Moscow without permission from the higher-ups, and one time a colleague, Agrippina Priestova, who was in Moscow with official permission, saw the permissionless Katznelson on Gorky Street. On her return, she thought it her duty to inform on him, and if this hadn't happened in America, you would have called her a "snitch." Katznelson was subsequently summoned to the personnel office. Recalling this incident, Valerian Avelianov called it a flagrant violation of Zhenya's civil rights, and said he wouldn't be a bit surprised if he found out Zhenya had taken off for Moscow after such a humiliation. On the other hand, someone, perhaps that same insidious Agrippina Priestova, allowed that Katznelson could have easily infiltrated the organization as a Soviet mole.

After these conversations, it became clear to everyone that interest in the affair had subsided, and that soon the whole community would forget about the missing Katznelson. It was just then that my wife unexpectedly discovered the address of the Katznelson condominium and went out in search of it, taking a friend along for protection.

She returned empty-handed, full of indignation about American procedures: this condo in Adams Morgan was like a fortress; it was impossible to get inside; nobody would ever open the door if the person you were visiting was not in. And as for the superintendent, he just shrugged his shoulders: he didn't have sufficient grounds on which to infringe on the privacy of a resident, since all the bills for the current month had been paid. Only if the payments were to stop might the homeowners' association, after conferring with the bank, consider putting before the appropriate authorities the question of a forced entry into the unit owned by Mr. Katzen. In the meantime, ladies, he had said, I can only advise you to go to the police.

So I went myself, and in a quarter of an hour arrived at the foot of an imposing structure five or six blocks away from the lively scene at Dupont Circle. The building was called the Victoria, a fact announced in big letters over the awning of the main entrance. The peak of the awning looked like the spread fin of a flying fish and was out of place against the somber façade and the narrow windows made of mirrored glass. This masterpiece of commercial architecture from the yuppie era was reminiscent of a model medium-security prison. All the necessary conveniences were implied, and in the inner courtyard—in other words, in the guarded space—there was supposed to be a solarium and a pool, all very carefully planned and comfortable, hinting at some as yet unnamed American socialism.

I already knew the number of the Katznelson unit, B-108A, and to clear my conscience I tried calling Gene from the entrance. I got his machine, where he very politely and without any trace of an accent apologized for his absence and invited me to leave a message. And then a black gentleman came out of his building holding the door open inquisitively: Well, are you coming in? It seemed that my appearance, and even more so the make of my car, which was parked at the entrance, didn't raise any doubts in him about my gaining access to this residential citadel. I asked him if he knew Gene Katzen from number B-108A. He didn't. Why don't you just knock on his door, he suggested. Maybe his phone isn't working, or some other nonsense. I entered.

It was around three in the afternoon, and it seemed the people who lived here all worked, since I didn't see a soul as I wandered through the lobby and some short hallways on the first floor. In such buildings, one must always be on guard so as not to fall into a claustrophobic trap. From one side of a door a doorknob might turn, while from the other side it might not, and you could find yourself in a dimly lit hallway for eternity. Nobody would ever respond to your cries for help. Perhaps Gene Katzen has been stuck in here somewhere, trembling, for three weeks now, I thought. Rushing about, I ran down a steel staircase, grabbing the doorknobs at every floor, all of them immobile. "Hey, is there anyone around here?" I yelled in a deliberately robust voice, while my insides were churning: You're in a scrape now. Suddenly, an illuminated "Exit" sign appeared, and it proved true to its word. Turning the doorknob and pressing against the door with my knee, I fell out into the inner courtyard of the Victoria. Just then, a formation of geese crossed the square of sky above, heading out to their favorite place in the Potomac Palisades, on the bank of the spacious, vibrant river canyon.

One side of the square was defined by the façade of a tall apartment building, while the three other sides were made up of rows of stacked units, each with its own entrance. Zhenya's place was in one of these rows—there. I began banging on the door. I felt as if I were knocking on a block of granite. No response. A Latino woman walked by, pushing a white baby in a stroller. In answer to my question, she threw up her hands: Don't understand, haven't got a clue. The baby showed me his rattle. He obviously wasn't privy to the secrets of this massive abode. One after another, several more of Katznelson's neighbors passed by. I dutifully asked each of them about the missing Katzen, so that in that distant place where these matters are taken into account, it would sink in that this one man was sincerely trying to find the other one. None of those interrogated knew the inhabitant of this town house, or had ever even seen him. Everyone shrugged their shoulders as if to say, "Why on earth should we know anyone who lives here?" And then the courtyard was empty, and the whole of the Victoria again became an alien monolith.

Good, so I'd done everything I could. At any rate, I had done more than all the other co-workers of the missing man put together. I had barely escaped from that claustrophobic snare! Couldn't really break down the door, now, could I? Let the proper authorities break it down, I thought. I can set out for home with a clear conscience, and think about the alienation of man in the modern world, about all this odious existentialism. I started back with all kinds of justifications for my decision. The car, with the calm befitting its model, continued to wait, its emergency lights flashing. When I was already almost out of there, it crossed my mind that this town house might have another exit out onto a parallel street.

The parallel street turned out to be one of those it is inadvisable to visit. In America it often happens that one street is considered "decent" and the next inadvisable to walk on. I drove over there and saw a group wearing baseball caps turned backward and bright pants. Well, it was obvious they were selling ecstasy powder. A metal fence stood in front of a dilapidated shack with a warped, rusty "Fish" sign. This was how the slummy side of the street looked, while the "decent" side presented a row of town houses from the Victoria condominium, with separate entrances. Slowly I rode alongside this row, checking the numbers: B-104A, B-105A, B-106A, B-107A. . . . The door to B-108A was ajar! Leaping out of the car, I was just about to fling myself into the apartment, but then the tendons in my legs prudently tugged me back. Katznelson had been missing for weeks, but the door to his apartment was open. No, I couldn't cross over the threshold! First of all, I shouldn't go in without the police, and, second of all, I should take pity on my nerves; who knows what I'd find in there.

While all this was passing through my mind, a young man came out of the neighboring door, marked B-109A.

"Excuse me, have you seen Gene Katzen?" I asked. The young man wrinkled his balding forehead, swaying on his sprightly, athletic legs: he was getting ready to go out for a run.

"Who is this Gene Katzen?"

"It's your neighbor, your next-door neighbor, after all, from over there!" I said, my voice rising unnaturally.

The young man winced slightly, glanced at his black watch with a yellow dial, and, at a loss for words, mumbled, "Thanks for telling me. I didn't know his name. What happened?" I explained that his neighbor had disappeared, but his door was ajar. Had the jogger (in his youthful absent-mindedness) noticed anything unusual? Sorry for all the trouble. He grabbed his left ankle with his left hand, and while pressing the ankle to his buttock reached his right hand behind his neck, making such a resounding crack that it frightened us both.

"Excuse me for doing this, it just happens automatically," he said. "By the way, I've noticed this door on the left has been open for quite a while. How long? Well, at least two weeks, if not three." With those words, he briskly ran off past the ecstasy venders, turning the corner into the "decent" streets. I was left alone by the door that gaped into the darkness like the entrance to a pyramid.

It didn't occur to me to call 911 and *Constitution* right away, but when I finally did I mumbled indecisively, because I didn't quite understand my role in this whole affair. In about fifteen minutes, they all arrived at the same time: the cops, and my colleagues from tyranny-monitoring—V. Avelianov, Klarissa Sonovna, Montassar Bdar, and of course the ever-present Agrippina. This last was making more of a fuss than anyone else, forcing herself on the cops, going on and on about Zhenya's "instability."

The police listened to everyone courteously, but with a decided lack of interest. Then they entered the apartment sideways, holding their guns over their heads. Barely ten minutes went by before they returned, calmly opening the door wide. There hadn't been a trace of any wrongdoing. They hadn't found anything, except a light layer of dust. Here's our phone number, ladies and gentlemen, let's keep in touch. In a few days we'll most certainly be able to answer your questions. In the United States, eighty-seven per cent of those missing are found sooner or later.

I forgot to mention that all this was taking place in autumn. The parks were turning crimson-purple and lemon-yellow, the leaves brightening into a graphic display; a cognac shade was thickening in the oak twilight. Not only the bronchial wisps but also the alveoli of the majestic mid-Atlantic flora began to shine through. With characteristic flightiness, the passersby had already managed to forget the gruelling steam bath of summer and were now enthusiastically starting up new projects: some busied themselves with love affairs, some with real-estate transactions. All took great pleasure in the cool, quickly darkening evening skies and from their still light coats worn with already warm scarves. In a word, bliss had arrived, which in some years could last many weeks and would not even be affected by political or sexual scandals on the Hill.

It was on one of these evenings that I dropped by a bookstore-café, to drink some cappuccino and leaf through some literary publications. As I stood in line at the coffee machine, someone called out to me in the Russian manner—that is, by my first name and patronymic. Behind me stood a large man with half-gray Rastafarian ringlets and a fleshy nose, which would have dominated his whole morose, stagnant face if it weren't for a silver earring in his left ear that at this moment happened to glimmer against the dying embers under the green sunset. It was as if the earring were chiming, Don't chase me away!

"I was walking behind you, but couldn't decide whether to call out to you. Figured you wouldn't recognize me. Well, do you?"

Of course I recognized him. A Muscovite with a strange last name. An art historian and a historian of art. Yes, precisely, Alexander Congusto. Alik. It had been twenty years since we had last seen each other. I held out my hand to him. He didn't shake it, but smiled amicably and joined me as I sat down at a table. "I'm so glad to see you, I don't remember whether we addressed each other formally or as friends. You're not going to believe this—I was planning to call you, but I couldn't make up my mind whether I should. And then here you appear, getting coffee right in front of me. I heard you're searching for Zhenya Katznelson, and I've just come down from New York to visit him. Well, yes, I just saw him an hour ago. The news is not good. He's dying. He's in Sibley Memorial Hospital, in the intensive-care unit. Well, yes, you do understand, you do know the story of our circle of friends. You don't? Well, he's got an advanced case of AIDS, which cannot be helped. As they say in Russian, SPID, in high speed."

> So it was such a simple story
> We got a bottle of wine
> The window like a faraway sea
> Was turning lavender this time.
> "You'll have to pay for all you've had in life,
> For what made you drunk on the earth,"
> Sang the Afro-Asian
> In a Dupont Circle café.

"We were all from the Moscow 'blue division,' and in the mid-seventies we all decided to emigrate," Congusto explained. "We couldn't stand being degraded by those disgusting 'law-enforcement agencies.' The criminal code gave the pigs the right to throw any one of us behind bars. And you do know what awaits a queer in the camps? Gang rape by filthy bastards who don't give a damn what they screw: a goat, a human being, or a telephone pole.

"All of our secret gatherings—Kuzmin poetry readings, Somov exhibits and Somov-like exhibits of etchings, with some kind of contraband cassette playing—everyone quivering at any sound from the door. . . . Throughout all this, we knew very well there was a burgeoning movement in the United States celebrating our culture. Of course, if the chance of clearing out hadn't come, we would have stayed and tolerated the situation, but the opportunity suddenly arose, and seven of us—the closest of the friends and lovers in the group—made up our minds to submit applications for Israeli visas. Everyone, of course, had discovered their Jewish relations, even the Russian aristocrats—you know who I mean. You don't? Well, Yurka Ludenishchev-Kurguzov, Vitasik Treshchokin-Sarantsev, and, well, Borka Gretsky-Sterzhen. . . . Didn't you know they were gay? I thought everyone knew all about us.

"We all got together in New York at the height of the gay carnival, in 1978. We had been told that freedom awaited us, but still we never expected it to be so carnivalesque. It was as if we were in a state of endless ecstasy. I would wake up every morning with ecstasy and go to sleep with it as well, if I slept at all back then. In fact, I copulated with ecstasy from morning to night and back again. Whatever guises it would don, it was still just ecstasy, and it and I fucked. Understand, old man? Well, it's just as well you don't.

"We were given a hero's welcome and dragged from city to city, from coast to coast—L.A. and San Francisco, Chicago, New Orleans, Cape Cod and Southampton in the summers, Key West in the winters—and we were surrounded by people just like us! Like us!

"A year passed this way, and another year, and then somehow, without even noticing, we ourselves began to shy away from the jubilant gay masses. Suddenly, something began to repel us in this boundless blue sea. The movement had turned out to be overly popular. In Moscow and Peter, homosexuality was taken as a sign of refinement—we considered ourselves the élite—and here we suddenly were among vulgar salesmen, roaring with laughter and yelling across the whole bar about who fucked whom and how hard up the ass. These festivals began to seem obscene to us, with all the frolicking backsides, and cat tails hanging from perineums. Someone from our group, maybe even Zhenya, once said, Hey, boys, don't you think that out of this ten per cent (at that time it was believed that ten per cent of the population were overtly or latently gay) the vast majority are not really gay but just doing it because it's the 'in' thing to do among the yokels?

"Here is a paradox of paradoxes: We suddenly remembered our secret gatherings in the Union with an almost hysterical nostalgia. Again, as in the old days, we read Kuzmin's poetry, as if officiating at a holy sacrament:

> Your tender glance
> Luring and clever
> What a pleasant dance
> Resounding with laughter
> Or Marivo's pen so impulsive
> Your nose Pierrot
> The curve of your lips so entrancing
> They spin my mind, like the Marriage of Figaro!

You see, we considered ourselves the revivalists of the Silver Age, the time of those famous Russian gays—Kuzmin, Somov, Diaghilev. . . . And no matter how inebriated we got after ingesting alcoholic Soviet sludge, we paid allegiance to the 'tenderness of the world,' to 'erotic kindness,' and 'the last infatuation.' We dreamt of flight, repeating the words of our idol: 'Dying every minute, will I see the new Arion?' And so we saw what really was the newest Arion, with frolicking mobs carrying political slogans on the shores.

"We began to avoid the various mass bacchanalia, but it was already too late to get ourselves out of that which in America is referred to by the nasty word 'promiscuity.' Well, and then that filty s.o.b. from Quebec, you know, that French-Canadian airline steward, flew into San Francisco with a new plague in his backside. While his plane was on the ground, that is, during the course of twelve hours, he managed to copulate with fourteen boys. You've probably read about all this? Incredible, you really haven't read or heard anything? And we believed the whole world was shaken by the collapse of our 'alternative' life style.

"Well, you know, just a few years after the first reported AIDS case in America, our Moscow social circle started to die off as well. First we tried to break off into pairs—Zhenya and Vitasik had it easier than the others, since they really had been in love for a long time—but the virus must have been carousing around our group for quite a while. First Mark Tumantsev left us, then Boris, then Yuri. A year ago Zhenya lost Vitasik, and now it's his turn. In a few days I'll be left completely alone. . . ."

We were already outside in the street when he told me the end of this story, walking along Connecticut Avenue, where the American Express agency, with its luminous red-and-blue-striped wall, made promises unto all the ages. Alik Congusto had left his car out there somewhere. He really did embody an alternative life style, with his Peruvian poncho wrapped around him, a pipe in his teeth, and the little sausages of his ponytail carelessly tied—as opposed to Katznelson, who had always appeared ordinary. Ordinary, that is, if you didn't look too closely. And, by the way, nobody had looked very closely.

For some reason, the end of this calm and almost rehearsed story shocked me less than the beginning. It seemed Congusto had noticed this and was looking at me in a rather perplexed way.

"Then, how was it that Zhenya went missing but his door was left open?" I asked.

Congusto started back at the beginning. "He moved here because of Vitasik," he said. "Vitasik got a job with the Post Office, and Zhenya managed to latch on to *Constitution*. Well, after Vitasik was gone, Zhenya was left here by himself and began to die alone. On the day he began to feel really awful, he couldn't find anything better to do about it than to call me in New York. And so I called the Washington emergency number. That's about it."

"That's about it, that's about it," he repeated several times while walking, and it again appeared to me that there was a certain rehearsed quality to all this, I dare say a kind of theatricality, although what sort of theatre could there be when, as Pasternak put it, "the soil was breathing your destiny"?

Then Congusto began again: "About the door, I just don't know why it was left open. Maybe the paramedics forgot to shut it."

He gave me a phone number where I could reach Katznelson. As was the custom in American hospitals, a dying person was allowed a telephone by his bedside. The dying, the administration might say, need a phone more than those on the mend: they need to sort out their finances and to impart a lot of instructions.

Congusto and I began our farewells. He bowed, as if emphasizing that we still hadn't switched over to less formal terms. I held out my hand to him. He declined my handshake with a faint smile. I suddenly remember that Zhenya had also (long before he went missing) strangely shied away from these rituals of the palm. Apparently this realization was somehow foolishly exposed on my face. Congusto grinned. "Yes, yes, me, too, although it's not in the advanced stages. Well, I'm H.I.V.-positive, I've got the virus—understand?"

"Yes, of course I understand!" I exclaimed. "However, Alik, it's of no importance, since it's not. . . ." and here I stopped short, barely suppressing my lack of tact. My hand still hung in the space between my raincoat and his poncho.

"Yes, yes, you can't transmit it through a handshake," he said, and, twisting his body politely, he seemed about to walk away, but after one step he relented. "I want to tell you one thing. Perhaps it will sound like a cliché . . . but I want to tell you anyway."

I could see that he was becoming very emotional, and I cursed myself

Yury Past (b. 1954)

NO OFFENSE IN LOVE . . .[1]

[Liubov'iu oskorbit' . . .]

Translated by Diane Nemec Ignashev

YURY PAST (b. 1954) writes of himself: "After graduating from high school, I went on to study physics at the university, then served in the army and worked in research laboratories; the idea that literature and writing might be my fate was hardly one I arrived at immediately. I read a lot, naturally, but began studying literature only in my thirties, when I enrolled at the Gorky Institute of World Literature in Moscow. Now, having finished the Institute, I write literary criticism, teach, and collaborate on several literary journals."

A ND ONE ONCE loved another. But the other didn't love him, it seems. And so one says, I'm leaving, Sasha. For a long while, maybe forever. To America. And then I smile. And Sasha says, Stay, Yura. Should I?

Sure, of course, but of course not, because he'll never say it, ever. But then I'm not going anywhere. But would I give up anything less either? As for America—that's just to keep from hanging myself. It means I'm alive, I believe in something, doesn't it? One once loved another. But the other didn't love him, it seems. But one didn't cry, because it wasn't the first time. And one smiled and was happy, when one saw him. And then one was sad. Evening after evening. How many more? Who knows? One told oneself, I can be patient.

And thought one to oneself, I'm intelligent, and good looking, and kind. Why doesn't he love me? If only I were young. . . . Sasha's twelve years

---

[1]Lope de Vega. *El perro del hortelano* [A Dog in the Manger]. Here cited from Lope de Vega, *El perro del hortelano, El castigo sin Venganza*, (Edición, introducción y notas de A. David Kossoff), 3rd ed. Madrid: Clásicos Castalia, 1986.

808 Diana   Fuera de que soy mujer
                  a cualquier error sujeta,
                  y no sé si muy discreta,
                  como se me echa de ver.
                    Desde lo menos aquí,
                  dices que ofendes lo más,
                  y amando, engañado estás,
                  porque en amor no es ansí,
                    que no ofende un desigual
                  amando, pues sólo entiendo
                  que se ofende aborreceiendo.

younger than I am. And he likes them younger. So I'm too old for him on two counts.

And, thought he, friendship perhaps might bring them together. And he began to seek the other's friendship. He told himself, I have to be patient. And I can't seem boring. And I can't let him feel like he owes me something, although it was true that he did. And he told himself lots of other things, but every time Sasha would leave me I would understand that he would forget about me completely even as he was leaving, and I would understand the entire hopelessness of my various calculations, and although I was no longer shedding tears or writing verse (I'd outgrown that), my heart ached, and ached.

And yet we continued to meet, because Sasha decided to study English, and I was teaching him. And I would await each lesson as if it were a holiday, something bright and long overdue. And then the thought occurred: what would I do if I didn't know English? Then for sure he'd never come. And, indeed, he didn't.

"Virgos are calculating," a female acquaintance once said. "My husband was a virgo." And he's a virgo, too. And so was Kolya, and Zhenya too. I haven't loved anyone else that way. Basically, I haven't loved anyone. They were born almost the same day: Kolya and Zhenya on the fourth, Sasha on the sixth. But virgos are also charming, aren't they?

But, after all, Kolya was, or rather, became my love. Or was he my loss? My victory or my defeat? My reason or lack thereof? But that's not entirely true either: he wasn't or didn't become anything on his own, I only made him up in my imagination and subjected myself to an imagined fantasy. But he was good. And I never wanted more than his friendship. Because I didn't hope, didn't dream of anything else.

After all, I'm incapable of loving a woman, and I'll never have children or grandchildren. . . .

Having spent her entire life pretending she wasn't Jewish, Evgeniia Nikolaevna died with a smile on her lips. She lay in her casket, eyes closed, and smiled ever so slightly and oh so craftily: I did it, I made it, I've passed myself on, I saved them. You, my children, my grandchildren, you go on living. I'm tired. . . .

That means, I'm left on my own. I have to make myself a friend. It seems like I've spent my whole life doing that, yet nothing comes of it.

A book can be a friend. But if I write it, will I read it? It's hard to say. But a friend like that won't betray me. At worst, it might get a bit boring.

And once one person saw another. And one's eyes hurt, he seemed so good. And he started to follow him, like a dog, and kept wanting him to fall in love with him and would have been delighted beyond all else to hear him say one kind word. Thus began their friendship, and at times it was even tender. We were students together at university. Kolya got A's, I did worse, and during final exams, the night before the last examination, Kolya would drop over to my place in the evening, after dark, and would wait for me to finish preparing sample questions, and then we would set off for a walk and would talk about something exceptionally fascinating and, likely, inconsequential (I don't even remember the words we used), and we would go our separate ways only when it was very late.

Kolya worked hard—he wanted to go on to graduate school—and he swam laps and even then lived the kind of calculated lifestyle that I have begun to live only now. And he went on and became a scholar and is as good-looking as he was then and has a wife, and a daughter, and, I bet, he's convinced himself that he's happy, but it seems to me that he's as unhappy as I am, although in his own way, of course.

It was a feeling I felt for the first time that strongly. Over and over again in my head, in unending repetition: Kolya, Kolya, Kolya. I would copy his gestures, his words, his opinions (likely, much has remained with me to this day). And once, when we went camping with a group I brought together and we were lying (I facing his back) next to each other on the blanket by our tent, I started to stroke his long fine blond hair which kept falling in my face, and he turned and suddenly kissed me on the lips (to everyone's amazement, for some reason), and it was a moment of innocent youthful eroticism (although mine was anything but innocent!), and I almost choked up and cried, my eyes filled with tears, and it was then that the clock ran out on my feeling, because Kolya fell in love with Irina, and I thought it would kill me.

A man fell in love with a woman. And a woman fell in love with him. But she was already pregnant with another's child. She was naive, inexperienced. While he, the other, had rejected her long ago, and she was alone. The man didn't know any of this. And somehow, after that camping trip of ours, Kolya had said, listen, let's go over to the university. And we went.

We're sitting at the entrance on the steps, and eventually I ask, so what are we waiting for, and he, for some reason too obviously embarrassed, says, maybe it's funny and stupid, but I really want to see Irina. . . .

I ran into her the next day, and we went over to the tavern on the other side of the pond behind the university and were sitting in the grass, and, it seems, I was drinking beer, and Irina, it seems, wasn't, and then she told me everything, and at that point I understood that I was losing everything, although it'd be more sober to ask: what was I losing? I really didn't have anything to lose. And Irina understood and took pity on me. . . .

She was to know happiness with Kolya, for a month or so, and then her stomach began to show, and he took offense and refused to have anything to do with her. Never again would he mention her. She loved him for a long time, maybe she still does a bit.

Then came two months of army reserve training after the university, and I went gladly, although I feared the army to distraction, but I couldn't bear to see them—not her, not him, or worst of all, the two of them together.

He and I drifted apart over time, gradually, year by year, and there were still times when I'd get asked at home why Kolya never stopped by anymore. And I'd think up something in response, and then he desisted entirely.

Several notebooks of my poetry have remained, together with our photographs, while of the books he presented me only the one about Chinese painting is left.

Maybe it's just a question of chemistry? The brain when in a state of grief, precisely the kind of love-bound grief I'm experiencing, gives off certain substances, and I've already grown accustomed to them and can't exist without them? A question of habit, like smoking?

If everything could be solved with a wish, with words, I would do nothing but tell him of my love, I would stop controlling my every move and, falling to my knees, would caress his legs and kiss the rough fiber of his jeans, all the time sensing the calm warmth of his body, stroking his hands, staring into his wonderful eyes as if into the sky or transparent running water. You are perfection, God created you, and I can't help but love you, Sasha.

Only it would be suicide, an overdose of a narcotic which even in small quantities—an encounter on the street, English lessons—comprises the very joy of my life. He would discard me, would start to avoid me, tire of me.

One once loved another, but the other didn't love him. Marina loved me. But not a single atom of my soul moved in response.

At first Marina didn't talk about anything, but then she could hold out no longer and started to send me presents—for New Year's, on my birthday—and, without insisting on or demanding anything, she wrote to me of her feelings, all of which I really didn't need, and I would give her presents to others and, as for her letter, I responded politely enough—thanks, you know, for the attention and all, but whenever I'd see her at the bookstore, if I spotted her first, I'd turn away cowardly and hide behind a shelf. Don't do it, Marina, I don't need anything from you, leave me in my single-sexed world, it's for me to leave it and not for you to be my companion. I don't feel for you, don't pity you, don't see your bitten lips and damning eyes, they don't exist for me, and nothing will ever come of this.

I also unloaded Zhenya's presents, after it became apparent that our split was final. So that nothing would remain, no reminders, no excuses for melodrama. And yet I unloaded them just as they do in bad Indian movies: at sunset out in an empty lot I set fire to the letters, the photographs. So that he should feel the blow, feel something. . . . Silly mysticism. I don't believe in it. But there's something to it, because Zhenya always sensed my gaze. He would, unfailingly, respond to my line of sight, even in a crowd; by that same line he could locate me. Once, it happened, he turned toward that seeming one-way glass through which I observed him, but he couldn't see me and craned his neck in confusion as if responding to someone calling him by name. . . .

Once Kolya found Gainesborough's "Lady Innes" among my journal clippings and took such a liking to it that every time he came over he'd ask me to show it to him. I gave it to him, and it stood on his desk and he would look at it as he worked.

I never thought it possible to fall in love with an image, one so infinitely distant at that, but possible it is. Call it a knight's love, a youth's love, a bookish love, a made-up love, there is no love purer. Only it's not a love for real life. In life everything was more tangible, harsher and senseless.

So what's new in that a love didn't "come together"? Nothing. I mention it only because you who hold this page before you are my only and most intimate friend. I have no one else, no one else at all.

It used to be I had a hard time with loneliness and wrote poems about it, but in fact I took it a lot easier then than I do now. There was a time when it didn't even cross my mind. But nowadays it's become more immediate, drawing closer all the time. There are times when I think I ought to get a dog. . . . Sasha once said more or less the same thing: when I get old, I'm going to get a dog. And I nodded and thought, take me instead. Only I'll get old before you do.

Sasha, you have such strong, true, and fine-tuned senses, why is it you can't sense how much I love you? Why doesn't the space around us transmit my embarrassment, my pain, my joy, my hope?

I'm always missing the mark. Only, most likely, I myself decided on this mode, or to be more exact, it was the space around me, manifest in me, that made the choice for me. Because, when I first saw Kolya in the corridor at the university, I didn't think for a second, or even half a second, about what was happening or how it would turn out for me, I didn't think because I didn't know anything then, just as I can't, for example, think in Chinese. Now I know, but that doesn't change anything.

So, there you have it. All that remains is for me to repeat the phrase one often repeated to oneself: "I loved him, but he didn't love me. Maybe I'll just stop trying, give up." At the same time he knew that he wouldn't give up, that he had to keep on hoping, and be patient.

Scene from the Moscow production of the play Slingshot, directed by Roman Viktiuk, 1993.
Actors from left: Sergei Makovetsky, Ekaterina Karpushina, Dmitry Bozin.

Nikolai Kolyada (b. 1957)

SLINGSHOT

[Rogatka]

Translated by Susan Larsen

NIKOLAI KOLYADA was born in 1957 in a small village in Kazakhstan. He embarked on a career in theater at the age of 15, when he enrolled in the Sverdlovsk Theatrical Institute. He subsequently worked as an actor in the Sverdlovsk Academic Dramatic Theater, where he played tragicomic roles from the Russian classical repertoire. Kolyada now teaches playwriting at the Ekaterinburg (formerly Sverdlovsk) Theatrical Institute and recently directed a production of his play *The Oginskii Polonaise* at the Ekaterinburg Dramatic Theater. He wrote his first play in 1986 and has now completed almost 40 others, of which at least 20 have been produced in theaters throughout the former Soviet Union, as well as in Italy, Germany, Canada, England and the United States. Kolyada's plays appear regularly in Russian theatrical journals, and a 400-page volume of his collected plays was published in 1994 (*P'esy dlia liubimogo teatra*), a rare event for such a young playwright.

Kolyada has had unprecedented success on the Russian stage and is considered the most popular Russian dramatist of his generation. In 1995 four of his plays were running in Moscow simultaneously, and an international festival of his plays was held in 1994 in Ekaterinburg. Kolyada's work has been championed by one of Russia's leading contemporary directors, Roman Viktiuk, who persuaded the San Diego Repertory Theater to stage the world premiere of *Slingshot* in October 1989. Since then, Viktiuk has staged *Slingshot* in Italy and Hungary, as well as its Moscow premiere in the fall of 1993, a few months after Yeltsin repealed the Russian law against homosexuality. Productions of *Slingshot* have also been mounted in other Russian cities, and in Europe.

Critical opinion of Kolyada's work is divided: Some critics have praised his theatricality and called him an "actor's playwright." Others have lamented the "stormy sentimentality of his plays" and their chaotic blend of melodramatic pathos with vulgarity. Most critics agree that Kolyada has a remarkable ear for the often inchoate, obscene and cliche-ridden speech of the Russian underclasses and a gift for writing "long, coloratura scandal scenes." Kolyada's work is often labeled "chernukha," or "black stuff," due to its focus on the darker or suppressed aspects of Soviet and post-Soviet society.

Finished in 1989, Kolyada's *Slingshot* itself was suppressed for several years in Russia, due to its sympathetic portrait of love between two men.

In contrast to many other contemporary Russian representations of homosexuality, *Slingshot* portrays the relationship between its two male heroes as redemptive and morally uplifting. Viktiuk foregrounded this aspect of the play in San Diego when he staged a pivotal sex scene to the music of the Russian "Our Father" and placed two giant pairs of "angel wings" at the center of the play's final scene. (Viktiuk's Moscow staging of *Slingshot* set all the "dream sequences," including the sex scene, to the music of Freddie Mercury's "Show Must Go On," a change typical of the generally lighter, more upbeat tone of the later production.)

About this translation:

This translation of *Slingshot* is based on the version that was commissioned by the San Diego Repertory Theater and incorporates suggestions made by the director, actors and other members of the crew during the rehearsal process, which I gratefully acknowledge here. Final responsibility for all interpretive judgments and any errors is mine. The text printed here has been abridged to meet the space constraints of this volume. All cuts are indicated by suspension points in square brackets; all other suspension points are Kolyada's.

Dramatis personae: Anton—age 18
Ilya—age 33
Larissa—age 35

The play is set in Ilya's apartment.

ACT ONE, SCENE ONE

Brakes shriek—it's deafening. The sound of breaking glass. This is the gong that begins the performance.
Semi-darkness. Ilya's tiny two-room apartment on the eighth floor. In the window hangs a sheer curtain with a big hole, darned carelessly with black threads. A mattress is wedged into the door leading to the balcony. This is how the apartment's owner keeps from freezing in winter. There's a chair with one leg tied on with string. From the ceiling hangs a tattered lampshade: it looks as if someone's taken bites out of it. [. . .] In the middle of the room stands a table covered with piles of trash, empty bottles, and murky glasses. Crumpled newspapers, magazines, and a few books have been tossed onto a bookshelf that hangs from the wall by a single nail. The wallpaper is peeling. [. . .] The second, coffin-narrow room holds a bed with graying sheets and a nightstand with a television. Evening. Outside on the landing the elevator makes sounds like thunder. Muttering, shouts,

gasping sobs, swearing. Someone can't get the key in the lock. It takes a long time to open the door. From outside on the landing, these voices:

ILYA: Now this I know for sure: everyone's lying, every last person—hiding his rotten little thoughts, keeping himself out of sight! Everyone, everyone, everyone! That's what life teaches everyone, the filthy mother! And do you know, what kind of life we have? One with class! Oh yes! Before we had color TV sets, people used to paste strips of plastic, all different colors across the TV screen. . . . Remember, ah? So the picture was . . . gray, but also—in color! And that's what we're all like—we're all hiding, each in our own swamp, crouched down out of sight, but on the surface—we keep drawing colored pictures, drawing and drawing. . . .

ANTON: Where's the light?

ILYA: That's it, that's enough. . . . (*after a pause*) You're a fine one! Go on, get out of here! . . . Feel sick enough as it is. . . . And I've told you plenty already. . . . Get out of here, I said! Done your bit for the invalid, now go! Get out! Get out! Get out!!

ANTON: Whatever you want. . . . *Pause.*

ILYA: What're you standing around for? What else do you want? Get out, I said. *Pause.* Aren't you kind . . . a regular Boy Scout. . . . If everyone had such kind hearts, we'd have built communism long ago. . . . Alright, that's enough, that's all! Shove me in the door and get out.

ANTON: Let me give you a hand . . . put you to bed! You're completely drunk . . . it's alright, alright, don't get so excited. . . .

ILYA: Who'd I tell: get out of here, ah, son-of-a-bitch, well? *But Anton has already found the light switch. A dim bulb illuminates Ilya's den. Anton looks quickly around, immediately grasps the situation. He opens the door wider and rolls in Ilya, who is sitting in a wheelchair. He pushes the chair so we can't see Ilya, only hear him swearing.*

ILYA: No you don't, you watch out, better watch out, what a snake . . . watch out, what a mother's helper, motherfucker. . . . So you rolled me home, rolled me home, what're you waiting for, what else?! Get out of here, well?! *Anton paces up and down the room. Craning his neck, he looks over the chewed-up lampshade. Anton is 18. He wears a white shirt and jeans. Women are crazy about him. But he lacks the insolence and arrogance typical of most "pretty boys." He's good-looking, well-built, with straight hair cut short at the neck.*[. . .]

ANTON: *Pause.* Live alone, ah?

ILYA: Well, sonny-boy, well, you son-of-a-bitch. . . . Is it any of your business, any of your business, well?! Shut the door from the other side, move it, I said! Who am I talking to?! Well?! *Anton is silent. Turns, sighs, goes towards the door.* Stop! *Anton keeps walking towards the door.* Stop, I said! Stop! Stop! Well?!

ANTON: What is it? [. . .]

ILYA: (*laughing*) Frightened him. [. . .] Calm down. . . . Listen, kid. . . .
Out on the balcony I've got a little something hidden away. . . . A bottle!
. . . On the balcony. . . . Get it out. . . . I always leave some for the night
time, hide it away—gets scary here by yourself. . . . Come on, come on,
drag it over here. [. . .] Don't act so stuck-up. . . . I'll fill your glass, too.
. . . We'll have a swig together. . . . Don't think I don't remember kindness! No sir! *Laughs.* For saving me I'll pour you a glass—a glass-and-a-
half! Young man! You've saved the life of a cripple, an invalid! Dear comrade citizen! We should plaster your personality in all the papers! Give you
a decoration! A medal! A wooden one! A weapon with an honorary title!
A gold watch! A certificate! Did you find it? Did you find it? *Ilya himself
turns the wheelchair. For the first time we see his face. His clothes are
filthy, his face—yellow. His eyes are black, spiteful and sober, but his
hands are drunk, flying back and forth. Ilya's hands are unusual: white,
slender, with incredibly long fingers.*
ANTON: (*digs around in the cupboard, which shakes and almost falls on
him*): This one?
ILYA: That one, that one. . . . Glasses are over there. . . . Leave them
alone, don't wash them! They're fine like that, don't wash them!
ANTON: They're dirty. . . .
ILYA: We won't croak. . . . I don't have AIDS. . . . No AIDS here. . . .
I'm not croaking and you won't croak. I eat, drink—never wash anything.
Come on, open it, open it, open it. [. . .] *Ilya drinks greedily. Wrinkles
up his face, drops his head on his breast, jerks his shoulders.* What a
bitch . . . disgusting . . . disgusting and delicious . . . and you?
ANTON: I'm not having any. . . . And you shouldn't have, either. . . .
ILYA: Oh, you! Giving lessons. . . . *Rolls away from the table, stares at
Anton. Surveys his face and clothing for a long time, with hatred.* Aren't
you something . . . still green behind the ears, and giving lessons to grown
up old men, bellowing away. . . . Look at you, aren't you fine . . . aren't
you fine. A stud with a Young Communist pin. . . . Oh we've seen perverts
like you before, seen you more than once. . . . You're really something,
aren't you? No, just look at the exotic bird that's flown into my mansion.
. . . Ruined plenty of girls, ah? They throw themselves at you, I bet, so
pure, well-groomed, clean-scrubbed, ah? Stand in line, don't they? Never
had anything like that here, just drunks off the street. . . . Oh, you're
something alright. . . . (*suddenly*) But you know, kid, I've never had a
woman, not once. . . . Never! Not once in my life! I've never slept with
anyone, not even once! I'm thirty-three years old, but I'm—still a virgin!
You understand, right? I'm talking to you seriously, after all, and here you
are laughing at me. . . .
ANTON: I'm not laughing. . . .
ILYA: Shut up when I'm talking! No, you tell me, why am I thirty-three
years old, and still a virgin? Why? Well? Why do you have everything, and

I—have nothing? Why've I got to wear myself out with masturbation, can you tell me or not? Ah-ah-ah! I've got it. It's all because I'm—a legless cripple, and you're—a two-legged animal! Bitch, how I hate you all, assholes, how I hate you all, if they only knew, how I hate, hate, hate you all!!!! *Takes a swing and hurls a glass at Anton. Anton turns away. The glass hits the wall and flies into small pieces about the room.* Go away, bitch. . . . (*quietly*). Go away. . . . Get out, or I'll kill you. . . . Bastard. . . . Punk. . . . Stinking communists, breed heroes like rabbits, Pavlik Morozovs—won't let a person croak—they have to throw themselves into the rapids, beneath the wheels of the train, into the burning house, under the car! They save everyone, everyone! Just so later someone'll write three lines about them in the paper: so-and-so performed a heroic feat, saved a human life! . . . Pigfucker, who asked you to save me, who, who, you bastard, who?! Get out of here, I said, or I'll kill you! . . . I'll hurt you, I tell you, you hear me?! *Pause.* Well, so what if you're standing up? Don't believe, I can crack your skull? Don't believe it? Or you think, I can't reach that far? I'm a sharp one. . . .

ANTON: Why are you like this . . . attacking people like a mad dog?

ILYA: Get out, I said!

ANTON: (*calmly*) I'll leave in a minute. Have to tie my shoelaces. Maybe, I like it here. Hit me, if you want to. I won't go. *SILENCE.*

ILYA: (*suddenly*) Well, stay then. Only watch out: I can stir up all kinds of trouble, and no one will blame me—I'm a cripple and only half-normal. . . . So you choose, it's your business. . . .

ANTON: Don't try to scare me. Been scared before [. . .] Listen, there's a cockroach in your kitchen that's hurled itself into a jar of water in despair. And drowned. He was looking for something to eat. . . .

ILYA: Got nothing to feed myself. Much less the cockroaches. . . . Turn out the light, youngster. . . . My eyes hurt. *Anton turns out the light. Semi-darkness. Anton sits in the only chair, looking at Ilya. Ilya is silent a long time. Smokes. Outside the window are the indistinct, strange, unearthly, incomprehensible sounds of the city at night. These two people are just as strange, as if silver threads were stretched between them, uniting them. . . .*

ILYA: (*not loudly*) [. . .] So, my eyes are full of spite, are they?

ANTON: Not now.

ILYA: It's dark now!

ANTON: I can see just the same. . . .

ILYA: Oh you, stray cat . . . he can see, just look at him . . . he sees in the dark, the stray cat. . . .

ANTON: And you—is it true?—you wanted to die?

ILYA: (*shrieks out*) None of your business! *Pause.* You're sneaking into my soul, motherfucker. Stop it! Stop it! Stop it! *A long pause. Ilya smokes, his hands are shaking.* It's all lies, all lies, got it, punk? It's just a screen of color, all this . . . all lies . . . I, I am telling you this. Remember this, learn it: people die—not like that, but—on the sly, secretly, in hiding. That's when they want to die—and they're not joking around. . . . But I—I just want to, for the hell of it: My soul—it aches, cries out, gasps for breath. Want to shove my rotten stumps in everyone's face. . . . So I carry on, serenading the streets and alleys. . . . No great loss if that truck had run over me, but I'd have known about it, known since this morning. . . . I'd have sensed it. Well, death, that is. . . . It lets you know ahead of time, I know. . . . I didn't sense it? Understand? I'm a coward. I can't stuff myself with pills and croak up here, I can't! A coward! Can't croak in this hellhole, on the sly, at night, I can't. . . . 'though it's time, long past time. . . . I'm afraid. . . . Afraid of those last three minutes before death. . . . I even dream about them. Dream about them often. Dream about a lot of things. Dream about everything. I dream about my whole life to come. Three years ago, think it was, dreamt that I'd be sitting here, just like this, and you'd—be there. I dreamt it. Just now remembered. You and I . . . sitting. . . .

ANTON: That happens with me, too, sometimes. . . .

ILYA: *Pause.* Ah? Well yes . . . yes. . . . *Pause.* I, when I was still little, had a dream, that once I turned twenty, I'd get in an accident, they'd cut my legs off, and I'd go rolling around in a wheelchair. . . . In the dream, I remember, I liked rolling around in the wheelchair . . . so much! . . . I was little! I woke up and laughed, rejoiced. . . . Ten years ago I had another dream . . . that my legs are made of wood and I'm lying in bed. In the room there's light—just like this, coming from the street. It's dark. No one around, and a sound in my ears, like drilling. . . . Well, then. . . . And the legs I have are wooden, and there's a beetle in them, some kind of maggots . . . they're in the wood, they're gnawing away at it. . . . I lie there, and my legs are breaking, falling apart, cracking to pieces—like some rotten, mouldering wood. . . . But the legs—they're mine, mine, they're alive and it hurts so much. . . . And realize—they're drilling holes in my legs, in my living legs. . . . I lie there—and I can't do a thing, can't move a muscle, a hand, not even a finger. . . . it's so frightening. . . . *Pause.* And you . . . do you have dreams?

ANTON: Often. Sometimes like that.

ILYA: (*rolls his wheelchair over to Anton and in a hoarse whisper, breathing into his face*): And do you dream . . . about naked girls?

ANTON: Sometimes. . . .

ILYA (*heatedly*): I dream about them, I dream about them every day! Every night! Lots of them, whole crowds of them, lots of them all around! Naked, beautiful, swimming, dancing, lots and lots! And right beside them —men, it looks like. . . . Also naked and also beautiful, swimming with us, rejoicing, leaping. . . . *Pause.* Shameful, ah?

ANTON: What's shameful?

ILYA: Well, that I'm talking like this—it's shameful, isn't it? A grown up old guy and . . .

ANTON: Nothing shameful about it. It's normal. I mean, you're talking to me. Not just anybody. And I won't tell anyone.

ILYA: I'm not talking about that, whether you'll tell or not tell. It's just . . . people don't say things like that out loud. It's shameful. Forbidden.

ANTON: If you trust a person, like you trust yourself, then you can talk. That's what I think.

ILYA: There aren't any people like that. None! None! Stop talking! That's enough! I'm almost twice as old as you. I know. *Pause.* And I'm still lying. I'm drunk. Spouting whatever comes into my head. But you—listen, listen to my lies. It's all nonsense. [. . .] You'll come back?

ANTON: You inviting me?

ILYA: I'm inviting you. You're good at being quiet. You're quiet a lot. I respect people like that. Other people sound off all the time about nothing. But you—listen. [. . .] Keep being quiet. I have a lot more to tell you. Myself. Here, I'll tell you about this other dream I had. Same kind, an interesting one. . . . I dreamt it a week ago. Dreamt I was—a crow. And I'm flying, flying above the city. Flying over my own building, past the balcony, flying, flying. . . . My feathers are black, and my wings—this big. . . . And I caw, I caw—like this: "I'm a crow! I'm no sex at all! Not male, not female! I spit on you all from this height! I look down on you with contempt! 300 years will pass and I'll still be flying and crowing about myself to you! I have 300 years left to live!" And then I go: "Cuckoo, Cuckoo!" Funny, ah? [. . .] Go on, go on, hit the road, before you get hit. I want to sleep! I need to sleep, get it? One way or another—I looked death in the face today. . . . (*laughs*) Go on. You'll come again?

ANTON: I will.

ILYA: When will you come?

ANTON: Well, tomorrow.

ILYA: At what time? Tell me exactly.

ANTON: In the evening.

ILYA: Exactly, I said, well?!

ANTON: Well, tomorrow, at nine. At nine!

ILYA: Go. . . .

ANTON: See you later. . . . *Anton goes to the door, turns around. Stands a minute or two. Exits, slamming the door.*

ILYA: (*calling after him, without moving*) Don't play tricks with me! Eh! You hear? Don't play tricks on me, I said! Well? Playing tricks on me— it's forbidden. . . . D'you hear or don't you? *Ilya drunkenly shakes his head, mutters softly.* May you have happiness, success in your work, and joy in the new year. . . . No, that's not it. . . . May you have happiness, joy in your work, and success in the new year. . . . You hear? D'you hear me? Don't play tricks with me . . . don't play tricks. . . . *Ilya shoves his*

*chair over to the window [. . . and] looks long into the city night. [. . .]
The red sign of a large grocery store somewhere far away now flares up,
then flickers out, flares up and flickers out. . . . Ilya dozes off, mumbling
something. . . .*

FIRST DREAM

*Voices and an answering echo. It's hard to tell whether people are walk-
ing about the room, or whether it's their shadows flying. Here comes Ilya.
He walks, smiling happily. He sinks onto his knees, to pet a cat that's appeared from nowhere. [. . .]*

ILYA: You, why're you walking around naked?
ANTON: Am I really naked? I'm dressed. You don't see me at all. You
need glasses. Oh don't, don't kill the cat. It's an old lady, a human being—
not a cat. You mustn't kill the cat . . . mustn't kill a human being. . . .
ILYA: And why are you so kind, feeling sorry for everyone? The cockroach
in my kitchen—you even felt sorry for it. . . .
ANTON: Because no one ever felt sorry for me. Ah-eee, the cat is on fire!
It's burning, burning, burning—black fire! Black! Aieeee! Fire! *The sound
of breaking glass.*

SCENE TWO

*The same apartment. The room has been hastily tidied up and the floor has
even been mopped. [. . .] Ilya sits in his wheelchair by the half-open door.
His head droops. He sleeps. Early morning. Sunlight shines through the
window. Anton has climbed up to the landing. Glances into the apartment,
sees Ilya, gives him a long look.*

ANTON: (*coughs*) Door's wide-open. Guess you're living the communist
life, ah?
ILYA; (*woke up immediately, gives a frightened smile*) You came. . . .
Hello! Hello! . . . And I expected you yesterday. In the evening. At nine.
But you didn't come. . . . So I fell asleep here, on the threshold. Left the
door open. Thought, it didn't happen. Thought, I was drunk, imagined it,
dreamt it. That happens with me sometimes. Were you here?
ANTON: Yesterday—no, I couldn't make it, old man.
ILYA: No, I mean, day before yesterday? Day before yesterday, were you
here, ah? With me, I mean, here with me? I was babbling on about something, I was drunk. . . . What I said . . . just forget it . . . alright? [. . .]

And what else, didn't I throw a glass at you, ah? Wasn't there something like that? I'm sorry, I was drunk. . . .

ANTON: Never mind. It didn't hit me. Here, I brought you something to gnaw on. From home. It's fresh, my mother made it. Don't be shy. [. . .] *Takes an apple from the bag and eats it.* The main thing is—you shouldn't drink. I know, I know—life is rough, but all the same—don't drink, you don't need to . . . take up some hobby, or something. . . . I don't know, wood-burning, maybe . . . or whittling. . . .How about it, shall I bring you a pocket-knife? I've got one at home, left over from grade-school. I mean, it's not fatal, that you're. . . .

ILYA: (*quietly and spitefully*) Alright, get out of here, you crooked asshole. . . . Get out, I said! Don't try that smarmy shit with me. One more missionary society has had its say . . . get out, I said, pigfucker. . . . I'll knock you one between the eyes, and you're a dead man, hear?! *Pause. Ilya rolls his wheelchair over to the window, looks through the curtain, lights a cigarette.*

ANTON: (*gaily*) [. . .] Come on, forget it. Forgive me, old man. I didn't mean to. My intentions were the best. Forgive me. Come on, all this is pointless anyway. *He walks over to Ilya, kneels in front of the wheelchair, looks into Ilya's eyes.* Well, peace? Peace? Come on, don't pout. Tell me instead what you dreamt today. Well? I like your dreams. They're—like the real thing. So strange, and alive. . . . Come on, ah?

ILYA: (*smoking*) Found yourself a new toy, haven't you? One that talks, right? A talking toy, only without legs, rolls around in a wheelchair. Isn't that it?

ANTON: Alright, cut it out. You're all puffed up like a mouse with a bellyache. What'd you dream about today, ah?

ILYA: (*looking out the window*) A black cat.

ANTON: A cat? A black one? That's a sign of bad luck! Really, Ilya!

ILYA: (*laughing*) You're like an old-lady fortuneteller. Want to hear more? Brace yourself. I dreamt, that you were walking around here without any clothes on. How d'you like that?

ANTON: (*seriously*) Naked? Completely? That's a sign of shame.

ILYA: (*smiling*) There was something else, too, I don't remember. [. . . .]

ANTON: (*eating an apple, looking at Ilya*) Want some?

ILYA: Hand it over.

ANTON: I don't have any more. Only this one. I already bit into it. You'll take it?

ILYA: Hand it over, I said. . . . *Ilya takes the apple, bites gingerly into it. Looks at Anton. Starts to cough.* Want it back now, don't you, snake. *They both laugh.*

ANTON: Uh-huh, I want it back. You'll burst from my apples, get fat. *Anton walks about the room, hands in his pockets. Looks at the walls.* [. . .]

ILYA: (*silent a bit*) Have a lot of friends?

ANTON: None that matter. Everything's so boring. Everywhere, it's all the same. I tried drinking—don't like it. Next morning your head hurts. Music—leaves me cold. Hobbies, all these amateur groups—you can have them. *Stretches.* All boring.

ILYA: What about girlfriends? A lot? Any?

ANTON: None. Did have one, but she got mad at me. It was my fault. *Suddenly sits down again next to Ilya, takes him by the hand, looks into his eyes.* If you like, I'll tell you about her, ah? I mean, about what happened with the two of us? I haven't told anyone about it, but you—I'll tell. You told me about yourself then, I believed you.

ILYA: (*takes his hand back*) I was drunk, lying. . . .

ANTON: You're lying now! Don't lie! You're like a snail—hiding in its shell again. . . . I want to tell you something, too, you'll understand me. . . . You know, nothing ever works out for me with women, nothing happens. . . .

ILYA: Well?

ANTON: Only don't start thinking that there's anything like, you know. . . . I'll tell you the truth, you won't tell anyone, I know. And you won't laugh at me either. It's scary for me, understand? Scary, when it turns out like that. I've been in bed three times with a woman and—nothing happens, understand? [. . .] In general, I'm just fine, everything works, you know, in the mornings, when. . . . well, everything's in place. . . . But like that [with girls]—nothing happens. Why, do you know? Should I see a doctor maybe? But I'm so ashamed. . . . What would I say? Why does this happen? From fear, ah?

ILYA: (*rolls his wheelchair to the side*) And why are you telling me this? Why me? . . . as if I knew anything about it. . . . Found yourself a real expert in that line of business. . . .

ANTON: (*silent a bit, looking at the floor*) Don't know. Phew! I told you about it—though I was ashamed, and right away, you know, I felt better somehow . . . you know? So tell me, you and I, are we alike?

ILYA: I'll tell you. Just alike. Two brother degenerates. Two half-wits. We're both idiots—all turned around like the fireman's trousers. . . .

ANTON: (*after a silence*) So tell me, what do you do, day in and day out? Sit here like this? Read books?

ILYA: I read alright—Mr. Fortified Red and Mr. Dry White. Sometimes I even get to Mr. Delirium Tremens. What books? What do I need them for? Get up in the morning—go to the grocery store. If the elevator's not working—that's bad. Lots of times I crawl downstairs by myself. Don't ask anyone for help. And if the elevator's still not working, I crawl back up the same way, to the eighth floor. Wanted to trade for a first floor apartment—nothing doing. Nobody likes this cage. And what do I care. . . . So I get to the store. Sit awhile, collect a little. People give me a lot, they feel sorry. They think—I was in Afghanistan. While you're young—

they give. I collect enough for a jug or two. Then I drink it. Alone. In the park. It's quiet there. [. . .] In general, life's just piss fine. Real high-class. [. . .]

ANTON: And the woman next door? You know, the one you talked about?

ILYA: Larissa, you mean? [. . .] The whole block knows her: "Legs-in-the-air-Larissa." That's her nickname. She latched onto me. She's one of those, you know—not nice, dirty. "Husband's away, wifie wants a lay." She's kind, it's true. Stops by, straightens up in here. I don't ask her to do it. Wants to get me hitched, get me into bed. Get her hands on my apartment. [. . .] She lives in a communal apartment right next door. Rents a room there. For thirty a month. Works in a factory, or something. I need her the way a goat needs bagpipes. And she needs an apartment, she doesn't need me. . . .

ANTON: I see. . . . What about a pension?

ILYA: I have one. Mailman brings it. It's a good one. Too little, all the same. From my old job. They broke some regulation or other—that's why my pension's so good. Up in Vladik—cable sliced my legs off. I was working on the docks. Long time ago that was. Thirteen years it's been since I came home to mother. That is, since they carried me home to her. *Pause. Ilya clenches and unclenches his fingers.* See—I've told you just about everything. Boring, huh? Nothing special, nonsense really. . . . [. . .] *Pause.* Listen, Anton . . .

ANTON: (*starts suddenly*) Ah? You wanted to say something, right?

ILYA: I'm talking to you: your name is Anton, isn't it? Listen, what I want to say is . . . I feel shy with you somehow. A little afraid. Come on, I'll have a drink all the same, relax a little and we'll talk a little more about something-or-other. . . . Like this—it's no fun—shameful, somehow. . . . Alright? You're not rushing off anyplace, right?

ANTON: No. Don't drink, Iliukha. You shouldn't, don't drink. Why do you do it?

ILYA: Alright, never mind, never mind. Wait. . . . To our acquaintance, how about, because, otherwise—I mean. . . . Just a minute, just wait. . . . *He rolls his chair quickly through the room. Finds a bottle in the cupboard. Hastily opens it with his teeth. Fills a glass, which was standing on the windowsill, drinks quickly. Breathes heavily.* Want to hear something funny? (*wipes sweaty hands along his trousers*) It's about what I said before, how dying is scary—I'm not just talking for the hell of it. Listen. Couple days ago I was drunk and fell down here. Well, fell asleep and fell out of my chair. My head landed over there, under the table. Uh-huh! Funny! I wake up and it's night—dark as can be. My head—dryg! dryg! And I can feel—boards on top of me. And I think: they're putting me in the ground, burying me, I think, like Gogol. . . . How I start to bellow, with all my might, bellowing away: "Eh, bastards, bastards, I'm alive, I'm alive, don't put me in the ground yet! Don't put me in the ground yet, bastards! . . . ,"

I bellow . . . *They both laugh.* Larissa came running, she woke up—that's how I was bellowing. She lives just the other side of the wall, after all. . . . And I'm bellowing the whole time: "I'm alive, alive, alive! . . ." *Pause.* And I cry a lot, too.

ANTON: Oh, cut it out. . . . You cry?

ILYA: Of course not! I'm not talking about that, about something else! It's funny, too. I'll have some vodka, you know, get to reading, oh, the Constitution or the Charter of the Communist Party—and I start to howl, tears all down my face, snot, too, all the way to the floor. . . .

ANTON: (*smiles*) But why?

ILYA: I don't know. Just feel like it. *They laugh loudly.*

ANTON: Don't drink.

ILYA: No big deal, a little bit won't hurt. *Pours wine into his glass, drinks.* It's good you came. Didn't play any tricks. You're so well-pressed, well-dressed, clean-cut. . . . Your eyes, you know, they're whoring eyes. . . .

ANTON: (*laughs*) What kind are those?

ILYA: You know, like yours. A ladies' man, aren't you? Well, that is, not really, but something else. That is—the women all like you, don't they? You're a happy man. I envy you. You go walking around over there somewhere, having some kind of conversations, some kind of things to do over there. . . . Over there—that's life. Isn't it?

ANTON: (silent a bit) No. Over there—that's not life. Here, where you are—that's life. Here, in this room—is life. *A LONG PAUSE.*

ILYA: What kind of life is this, here in this rathole. . . .

ANTON: Well. . . . You have dreams . . .

ILYA: Dreams—that's not life.

ANTON: All the same, you're special somehow. Not like other people.

ILYA: Unhappy, you mean to say? Unlucky?

ANTON: What do you mean unhappy? Stop acting so miserable! Cut it out! You're normal, normal! Not like other people, and thank God you're not! You and I are exactly alike. In everything. Cross my heart. When I talk to you—it's like talking to myself. It's so easy. Here, how old are you?

ILYA: Thirty-three . . .

ANTON: And I'm—going on nineteen. . . . So, you're only thirteen years older than I am!

ILYA: That much!

ANTON: Uh-huh, that much! And not that much, but only, only thirteen years older. That's why, you know, we're so alike. Alike in everything, in everything. . . . *Pause.* You know, I also often, often feel like dying. . . . *Anton sits on the floor against the wall, looks at the ceiling, dreamily.* I will die . . . in a car accident. I even know how it will happen. Just imagine: I'm crossing the street on a red light. Here comes a truck, right at me— a hundred ton, a huge truck. . . . I turn my head, see the truck's bumper, its headlights coming closer, coming closer. . . . Through the glass I see

the twisted face of the driver. . . . The glass shatters into smithereens—
that's it! The wheels are crushing, crushing the back of my head and I still
have time to notice, at the very last instant, to see, how my brains are
squeezing, like paste from a tube, out of a black box, from my eyes onto
the filthy earth. . . . And blackness! And darkness! And death! How beautiful it is! Ah? Class! *Pause.*
ILYA: You what? You . . . You want to die? Is that true?
ANTON: So what? Living—is it so good? Ah? What's good about it?
There's no reason to live. No-reason-at-all. And that's that. *Ilya rolls over
to Anton, who's sitting on the floor and begins to slap his cheeks, to pound
Anton with his fists.*
ILYA: Miserable louse! Lousy punk! Out, motherfucker! Out! Motherfucker, crooked asshole, get out of here, son-of-a-bitch! You carry on
about your own two legs, like they were the be-all and end-all, motherfucker, get out, out, out, out, out!!!! *Shoves Anton out of the apartment,
slams the door. Breathes heavily. Pushes his chair over to the table. Fills
his glass with wine, drinks. [. . .] The doorbell rings. Ilya doesn't move,
looks senselessly out the window. . . . Darkness.*

SECOND DREAM

*The sound of breaking glass. Ilya walks around the room, stepping care-
fully on his toes. A black dove beats its wings against the windowpane.*

ILYA: Do you see? A black dove beats its wings against the window. . . . It
wants to fly in to see me. . . . Eh! What do you want here?
ANTON: Who are you talking to?
ILYA: To you. I'm talking to you. And how did you get here? Didn't I kill
you? I saw your blood. . . . How can you be alive?
ANTON: It's impossible to kill me. Because—I'm alive. [. . .] These
aren't just leaves of paper. This is my novel. I've been writing it all my life.
Ah-eee, the wind, the wind! It's a whirlwind! The wind! It's carrying away
the pages of my novel, carrying them away! Now I never will collect them,
never! . . .
ILYA: It's beautiful, isn't it? . . . The white pages flying through the dark
night. . . . Like a movie. . . .
ANTON: That's my blood flying, flying away, pouring out, spouting tor-
rents, my blood, blood, blood. . . .

SCENE THREE

Three days have passed. Late evening. [In the beginning of this scene Larissa tries to persuade Ilya that she loves him and would make a good wife. As Ilya repeatedly rejects her, she explodes and tells him he will "croak" in his apartment. She storms out when Anton arrives, a little drunk and in a good mood. Ilya is happy to see him.]

ANTON: I've been remembering you these last three days. Been thinking.

ILYA: Me, too—about you. Been thinking.

ANTON: And what did you think?

ILYA: You go first.

ANTON: No, you! I asked first!

ILYA: Well, I thought, that you're—educated, and I'm—not.

ANTON: How am I educated? I'm completely—completely in the dark, stupid, and uneducated! (*he laughs*)

ILYA: Oh yes. You just pretend to be stupid, try to use words like I do when you're here, but really—you're educated. And some of the words you use—I don't know what they mean, never heard them before. I had eight years of school, and they showed me the door. But you—your parents are teachers and yourself—you're over there in the institute. . . .

ANTON: Just cut it out. That's all nonsense. Educated, uneducated. . . . All people are alike. There are only kind people and spiteful ones. Those who had more luck, and those . . . who had less. . . .

ILYA: I've been unlucky and that's why I'm spiteful? You had me in mind when you thought that, ah?

ANTON: You haven't been lucky—that's true. But you're not spiteful. You've just been made spiteful—infuriated! You are so in-fur-i-a-ted sometimes, you are, you are! *Laughs.* And I thought . . . I thought, it would be good, if . . .

ILYA: Well?

ANTON: Only don't start squirming, please. It would be good, if I could help you somehow. . . . Pancake-soul, I know, worn-out, pretty words, but—it's true! It would be good, if I could help you, ah?

ILYA: But you do help. Now I'm always looking out the window. Waiting for you.

ANTON: Well and what do you see from the eighth floor? (*laughs*)

ILYA: I can see everything from above, let me tell you! And you, when I look at you, my soul gets more peaceful. Sometimes—it's empty—empty. But when you're around—it's peaceful. I even talk to you late at night, I've already told you everything—my whole life. . . .

ANTON: And I—you . . .

ILYA: Tell me again. . . .

[After talking more about their childhoods, favorite toys and similar memories, Anton pushes in an ancient washing machine that Ilya uses as a makeshift still for his homebrew.] Anton and Ilya laugh loudly, joyfully and infectiously. Anton turns on the machine and it howls like an airplane at take-off. Anton kneels in front of Ilya's wheelchair. They both talk a long time about something, shouting, laughing, waving their hands. It's as if Ilya is lit up from within: that's how his eyes seem when he looks at Anton. Suddenly Ilya turns off the washing machine. Runs his hand through Anton's hair.

ILYA: Poor thing, you poor thing. . . . What hair . . . you have. . . .

ANTON: Your fingers . . . long fingers. . . . *Pause. It seems as if something may explode any minute—they're both so wound up. Anton suddenly jumps up, starts slapping his pockets fretfully, getting ready to leave.*

ANTON: I . . . You . . . I'll be off, I guess. . . . Time to go. . . . It's late. . . . I should. . . . I'll go, I guess. . . .

ILYA: Stay a little longer. . . .

ANTON: I . . . I'll come . . . tomorrow, I'll be back. . . . I'll definitely be back. . . . I should go. . . . I'll be back. . . .

ILYA: Just don't play any tricks on me. . . .

ANTON: No, no. I won't play any tricks. . . . I'm off. *Walks towards the door, silently. Turns around.* Listen, isn't it good, that you and I met, isn't it? (*fretfully*) Remember, how I dragged you home, and you go: "Done your bit for the invalid, now get out of here!"

ILYA: And you go: "This your place?"

ANTON: And you: "Mine! I rent it! 300 a month! Shut the door from the other side. Get out, motherfucker! . . ." And I left. . . . *Anton goes out the door.*

ILYA: And I shout—Stop! (*louder*) Stop! Stop! Stop! *Anton is gone. Ilya in terror rolls his chair to the door, gets tangled up in the cord of the washing machine, falls out of the chair, gasps, crawls to the door:* Stop. . . . Stop. . . . Come back. . . . Stop. . . . Come back, I beg you. . . . I'm begging you, come back. . . . Oh come back. . . . Stop!!!! I can't get along without you now. . . . Stop! Stop! Come back!!!!!!! *Darkness. Curtain.*

ACT TWO, THIRD DREAM

Ilya's apartment. Semi-darkness. The windows are wide open and the curtain is flying in the wind. Someone's bare feet slap against the moonlit squares on the floor.

VOICE: I feel good like this. . . . You feel good?

VOICE: Never felt so good before. . . .

VOICE: The moon outside—it's gone crazy. . . . there's light, heat coming from the moon, everything burns. . . .

VOICE: What freedom. . . . I'm happy. . . . I feel so good. . . . Happiness. . . . I'm dreaming this, ah? Tell me, am I dreaming?

VOICE: You're dreaming, dreaming, dreaming. . . . Sleep. . . . We dream everything. . . . There's no life, only dream. . . . Sleep. . . . We dream everything, dream, dream everything. . . .

The curtain flutters at the window. Happy laughter, whispering. Darkness.

SCENE FOUR

Morning. Ilya's apartment. Ilya is sitting in the wheelchair—clean shaven, washed and in fresh clothing, smiling awkwardly. On his knees— a pile of photographs. These are constantly falling to the floor and Ilya picks them up with difficulty. Anton stands beside Ilya. He's all in white—shirt, pants and sneakers.

ANTON: Why don't you buy yourself a photo album? Photographs have to be taken care of. Each is a memory you'll keep your whole life. A moment frozen in time. See how the corners are bent. There's a pretty one, you should put it in a little frame, you know, and hang it on the wall— just like in a decent house. Look, they're all crumpled. Why don't you buy yourself a photo album, I'm asking you?

ILYA: (*smiles*) I will buy one—now.

ANTON: (*looking through the photos, dropping them on the floor*) Now! Now—it's clear! It's clear it's a bull—once you can see its horns! Should have thought of it earlier, earlier, understand? See? Everything's falling to pieces, torn apart, everything, everything, everything!

[*Anton starts picking at Ilya's manners, grammar, behavior. He is loud, deliberately crude, but never mentions the preceding night. Ilya is fighting back tears. After a promise—or a threat—to bring some girls over to Ilya's place for an "orgy," Anton notices a slingshot.*]

ANTON: And what's this? (*laughs*) What do you have this for, Iliukha, you a kid, or something? Why do you keep this around?

ILYA: It's a slingshot. My slingshot.

ANTON: What's it for, I'm asking?

ILYA: I shoot at windows. (*hoarsely*) I roll around the streets at night and I shoot at windows.

ANTON: We-ell, pancake-soul! Madman, what for?

ILYA: (*silent a moment*) So people won't live so fine. Everyone's got to living awfully fine.

ANTON: Wh-at?

ILYA: What you heard.

ANTON: And you're an idiot . . . Ah? What an idiot! I mean, they'll catch you someday after all, beat your butt, and what'll you do, Iliukha? I mean, you can't run away after that little trick, can you, what'll you do? *Anton laughs, wipes away tears.*

ILYA: But I don't run. I take my shot and wait, wait 'til they run out into the street. They shout and bellow, but no one gives me a thought. I tell them: "That-a-way, that-a-way, he went that-a-way! Catch him!" And they—run that-a-way. And me—they don't touch me.

ANTON: Well, you are an idiot, Iliukha, an id-i-ot, I mean, i-di-ot. . . . No, really, you just had to think up something like that! Look what a fine trick he plays on people, ah? What an animal. . . . But did you think about the people? That they'll have to sleep all night with a broken window? And what if there's a draft—and children, too—they'll catch cold! Well, what a shit, ah? What a vicious animal! Just look! And what if they did the same to you, ah? To you, shit? If I take five kopecks, put it in the sling-shot, and—bang!—at your window? Take it and—bang! Look, I'll take it and—bang!—you'll feel fine, ah? Fine, right? Take this, animal, take this, take this!!! *Anton, in a fierce and venomous rage, fires a five-kopeck piece at the balcony door. The sound of breaking glass. A LONG PAUSE. SILENCE. Anton wipes the sweat from his brow.* (*quietly*) That does it. Bye. I'm off. Take care, my lord. . . .

ILYA: Wait . . . Wait a bit, Antosha. . . . Antosha, don't go. . . . Wait. . . . Please, stay. . . . I beg you. . . .

ANTON: (*in a shriek*) This makes me sick! It's disgusting! As if I'd been fed shit! It's sick! It's all so revolting. . . . Why did this happen? Why?? Why did this happen, why, why, why?! What vileness, what shame. . . . Oh, Lord, it's like a dream. . . . I could croak. . . . Vileness, vileness, what vileness. . . . It's that homebrew of yours, there's craziness in it . . . filth, vile filth. . . . As if spiders were crawling all over me, it's obscene . . . obscene . . .

ILYA: (*quietly*) You had a dream about something? Ah?

ANTON: Shut up! Shut up, animal! Don't play stupid! Don't fuck with my head! What're you trying to pull with this idiot act, wha-at? Oh, you don't understand anything, do you?! It doesn't make you sick, does it?! He's just a boy, just a boy still. . . . Pure and innocent! You make money with this business, ah?? Lord, Lord, how vile, how loathsome. . . .

ILYA: (*insistently*) You dreamt something. You were dreaming. In this apartment, people always dream. . . .

ANTON: Aha, so this business goes on here all the time, does it?? You lure everyone up here, is that it?! Oh, what dirt, what filth, what vileness. . . . You're a fucking animal yourself, motherfucker!! An animal yourself!!!

ILYA: (*continues, without listening*) Very strange dreams, that look like the truth—everyone dreams like that in this apartment. . . . Almost anything can happen in a dream. . . . The most unlikely things. . . . I dreamt about something, too, but now I see, now I'm awake, that all the words, every-thing, everything that happened—it was all lies, a fake, a dream . . .

ANTON: Shut up! Shut up! I didn't dream anything! Everything really hap-pened! I remember everything perfectly!

ILYA: You had a bad dream? It's not my fault. . . .

ANTON: (*mocking him*) A bad dream, a bad dream! You let loose a cloud, a cloud of words! You mixed some kind of poison into that moonshine of yours, sorcerer, legless wretch! I hate you, snake, hate you, snake, hate you!!!! . . . *He slams the door, Ilya sits for a long time in silence, his head drooping. Rolls the wheelchair over to the balcony door. Wipes away tears. Begins to pick up the broken glass. Cuts himself. Blood runs onto the floor. Ilya doesn't notice. He throws the pieces of glass aside.*

ILYA: (*quietly*) Just so he doesn't do anything to himself. . . . He'll come back, he'll come back. . . . Just so he doesn't do anything. . . . He'll definitely come back. . . . Otherwise. . . .I've no reason to live. . . . He'll come back. . . . *Darkness. The sound of breaking glass.*

FOURTH DREAM

Once again indistinct shadows wander through Ilya's room. And here he is, hiding, pressed up against the wall. Larissa enters from the balcony.

LARISSA: So, that's where you've hidden, ah?? Want to run away? Can't run from yourself. . . . Won't work out, friend. . . . Now I know all about you, all your dark secrets, every last one of them. . . . And here I'm thinking—what's going on? And now—I know everything. . . . Everyone knows about it, the whole town. . . . What scum you are, worthless, revolting scum . . .

ANTON: Scum, you're scum, lousy scum, pigfucker. . . . I wouldn't wipe my feet on you. . . . Playing stupid here . . . throwing dust in my eyes . . . lousy scum. . . . Worthless scum. . . .

ILYA: You should understand everything and forgive everything. . . . You know how to do that, after all. . . .To understand, to forgive. . . .

ANTON: Scum, scum, scum. . . .

LARISSA: Rotten, mouldering, maggoty scum. . . .

ILYA: Ah-eeeee! Look—there it is again! The black dove beats its wings again outside my window! He wants to fly in through the vent! There's no glass there, why doesn't he fly in?

LARISSA: He'll fly in, fly in, never fear! It's death, after all, has come for you, your death. . . . It's done beating around the bush, all done. . . . Long ago, you should have met with it, sat down with it long ago. . . . It's your death, death. . . . *The sound of breaking glass.*

SCENE FIVE

A week later. Evening. Ilya's room. Everything is just as it was. Things have been straightened up, it's true. The broken window is covered with cheesecloth. There's no dust in the corners. Ilya is walking around the room. These steps cost him dearly. Heavy, ironlike prostheses barely move him from one place to another. One step, another step. . . . The doorbell. Ilya starts to fret—turns his body first forwards, then backwards, now towards the table, now towards the door. Almost falls. But keeps his balance. Makes it to his wheelchair. [. . .] Anton kicks the door wide-open. He's drunk. His hair is flying in all directions. He's wearing a blue t-shirt and jeans. Walks into the room, without looking at Ilya.

ILYA: Hello . . .

ANTON: "Here's my village, here my native home!" Haven't been home for a long time, have we! Well, how're you doing, how's your tummy, what about your head—does it hurt? Well? *Sits in the chair, puts his feet on the table, smokes, scattering ashes on the floor.*

ILYA: (*smiles*) You act like you're in America. . . . As if you were at home. . . . It's good you've come. . . . We can talk a little. . . . Want something to eat? . . . I'll fix it right away. . . .

ANTON: (*curls his lip*) Don't speak low, we're all friends here. . . . What're you doing, ah? Brought you some fresh jokes. Guaranteed to crack you up. Two chickens meet, and one says to the other: "How much do your eggs bring?" The other one answers: "A ruble thirty. And you?" The first chicken says: "A ruble five." "And why so little?" asks the second chicken. "Eh," answers the first, "Why should I bust my ass for twenty-five kopecks?" *Anton laughs loudly.* "Bust my ass?" get it? Classy stuff, ah? Keep listening! [*After several similar jokes, Anton is "laughing wildly, on the verge of tears"*].

ILYA: (*laughs, too*) Want some tea?

ANTON: I come for tea! Bring on the glasses! We'll have a bang! Let's you and I bang away, friend Iliukha! Bang away! Bang away! Bring in the glasses! *Once again something amuses him, he laughs till he almost chokes, almost in hysterics, falls from his chair onto the floor and pounds the boards with his fists. Ilya brings in the glasses, puts them on the table, looks at Anton.*

ILYA: (*laughs*) And here I am waiting and waiting for you, for when you'll stop by. . . . I wait and wait, and you don't come, don't come! I thought, maybe something had happened. . . . I've been waiting all week . . . waiting, waiting, waiting, and you don't come, you don't come. . . .

ANTON: Haven't seen you myself. What is it, not sitting outside the grocery store, now, eh? Ah? Not working, or something? Goofing off? (*laughs*) Should've sat down, collected enough for a jug, what else is there?

Or have you come into a lot of money, is that it? An inheritance fallen from the sky, ah, Iliukha? Why aren't you working?!

ILYA: No, no inheritance. . . . Somehow, Antosha . . . you know, somehow, I just didn't feel like it, Antosha. . . .

ANTON: Oh-oh. Your highness. Don't start getting familiar. A fine Antosha you've found yourself. You talk trash like Trotsky. . . . Well, shall we drink? *Pulls a bottle of wine from his plastic bag, opens it with his teeth.* Today's a day that positively calls for celebration! A red letter day! I'll remember it for the rest of my life, all the rest of my life! I have to! Can't forget a thing like this, no way, right, Iliukha?

ILYA: Passed an exam, ah?

ANTON: (*laughs loudly again, crawls on the floor, pounding his fists*) Exactly! You hit it on the nose, exactly! That's it! I passed an exam! Exactly! And I got . . . an A! An A-plus! An excellent! In my long report card—the first mark—is an A-plus! Excellent! My very first teacher signed her name to it! That's what she said in parting: "Antonchik, you're brilliant, just brilliant. You're the most brilliant student I've ever had in my life!" *Ilya laughs too, infected with Anton's mirth, but doesn't understand what he's talking about. Anton keeps laughing, filling the glasses with wine.*

ILYA: Well, congratulations, then, since that's how it is. . . .

ANTON: Thanks, old man! Thanks! Thanks for the good word. . . . Thanks! You've made me laugh! Now, as one man to another—congratulate me on this business! On passing my exam, that is! Ah? Well, are you and I men, or are we old ladies, goddam it? Let's have a toast! We—are men! When you drink to women, sir, that is—to ladies—you have to drink standing up! That's the tradition! If we have any respect for ourselves! Never mind, never mind, you go ahead and sit, sit, I'll let you, go ahead, sit. But I'll drink—standing! (*cruelly*) Standing! To women, sir! That's all! The past is no more! To women! Oh yes, "Our t-shirts say 'Adidas,' any babe will do us. . . ." Right?! Well, are you and I men? Are we men or aren't we? What're you so quiet for? Men, are we men?

ILYA: Men.

ANTON: So, let's drink then! Get on with it! *They drink. Pause. Anton chews some bread, without blinking, he looks at Ilya, laughing uncertainly. Both of them are silent a long time.* Listen, Iliukha . . . I didn't show up here for no reason. . . . No-o, not for no reason!! I don't do anything—for no reason. . . . [. . .] You know, I came here to blackmail you. [. . .] And what can you do about it? Nothing at all. Live with wolves—you end up howling like one. So, you choose: one in the hand, or two in the face . . . your face. Well? Why're you so quiet? Don't you get it?

ILYA: What do you want?

ANTON: As if he didn't understand! If you pay me—I'll keep quiet. Got it? Or not?

ILYA: No . . .

ANTON: Ah, you don't get it. . . . Well, well. I'll try again using simple words. See, I'll just go and start telling your neighbors, the whole building, the whole street—tell them just who they've been warming in their bosoms, just who it is that lives here. . . . Let them put you in the nuthouse. . . . That's what'll happen—if you don't pay up. But if you do pay up—then I'll keep quiet. Well?

ILYA: (*quietly*) No money. . . . I don't have any money right now . . .

ANTON: Well, that's right! And there won't be any! You haven't been going to work, after all! And you've got to go to work, every day, go and sit there, and beg, beg it out of them! You could earn tons, tons! [. . .] I won't let you starve. You're my meal ticket! Well? Come on, say you'll do it, Ilya Ivanovich! Or else, you know, I'll go and tell everyone all about you—all, all, all about you!

ILYA: (*quietly*) Anton . . . you mustn't . . . You're not, not like that. . . . *Ilya's throat convulses, he's almost sobbing.* You mustn't. . . . You . . . you're . . . an angel. . . .

ANTON: (*shouting viciously*) Ai-ai-ai! What did we say? What fine words we know, right out of a book! First it's—we can't put two sentences together in Russian, have to use our hands, our hands to help us speak, then—all of a sudden—an angel! If you want, I could tell you a joke on that topic! A per-fect-ly - bril-li-ant joke! Simply brilliant! About an angel! Angel. . . . Oh you, really. . . . Hey, gave you a scare, ah? You were frightened, frightened, I can tell by your eyes, how you took fright right away, right away started speaking so fine. . . . Well, alright, listen. Imagine this: a canal full of muck and slime. Although why imagine anything? Your apartment looks just like it! 100% like! (*laughs loudly*) And in this canal—all kinds of shit is floating. Big chunks and little pieces. . . . A whole canal full of shit! And plowing through this shit, choking, arms and legs flailing, comes a rat—dirty, no fur left on its back. . . . And her eyes. . . . Oh, they're just like yours, 100% like: spiteful, oh so spiteful, and tiny, oh so tiny. . . . Full of spite, scared to death, sparkling eyes. . . . And on the rat's back sits a little baby rat: filthy, covered with scabs, scales, sores. . . . Suddenly, above the canal, a bat flies over—and it's just as dirty, stinking and tormented. And the baby rat pokes up its head and cries: "Mama, look, it's an angel, an angel!" *Laughs loudly.* Brilliant joke, ah? About our life exactly, yours and mine. . . . Very, very, very, like. . . . *Pause. Silence.* Well, what're you looking at ? What is it you're peeling and peeling away with your spiteful little eyes, like a wild chicken, ah? There's something you don't like, ah? Well, what is it, what don't you like, what fails to meet with your approval? Well, speak up, speak up! You don't like me, ah? Speak up, I said!

ILYA: I like you . . . a lot . . .

ANTON: (*shrieks*) Shut up! Shut up! Shut up! Or I'll kill you!

ILYA: Kill me, then.

ANTON: (*silent a long time, walks quickly about the room, pulling at his hair*) By the way. Although it's completely off the subject. But no matter. No matter. I still haven't told you, where I've come from, where I've been, what I've done and why it is we're having this little drink today. I forgot the most important thing. Overlooked the elephant under my nose. Yes, yes. You got it right, you guessed correctly, when you said—I passed an exam today. With an excellent mark! Stay calm! Stay calm! Dear Lord, what an idiot! What an idiot I am! Because of those three times, I was so afraid, so shook up, and it turns out—those bimbos, those broads, they were to blame themselves, themselves! They were just like logs! And they only had to do just a little, just a little bit to help me out, but they're— uneducated idiots when it comes to sex! Understand?! In brief. Remember, I told you about Sveta, that fox I know? Well, the one who's got what it takes? Remember? Don't pretend you forgot, you remember! Never mind. So. Today mama and papa—bless their hearts, God give them health!—went out to the dacha. I invited Svetochka over to our place, to drink coffee, watch videos. . . . I wasn't even thinking about that, not even thinking! She herself suggested it! She did everything! Everything! Seventh heaven! Ecstasy! And I—I had what it takes! Do you hear?! She even said later that she'd never had a man like me in her life! No one had ever pleased her as much in bed, as I did! She said, that I have a beautiful body, beautiful hair, that as a man—I am irresistible! As a man! And she told the truth, the truth, do you hear?! I believe her! She put strength into me, she made a person out of me, now I am calm, calm! Completely calm, calm like an Olympian! Because I was losing my mind, tossing back and forth, like an idiot, an idiot! I wanted to go to the doctor—thought I was impotent, affected by radiation or something down there! I even wanted to throw myself in front of a car! Idiot, idiot! But it turns out—it's possible, possible, so long as everything is beautiful! And, afterwards, it's not shameful at all to look her in the eyes when it's—like something ordinary, understand? You do it—like something ordinary! And I thought—I was sick! But I'm healthy, healthy as a bull, as a horse, as a moose! In two hours—four times! Four times! Four times! Understand?! She was floating on clouds, she was so satisfied! That's right, that's right! And I will have children, I will, I will! I love children! I love children so much! I really, really love children very much! I will, I will bring children into the world! My wife and I will have lots of children! Five, six, eight of 'em! Every night I'll come home from work, and they will run and jump and hop and race all around me! Around me! Around me! My children, understand? I will, will, have them, my children, my children. . . . I will have them, I know—I will!!!! *Silence. Anton brushes away tears.*

ILYA: (*not loudly, with a cough*) And I—too . . . also did . . . the very same, as you. . . . Only yesterday. With Lariska. Come on, let's drink. Pour. She came over and I did it. Of course, not like you, the way you did. . . . Worse, of course. . . . But everything worked out. Everything was normal! Come on, come on, come on, let's hurry up and drink! If everything's turned out so well for you—we should celebrate this business right away, such a thing happens only once in a lifetime, we've got to drink more, drink more! Come on, come on!!!! *Anton believes him immediately, talks rapidly, without stopping and without looking Ilya in the eyes. [. . .] They drink in one gulp. Someone's teeth knock against the sides of a glass—either Ilya or Anton is trembling. SILENCE.*

ILYA: Night already. . . . Turning cold. Fall will be here soon.

ANTON: (*quickly*) You did the right thing with Lariska. . . . The right thing! Good boy! Class, ah? Should have done it long ago, long ago! That's right, Iliukha, that's the way, that's the way!

ILYA: I haven't had anything to drink in a long time. . . . My head is swimming . . . everything's spinning. . . . *He laughs, clutching his head in his hands.* You know, I just now remembered, all of a sudden remembered: My mother once stole a chicken from somewhere. . . . A live chicken that she swiped from someone! I was little, she brought it home. . . . *Anton also laughs loudly.*

ANTON: A chicken? A live one?? Really?

ILYA: Right, a live one! My mother named her Esmeralda! Esmeralda—a chicken! She sat there until evening, under the bed. . . . Messed all over the place, and then . . . (*gasps with laughter*) . . . And then my mother put her on the stool . . . she put her on the stool and with an axe . . . her head . . . her head . . . with an axe, with an axe . . . one, two, three. . . . She's jumping, racing around. My mother falls on the floor, she's cursing, and the chicken is running her neck into the wallpaper here, there, in this room, and that one, with her neck, her neck . . . here, here, here. . . . And I hid in the bed and watched and laughed at my mother, and laughed at the chicken thrashing against the wallpaper, the wallpaper, the wallpaper. . . . *They both laugh.*

ANTON: (*through his laughter*) Listen, Ilya. . . . Come on, let's come to an agreement here, on the brink. . . . Let's make an agreement, come on, listen!

ILYA: (*laughing*) Alright! Alright! Alright!

ANTON: Listen. . . . You did it, and so did I . . . Understand?

ILYA: (*chortling*) Well yes!

ANTON: Wait, hold up. . . . That's all! (*crosses his arms*) That's all—understand? That's right—that's all. Because, what happened with you and me—we have to forget that, rip it out, and forget it, forget. . . . You said it right that time—it was a dream. It's just that you and I, of course, had too much to drink. . . . Things like that only happen when you're drunk, understand? Let's forget it, ah? I won't come to see you anymore, never! What for? You'd be ashamed, and I. . . . It's forbidden! It's revolting, sickening. Shameful. Between men—you don't do that kind of thing, understand? It's indecent, see? You and I—we're men, understand?? It's shameful, forbidden, shameful, forbidden!

ILYA: I'm not ashamed.

ANTON: (*quietly*) Be quiet, be quiet. . . . Don't let anyone hear that! . . . Be quiet. . . . You're a grown up old guy, but I'm just a kid—trying to persuade you, or something, teach you how to live. . . . It's your business, of course, you can carry on like this with anyone you want, but I . . . I made a mistake, understand?? It's awful, awful, you can't do things like that, it's shameful, disgusting . . .

ILYA: I don't need anyone. Only you.

ANTON: (*shouts*) Shut up!!! Shut up!!! Be quiet!!! *Walks rapidly up and down the room, pressing his head between his hands, swaying from side to side. Whispers:* Quiet, quiet . . . stop it, stop it. . . . It was just a moment, some kind of fire blazed through, a magnet or something—pulled us to each other, that's all. . . . Blindness! This all happens from loneliness, loneliness! You have it rough, and here I show up—going on about my kid's worries and torments, so stupid, stupid. . . . Understand, this is vile, sick, revolting. . . . Vile, vile, vile. . . . That weakness, I curse myself for it—it makes me wretched, wretched—wretched that I was so weak, that wasn't the way. . . . All these days I've been thinking about it: wanted to do away with myself, stuff myself with pills, do . . . I don't know what with myself. . . . And if it weren't for Sveta today—I would have, for sure, because I can't, can't bear that night in myself. . . .But today—today I freed myself from that dirt, washed it away! After Svetka I went into the bathroom and washed myself, washed myself, scrubbed myself with a brush! Washed all the dirt away! I won't be with anyone else now, do you hear, not with anyone! Not until my wedding day! With Sveta—it was so, so simple—I proved to myself, that I can do it—and that's all! That's all! I'll cut myself off from everything now, keep myself pure for my wife! I'll be pure! Find myself some good girl, marry her, and tell her, that I'm—just a boy, that I've been saving myself for her! I want to wipe out what happened with you and me! It makes me sick to think, that my hands, that . . . that touched you, are going to touch her, the mother of my children, understand?! And my children—I'll caress them and kiss them with lips, lips that. . . . Vile, vile, how vile and rotten!!!! *Pause.*

ILYA: (*quietly*) Then you weren't lying?

ANTON: Listen, you, maybe you could go away to another city, ah?? I'll get some money for you, I'll get a lot, really a lot! Just so you vanish, disappear, cease to exist altogether in this town?! Could you disappear?!

ILYA: (*shudders*) What for? I won't tell anyone anything . . .

ANTON: Well, that's right, sure. . . . Right. . . . Why would you . . . about your own self. . . .That's right, what you said. . . . Alright, alright. . . . You're a decent guy, kind. . . . You'll understand, I think, why I'm so upset. . . . You'll understand. . . . You . . . here's what: starting today, you and I don't know each other, understand? Wherever we meet, whenever we see each other—not under any circumstances! We don't know each other—period! Ten years will pass, twenty—never! Never, hear?! . . . And if—God help you, you should suddenly. . . . Well I'll . . . you . . . I'll do . . . You'll get. . . . You understand, right? I just don't know what I'd do with you then. . . . Can you promise me right now that you'll never let on that you know me, can you?!

ILYA: (*silent a bit*) You're all worked up. Save yourself. For your future life. It will be long and complicated enough as it is. . . . What are you so frightened of? I promise—we will never, never, never meet each other, and if we do meet, I won't make a sign. . . . *Laughs hoarsely*. We'll meet in the other world. . . . If, of course, it exists. . . . There, I suppose, I can let on that I know you?

ANTON: Alright, alright. Don't be an idiot. That's all. That's all, Iliukha! I'm leaving, old man. Come on, don't start sniveling and don't be an idiot. Everything will be all, all, all, A-OK for you, too, I have no doubts. So!

ILYA: Wait . . .

ANTON: (*on the threshold*) No, no, don't hold me back, old man, you mustn't, it's time for me to get home, it's late, see you later, it's time, that's all, see you later. . . .

ILYA: Wait, I said. Don't be afraid for yourself. . . . [. . .] Wait . . .

ANTON: (*shouts*) What are you tormenting me for, what do you want—what, what, what?

ILYA: You shouldn't get so wound up. Your children will grow up touched in the head. Like their father. You haven't promised me the same thing.

ANTON: What, what, what is it!

ILYA: You haven't promised me . . . not to recognize me. I promised you, but not you—me!

ANTON: (*with a sigh of relief*) We-ell—you needn't worry about that! Put your mind at ease! God help me! Not only will I never recognize you, I won't throw you a broken kopeck, not once in my life! Not a one, God save me! (*laughs*) That's all, old man. Later, alligator! See you, old man. So long. I mean, good-bye! *Slams the door. Ilya sits a long time without moving. Then he turns the wheelchair around and slowly rolls to the window. Looks at the sky and whispers softly:*

ILYA: Dear Lord, hear my curse on him, hear it! May he suffer torments the rest of his life for his cruelty, may he pay for it! May his dreams be unquiet, may he see nightmares by day and by night, may he wake up in a cold sweat every day of his life, every day of his life! Cruelty—must be paid for! Even childish cruelty, a drowned kitten, a stone through a window, everything, everything—must be paid for! May he pay all his life! May you be cursed, cursed, cursed. . . . *SILENCE*. Oh Lord, what am I saying. . . . No, no, no, no, Lord. . . . Help him to live. . . . May he never find an evil person at his side. . . . May he always be as beautiful and defenseless as a child. . . . May his soul never darken. . . . May everyone love him, and everyone pity him. . . . May he never more bring anyone grief. . . . never more—not to anyone! Lord, Lord. . . . You and I will meet each other, Anton, we will meet. . . . You will never forget me, never. . . . We will meet. . . . You will not forget. . . . You must not forget me. . . . We will meet. . . . Forgive me, forgive, forgive me, forgive, forgive. . . . *Ilya opens the balcony door. Wind blows through the room, fluttering the curtains. Ilya slowly crawls from the wheelchair. Darkness. The sound of breaking glass. The night wind rustles the newspapers.*

SCENE SIX

Six months later. Winter. The landing. Anton is slowly climbing up the stairs. [. . .] Upset and frightened, he is clearly forcing himself to come here and ring Ilya's doorbell—as if a magnet were pulling him. [. . .] He takes off his mitten to press the doorbell, jumps back when he hears movement in one of the neighboring apartments. Anton quickly heads down the stairs, then turns around. Larissa comes out with a trash bucket in her hands. She's in slippers and a robe, her hair uncombed. Meeting Anton's eyes, she takes fright.

LARISSA: Dear God, you frightened me. . . . What do you want? Coming and going. . . . Elevator's broke again . . . always coming. . . . So what do you want? Come to see him, ah?
ANTON: (*with a dry throat*) To him.
LARISSA: You make me sick, alcoholics. . . . Everyone's known for ages after all—he's gone, not here anymore! But still they come. Touring your old hang-outs, ah? What do I have to do, hang a sign out downstairs, ah? He's gone, see?
ANTON: But where is . . . Ilya?
LARISSA: Where, where. . . . Back in his mother's cunt, that's where! Get out of here!
ANTON: He moved? Then, his address, could I . . .
LARISSA: Uh-huh, moved! Out of the city, for a lark, to the North Sea! He's a louse, your Ilya! How I begged him, how I tried to persuade him to register the apartment in my name—it's all gone to hell! They sealed it up, see? The City Council sealed it up!
ANTON: What . . . what happened? Something happened? Put him in a home for invalids, ah? Where is it?
LARISSA: He croaked, I'm telling you, croaked! The drunk, he had too much, fell off the balcony! Lived like a cockroach behind the stove, and that's how he croaked! Go on, get out of here, before I throw this at you! Coming and going, dropping cigarette butts all over the place. . . . Go on,

get out, ah?! He croaked, he's no more! *Anton heads downstairs. Returns, comes back up.* What are you looking at? What is it?? . . . No reason to look at me. . . . No reason. . . . What is it. . . . What? I'll call the cops on you right now. . . . I'm telling you, he croaked, he's no more!! *Anton presses Larissa up against the wall, starts hitting her forcefully, insistently, methodically.*

ANTON: Lousy whore. . . . Lousy whore. . . . Lousy whore. . . . Lousy whore. . . . You killed him. . . . You. . . . Not one of you loved him. . . . Not one of you knows how to love. . . . Lousy whore. . . . Lousy whore. . . . Lousy whore. . . . *Larissa shuts her mouth tightly, doesn't even cry out, slips down the wall to the floor. Anton hurls himself at the door, with all his strength, shouts:* Ilya! Ilya! Where are you, Ilya! Open up! Open up! Open up, Ilya! I've come to see you, Ilya! Ilya! Ilya?! Ilya?! Ilya?! *Hits himself on his cheeks, weeps like a little child.* Ilya, brother! I'm here, Ilya! Where are you, Ilya! Ilya, I'm here! Ilya?! Ilya?! Ilya?! . . . *Sits on the threshold, weeping. Beside him—Larissa. Also weeping.*

FIFTH AND FINAL DREAM

White twilight.

ILYA'S VOICE: But I know—what death is like. . . . Death, they say—it's darkness, blackness, night. But, that's not true. In childhood, an electric shock almost killed me. A white, white gauze hung in front of my eyes. And I saw . . . some kind of dead end . . . a corridor. . . . A white, white corridor. . . . They pushed me back. . . . What for?? I should have gone down that corridor then, into the white twilight. . . . Not caused myself such suffering, and others too. . . . No, the main thing is—to spare others suffering. . . . They mustn't suffer. God punished me for everything. . . . God punished. . . .

ANTON: I didn't come to see you for half a year. . . . But then I came . . . to stay forever. . . . I was coming to see you, but I knew myself, that you —were no more. . . . That day, when you were no more, I knew already, I knew. . . . Will we meet? Tell me, Ilya, will we meet? Just say one word, Ilya: Will we . . . meet?

ILYA: We will meet. . . . We . . . will definitely meet. . . . *Darkness.*

Sergei Rybikov (b. 1962)

LAYS OF THE GAY SLAVS

[Pesni gei-slavian]

Translated by Anatoly Vishevsky and Michael Biggins

SERGEI RYBIKOV (b. 1962) lives in Moscow. "I collect plots and creative ideas from the lives of my friends and acquaintances, after which I lose all interest in them. I am the lyric hero of my own works. Outgoing, friendly, talkative. But rude. I like new friends and fresh meat." "Lays of the Gay Slavs" first appeared under the pen name "Werewolf" in the gay collection *Drugoi* (Moscow, 1993).

To the real Yura, Alyosha, Dima, and many others, the author dedicates this work.

INTRODUCTION

EVERY SELF-RESPECTING people has its own mythology and folklore. In this sense the Gay Slavs are no exception. The only thing that distinguishes them from the world's other ethnic groups is their lack of a literary heritage. The present collection of lays, legends and *bylinas* (epic songs) of the Gay Slavs, it is hoped, will serve, if only in part, to fill in this gap in Gay Slavic studies.

Of course, this humble work makes no claim to being comprehensive, for folklore is inexhaustible and its greatest discoveries still lie ahead.

LAY THE FIRST: "YURA AND ALYOSHA"

1. There lived in Sokolniki a boy named Yura. He was handsome, strong, and masculine, so that

2. none of the people around him, not even his closest friends, would have guessed that he was gay.

3. More than anything in the world, Yura was afraid that someone would find out. And he even started dating a

4. girl from his school, and he wanted to marry her. But in fact he would time and again fall in love with his friends and at night he would

5. quietly cry into his pillow over his bitter fate. But then it came time for him to join the army.

6. Yura was sorely afraid that he wouldn't last long there, among so many young fellows, but what was to be done? He was in perfect

7. health, and they took Yura into the marines. Time passed, and he did his service. At the

8. beginning Yura couldn't even think about anything, only about how hungry and sleepy he was. And even in the

9. bathhouse the young soldiers' bodies stirred absolutely no feelings in him. But then a year passed,

10. and Yura managed to find a comfortable niche for himself in the company headquarters, and other thoughts and desires started to visit him.

11. Except that no opportunities presented themselves. But then one day they brought new recruits onto the base,

12. totally green kids, and Yura started processing their papers and filling out all kinds of forms.

13. And among the recruits he saw one young boy, and he felt that he couldn't restrain himself anymore.

14. He stood and smiled at the boy, and the boy smiled back at him. Not much time passed, and Yura had

15. convinced his superiors to assign the boy to him for training as his assistant and substitute. And then one word followed another,

16. and one thing followed another, and they got together. Of course at headquarters things were so much simpler. How Yura enjoyed living freely.

17. And Alyosha (that was his name) turned out to be such a sensitive boy, and more than once he said to Yura,

18. "There's no life for me without you. When I get discharged, I'll come to you, and we'll be together for the rest of our lives." Yura would only smile

19. at these words. Day by day, month by month, Yura's hitch ran out. Well, he thought, tomorrow I go home.

20. That's where my friends are, where life is free. Just one thing bothered him. A year is a short time, and what if Alyosha suddenly

21. did show up at his house? Yura thought and thought how to avert such a disaster, and at last it came to him.

22. Just before his departure he told several of the men that Alyosha was queer and had been following him

23. constantly. He told them, and then he left for home. And he was expected there, by the girl from school who was making preparations for their wedding.

24. In short, there was nowhere for Yura to turn and he got married. And in the meantime Alyosha began to live through hard times.

25. The men, of course, didn't keep the news to themselves, but told others, and the news continued to spread. One night the men

26. caught Alyosha in the latrine, and they let themselves go: they beat him to a pulp, they violated him, and then they even warned him

27. not to tell a soul. Alyosha returned to the barracks pale as death,

went to bed in silence, and during the night he had

28. something like a fever. He cried constantly, biting his pillow and plaintively whispering, "Yura, Yurochka." And then

29. he went to the latrine. They found him there in the morning, hanging by his belt. That night Yura had a dream, as though he were standing

30. amid a snow-covered steppe. The wind whipped his face, and up ahead a familiar figure beckoned to him. And it was as though

31. Yura took a closer look, and it was his Alyosha. Yura was overjoyed and ran after him. And it was as though he was running as fast as he could,

32. but couldn't catch up. He tried to reach his hand out to him, but it just passed through him as through a fog. And Yura saw

33. Alyosha turning to him, laughing, and then suddenly turning serious and saying, "You won't catch me now,

34. and you won't reach me. I used to love you, and I was fine. But now I don't love you at all, and that's even better."

35. And in the dream Alyosha opened his overcoat, revealing a uniform belt taut around his neck. Yura awoke beside

36. his young wife, remembered the dream, realized that Alyosha was no longer alive, and cried most bitterly.

LAY THE SECOND: "MISHA"

1. Then there was Misha, the son of important parents. And as often happens, he was bored of the luxury, affluence and wealth

2. that had surrounded him from the cradle; bored of his teachers' sycophancy; but most of all he was frustrated by the fact that he simply

3. couldn't find a friend equal to him, not in social status, but in the degree of his inner freedom. All of his

4. friends were either too self-important and boring or too messed up. And so Misha

5. approached his sixteenth birthday having loved no one, when a most unusual thing happened to him.

6. One day his father's driver did not come for him after school, and Misha decided to walk home alone, especially since he didn't live

7. far at all. And as he was walking down a side street—Trekhprudny, most likely—a bum who lived there in a musty, filthy cellar

8. caught sight of him. He could see this was a clean-cut kid, and the clothes he was wearing were also first-rate.

9. He threatened Misha in such a way that the boy couldn't move, then he grabbed him by the waist and dragged him into his cellar.

10. He beat him up, of course, he took off his jacket and pulled off his jeans, and when he saw the boy's young and pampered body,

11. his long-dormant passions started to stir. He got on top of Misha and raped him,

12. and then fell asleep on him. Misha tried to push the heavy, foreign body off of himself, but his arms were too spoiled and weak.

13. He cried for a while and then fell asleep, too. In the morning Misha awoke in the dank, filthy cellar, and the bum said to him,

14. "Get out of here," he said, "go home. But if you blab, I'll kill you. So tell your parents any lie you want." And Misha

15. answered him, "I'm not going to leave, because I love you." At this the bum grew even angrier than before

16. and beat him up, but let him stay. And so Misha came to live with the bum, and he survived on thievery and panhandling,

17. because the bum didn't bother to feed him, but beat him at the slightest provocation. But Misha seemed not

18. to notice the beatings at all, and could only dream of when night would come and the coarse hands of his beloved would sweetly

19. squeeze him again. Meanwhile, Misha's parents had naturally reported him missing and set the entire police department out

20. searching for him. Time passed, and eventually they found Misha. Misha's parents, as I have already said,

21. were important and influential people. The charges against their son were suppressed, and the bum was put in jail for vagrancy,

22. theft, and extortion. When Misha learned about this he cried bitterly, since he had

23. never loved anyone, but anyone, as much. Then one night he got dressed, left the luxurious apartment, and set out for wherever the road would take him;

24. clearly, he wanted to find his beloved, though he had no idea where to look for him, nor where he came from, nor even his name.

25. I don't know whether he found him or not, but since then no one has seen Misha again.

LAY THE THIRD: "DIMA AND VALERA"

1. There once lived an unmarried woman. And she had an only son whom she loved more than life itself.

2. And it wasn't for naught that she loved him, for you could have searched far and wide and not found another like him: for he was winsome, and handsome,

3. and kind. And his name was Dima. To his mother's delight, Dima grew to be clever, obedient, and industrious. Only one thing

4. darkened his mother's happiness—Dima didn't have a girlfriend. And however much his mother tried,

5. even trying to matchmake with her friends' daughters, it was all for naught. Not one of them appealed to Dima. His mother fell to thinking,

6. her son was already twenty-two without even a hint of a girlfriend.

And so she started to look for a reason.

7. The reason was not far to find. For Dima already had a love, and what a love it was! Stronger than strong and greater than great.

8. This love's name was Valera. Valera lived across the street, but the two seldom saw each other, so as

9. not to provoke suspicion. And they made love even less often. But when such happiness would come,

10. they would cling to each other so that you couldn't pull them apart with a team of horses. They were a perfect match, beautiful as

11. heavenly angels. But even this furtive happiness didn't last long. Dima's mother somehow managed to find them out,

12. and then began what no tale can tell nor pen can write, and Dima's mother began to raise a ruckus,

13. following her son's every move and turning to doctors. But Dima paid none of this

14. any heed, he just lost weight, grew pale, and fell more and more silent. And then he succumbed

15. and fell gravely ill. He lay lifeless in bed, neither eating nor drinking, breathing with difficulty.

16. His mother began calling in doctors again, but they could only shrug, and nothing was of any help whatsoever.

17. He expired like a candle in the wind. Then once the doorbell rang, ever so timidly. Dima's mother opened the door,

18. and in the doorway stood Valera. He was clearly frightened of the stern woman, but wanted to say something

19. important. "Let me in to see Dima," he said, "and he will get better right away. It is me that he misses so much."

20. Dima's mother got angry. "What kind of nonsense is that," she said. "Now get out of here before I call the police."

21. What was there to do? Valera wavered and went home. Dima's mother returned to her son's room, looked

22. and saw him sitting on the bed, his eyes glistening with tears. And he said, "Mom, who was that at the door?" And she replied,

23. "Nobody, son, just somebody who got the wrong apartment." Dima moaned frightfully, collapsed in his pillow and fell as silent

24. as the dead. His mother took fright, touched her son, but he was now truly dead as a doornail. And now the poor woman

25. realized that she had destroyed her virtuous and beautiful son, with her own two motherly hands she had

26. destroyed him—and she cried disconsolately.

LAY THE FOURTH: "THE TEMPTATION OF ANTON"

1. And now, my friends, let me tell you a wondrous and unusual tale. There once lived a boy

2. whose name was Anton. Actually there was nothing so unusual in that; people are named

3. all kinds of things. What was unusual about him was the fact that he yearned for everything Arabic, although

4. it wasn't some Istanbul where he lived, but in the Moscow quarter of Presnya. More than anything in the world, this Anton loved the Tales of

5. a Thousand and One Nights, which, as everyone knows, is about all kinds of genies, and

6. exotic, adventuresome youths in turbans and billowing pantaloons, which is to say, totally shirtless. Anton was utterly

7. taken with these stories. And he empathized with them so much that even at home he paraded around à l'arabe: in sweat

8. pants and with a towel on his head. And he even began to think and speak in ghazels. And Anton would still be living like that,

9. obsessed with Oriental princes, if the most unusual thing had not occurred to him. One day he was walking down

10. Tverskaya Street, and, imagine this, suddenly he found himself in front of a guy with the face of an Arab prince straight out of a

11. story book. His eyebrows had grown together and his eyes were slanted. Anton stopped

12. riveted to the spot, staring wide-mouthed at the prince. But Tverskaya is a busy street, bustling with crowds, and people began bumping into

13. Anton and swearing, naturally. But he stood daydreaming, not noticing a thing. What happened next

14. was just like in an Arab fairy tale. The prince was looking at Anton with his debauched, slanted eyes, and

15. said to him penetratingly, "Young man, let's get acquainted," and he smiled at him that

16. way. Anton very nearly collapsed on the spot. For even if he had just then seen the fairy tale bird Simurg

17. shitting on the head of the bronze Pushkin statue, he wouldn't have been so surprised. The Arab prince, noticing Anton's confusion,

18. with a mellifluous smile took him by the arm and led him straight to the "Lebanon," a hard-currency restaurant. And there,

19. naturally, the fairy tale continued to go on. They sat at low-slung tables, and the genies and other spirits in

20. uniform couldn't bring them all manner of delicacies and wines quickly enough. Anton slackened from all of this luxury.

21. His eyes glazed over, either from Russian sloth or Oriental sensuality. The prince didn't miss his chance. He took Anton

22. out of the restaurant, put him in a taxi, and more quickly than any flying carpet, brought him to his palace in an eighth-

23. floor walk-up in the suburb of Sviblovo. There he of course dispatched Anton to the shower, and then he single-handedly

24. dressed him in translucent, billowing pantaloons, wrapped a turban around his head, lay him on a rug, stuck a hookah pipe in his mouth,

25. and then absented himself to take a shower before making love. Anton lay on the rug in pantaloons and turban, exhaling smoke through his nostrils

26. and towards the dirty ceiling, as though he were some kind of fakir, pardon the expression, waiting for his most gracious prince to return.

27. And then he entered, imagine, almost naked, except for a tray of peaches that he was

28. carrying. They lay together on the shaggy Persian rug and started devouring peaches.

29. And these peaches caused Anton, who rarely ate them, to experience an itching and rumbling in his stomach, and other things that are too indelicate to mention in

30. public. Forget about your Arab love. There was simply no way to get a move in edgewise.

31. And when Anton managed to return to the room, he saw that his prince had smoked so much in the meantime that he couldn't

32. put two words together. Then Anton quietly gathered his stuff and got the hell out of there, just as he was,

33. mortified, and in the translucent pantaloons and turban. He barely made it home, and from that time on, believe it or not,

34. Arab fairy tales have simply turned his stomach.

LAY THE FIFTH: "PORN"

1. Once a group of students got together at the luxurious dacha of the parents of one of them, where there was a fireplace and

2. fine china and, among other wonders of the world, a VCR. As if to spite them, the group happened to be all

3. male. And then one of them up and volunteered, "Hey let's watch some gay porn." At first they all naturally

4. squawked, "Oh, come on, what's with you, and where could we get it, anyway?" In the first place the one who had made the proposal

5. was the class president, and in the second place there suddenly out of thin air appeared a cassette with that very porn.

6. And the passions subsided. But before watching it they decided to drink something to bolster their courage, but

7. something, mind you, quite special, and they started to rummage around. But all they could find was vodka and cognac,

8. and to their great dismay only thoroughly domestic stuff, at that. They couldn't very well watch porn with Moscow vodka,

9. much less gay porn. Finally they came up with an idea. They brought in an empty three-liter jug, emptied the vodka and

10. cognac into it, and for greater exotic effect, they broke into the vanity of the lady of the house, and they poured all of the perfumes and lotions—in a word, everything that

11. smelled of wine—into the concoction. The mixture proved to be a fiery one, even if a bit revolting.

12. But they gagged and drank it—after all, they had to uphold their reputations. And each of them began to feel distinctly

13. that this booze was getting them into a state where the only thing to do was to watch gay porn.

14. Whether from the perfume or not, right and left they got into some real debauchery. With forks and knives they pried open mother's

15. wardrobe. They dressed up in whatever they could find. They painted their lips and in these vile, outrageous get-ups they chased each other

16. around the house, first drunkenly, then mischievously, and then with the goal of making sexual contact.

17. The one who had originally suggested watching gay porn—the class president—wound up with none of mother's

18. things, except for a girdle and black nylons. He put them straight on his naked body, but didn't even cover himself with

19. a serving tray, the fiend. And would you believe it, half the house was chasing after him. What came afterward, and what kinds of multi-figured

20. compositions took shape could only be described by the jaded pen of the Marquis de Sade. In the morning everybody came to their

21. senses, and most importantly of all, every single one of them was wearing skirts and bras and covered in lipstick, and not a one of them could quite remember what happened.

22. They got up and talked among themselves, saying, "wow, what disgusting stuff that gay porn was that we saw last night.

23. We ought to throw that thing out." And the funniest thing of all was that there wasn't even any trace of porn on that cassette:

24. just some fruity kids' cartoon, like Wolf and Rabbit.

Notes for the clueless: "ghazels" in their Arabic sense are not wild goats but elegant poems reminiscent of our limericks; "fakir' in Arabic means a wonder worker and not what you thought.

Dmitry Gubin (b. 1967)

THREE POEMS

Translated by J. Kates

DMITRY GUBIN (b. 1967) lives in Ufa, in the Urals, where he works as an emergency services doctor. These poems appeared originally in the Russian gay journal *Kristofer* (1992).

After an enchanted night
Morning rises pink and blue,
But ordinary, nothing new!
No help for such indifferent light . . .
After that enchanted night.

I dress in haste, while trying not
To look at you, and gulp my coffee,
And burn my tongue, while it's still hot.
You—and one last smoke—hand me
my overcoat. Full morning now,
And we have different ways to go.

We've said goodbye. And moved apart.
What's gnawing, gnawing at my heart?
Perhaps it was an idle match
We played—but it was sweet to play . . .
We told each other much too much.

Better if we'd had less to say.
And parted less as strangers?

Yesterday it all was clear:
We were not lovers—no such danger—
I stayed with you until the morning,
Drunk on the enchanted night.
"Trust me," I still can hear you whisper . . .

So why was everything so sweet?
And why right now is it so bitter?

* * *

You, I see you once and only once.
Forgive me, if I can not tear my look away
From your reflection in the window glass
Amid the darkness of the trolleybus.
Your face, so new, completely unfamiliar,
But something in it, achingly dear to me.
No indifference or tension in its play.
A single look, and then you turn away,—
Attentive, stern,
But your own glance was lingering—
I'd stake my life on it!
Our souls, I'm sure, flinched from one another,
Our barefoot angel reached back for his arrow.
But did not lodge it in our hearts.
. . . No, I will not go on being sorry
for a fantastic dream that cannot work.
Nor do I forget your face before me.
Or pardon fate for this malicious smirk.

* * *

When you sit down beside me, with your face
Carefully set to boredom, as if by chance,
I move my hand and deliberately place
That ring where it will fall under your glance.

Unwilling to trust my eyes, I natter on
To others about everything, about nothing at all.
And you are so lively with that other one
Next to you—I wish you both in Hell.

Only my cowardice is courageous now!
I make small talk and listen with half an ear.
The other half is taken up with you,
And knows no peace at all today, not here . . .

But, oh, I hope to God you won't catch on
How much it costs to keep up this pretense,
How awkwardly I hide barebones confusion
Under a mask of proud
Indifference.

Dmitry Kuz'min (b. 1968)

TWO POEMS

Translated by Vitaly Chernetsky

DMITRY KUZ'MIN was born in 1968 and graduated in philology from the Moscow Pedagogical University. He is a poet, critic of contemporary poetry, and editor of *Vavilon*, a young writer's magazine and *Risk*, a gay literary magazine. The poems printed here appeared originally in *Vavilon (Babylon)* no. 3 (19), Moscow, 1995.

Kostroma,* where the boys don't wear shorts,
and the girls don't wear them much either,
consequently, there, little tattoos on calves
cannot be seen, and the air
doesn't move, there in Kostroma,
where the boys don't get
little tattoos on their tanned calves,
only on their upper arms,
and wear T-shirts, uncovering
only arms, not legs (and the girls, too)
but no, they don't even uncover their arms,
or rather, they do, but only slightly above the elbow,
and these boys' arms are strong, used to rule and steer,
like a coachman—thick upper arms
and round shoulders, only they are invisible—
except if you look into the window
in the farthest house, where the lights aren't out,
all alone
there shoulders, calves and thighs are uncovered,
the timid line of hair
that rapidly thickens going down . . .
oh my God, in the last house, there,
where boys don't walk around,
the lights go out, everyone's asleep
in Kostroma, so cheerful only yesterday.

*   *   *

*Kostroma is a small industrial city about 200 miles northeast of Moscow; founded by Yury Dolgoruky, ca. 1152.

A tall boy
in a black T-shirt
is shivering strongly
(escaping from a sudden shower,
he jumps into the trolley car).

Goosebumps on tanned arms,
because of them the little hairs,
slightly bleached by the sun,
are more noticeable.
If you were to caress his head
with its haircut that's too short—
he would hit you in the face.

I stand next to him silently.

He gets off.
I see in the window:
he walks deliberately, slowly.
It pours.
It pours.

Drawing by Imas Levsky.

Gennady Trifonov (b. 1945)

TWO BALLETS BY GEORGE BALANCHINE
Selections from the novella

Translated by Michael Molnar

TRIFONOV began to write during the Soviet period and has continued with his writing in the New Russia (see the biographical notes on his life on page 226). The present novella dates from the early 1990s and was published originally in the St. Petersburg magazine *Gay Slavyane*. This translation appeared first in the gay issue of the journal *Index on Censorship* Vol. 24 No. 1 (London, 1995).

THE BOYS THREW their bikes into the bilberry clumps by the shore, frightening some sleeping ducks, then instantly stripped off their cowboy shirts (all checked men's shirts were called that in those days) and their shorts as well, and Ilya stripped off his swimming trunks too, somewhat to Irsanov's embarrassment, for during the winter he had grown more manly and had now entered into a cautious, delicate relationship with his own body, and had begun seeking explanations in his father's books for the changes that were taking place in him.

He was a head taller than Ilya. Thanks to swimming and to the basketball which he had been playing all winter in sport at school, his sinewy, muscular body had grown, but his shoulders, like all swimmers', were broad and the muscles of his neck, arms and chest stood out in clear relief. This disturbed Ilya and during the day that disturbance had been unconsciously communicated to Irsanov too. Several times Irsanov had caught Ilya watching him. From time to time he had fluttered his thick eyelashes at Irsanov and smiled at something or other, and Irsanov smiled back, but felt his cheeks burning, his palms moistening and his breathing catching. This was not lost on Ilya. When he had deftly mounted his bike and headed off, standing on the pedals, Irsanov had raced after him, and as he gradually caught up, thought to himself: "It would be nice if he didn't have a bike. Then I could sit him on the frame of mine and we would be close together now." Such ideas made Irsanov's head spin and twice he even lost control of his bike and almost crashed into a thick pine tree. Ilya noticed and, bursting into laughter, dashed on ahead. . . . Glancing round, Irsanov decided to follow Ilya's lead and stripped off his new, bright red swimming trunks, then hurled himself into the dark water, noisily cutting through it with powerful strokes. But then he noticed that Ilya swam much worse than he did, and not wanting to demonstrate his mastery, began swimming "like everyone else," calmly and quietly.

The lake was warm, its surface darkened and silvered as it reflected in turns the sky or the surrounding woods, ducks that had landed on the water, a bonfire glittering on the far shore and the thin ribbon of smoke that rose above it; and even the words of a song around the campfire could be heard, and suddenly a little boat appeared on the smooth lake, with a lone angler concentrated on his task, and a lone bright star glinted in the sky and on the dark ripples. . . .

Ilya emerged first from the water. Climbing onto the bank, he looked round and called to Irsanov, his arms wide. Irsanov now saw him in the all in all and the sight confused him. He suddenly remembered once seeing such a boy, or more exactly, a half-girl, half-boy with shoulder-length hair, in one of the galleries of the Russian Museum. That marble youth was sitting on a tree stump, legs wide apart, a warrior's helmet on his head, and he was smiling mysteriously—just like Ilya today. And then, in the Hermitage this time, Irsanov had seen another such boy. He was standing, leaning against the trunk of some sawn-off tree, soft and graceful. He wore a curious cap on his curly head. With his right hand he was pouring water from a pitcher, and in his left hand he held a little bell. It was Ilya's raised arm that reminded Irsanov of Thorvaldsen's Ganymede, who had been kidnapped by an eagle at the whim of Zeus and carried off to Olympus, where Ganymede became his wine bearer. There, in the cold luxury of the Hermitage, which Irsanov had visited fairly frequently that winter, he had wanted to become Zeus and like him carry off that marble boy, to stroke him lightly with his palms. . . .

However, Irsanov was in no hurry to get out of the water. He had a particular reason. Now of all times. Now of all times his own nakedness caused him embarrassment in front of Ilya who was standing on the shore, slowly drying himself with a long checkered towel, drying each leg in turn, now with his face, now with his back to Irsanov, while Irsanov waited for the moment when he would turn his back, so that he could emerge from the water as quickly as possible and unnoticed. The moment occurred. Irsanov leapt onto the bank and to Ilya's side, seized the towel and began quickly drying himself, not noticing that as he dried himself their bodies were brought closer together. "Lord," Irsanov thought at that moment, "what's happening to me? . . ." But Ilya did not allow him to finish his thought. Suddenly he pressed himself firmly against his friend and Irsanov, without the least erotic movement, pressed himself against Ilya, and with his hand, now free of the towel, stroked Ilya's damp locks. . . . He no longer noticed the towel slipping from his fingers and his palms were stroking Ilya's cool skin, first around the shoulder blades, then finding their way lower, halting a little below the waist. . . .

Ilya suddenly shivered all over from these movements and, clasping Irsanov round the neck with both arms, pressed hard against him with all his cold body, that suddenly grew warmer, burning even. . . .

—Kiss me now, please. . . . Ilya uttered in a low whisper.

—But you aren't a little girl? Irsanov said loudly, recoiling a little. But his arms did not obey him and clasped Ilya's body all the harder. . . .

—Kiss me, kiss me, whispered Ilya feverishly. Irsanov kissed him lightly, hardly touching his full red lips.

—Not like that, Ilya said.

—How? Irsanov asked loudly and, unaware what he was doing, raised Ilya to the level of his face so that now both Irsanov's palms rested agsinst his broad buttocks, that quivered, tensing and slackening under Irsanov's strong fingers. . . .

—Properly, hard, Ilya said, this time aloud, and closed his eyes, his lips against his friend's half open mouth. . . . Fixing his lips upon Ilya's, Irsanov gave him a prolonged kiss, and felt the tip of Ilya's tongue against his palate.

—That's it, that's it, harder. Can you? Ilya said rapidly, gratefully kissing Irsanov's cheek and eyes.

—I can, Irsanov said. But instead of his lips, he began kissing his face, hungrily moving down to Ilya's cheeks and shoulders. . . . At that moment his tense body was suffused by a sweet pain, already familiar from his dreams at night. His heart throbbed rapidly. It was as if something had burst in his head, hs legs gave way as if under water. At that moment Ilya moved his left hand from Irsanov's cheek to his back and tightly, tighter than before, pressed himself to the bursting Irsanov.

All at once Irsanov realized what had happened to him and fell away from Ilya, blurting out:—I'm sorry, Ilyusha. I didn't mean to. . . . How horrible . . .

Irsanov snatched the towel to wipe Ilya's belly, down which an acrid milky liquid slowly dripped. . . .

—Nothing horrible about that, Ilya said, loud and boldly—I'll dry it off myself, Yura. It's not horrible at all.

—What is it if it isn't horrible? Irsanov said dully, stopped looking for his swimming trunks, and sitting on his shirt, dropped his head upon his knees.

—I don't know, Ilya pronounced, whispering again for some reason, and he stretched out full length on the spread towel, his curly head resting on both arms and turned towards Irsanov.—Let's just lie down together. I'll turn round. Lie down. Turning on the spot, resting on his arms, Irsanov lay down beside Ilya.—There, see, that's comfortable.

For a time both boys lay in silence: Ilya did not move and Irsanov lay on his back now, his arms behind his head and stared with wide open eyes into the night sky that was beginning to grow lighter.

—It's funny, isn't it, Yura, that there aren't any mosquitoes. This is Komarovo and there are no mosquitoes. [In Russian "mosquito" is *komar*:

translator's note]

—That's true, Irsanov said quietly. He wanted to say something completely different, but did not know exactly what, and so fell silent again.

—You're not asleep, Yura? Ilya asked quietly, seeing Irsanov with closed eyes.—You're not cold, are you?

—No, I'm not asleep. It's really warm. Hot even. Why?—Did you like it when. . . .

—What do you mean "when"? Irsanov interrupted and his breathing became intermittent again.

—When you kissed me? And then . . .

—A lot, Irsanov answered, for some reason in a whisper again.

—Do you want to do it again?

—I don't know.

—I do.

—Can I? Irsanov asked for some reason.

—You can, you can, Ilya said excitedly, and leaned over on his elbows, although he could get no nearer to his friend's lips. . . .

—All right, Irsanov agreed and smiled at him. He kissed his Ilya slowly now, interrupting the kiss with a happy smile. Again his arms pressed the wild Ilya to him and again Ilya's body burnt his fingers, literally to the very tips. "How beautiful you are, Yura!" Ilya whispered to his face and heard the answer: "You're beautiful, just like a girl." "But I'm a boy, Yura, I'm a boy." "So why are we kissing?"

They fell silent again. Again Irsanov's head was spinning. Again his temples were throbbing. Again his whole body tensed. Again his legs began giving way.

Ilya's hot lips were once more kissing Irsanov's chest, all his belly, down which a dark hairy track had appeared that winter, beginning at those light, firm hairs which bore witness to many things, and above all to the readiness, the necessity, to become a man.

—What are you doing! What are you doing! You can't! Irsanov exclaimed as Ilya's nimble fingers and lips found themselves down there, where, according to Irsanov, "you can't." He even raised himself on his elbows.

—You can, Ilya said firmly. If you like it then you can. Do you like it?

—I don't know. Probably. Yes. O-o-o . . . Ilyusha . . . Ilyushenka . . .

Irsanov gave a low groan. His hands again sought Ilya's body. Finding it, they firmly pressed Ilya's thighs and his lips stretched towards his lips.

—Again, please, Irsanov whispered. Just once more.

Irsanov did not know whether he was now exhausted by Ilya's caresses. He lay on the narrow band of checkered towel, thinking of nothing. Perhaps he was even dozing. But when he came to, opening his eyes wide, he saw that Ilya was half lying next to him and stroking his belly with a blade of grass.

Irsanov slowly stood up and without saying a word, simply smiling broadly at Ilya, he took his hand and led him to the water.

He carefully lowered Ilya into the water and they both began quietly swimming, trying to remain as close as possible to each other.

—I've liked you for a long time, Ilyusha. A very long time.

—And I've liked you, ever since Ozerki.

—Why didn't you say anything then? I would always have kissed you, as much as you wanted.

—Really?

—Honest.

—I was embarrassed, Yura, I was too embarrassed.

—And you're not embarrassed now? Irsanov asked slyly and swam up to Ilya's back. Having swam into the shallows, he pressed firmly against Ilya, and with his whole being sensed Ilya's readiness to resume their games.—You can see, I'm not embarrassed now. Having said that, Irsanov released Ilya from his grip, showing himself to Ilya without any embarrassment.

There was no point in drying themselves with the towel. It lay on ground covered with fir needles which could not be shaken off. Once again the boys lay on the towel and began to dry.

—When did you know that you were already grown-up, Yura?

—Properly, today with you.

—I thought so, Ilya said with conviction.

—Why? Irsanov asked in amazement.

—Because . . . Because I love you, Yura, Ilya burst out. And I always want to do that to you.

—What's "that"?

—What you want. Always, always. Only with you.

—Is there anybody else? Irsanov was troubled and raised himself over Ilya.—Is there? Tell me. Can there be?

—There isn't, Ilya said with conviction. And there never will be. With these words he pressed his lips to Irsanov's, not as if kissing but with another intention in which Irsanov read Ilya's affection and faithfulness.

—This is like a dream, Iyusha, Irsanov whispered, throwing his head back upon the short grass and looking up.—Once I dreamed that we were kissing . . .

—And I dreamed that. Often. I dreamed that we were caressing each other like today and kissing and I was kissing you too, all over, you understand?

—I understand.

—And I dreamed as well that you . . .

—What was I doing? Irsanov asked, agitated and interested.—Well, that you, Yura . . . That you . . . That you were very nice.

—You're nice too, Ilyusha. The best. The best of all. Having told each other that, the boys again felt an intense attraction to each other. But Irsanov now wanted Ilya to look at him and admire him, his masculine strength. And Ilya wanted the same.

Both now wanted this bright night never to end, this night in which they had discovered a previously unknown aspect of each other, an aspect that corresponded to what had previously been no more than guesses about each other. They did not, could not even, think that life, our cruel stepmother, would one day, perhaps quite soon, part them and that they would never again experience, never again feel, never again know such a night.

—We'll always be together now, Yura, won't we?

—Of course, Ilyusha. Of course.

—I won't let anyone else have you, you're so beautiful and good. Nobody at all. I already saw the girls squinting at you at Ozerki. Today in Komarovo and there, at Zelenogorsk as well. And it hurt me then to think of it. It hurt me a lot, Yura.

After this strange confession, unexpected even for the talkative Ilya, there was a silence between them, filled with inexpressible feelings that only visit us in our youth when we are next to our first love.

—Do you like other boys? Irsanov asked quietly.

—To tell you the truth, I liked one fellow in our class. Last year.

—Did you go swimming with him at night?

—Of course not! Once at gym, in the changing room, I saw him kiss a girl. I hated him for that straight away. For the rest of my life.

—But it wasn't his fault, Ilyusha.

—Yes, it was. It was! I liked him a lot and he never noticed me. I gave him all my lessons to copy out. All the tests.

—Well then, when the summer's over you'll go back to school and make friends with him. Is he handsome?

—I don't think so now, for a start. Secondly, he's an idiot. And thirdly, this year my parents are moving me to the English school. Mum is going to teach English there and my last two years will be in English. Then I'll enter the Herzen teacher training college. What about you?

—University. Next year already. Let's go together, eh?

—They'd see there. Like parents.

Returning the conversation to its previous course, Irsanov asked Ilya:

—Have you ever kissed a girl?

—What for? And you?

—Three times. She said she'd drown herself in the Smolenka river if I didn't. It's only a little stream on the Vasilyevsky Island, very picturesque.

—Well, you should have let her drown herself, Ilya said, adding— although in her place I would probably have drowned myself too. And with these words he pressed himself to Irsanov and laid his head on his chest. The boys fell silent again. Now both of them were half asleep and both thinking of the other with sheer gratitude.

Although now dozing, Irsanov still sensed the physical proximity of his curly little Ilya with the whole of his strong young body. He sensed his hot breath, his smooth, soft skin, all the muscles of his extraordinary body, the quivering of his back, his thighs, his graceful legs. . . . He sensed Ilya's wily hand passing over his chest and belly, carefully and lovingly touching those spots where his power, energy and beauty were concentrated at that moment. And he was grateful to Ilya for that too. He was happy now and therefore tensely calm—confident and virile. For this affectionate little boy with his sensitive mouth, with the curls hanging to his shoulders, had aroused a moral sense of gratitude in the 16-year-old Yura Irsanov, who, though intellectually and physically already fully grown, had never before experienced it—gratitude for the ecstasy they had felt, for the confidence he had inspired, for their mutual understanding, for that fusion both with the natural world around and with those emotional and physical impulses which both of them now felt to be natural and fundamental.

Photo by O. Kaminka.

Efim Yeliseev [pseud.] (b. 1940s)

THE BENCH

[Skameika]

Translated by Anthony Vanchu

"EFIM YELISEEV" is the pen-name of a Russian writer, born ca. 1948, who was living in the city of Penza (about 400 miles south-east of Moscow) at the time this story originally appeared in the gay paper *Ty (You)* in Moscow, 1993.

Going to the bathhouse (banya) in Russia is not what gay American men might think. The weekly trip to the bathhouse was a traditional part of the Russian peasant's hygiene, although it was not an exclusively rural phenomenon by any means. Both men and women would go, usually separately, since one must get naked (if the banya is co-ed, then individuals wear bathing suits). The Russian bathhouse can be as simple as a wooden shack in a back yard, to something as elegant and ornate as Moscow's Sandunovskaya Banya. In its most elaborate form, a men's banya consists of an outer room where they change out of their clothes and sit, wrapped in sheets, drinking, eating, chatting, playing chess, etc. Beyond that is a room with showers, tubs, and benches where it is not uncommon to see men soaping each other down, although there is nothing overtly sexual about this activity. The heart of the banya is the parilnya (steamroom), something like a wet sauna. This room has various elevations, and the higher one ascends, the hotter and steamier it will become. In the parilnya, people swat themselves and each other about the body with veniki, little bundles of birch switches (leaves intact), usually sold outside the entrance to the bathhouse. The sap emitted from the birch is said to have a salubrious effect.

Some public bathhouses have small rooms with bathtubs that are available for rent. Given the difficulty of finding places to have sexual encounters, it was (and still is) not uncommon for two men to rent such a room on the pretext of bathing together. Most bath attendants know, of course, what is going on, but usually look the other way.

Sashka's status as a soldier merits brief commentary. As is the case with American armed forces, there is a considerable amount of homosexual activity in their Russian counterparts, although it is, of course, officially forbidden. Supposedly "straight" rank and file soldiers are rumored to be more than willing to dispense sexual favors (often in a "rough trade" fashion), although usually for money or a "gift." This reputation extends well beyond Russian borders. When the Soviet troops left the Warsaw Pact countries, Moscow gays joked that the only people in those lands who regretted their departure were gay men.

ALL THE SAME, Sashka went out by himself. No matter how much the other guys insisted on him coming with them, he still decided to spend his first liberty on his own.

Mother Nature had given him everything: he was tall, with broad shoulders, and a rather handsome face. . . . The only thing she hadn't bestowed upon him was an out-going personality. He was really quite shy! Ever since early childhood he hadn't liked being with large groups, usually preferring to be on his own. In the village where he was born he had only one friend, and lately even he had begun distancing himself from Sashka—he'd become boring to be around. In fact, how could it possibly be interesting to spend time with someone who's always quiet and hardly ever even smiles? Sashka understood that and took it all in stride. Nevertheless, every human being needs contact with his own kind. It became especially difficult for him after the first time a girl really took a liking to him. Of course, nothing ever came of it. She called him a bump-on-a-log. But Sashka wasn't offended. Even he considered himself a slow-witted bump-on-a-log, fit for nothing. And so he lived like this until he came of age, when he joined the army. He'd been lucky. Fate destined him to serve within Russia, and thus he remained on his native Russian soil, among his own people. Sashka ended up in a small unit located in a small district town, somewhere in the Middle Volga. On the very first day one of the soldiers who had been around a while had tried to "do him," but a couple of blows from Sashka's massive fists—and then everything was set right. They began to respect him and he even had gained some influence. Even the more senior soldiers didn't allow themselves any liberties in their relations with him and gave him the nickname of "The Silent One." Indeed, Sashka spoke very rarely. He liked to listen to the guys who chattered a lot, especially to the bacchanalian tales of their sexual debauches, although he took it all at face value. At those moments he realized his helplessness even more strongly in as much as he not only hadn't been with any women, but also had never even really touched one. Once, when he was still in grade school, he had tried to hug a girl he liked very much, but nothing came of it. Poor Sashka, he even suspected that ninety percent of the soldiers' tales were sheer fantasy, and that these would-be "Don Juans," with their descriptions of women's bodies and how they had come to be with them, had actually seen naked women only in pictures and in copies of photographs from pornographic magazines. He imagined them masturbating in desperation while looking at these pictures, locking themselves in the toilet, or stealing away to barns or attics, out of the sight of their vigilant mothers.

Sashka did not yet have any real friends in his unit. He hung out with a couple guys, but that was more out of necessity than anything else. Sashka spent his free time writing letters home to his mom and dad. He was a fine, respectable son who loved and cared about his parents a great deal. He was the only child in his family but, as they say, he had done well. He understood that there could be no one closer than one's mother, and he tried to warm her heart with his letters as often as possible. He described everything that happened each day in order, without hurry, knowing that his mother was interested in everything, even the smallest detail of his life in the army.

And so here it was—his first leave! Sashka would be a free man for an entire day—he couldn't believe it! He spiritedly strode down a street in the town where he was stationed, inhaling the warm spring air. Soon the long-awaited summer would begin. The trees had already started to turn green, the temperature was already in the high eighties, and Sashka's youthful blood had begun to stir. He enjoyed looking at the local girls and catching their coquettish glances; yet he always ended up feeling distraught on account of his damned shyness. Why couldn't he at least work up the nerve to approach that enchanting blond walking in front of him over there and introduce himself. . . . Well, no matter, Sashka didn't lose faith that fate would eventually smile upon him and send an interesting acquaintance his way. But when would that be? After all, his whole youth could pass by in obscurity. Everything interested Sashka—people, buildings, even dogs and cats. He had no idea where he was even headed. Having no particular destination in mind, he just walked on straight ahead, making no turns of the street. No matter what might happen, life was great! He was in an extraordinary mood. A two-story yellow-brick building on the right-hand side of the street caught Sashka's attention. Upon coming closer, he read the sign on it: "Bathhouse." Sashka remembered the cozy little bathhouse in their yard back home, the fragrant birch-leaf switches they'd use in the ablutions, the splashing of the hot water. The house of his youth was so far away now. . . . A thought entered his head—why not go in? He went in and stood around a while in the entry hall. There weren't many people there. And suddenly, Sashka's imagination drew for him a picture not of the sauna, but of a large bathtub, full of hot water. Never before in his life had he soaked in a warm bath. Some unknown force pushed Sashka toward the cashier. He made his way up to the window and asked:

"Do you have a small room with a bath available?"

"Yes. You can go on in right away."

Without thinking he paid, bought a towel and a piece of soap as well, and went where they told him to. He gave his ticket to the elderly bath attendant and entered a clean and cozy little room with a new, clean bathtub. Looking around him, he sat down on the bench, slowly undressed, and turned on the faucets. The soothing water began running into the tub. Sashka stopped up the drain with a large wooden plug and the tub filled up quickly. The gurgling water calmed and soothed him. This was great! For some reason Sashka remembered a phrase from a schoolbook: "Water is the cradle of life on Earth." And truly, it was like a cradle. The tub filled up, and Sashka dropped down into it. What bliss! His whole body began to shake, to tremble, reveling in the caressing warm water. He closed his eyes and relaxed. There were, after all, many people who partook of this pleasure every day and even used fragrant bath oils. . . . How lucky they are! Perhaps one day he, Sashka would have his own apartment with all the modern conveniences and just such a bathtub with clean shiny tile and a large beautiful mirror. And he would engage in this fantastic pleasure, imagining that he was a millionaire in the West. Sashka became lost in reverie. People such as he are by nature dreamers. He totally submerged himself in the water, keeping only his face above it, resting to his heart's content. Then he sat up and opened his eyes. With relish Sashka scrubbed his legs, his feet, his knees. . . . When he got to his thighs, he began to feel particularly good. Just then Sashka felt his member begin to stir and impetuously become erect. In an instant it became hard and engorged. "Oh well," Sashka thought, "once again I've gotten an erection." This had been happening to him a lot this spring, a few times every day. To the point of hurting. And in the morning, to the point that he wanted to cry out for help. Sashka began masturbating with all his might. His father had once caught him in the act and had given him a good cussing out, telling him that it would ruin his health. His father's words had taken firm root in Sashka's mind, although he had despairingly tried to forget this lesson. But sometimes his patience ran out and the poor fellow could bear it no more. When it was all over, Sashka would always be in a particularly foul mood. Then once more there would be long days of self-restraint, but eventually his hand would refuse to obey his head—it truly seemed to have a mind of its own. Sashka's fingers caressed the head of his penis. It shuddered, as if asking, "Master, please, don't torment yourself. . . ." Sashka grimaced. God, how tired he was of this torment! He tried to distract his mind with other thoughts—he thought of his home, his mother, about the military; yet his accursed hand had no intention of releasing his straining tool. Of their own accord his fingers kneaded the head of his penis, the shaft; stroked his balls. Well, what could he do, nothing helped. It was with great force of will that Sashka removed his hand from his member. He took a deep breath and loudly and clearly said out loud:

"No! I won't masturbate!"

He took great pleasure in such moments when his strength of will won out. He understood that this wouldn't last forever and that sooner or later he would once again give himself over to his weakness. But how pleasant it was, even if only for just a moment, to feel he was the master of his desires, how gratifying it was to realize that he was a strong person! Sashka felt the excitement gradually weaken and his tool subsided. The head of his penis bowed sadly downward, having not received its desired satisfaction. Sashka decided that now would be a good time to douse himself with cold water so as finally to conquer his arousal. He was about to empty the water from the tub when suddenly his gaze fell on the wall that was right before him. His attention was attracted by a small luminous flickering point.

"What's that?" he thought.

Sashka moved forward and saw a small hole someone had made in the wall. And that glow was the light in the room next door. His heart stood still as Sashka gazed into the opening. It was clear that whoever had made it had taken great care in doing so. It would have been impossible to have picked out a better height and angle. Nearly the entire room was visible. What Sashka saw forced him to freeze in astonishment at the wave of contradictory sensations he experienced. He had never felt anything like it before. There were two youths in the room, boys no more than fourteen or fifteen years old. Both had raging erections. They were lolling about and joking with one another. Although Sashka couldn't hear their words, he could see everything perfectly. In the meantime, one boy grasped the other's member and began playfully to masturbate him. And the other, to be sure, saw nothing out of the ordinary in this, because he himself extended his hand and seized his friend by his member as well.

"Oh yeah, that's it! Man, those guys are really going after it!" thought Sashka.

The boys continued at their play. Their hands became ever more active and inventive. First they bared the heads of their members, then jiggled their fingers along the shaft, and then gently began kneading each other's balls. Sashka was unable to tear his gaze from this spectacle. Some sort of unknown force wouldn't allow him to leave, to turn away from that small crack in the wall. He felt his manhood swell again, like a spring bud. Seemingly on its own, his right hand embraced the shaft and started sliding smoothly—up and down, up and down. Then Sashka saw one boy get down on his knees and bring his face nearer the other's member. Sashka got a lump in his throat. What was going on here? And then the boy closed his eyes, opened his mouth a bit, and the head of his partner's tool slid smoothly past his lips. Sashka understood what was going on and instinctively began working over his manhood with even greater force. And the boy's lips, pink and moist, kept sliding along his partner's member, caressing it and fondling it. Then his tongue came out and, with the very tip, he tickled the head and its opening. A few minutes later the guys changed positions. Already another tool was flicking in and out of the other's lips, even more energetically. Sashka beat off with abandon. Never before in his life had this activity afforded him such intense pleasure. He gave himself over completely to his masturbation, forgetting about everything else in the world. He couldn't even begin to think about how he might get together with these boys—how could he! Such a thought was so totally alien to him. It was simply that the sight of these two had excited him so much that his tool now raged as if possessed, his hand banging away like a piston. These two guys kept on sucking each other. They switched positions with greater frequency and became ever more inventive at how they did it. Sashka saw each drop of saliva that fell from their lips, each vein on their members, and he just kept on beating off, beating off, beating off. . . . Suddenly one of the guys grabbed the other by the head and plunged his member into his mouth, right up to the balls. He tried to resist, but his partner's strong hands didn't allow him to spit it out. And so they went on for a few seconds. Then his hands left the other's head and fell in exhaustion to his side. Sashka saw the boy who had been on his knees spit out some milky fluid. And then he realized that this wasn't spit at all. His mind hazed over and everything around him began to float. Huge quantities of sperm gushed forth from Sashka's tool, falling into the water in formless blobs. His knees shook in frenzy, as if an electric current had been shot through them. He squinted and no longer saw anything; he then began quaking in an orgasm so intense that it was almost painful. The sperm continued to flow and flow across his hand. It remained there, looking like drying glue. When Sashka regained his senses, the boys in the next room were no longer there and the water had stopped running. Either they had finished with their games and had gone into the dressing-room to relax, or else they had left altogether. One way or another, the room next door was empty. Sashka stood around for a little while, rinsed his hand, washed the remains of semen off his tool, and picked up a piece of soap. He washed very slowly, as if in a trance. A heavy fog hung over his brain, his ears rang. And in his imagination he kept playing over and over the picture he had just seen. Sashka tried to comprehend what had just happened. Could such a thing have happened to him when he was that age? Hardly. And with such intensity? Most certainly not. He thought of his friend Slavka. While Sashka himself had quite a large tool, Slavka's was even larger. They had been to a bathhouse a few times together, and once Slavka had become completely erect. Sashka smiled, remembering how his friend sat on the bench all huddled up, trying in vain to hide his protrusion. And now at last Sashka admitted to himself that just then he really had wanted to touch Slavka's tool, even if only in jest. But of course he didn't. And that night, when he had gotten home, just before going to sleep, he beat off with great rapture, imagining that he had done so with Slavka—that he had beat Slavka off and Slavka him. However that never happened. But then that wasn't the point of it all. Now Sashka understood that he really had wanted to do this. What was the point of denying it—he wanted to do it! Yes, all of that could have been a reality. But fate had simply dictated otherwise. Sashka concluded that the same thing was happening all over again. It was unpleasant even to think about it. Maybe that's the way it had to be? Yet there was something that he hadn't gotten to experience. And at this thought, he was beset by such profound bitterness that he blurted out: "Aw, what the fuck, those guys are sucking off each other for all they're worth now, and then in a year or two they'll start hanging around with babes. But me, I've never even beat off with another guy—I'm always alone, always alone. Well, why can't things turn out for me like they do for other people?" His mood had soured altogether. Sashka wiped himself off with a towel and, leaving it on a bench, got dressed and left the room. Out in the hallway he went to the soda machine and drank down two glasses in quick succession. He felt a bit better. Sashka had already turned around and was headed toward the exit. By the wall there was a large wooden bench, and sitting there were . . . those two guys. The very same ones! Sashka recognized them immediately. They were again chatting away contentedly, running their hands over their taut faces and freshly-washed hair. Sashka approached and sat next to them. Why? He himself didn't know. He sat down, propping up his head with his hand. He half-listened to the boys' conversation. Some sort of school gossip—teachers, classmates. . . . And all the time they were laughing, giggling. An indescribable knot of sensations began to well up inside Sashka. He nearly became sick. First of all, he felt an insurmountable curiosity for the unknown. An unhealthy curiosity. Secondly, there was this longing that was both profound and repulsive. And all of this was fed by a most genuine gnawing and reproachful envy. Yes, Sashka had caught himself; he knew full well that he secretly envied these guys, envied not so much their age as their uninhibited and cheerful spirit. So why did he, Sashka, have so many problems in this area? But these kids, still wet behind the ears, everything was simple for them. They were so lively and buoyant, their eyes gleamed slyly— they didn't experience the same longing and sadness. He was sick and tired of things being like this!!! He could take no more. Sashka spoke. Or more precisely, not he, but his lips and tongue. And they didn't speak, but rather whispered into the ear of the guy closest to him:

"Excuse me, what's your name?"

The boy turned around and looked at the tall soldier in surprise:

"Sanka."

"Well, so we have the same name."

The soldier and the boy shook hands. At that moment the unhappy soldier again felt a sturdy erection. All the taboos had been forgotten, all borders dissolved.

"Sanka, you know, I need to tell you that . . . I . . . uh, quite by chance happened to see . . . well, what you and your friend were up to in your room there . . .

The boy's face flushed red immediately. But the soldier wasn't about to stop there.

"Don't be afraid. . . I'm not going to tell anyone. It's just that, you know, . . . how can I say this . . . you see . . . I want to try that too. Very much. I've never done anything like it before. . . . If you'd like, tell your friend, and I'll be agreeable to anything. . . . We could go off together sometime, the three of us . . .

"Okay, just a sec. . . ." the boy muttered. He elbowed his friend and they got up and walked off to the side. Sashka's heart began racing so wildly that he pressed his hand to his chest. The guys talked for about a minute. During this strange conversation, Sashka felt the other boy looking over at him. His glances weren't at all friendly. In fact, they began to make Sashka feel quite ill at ease. Finally this Sanka came up to Sashka and blurted out:

"We'll be there in a minute."

After this the boys quickly went out onto the street. What the hell was going on?! Instinctively Sashka ran out after them. A wild thought flashed through his head. . . Exactly! That was it! With terrifying speed the boys ran down the sidewalk and away from the bathhouse, away from the luckless soldier, and then quickly disappeared around the first corner. Sashka stood there, crushed by feelings of betrayal and helplessness. What should he do? Run after them? That would be a dumb thing to do! What a hick he was! A total hick! Poor Sashka wanted to let out a roar and break down sobbing. He rocked back and forth, watching the possibility of pleasure receding into the distance, the possibility upon which he had pinned so much hope!

Suddenly, simply dreadful thoughts came to him, one after the other. Where had the boys run off to? Maybe they hadn't just gotten scared, but had taken off for some other reason. Who the hell knew what they were thinking. . . . And now they'd bring someone here—a bunch of their buddies, or maybe even their parents. . . . Or even the police! Sashka was horror-stricken. In his mind he saw a picture of two police informers leading him back to his unit in handcuffs. What would happen then? Such a nightmarish feeling of fear and shame gnawed at his soul that he now moved ahead mechanically, as if in a trance. Sashka didn't walk but almost ran in some sort of thieves' trot, cursing this bathhouse and himself. A nervous shaking struck him and his teeth clenched down tightly, like a vise. He was no longer himself, Sashka, but some sort of bizarre entity, trying to run away from itself. He felt like a rabbit on the run—running away not from the wolf itself, but running in anticipation of the wolf's pursuit. Sashka ran off blindly, hardly taking in the buildings and streets he passed. Fear and shame drove him like a relentless engine; he became smothered by bitter, but in his mind appropriate, feelings of guilt. He blamed no one other than himself and prepared for the worst case scenario. God knows how much time passed like this. The poor guy took quite a while to calm down. He finally got tired of running this marathon and slowed down, catching his breath. At last his brain began seeking a solution. Okay. This was all behind him. He calmed down. What had happened back there? Nothing at all. It was impossible to prove anything. I wasn't the one who was in the bathhouse! Not me! It was some other soldier. We all look alike in uniform. But all the same what an idiot I am! Blockhead! Did you have to go so far with it?! . . . Okay, best just forget about it. Good God, what an ass I am! They wouldn't come after him with anyone. Besides, how do they know what I did? I'd off and tell what they were doing, since I'd let them know that I'd seen everything. What a jerk I am! They just got scared because I'm an adult. Of course! Why would they want me? They probably keep what they do there secret even from their own friends. They go to that bathhouse on the sly, or else they go off to some attic or a cellar . . . and everything's kept quiet, no one knows anything about it. And then suddenly I appear on the scene . . . Laughter! Sashka actually burst out laughing—it finally helped him calm down. That's that! Forget it completely! Throw it out of your memory forever! It never happened! Sashka set off for the bazaar, bought some sunflower seeds to munch on, and met up with two soldiers from his unit also on liberty and roaming about town. The guys invited him to go get something to eat with them, but Sashka said no, making up an excuse. He was quite nervous and really didn't feel like eating at all. Moreover, he honestly couldn't bring himself to talk with anyone right now—he needed some time alone. He thought of his stomach only in the latter part of the day, when it began to rumble discontentedly. Sashka went to a bakery and bought himself three rolls. He stood on the sidewalk and worked his jaws with pleasure. He had a few hours of liberty remaining. But Sashka was already thinking about going back to base. It's better there, more peaceful. . . . Ahead of him along the street, about twenty meters off, Sashka saw a sign, "Movie Theater." He went closer: it was a small old movie theater called "The Worker." A tattered poster beckoned potential viewers: "The Fateful Step. From India. In two parts." Alright! That'd be just great. A film about love. He could relax some. Sashka glanced at his watch. A showing had started just twenty minutes ago. The next one was in two hours, at 8:30. He'd be able to see it and get back to his unit in time. He still had some money, so he bought himself a ticket and went out onto the street, munching his last roll. His legs throbbed from fatigue. And he still had to find somewhere to hang out for two hours! Sashka looked around for some sort of bench to sit down on, but there weren't any. . . . Then suddenly he remembered that he had just passed through some sort of little town garden. Which way was it from here? That's right, it was over there—to the right and then up one block. . . . When Sashka finally plopped himself down on a bench in the garden, he felt an even greater sense of bliss than in the bathhouse. Finally! Sashka sighed deeply and stared off into space. The fateful event of the day had already receded into the background, but his memory continued to replay all those images with great clarity. Ah, yes. . . . Oh well, there are far worse things. But today Sashka had come to realize that he didn't really know himself very well. Did he think, did he suppose that something like that could even happen to him? That's the way it was. He had to be more careful and take better care of himself in such delicate situations, keep his head on his shoulders. Otherwise he might get himself into such a mess that

he'd never find his way out. Sashka thought about how nice it would be,
sitting here on this bench, to be having a cigarette and blowing smoke rings.
But he didn't smoke. He'd tried taking a drag off a cigarette a few times,
but each time he did, it was just nauseating, really awful. So he hadn't tried
it again. Apparently for him it just wasn't meant to be, like so many other
things.

"Would you like a smoke?"

Sashka shuddered in surprise. The clear and pleasant voice that had
spoken these words seemed to have arisen out of nowhere. Sashka raised
his eyes. A guy stood before him and offered him an open pack.

"I don't smoke," Sashka smiled.

"You should. That's something you don't see often. . . . A soldier who
doesn't smoke! Not even Marlboros?"

"Not even Marlboros."

"Oh well, too bad! Can I sit down here with you?"

"The bench doesn't belong to me."

"Thanks."

The guy sat down next to Sashka and lit up. Sashka looked him up and
down from out of the corner of his eye and concluded that they were about
the same age. The guy was average sized, on the thin side, lightly complected, with a rather handsome face. Sashka noticed that this guy also
seemed interested in him. Their heads gradually turned toward one another
and the gazes finally met.

Sashka felt self-conscious and shy with him. On the other hand, he
wanted to talk with this guy.

He smiled a lot and seemed to want to talk.

"Where are you from?"

"Near Tambov. I'm stationed here."

"And how do you like it?"

"It's not bad. Could be worse."

"No kidding. Is this your first year in the service?"

"Yes, I'm just starting out."

"Feel homesick?"

"Of course. There's nothing better than home."

"To each his own. I was born in this godforsaken place, grew up here
and, I can say, actually love it. But I could never say that there's nothing
better."

"And what would be better for you?"

"Moscow! For me, it's better than anything else on earth. To live in
Moscow is my secret dream. If it ever happens, I'd be the happiest person
on earth. Have you ever been to Moscow?"

"No, never."

"Then you wouldn't understand what I'm talking about. If you go to
Moscow just once—you'll fall in love with that city. It's very hard for me

every time I have to leave Moscow. I feel like jumping out of the train and running back.''

"Do you go there often?'' Sashka asked with envy.

"Yes, often enough.''

"Do you just go there for the hell of it, or do you have some sort of business there?''

"I go there mostly on black-market business. Buying and selling clothes, shoes, perfume . . . they used to call it 'speculation,' but now they call it 'commerce.' Of course when I'm there I also take it easy, breathe the air of the capital, and relax.''

"Good for you. Seems like a nice life. . . . Must be interesting.''

"And your life isn't interesting? Are you bored?''

"Well, you know, I'm kind of unhappy. Whatever I try to do, it never seems to work out.''

"What do you want to do? Maybe meet someone fun?''

"How did you know?''

"Soldiers are all alike when it comes to that. You haven't gotten together with anyone yet?''

"No, you're the first.''

"I meant getting together with a girl.''

"No.''

"It's not easy for you soldiers. Girls like to be taken out to restaurants, driven around in cars, given expensive clothes. But what does a soldier have to offer?''

"I suppose you're right,'' Sashka sighed. The guy then continued on with a meaningless chitchat. He spoke reasonably, plainly, his words right on the mark. And he spoke in such a tone, that it was impossible to disagree with him. It was as if he wasn't eighteen, but a middle-aged man of fifty or so. His lips froze in a half-smile, and his eyes looked straight ahead. But Sashka subconsciously felt that his eyes were fixed upon him, and that he kept following him out of the corner of his eye. Following him very closely.

Suddenly Sashka remembered that they hadn't yet introduced themselves.

"What's your name?'' he asked. The fellow smiled and turned his entire body to face Sashka.

"Really. We've been chatting a half-hour already, and we still haven't introduced ourselves. My name's Yegor. Not a very fitting name, is it?''

"What do you mean?''

"Well, everyone says that Yegor's a name for a large, burly peasant—but I'm just a little grasshopper . . .''

"Nonsense. Different people have different names. My name's Alexander.''

"Oh boy . . . that's not a name—it's a burst of gunfire!''

Yegor smiled again and Sashka noticed that he had a very pleasant smile. When he smiled, his face became so childlike, even somewhat feminine. They stayed there another half-hour, their conversation flowing at a measured pace, unhurriedly, like a little stream. Sashka noticed that the theme of their conversation increasingly seemed to center around his sore spot—sex. Sashka really liked everything Yegor had to say—it even aroused him a bit. There was nothing left for him to add—he just nodded in agreement. Then he admitted to Yegor that he hadn't yet been with a woman, and that this weighed heavily upon him. Yegor smiled again, saying that it must really be unpleasant, and that he must really be fed up with it. This Yegor —with only a couple of phrases—had the astonishing ability of getting to the heart of matters. Sashka felt at ease and carefree in his company. There was a slight pause in their conversation. Sashka saw that Yegor was looking at him in a particular way, straight into his eyes, and the latter calmly addressed him:

"Sashka, I want to ask you a sensitive question."

"Go ahead."

"Have you ever fooled around with boys?"

A lump of sweet anxiety welled up in Sashka's chest and an image of the boys from the bathhouse suddenly ran through his mind. He wanted to tell Yegor everything, the whole truth, from start to finish. But something inside him whispered: "Why shame yourself? Keep quiet."

"No," Sashka replied, "never."

"And what would you think about that?" Yegor continued.

"Oh, I don't know. Guess I'd never thought much about it."

"Well, does it make you angry or turn you off like it does other guys?"

"No."

Yegor looked once more straight into Sashka's eyes with his strange and quizzical look.

"Listen, Sashka . . . I've been talking with you for a while already, and it seems to me like you're an open-minded kind of guy. I've got a proposal for you. . . . If you wouldn't be against it, I'd like to give you a minette."

This abrupt and unfamiliar word struck Sashka over the head like a stick. But he also felt as if this unusual word was not at all menacing.

"What's that?" Sashka half-whispered.

"Sorry, I should have suspected that you wouldn't know that word, and I'll phrase it more simply. Or maybe I should just explain what it is. A 'minette' is an intimate sexual act carried out by taking the male sexual member into one's mouth. That's a clinical description. But in simpler language, the name for it sounds rather vulgar. I hope you know what I mean?"

Sashka nodded. His tool once again began to strain impetuously, sending lustful signals to his brain; his eyes half-closed. Sashka was ready for anything, although he was just a bit afraid for himself. Would he burn up?

Would he make a bad impression? Yegor awaited his reply.

"Uh, well, where would we . . ." Sashka sighed.

"How about over there, where there's some nice dense bushes. They're quite full."

Right behind them spread a sizable thicket. It had, so it seemed, been specially designed as a place for secret trysts and carryings-on. Not waiting for Sashka to reply, Yegor silently held out his slender hand. Sashka hesitated a second, but then gently took hold of it with his large paw. They looked at one another and, without a word further, they set off into the embrace of the shrubbery. The branches and their leaves tenderly pressed against Sashka's cheeks, as if to calm the soldier: "Don't be afraid, everything will be fine . . . you'll enjoy it . . . we know you will. . . ." Yegor went right up to Sashka and placed his hand on his chest.

"Sashka, what's the matter with you? You're trembling. Are you afraid?"

"No . . ."

"Don't worry. Relax and don't think about anything at all. I'll try to bring you more pleasure than any girl ever could."

"I . . ."

"Quiet. You don't have to say anything. Don't try and talk sense just now. Try to relax as much as you can and tune out the rest of the world."

"I'll try . . ."

Yegor kept looking into Sashka's eyes. And Sashka couldn't tear himself away from his stare. He felt one of Yegor's hands slide down his belly, gently unfastening his belt-buckle. Sashka stirred, trying to undo the buttons.

"That's okay," Yegor said, "I'll do it all myself."

Slowly, deliberately, Yegor liberated Sashka from his plain soldier's garb and with one brisk tug pulled his pants, along with his underwear, right down to his very boots. Sashka stood before him in all his beauty. Yegor touched Sashka's tool, ready in choice fashion for its first examination.

"You've got quite a boner there, there's no denying that. It's long overdue to be put to good use."

And with these words Yegor squatted down. Inside Sashka everything pounded, his heart jumped. Yegor opened his mouth and stuck out his tongue. With the tip of his tongue he began tickling the head, all the while looking up and monitoring Sashka's responses.

"Does that feel good?"

"It's great!"

Yegor took Sashka's hands and put them on his head, at the same time grasping his manhood with his lips and taking it into his mouth all the way down to the balls. For the first time in his life Sashka's tool felt the warmth of a mouth, the caress of lips and a tongue. He squinted with pleasure, like a cat basking in the sun. Yegor kept his eyes fixed on Sashka. He began playing with his tool as if it were a toy, licking up and down, nibbling on it. . . . Sashka liked everything he did. Then with one hand Yegor began to massage his balls ever so gently and let his fingers roam along the area between his balls and his ass. Sashka, without even noticing, stroked Yegor's hair and fondled his ears. Yegor took Sashka's member out of his mouth for a second and said:

"Sashka, don't forget to keep a lookout for anyone passing by, okay?"

Sashka nodded and his tool once again was enveloped by the moist warmth of Yegor's mouth. No, no one would bother them. Sashka could be seen through the branches of the bushes by the occasional passer-by, walking along the lane. But they never looked over toward the bushes. Sashka also watched Yegor with interest.

"That's so wonderful! . . . It's great!" Yegor whispered.

Sashka ran the palm of his hand across his forehead and thought: "He sure knows what he's doing—it's as if he didn't have any teeth." This kept on for some time, until Sashka noticed that Yegor was starting to tire.

"Would you like to rest a bit?" Sashka asked. Yegor stood up and wiped his lip with his hand.

"Sashka, don't worry about it. This is your first time, so you might take a while to climax."

"But why?"

"Well, you know, an orgasm is a rather complex thing. It might be more difficult for you to have one under these conditions, since it's all new to you. I've been with soldiers who've done this for the first time with me, and one of two things usually happens: either they climax right away, or else it lingers on for almost a half-hour. The important thing is for you not to worry about it. Everything'll be just fine."

"Listen Yegor, where should I shoot?"

"Into my mouth, of course."

"That won't sicken you?"

"What a dummy you are. . . . I'm hoping for just that. Well, I guess I can't really expect you to understand—but then again, you don't really need to."

They rested a while longer, talking about this and that, and then Yegor once again squatted down in front of Sashka. Yet it was strange—although Sashka felt a certain resilience in his tool and the sensations were pleasant, he couldn't climax for anything. There were moments when he felt the inevitable approach of an orgasm, when his sperm should have been just about ready to gush forth, but each time it receded somewhere, and he felt only a bit of pressure. Sashka saw that Yegor had had enough, that he was now moving his mouth mechanically, no longer deriving any pleasure from the act. With all his might Sashka tried to finish it off, but things just got worse the more he strained.

"Enough, I can't do any more," Yegor said. He removed Sashka's tool from his mouth and, with a grunt, got up on his feet.

"For some reason it's just not happening for me," Sashka said, almost in tears.

"Somehow you just don't seem to be able to let go. Maybe the conditions aren't right, or else you need to be in a different position, sitting down or lying. . . . Who the hell knows. . . . But I'm not in the mood any more. . . ."

Yegor's last sentence left Sashka crestfallen. Here it was, his long-awaited first sexual contact. It was at least something other than masturbation! But once more nothing happened. The poor guy felt like there was some sort of curse on him.

Yegor took out a cigarette and lit up. Sashka looked at his absurdly erect manhood and sighed quietly. He really did want to climax one way or another. But he couldn't bring himself to beat off in front of Yegor. Yegor let out a bit of smoke and put his hand on Sashka's shoulder:

"Do you have some time?"

"About an hour or so."

"Is that all?"

"Well, I have a ticket for a movie at eight."

"What the fuck are you talking about. . . . Which movie theater?"

"The one over there, 'The Worker.' "

"And what time do you have to be back to your unit?"

"Around nine."

"Great. To hell with your movie. Let's go to this place I know."

"Where is it?"

"Right over here, two blocks away."

"What kind of place is it?"

"There's a guy there. . . . Don't worry, he's cool. He lives alone. We have to get your rocks off somehow!"

"But maybe it would be awkward for us to go there?"

"Once I make a phone call it won't be."

Sashka hesitated. He had experienced so many different things today that he already felt a little overwhelmed by it all.

"Maybe it would be better to go another time? I'll just go to the movies, okay?"

"All right. I get it, every kopeck means a lot to you right now, doesn't it. Well, here's enough for you to go to the movies ten times over."

Sashka was about to protest, but Yegor foisted the money on him. They left the garden and set off down the street. No, Sashka didn't care about the movie he'd miss; he simply felt like this was all so completely alien to him; he felt like a fly that had landed on the smooth surface of the water in someone's aquarium. He didn't know how to behave, what to say, and more to the point, he had no idea how this was all going to turn out. But he walked along with Yegor, walked, blaming himself for these base passions that reared up from time to time in most anyone. After they had walked a block Yegor stopped at a pay phone.

"Let me give him a call. He's usually at home, but anything can happen. He might have decided to take off somewhere all of a sudden. . . ."

But it turned out that he was home. Sashka stood alongside Yegor and listened to their conversation. Yegor spoke in a different tone, very chummy, even kind of crude:

"Hey there buddy . . . I'm coming over to see you right away. . . . No, there's two of us. . . . You'll see, you'll like him. . . . We're just around the corner. . . . We'll be right over."

A minute later they entered the gateway of a well-kept five-storied building. There weren't very many buildings like that in the city.

"Which floor?"

"Third."

They walked up the stairs and Yegor rang. Sashka expected to see any other sort of person except for the one who opened the door. . . . It was a boy who opened the door for them—quite young, no more than 16 or 17. Sashka was dumbstruck and asked Yegor softly:

"How old is he?"

"Sixteen," Yegor snorted, "he's young, but precocious. And there's no need to be bashful in front of him, he's cool."

"Does he live here alone or something?"

"What are you talking about, he lives here with his parents. But they're away—and won't be back for a week."

Sashka entered the room behind Yegor. They sat down on a couch. The room was well appointed, tasteful, but not too luxurious. There was a nice wall-unit . . . soft furniture, a beautiful large clock, a television, two carpets. . . . but what was most striking was how clean it was. There wasn't a speck of dust on the furniture, and the air was fresh. Behind the couch stood a small table on wheels with two bottles of champagne and a large box of chocolates. The kitchen door opened and the host returned. Sashka felt bashful in front of him. . . . Well, he was just another guy, nothing more. . . . The boy looked at Sashka with his large black eyes and offered his hand:

"Koba."

"Excuse me?" Sashka didn't understand.

"Koba. I have a Georgian name: my mother's Russian, my father—Georgian."

Yes, of course. Now Sashka noticed a distinct hint of Caucasian blood in him. Koba was handsome, that's all there was to it. His hair was almost completely black; he had a swarthy complexion, long eyebrows that extended nearly to his ears. But the most exceptional feature of his face was, of course, his eyes. Robust, black as black could be, yet very sad. Some kind of velvet melancholy enshrouded and possessed these eyes. Koba took three crystal champagne flutes off the shelf and set them down on the table. Yegor opened up the champagne, and they toasted their getting to know one another. Then they started up a simple conversation. Yegor yammered on about this and that; Koba smiled every once in a while, although when he smiled, his eyes became sadder still. Koba certainly didn't seem the master of this house. All the time he seemed bashful, even more so than Sashka. But on the other hand, Yegor was quite at home. He loosened up from the champagne, his eyes shining contentedly. A half-hour or so passed like this.

Time was growing short for Sashka. Finally, Yegor stretched out and said to Koba:

"Okay, time is money. And our soldier here doesn't have much time to spare. Change the lighting and turn on some music."

"Should I turn on a soft light?"

"Better the television."

Koba switched off the overhead light, turned on the television with the sound off, and started up a small Japanese tape recorder. Yegor quickly unbuttoned Sashka's pants and began sucking. Sashka had never felt more ill at ease in all his life. Koba sat down beside them and watched television. Sashka didn't feel even the slightest bit aroused. It was actually quite unpleasant for him. He couldn't even begin to get an erection. But this didn't seem to bother Yegor in the least. He kept on working Sashka's tool, paying attention to no one and nothing. Out of the corner of his eye Sashka looked at Koba, who sat there like a statue. It didn't even seem like he was breathing. More than anything Sashka wanted to knock Yegor off him and button up his pants. After a little while Yegor tore himself away, stretched out, and shot out gruffly to Koba:

"This guy's burned out. And I'm exhausted. Come on girlfriend, have a go at it."

Koba didn't move a muscle.

"Are you deaf or something? Have your ears rotted out?"

"I can't just do it like that," Koba said in a subdued voice.

Yegor burst out into loud laughter.

"Stop," Koba said, in an even quieter voice.

"Well then, get the hell out of here and go into the other room, don't get in the way."

Koba got up and went out the door on the left. Yegor again climbed over to Sashka. The exact same movements with the exact same result. Sashka winced. He couldn't bear this coarseness any longer—he'd been raised differently. He never behaved crudely and couldn't put up with it in others. It was especially vile to hear Yegor address Koba as if he were a girl. Sashka waited a few minutes and then firmly shoved Yegor aside:

"Why do you act so appallingly toward him?"

Yegor hadn't expected a question like that. He raised his head and looked at Sashka, dumbfounded:

"Oh. Well, I guess I didn't tell you about that. I've known him for a long time, and we have our own sort of relationship. . . ."

"Still . . ."

Sashka got up from the couch and buttoned up his pants. He was disgusted. The clock said ten till eight. He still had just a little more than an hour left. It was a good twenty-minute walk from here to the base. "I'm out of here," he decided. It would be better to walk it at a slow pace than to work up a sweat hurrying back. He was just about to open his mouth to say good-bye to Yegor, and then suddenly remembered Koba. He ought to say good-bye to him as well. Sashka opened the door to the other room where his swarthy host had gone. In this small, dark room that looked like a bedroom, a pleasing pink night light glowed. Koba stood next to a large wall-mirror. He was standing in a position where Sashka could see his face in the mirror. Koba was crying. Softly, silently. . . . Upon seeing Sashka, he turned around and quickly wiped his eyes. But Sashka, having seen this, completely forgot that he had come in to say good-bye. He went over to Koba and said:

"Why do you let him talk to you like that?"

"I can't take it any more," Koba said, and another tear rolled out of his eye. "It's been like this for some time already. . . . It'd be okay if it happened only when we were alone, but in front of others. . . ."

"But why do you put up with it?"

"It's just my nature . . ."

"Your nature has nothing to do with it. . . . It's disgusting how he acts toward you, and you don't say anything. What is he to you—your brother, a relative, a boyfriend? . . ."

"Don't call him my boyfriend. I guess . . . it's our past that keeps us together. . . . He seduced me. . . . I was still a child then. Do you understand?"

"So that's how it is," Sashka frowned, "well, are you tired of this guy? Or are you going to let him keep on like this?"

"I don't know. . . . It's all so sickening every time it happens. I don't even want to see him any more."

Sashka tilted his head to one side.

"If you want, I'll get rid of him, if he's annoying you."

"How will you get rid of him?"

"Elementary. Properly, calmly."

"Altogether?"

"Well, I'm not sure that's exactly what you want. But he does need to be taught a lesson."

"You think so?"

"I'm sure of it."

"How will you do that?"

"That's up to me. But I need for you to give me the word—remember, you're the master of the house here."

"Gee, I don't know . . ."

"Don't be a wet rag, make a decision. Yes or no."

Koba hesitated a bit, and then finally managed to squeeze out a "Yes."

Sashka went into the living room. Yegor was lazing about, sitting on the couch and leafing through a magazine, evidently not giving a damn about any of this. Sashka's deep and firm voice resounded through the room:

"Yegor, the master of the house requests that you vacate the premises."

Yegor slowly turned his head and stared at Sashka with an expressionless gaze. After a rather long pause, he answered:

"What, has the master's tongue dried up?"

"He just can't come out."

"Has he been struck by paralysis?"

"I don't think so. He just doesn't feel like coming out here."

"So that's how it is. . . . Well, we'll just have to ask him what he wants. Koba! Do you hear?! Come out here, Koba!"

Koba came out into the hallway and stood alongside Sashka. The smile that spread across Yegor's face thoroughly disgusted Sashka. Yegor suddenly seemed to have aged 15 years.

"I've been told that you've requested me to vacate the premises, is this correct?"

"Yes," Koba replied, quite firmly.

"And what have I done to incur his highness's wrath?"

"I can't put up with your boorishness any longer."

"Boorishness? You consider it boorishness that I call a spade a spade? Why don't you say it more directly, that I'm in the way here, that you're falling head over heels for this soldier boy."

"Shut up," Sashka growled.

"Oh yeah, looks like it's big time love here. What the hell. . . . I'll just have to step back for now."

Yegor got up and headed for the door.

"Only you'd best hurry up, my little Georgian," he said, putting on his shoes, "you hardly have any time left. It's already after eight. You know they say that a soldier's love is over with quickly, but maybe it'll be different here. Although . . . maybe you can try giving your uncle a call. I wish you all the best. Take care, soldier!"

Yegor slammed the door so hard that you could hear the neighbors opening their doors and looking out into the stairwell, wondering: "What happened?"

"Jerk," Sashka said.

Koba looked at the door pensively.

"No, he's not a jerk. He's just very lonely and unhappy."

They returned to Koba's room. Sashka understood that Koba was upset now, but time was growing short.

"I've got to be going soon, Koba."

"Yes, I understand. And once more I'll be left alone. I don't want that to happen!'

"I'd really like to stay, but I can't—I'm on duty."

Koba looked at Sashka anxiously, pleadingly:

"Tell me truthfully. Promise me that right now you'll answer my question in all honesty. It's very important to me."

"I promise."

"Do you really want to stay, or are you simply saying that so you can leave more quickly? Only tell me the truth, I won't get mad."

"Yes . . . I really . . . don't want to leave you."

And suddenly Koba's eyes changed. Sashka noticed this straight away. They became dewy and more gentle. Koba smiled.

"I'm not quite certain, but it looks like I can arrange it so that you don't have to rush back to base. Would you stay if I could?"

"But how?"

"Did you hear Yegor mention my uncle?"

"Yes."

"We've got him to thank for putting the idea into my head. I wouldn't have thought of it myself. The commander of your unit happens to be my uncle."

"Sherikadze?" Sashka asked, asonished.

"Yes. Dato Grigorievich. He's my father's brother."

"And what do you propose?"

"I'll call him up and ask him to allow you to return to the unit in the morning."

"How are you going to explain this to him?"

"Very simple. I'll tell him we've got some people over here . . . some girls . . ."

"He won't allow it."

"I've never asked him for anything like this before. But I don't think he'll refuse me. Will you stay then?"

"Well, then I could. . . . But you won't be able to do it."

"Let me try. It should work out."

Koba once again smiled and picked up the receiver from the phone. He'd already begun to dial the number, but suddenly pressed down the lever and . . . burst into laughter. Sashka was quite surprised.

"What's with you?"

"You're going to laugh, but I don't know your name."

"What, I didn't introduce myself?"

"I'm sure you did, but I must have forgotten."

"Sorry. It's Sashka."

"A wonderful name. Simple and gentle. Okay. Wait a minute—it

doesn't make any sense to call the base now, since he'll already be home."
Koba dialed his number:

"Good evening, Grigorievich! Recognize your favorite nephew's voice?
. . . How are things? . . . Yeah, same here. . . . Listen, uncle, I have a
favor to ask. I've made the acquaintance of one of your soldiers. . . .Well,
you know, we've got a nice little party going here. . . . What I really need
is for you to be a friend here. Could we somehow arrange it to extend his
liberty until morning, since it's almost over. . . . Yes, he's at my place.
Well, I'd really like for him to be able to stay. I'm asking you, please. . . .
What? His last name? Sashka, what's your last name?"

"Skvortsov," Sashka answered.

"Skvortsov, Aleksandr. . . Okay, got it. Sashka, your company, platoon, and section."

"Second company, first platoon, third section."

"Uncle, second company, first platoon, third section. . . . Okay. I'll
wait."

Koba hung up the phone and joyfully turned to Sashka:

"First he'll call the unit, and then back here."

"Do you think it'll work?"

"Now I don't just think it'll work, I'm certain of it."

"He seemed to agree rather quickly."

"Well, you know . . . I really shouldn't be telling you this, but, well—
you have to promise to keep it between you and me. The fact is that he owes
me a bit of a favor. Things haven't been going so well between him and his
wife, and so he has this woman friend. My parents often go away for a few
days at a time and let him and his woman come over here when I go out.
No one besides me knows anything about this. So I ask you, please . . ."

"Of course, don't worry about it . . ."

The phone rang, Koba picked up the receiver and in a flash all their
problems had been solved.

"Everything's in order," Koba said, "you have to be back on base
tomorrow at nine in the morning."

"Great! I can't believe it!"

Sashka felt a flood of fresh energy. Twelve extra hours! Koba was positively glowing.

"So. Today we're going to kick back and take it easy."

He held out his hand to Sashka. Sashka clapped his hand into his.

"Right—we'll kick back and take it easy."

"And have some fun. We'll go through all the champagne."

"We don't have to."

"We must! We live but once. Now off to the tub with you for a bath."

"I've already bathed today."

"In a bathtub?"

"In a bathtub."

"Where was that?"

"At the bathhouse—I rented a room with a tub."

"That's nonsense. I'm going to draw a bath for you that you'll never forget."

Koba went out. Sashka felt like he had just drunk the strongest coffee ever brewed. His fatigue disappeared, he felt easy and carefree. Koba returned a few moments later:

"Everything's ready. Let's go."

When Sashka went into the bathroom, his jaw dropped to the floor. The room was done all in blue and black imported tile; they were beautiful and sparkling clean. There were also two enormous mirrors and shelves brimming with vials containing potions from abroad. But the best part was the fragrance. The bathroom was redolent with the aroma of fresh strawberries. Yes, yes, strawberries! And from out of the bathtub, almost to the very top, there rolled a bright pink foam.

"It's berry-scented bath gel—strawberry—from France," said Koba.

"Well, aren't you something," Sashka said in amazement.

Koba lowered his head:

"If you come by again, it'll smell of currant or apple."

Sashka suddenly wanted to put his hand on Koba's shoulder. He did so, and then said:

"But maybe you won't want me to come by again."

"Don't be a fool," Koba said softly and left.

Sashka grinned and began undressing. What a day he'd had! All kinds of things happening: in all his life he had never experienced so much. Sashka sunk down into the pink foam—it was like fresh strawberry preserves. He'd always dreamed of taking such a bath. . . .

Koba came back and hung up a terry robe. And then he left again. He was so young, yet so self-reliant. . . . He should be the one getting into the bath, having a nice soak, and putting on a terry robe, but he was thinking about others. Sashka got out in about twenty minutes. Before the sofa stood the very same little table with wheels, but this time it held a large bowl of steaming borsch, next to which were neatly cut slices of bread, a fresh salad, a bowl of sour cream, and, on another plate, a large piece of meat with fried potatoes.

"Hey you . . . why so much," Sashka said.

"Well, you really haven't had anything to eat today. We can't have that, you need to eat right."

"And you?"

"I had my fill just before you came. Eat up, and I'll go into the kitchen—I need to grind the coffee."

Left alone, Sashka thought: "He went out just so I wouldn't feel awkward eating in front of him." He ate up everything, in the literal sense of the word, wolfing it all down, and then brought the empty dishes to the kitchen. And wafting from the kitchen was the heavenly scent of coffee. What a kitchen! Everything in it was imported.

"Koba, who are your parents?"

"They're in the trading business."

"And where are they?"

"In Moscow, Petersburg. . . . They're off on a buying trip. They travel a lot. Here, everything's ready. Let's have some coffee, and I also have a pie."

He picked up a large pot of Turkish coffee, a tray with the pie, and went out to the living room. Sashka followed. Koba got out some cups and they settled in on the couch.

"Sasha, how do you know Yegor?"

"We met just today. On a bench, in the public garden."

"Tell me, what he was doing to you here in the living room . . . well, was it very unpleasant for you?"

"You know, it was the first time for me, and. . . . You know, I just can't do it like that, with someone else there."

"Me too. I can't do it when someone's watching."

"That's why I couldn't come."

"So you didn't come?"

"No."

"And before today you had no idea that there could be this kind of intimacy between men?"

"Well of course I thought there might be."

"But you didn't know how it all happened, did you?"

"No."

"Okay, now I'll show you. I keep this video very carefully hidden from my parents."

Koba went out into the bedroom and returned with a videocassette. Only now did Sashka see the Japanese VCR atop the television. Koba loaded the cassette and then poured some champagne, opening yet another bottle. But Sashka couldn't swallow another drop of the heavenly nectar. His eyes were literally glued to the screen. Before Sashka flashed the fairy tale-like beauty of boyish bodies, the most beautiful faces, enormous erect members and music . . . such music. . . . It was piercing, captivating, mocking the idiotic government under which this was all forbidden. . . .

There was no end to the caresses and tenderness that flowed like a river from the screen straight at Sashka. He shuddered when fantastic fountains of sperm, inconceivable and unimaginable, shot upward. The champagne flute in Sashka's hand was frozen still, its bubbles, dancing about, long forgotten. Trembling members appeared in every orifice of the human body, moving into any that they possibly could. It seemed unfeasable, physically impossible, and yet it was done with such playful ease and shown in close-up so that deception didn't seem possible. This went on and on. One segment would end and then another would immediately follow, even more captivating and explicit. And then it was not just a pair of guys having a go at each other, but a threesome . . . a foursome . . . a fivesome . . . a whole crowd. It was a totally new world. Everything was different.

Sashka closed his eyes and hung his head.

"What's wrong?" Koba asked.

But an answer wasn't forthcoming. Sashka simply gathered him up into his ample arms and hugged him tightly.

"Hey, don't suffocate me," Koba whispered and hugged Sashka about the neck.

"I'm sorry, I just can't stand it any more. . . ."

"I understand. . . . Do what you want to with me, only don't deprive me of life. . . .

Koba kissed Sashka on the lips; Sashka didn't move away. He hugged the boy closer still and groaned lightly. Koba ran his hands along Sashka's chest, and Sashka began quivering all over.

"Sashenka, are you okay?"

"Too okay. I'm going to come."

Koba quickly went down on Sashka's manhood—he barely got there in time. His tool began spurting in such a frenzy that it should have been captured on video. Koba opened his lips and Sashka saw sperm flying through the air, into Koba's mouth. Some of it fell on his chin, his nose, his cheeks. Sashka dropped his hands, now lifeless, to his side.

"You came so fast. . . . You got too heated up watching that video, poor guy," Koba smiled.

He ran off to the bathroom, washed his face and returned. Sashka held out his hand, and Koba pressed to him.

"Koba, turn off the television, that's enough for today."

"I think so too."

The screen went dark and they continued drinking champagne. Sashka looked into Koba's shining eyes—he simply got lost in them:

"How beautiful you are . . ."

"I know. I'm sick of hearing that, though. I don't want to be beautiful."

"Then what do you want to be?"

The spark disappeared from Koba's eyes and once again they became sad.

"Happy . . ."

"Well, that's more complicated."

"You know, that's funny, because for me, it's very simple."

"Really?"

"Yes. I really don't need very much."

"Just one man who wants me. I'm not like Yegor. I'm very domestic, I don't like having all kinds of sexual adventures out there. I don't judge him for it, I'm just different. And that's precisely what annoys him the most—that I'm not like him. Do you understand?'

"I understand."

"So he tries to belittle me. The only thing he really needs is sex. In any way, shape, or form—if in a bed, then in a bed; if in the bushes, then in the bushes; if in an entryway, then in an entryway. But me, what I need most of all is another human being."

"So you mean you're not really interested in sex?"

"No, I like it a lot, only with someone I care about, someone I want to be with."

"Does that person have to be a man?"

"I don't know, maybe I'll fall in love with a woman some day, but for now, that's not happened to me."

"The same with me."

"Really?"

"Absolutely. You know today was the first time ever for me. . . ."

"What? . . ."

"I was introduced to sex.'

Koba smiled pensively.

"That means Yegor was your first? Well, I guess that's not so bad. Don't think badly of him, okay? He doesn't have an easy life. You know, tomorrow you'll leave, and we might not see each other again—but he's not going anywhere, regardless of what he's like. Yet I can tell you this much— I won't allow him such liberties any more. You were right about that."

"Why did you say that we might not see each other again?"

"Don't you think that might happen?"

"Well, everything depends on you. You're the master of the house."

"Sashka, I'd really like for us to see each other again. But I was afraid even to bring it up. Do you want to keep seeing each other?"

Sashka was silent a moment and then replied:

"Yes . . ."

"Is that the truth?"

"Yes. Only I don't want Yegor to . . ."

"Well, that's your right."

"Please don't get mad, it's just that it's very difficult for me right now. Only a couple of hours ago, there was nothing like this in my life, and now, everything's different."

"I'll also need time to get used to you. Sanyechka, you should get some sleep. You've had quite a rough day."

"I don't want to sleep."

"Well, what do you want?"

"Just to sit and talk with you. And once more . . ."

"What?"

"To kiss you."

"Well, go ahead and kiss."

It was no longer lust. Gently, softly, tenderly, Sashka kissed Koba on the forehead, the cheeks, the lips. . . . Savoring him like champagne. He got used to Koba, and Koba to him.

"Sashenka, you're so tender and gentle. . . . It's hard to believe that today was your first day."

Sashka smiled and pressed the boy's face to his chest. Koba heard the beating of his young, strong heart. More than anything on earth Koba wanted to freeze this moment, to hear this sound forever. Without a moment's hesitation he would give all of his tenderness, affection, and devotion to Sashka. They kissed and kissed one another. Sashka was once again aroused to the straining point.

"Sashenka, you think you could do it again?"

"I could."

Koba got a package of condoms from the table drawer, and lovingly put one on Sashka's tool.

"It's better to get used to rubbers right away. They're a little inconvenient, but they'll save you from all kinds of troubles."

And Koba sat on top of Sashka. His manhood slid in smoothly, and Sashka filled the boy up. It was warm. Tenderness . . . Affection . . . Sensual movements. . . . Then Koba lay down on his back, with Sashka on top. Koba put his legs up over Sashka's shoulders—and Sashka pushed into him, and kissed him, and hugged him. . . .

In the morning they stood for a long time on the threshold, hugging. Koba cried a bit and then raised his head to wipe away the tears:

"God. It's time. I'll wait for you."

Sashka left. He walked past the garden, passing that bench, He grinned —if not for that bench, then none of this would have happened. He remembered Koba's face, his eyes, his voice. God, he couldn't wait to see him again! . . .

I want to be with him! Just to hug him and be still. Not one word need be said.

Sashka had already learned the cherished phone number by heart, and decided to call from the first pay phone! Sashka bolted over to it:

"Hello! Is that you?'

"It's me. What, are you already back on base?"

"No, I haven't made it back there yet."

"Be careful that you aren't late!"

"Koba, I wanted to tell you . . ."

"Tell me."

"I don't know how to say it . . ."

"Just say, how you feel."

"My Kobochka, I . . . I . . . I . . ."

. . . And three simple noble words rang out. . . .

Drawing by Imas Levsky.

"Vitaly Yasinsky" [pseud.] (b. 1946)

A SUNNY DAY AT THE SEASIDE

[Solnechnyi den' na vzmor'e]

Translated by Anthony Vanchu

VITALY YASINSKY (pseudonym) is a journalist currently working for the "red" press. He lives in Moscow, where his hobbies are, in his words, boys and painting. "A Sunny Day at the Seaside" was published originally in 1992 in the literary supplement to the gay magazine *1/10*.

VAGIF USUALLY took his student holiday in June. After the trials and tribulations of life in the capital, and his studies at the conservatory, he would feel quite at ease in his quiet seaside hometown.

He had just completed his third year at the conservatory. In the fall, I had joined the army. Each of us understood that we wouldn't see each other for a long time, and thus decided to arrange to spend June together at the seaside.

My friendship with Vagif, at first purely boyish in nature, had become something more. I had never had any friends. I shunned the company of other boys, didn't like getting into fights, and tried to avoid altogether those street encounters on the street where things were resolved with irreconcilable ferocity. In a word, I was shy and closed off, constantly subjected to ridicule and mockery. It was hard for me to take it, but I had neither the character nor strength to defend myself.

And so it happened that Vagif had become my sole friend over the years. It all began one day when, on the way home from school, some boys from another neighborhood were pestering me. A fist fight was in the making, with an undoubtedly dreadful outcome for me. Suddenly there appeared a tall, darkly complected youth. He chased off my attackers, helped me gather up my notebooks, which had been scattered about the grass, and took me over to his house. We gorged ourselves on apricots from his garden; later on, we drank our fill of tea, ate cake, and watched videos until late that night. I felt a sense of ease and well-being that day . . .

Ever since that episode, I would always leave a half-hour early to meet Vagif and we would walk to school together. He was two years older—a difference that seemed like an eternity to me. But Vagif treated me as an equal. And he had my unspoken thanks for that. Suddenly, I had a friend. I tried to keep up with him as best I could. He did gymnastics—and so did I. He took up soccer—and I was there with him. The huge library and piano in his house also attracted me. For the first time I realized that there existed literature other than *The Dagger* and *The Three Musketeers*, that there were other books that you could lose yourself in until the morning. I would also listen to the piano as Vagif, my savior and idol, sat and played. He had saved me from loneliness and humiliation.

As it happened, I was at the age where you begin talking about "it." Vagif was the first to tell me about Freud, whom he had already managed to read in full. Our talks aroused strong feelings in me, awakening sweet and sinful desires . . .

That summer we found a quiet and secluded spot on the beach. There was a hanging cliff, a steep shore and strips of wondrous fine sand. But most important of all—there was not a soul around. It was as if we had recaptured our childhood—we were free, young, and strong. We were extraordinarily contented.

Stretching out on the sand, I waited for Vagif to make his way out of the water. I had dozed off. I dreamt that he put his hands, cold and damp from the sea water, on my chest, I shuddered in amazement, trying to free myself from this weight. But it pressed and pressed upon me heavily. And those black eyes, full of lustful languor, pressed upon me as well. His gentle, thin musical fingers had suddenly strengthened, becoming full of desire. And then there was that body, beautiful, powerful, hanging above me.

"Vagif!" I said, gasping for breath, not yet realizing that, unbeknown to my conscious mind or my will, something unexpected was taking place, something that would destroy the past. And I became afraid for myself, for Vagif, for us both.

I involuntarily attempted to hunch up as his masculine hands began to travel along my body in endless waves. His light, tender caresses gave place to a powerful and insistent haste; they were intoxicating, sending a chill throughout my entire body, depriving me of my will.

My wide-open eyes unconsciously gazed into the high blue sky. Not a single cloud there. And here, on the earth, there was an emptiness, ringing and ominous. How could I tear myself away from it? To whom could I call out for help? Where could I run? But I was afraid to stir, because now it was no longer Vagif's hands, but his moist, juicy lips caressing my body. They tenaciously descended lower and lower. I felt their anxious breathing on that place where my impassioned blood had wandered and, with leaden weightiness, had poured itself into my flesh. I instinctively and obediently spread my legs, powerless to resist this invasion any further. Then suddenly Vagif, in one single motion and with inexplicable brutishness, tore my bathing suit from me. Having broken loose to freedom, my member rose up to its full height, effortlessly and shamelessly.

And again, those hands. What were they doing to me?! It was as if they were playing, pressing down on invisible keys. I was entirely in their power. Vagif's thin fingers gently caressed my foreskin. Burning, pulsating currents of blood came alive; my temples reverberated with a dull pounding.

My flesh was filled with some kind of unearthly, unnatural power. Something irreversible and terrifying was about to happen.

But perhaps this wasn't really so irreversible, so tragic. The fear that had taken hold of me was still present, but something else had begun to make its presence felt, something I had never known before. A sweet and delightful languor slowly crept through every pore. My trembling subsided. The cool sand pleasantly tickled my enflamed body. My hands firmly embraced Vagif's pitch-black head, tugging at his hair, caressing his shoulders. And then I felt a hot and gentle touch, the kind of touch that makes the soul seize up and the heart stop beating. His hot, thirsting lips touched my member, this trembling lantern, and took it into its embrace. They enveloped it carefully, unhurriedly, as if fearing they might harm something frail and tender. Giving themselves over to desire and instinct, they began their agonized and anxious movements, raising up from far-off depths my long-slumbering juices.

Everything inside me was tense, like a taut string. It was as if I was all afire—my face, my body, and my member, that triumphant and joyful erection. My torso tore itself from the earth, raising itself higher and higher, urging my flesh on toward something unattainable and captivating.

. . . The earth shuddered beneath me, and the fiery lava that had kept itself hidden somewhere unknown suddenly gushed out with such force that I no longer saw either the blue sky or the bright sun, and could not hear the surf's dull crash. A scorching wave rolled across my body again and again as I lost myself in excruciating exhaustion.

. . . I opened my eyes slowly. It was still the same sand beneath me, dry and hot. Still the same sky, still the same blinding sun. And the eternal roar of the surf. My world had not come crashing down. But what had happened to me? Had my past life ended? What had just burst into it? I didn't understand. How could I unite these thoughts about tragedy, depravity, and sweet delight flooding over me?

Vagif lay alongside me. Frozen to the spot, I looked at his bronzed legs, spread wide, the black hair lightly winding between him and his flesh, powerful, rearing up, beautiful and proud. I couldn't take my eyes off it, nor could I control myself. What sort of forces, what sort of secrets did it possess? Why did it bewitch and attract me so?

My fingers growing cold, I impatiently embraced his manhood. My hand descended involuntarily. As if tearing away the veil from the face of an unknown beauty, I gazed, enchanted, at the delicate pink head of his quivering member, at the solid furrow that ran from below, at the small darkened funnel at its very end. Through his skin, I could feel how his blood boiled. But then maybe it wasn't really blood, but molten metal? And again my hand, now with a cruel vengeance, went up—and then down. Once more I looked at his naked, defenseless flesh. I wanted to possess its strength, power, and passion. I pressed up against his body as it sprawled out on the sand. I pressed against him—he who had become excited and impassioned, so close to me and so desired by me.

I was feeling good. I felt his broad chest stick to my back, the quickened beating of his heart, his searching, agitated flesh. It burned me, like a heated wedge. It was reckless. It was gentle.

Vagif's hands again caressed my body, now compliant, seeming to lack a will of its own. Effortlessly they pulled my torso up from the ground. All I could see now was a strip of golden sand and a bitter wormwood bush. I felt this impatient and thirsting body above me; it smelled of salt water, sun, and wind. I was afraid to admit to myself that I was anticipating him. It was the first time I had felt this thirst in me, and at that moment, I lived only for it.

Vagif grasped me about the shoulders and pushed himself away; he raised himself up some more so as then to lower himself onto me with the insatiable passion that accompanies only love.

A moan burst forth from inside me. I gasped for breath in passion, joy, and pain. I could no longer restrain the passion raining down upon me—it was something primal. Its incinerating fire spread across my entire body. I could not tell whether it was burning sweat or tears flooding my eyes. I could not even hear my own moaning, hysterical, joyful and grateful.

Did all this really have to come to an end? The world around me had ceased to exist. I didn't belong to it, I just no longer belonged to my self, enslaved by the call of life's passions.

Vagif's ardent hands entwined my body—tenderly, tremulously. Then I grasped him with my thighs, a steel hoop, and began my violent yet pleasure-filled movements with renewed force. I felt every cell of his powerful, strong phallus, its joy and triumph. With every passing moment it became more rapturous and insistent. Vagif surged forward, as if trying to raise me up into the cloudless blue sky. I felt his heated panting, his trembling shiver in the depths of my very heart.

How long would I be able to hold on to this feeling? How was I to know? I was prepared to suffer, prepared to endure all imaginable torments, prepared to refuse all other joys if only what I felt right now would remain.

What would happen next?

My last bit of strength had deserted me. In my fog, I felt convulsions racking Vagif's body and then a surging, burning stream gushed forth into my being.

I accepted this gift. And no one, other than I, knew how bright and clear this day had been, how beautiful this little wormwood bush, how brightly the sun shone in the blue sky.

. . . What a simple thing it is—happiness. In a single instant, a chance encounter on the street is sometimes all it takes to gain it or lose it forever.

"K.E." [pseud.] (b. 1962)

THE PHONE CALL
[Zvonok]

Translated by Anthony Vanchu

"K.E." is the pseudonym/pen name of Ella K. who lives in the city of Oryol south of Moscow and works as a librarian. "The Phone Call" appeared originally in the gay collection *Drugoi* (Moscow, 1993).

The gay community in Russia long thought of AIDS as a "foreign" disease, i.e., Russians got it only if they traveled abroad or consorted with foreigners. "The Phone Call" is significant not only because this attitude is totally absent, but also because it deals directly with the effects of the disease on this young man's life from a very personalized point of view.

A PHONE CALL woke him up. . .
He picked up the receiver.

"Hello. Is Nikolai there?"

"This is Nikolai."

"Ah . . . it's you. Great. Can we get together? Are you busy today?"

"Who is this?"

"It's . . . (there was a short hesitation on the other end) Seryozha. We got together once. . . . You know, we met at that place . . . about a year ago. Don't you remember?"

"No . . . and I don't recognize your voice either. But maybe we. . . . So we got together, you say. . . And why haven't you called since then?"

"I'm down here on a business trip. . . ."

"Ah . . . I see. Where are you right now?"

"I'm at the Salyut Hotel. . . . Maybe we could meet somewhere this evening. . . ."

"You know, I'm really not in the mood right now. . . . You woke me up. . . ."

"We can get together this evening. . . . I'll wait for you outside the hotel around six. Okay?"

"Sure . . ."

Kolya threw down the receiver rather rudely and once again curled up in bed. But sleep no longer came to him. . . .

He really couldn't place the voice or the name. Yet the whole thing rather fascinated him. In his mind he went through a number of faces, various situations. . . . Oh well, did it really matter? . . .

At six o'clock he was outside the hotel.

Standing there was a darkish, rather nice-looking young man.

"Hi. Are you Seryozha?"

"Yes . . ."

Seryozha smiled sweetly.

It seemed that he was a bit embarrassed.

No . . . he hadn't seen him before. Or maybe he'd simply forgotten him. . . ?

His memory drew a blank . . . not even a glimmer. . . . But did it really matter, especially now that they'd met up. . . ?

"Well, shall we go up to your room?" Kolya asked.

But it seemed that something was making Seryozha feel embarrassed. Interesting, was he so embarrassed the last time?

No, he really didn't know who this guy was . . .

He wouldn't forget such a nice-looking man with a trim body. . . . And his eyes . . . he could hardly have forgotten those eyes . . . so expressive . . . dark, beautiful . . . sparkling . . . and such thick black eyelashes. . . . He sort of looked like a Jew . . . like a handsome Jew.

"How long will you be here? . . ." Kolya inquired.

"A week. . . . Maybe we could take a bit of a stroll and talk some?" he suggested.

"Sure . . . let's . . . if that's what you'd like. And what . . . what kind of business trip are you here on?"

"I'm an engineer . . . a construction engineer."

"Aha. . . . Well, I'm not at all interested in technical things. So you needn't tell me anything more about what it is you do. . . ."

In fact nothing really seemed to matter to Kolya. . . . He didn't even really need to know this man's name. . . . Moreover . . . he wanted things to happen quickly . . . and get the whole dreary process of getting acquainted over with. But Seryozha, it seemed, needed some time to get over his initial shyness. He wasn't behaving like an old acquaintance at all.

Maybe someone else had given him his phone number?

While that was possible, it didn't change anything. It didn't really matter.

Kolya surprised even himself a bit with his own indifference and lack of desire to know anything more about his old-new acquaintance.

What was there to ask about anyway? He'd be gone in a week. Hello and good-bye. And then maybe he'd call again sometime, the next time he was in town. . . . Or else he wouldn't call. No one was obliged here.

After a rather short and meaningless stroll, they ended up going not to the hotel room, but to Kolya's apartment. It would be more peaceful there.

Sergei pulled a bottle out of his briefcase . . .

Kolya offered up some scraps out of the refrigerator.

He pulled the shades down, turned on a soft light.

They sat down at the table . . .

"And so, the last time . . . where was it that we got together?" Kolya inquired. "Somehow it's slipped my mind. Besides. . . . Did we see each other much?''

The other man kept silent, and then admitted what Kolya had suspected all along.

"I'm sorry. . . . But I don't really know you from before. I got your number from . . . Volodya. Do you remember him?''

"Which Volodya are you talking about. . . ?''

"You know, he's got a really solid build, and is a bit taller than I am . . . he's a real fun guy.

"I don't know. Maybe I remember him, maybe I don't. . . . There are lots of real fun guys. . . . A solid build, you say . . . is he blond?''

"Well, almost . . . he has gray hair. . . .''

"No, the one I'm thinking of . . . he's quite blond.

They ate and drank disinterestedly.

Kolya looked into Seryozha's eyes. . . . He liked his eyes. A nice fellow. . . . but with just a few complexes. . . . He'd have to work on him some.

"If you'd like, I can turn on the TV.''

"No, that's okay . . . you don't need to . . .''

The bottle had been drunk up, the snacks eaten—there hadn't been much of them anyway. . .

Somehow Kolya wasn't really in the mood . . . to get things going. It was strange . . . for some reason . . . he just wanted to hug this Seryozha . . . lie down in bed with him, and simply lie there next to him. Gently, they slowly caressed one another. . . . He didn't even want to get undressed.

But time passed.

He had to do something.

Besides, they still had a lot of time. . . .

Sergei spent the night with him. . . .

He left in the morning. Business to attend to. . . .

Kolya couldn't sleep any more. . . .

He'd been feeling despondent for some time now. . . . Such sadness . . .

He would get aroused, but it didn't last long . . . he'd get aroused, but only physically. Inside—it was as if he didn't even have a soul. . . .

His indifference was profound. How long would it go on like this? His illness gnawed away at him. . . . But his own health didn't matter to him. . . . Tell him tomorrow that you have AIDS . . . surely that wouldn't faze him at all.

There had, however, been a time when he'd had hopes and dreams. . . . When he was looking for someone. . . . He used to believe. . . . And cry. . . . At one time he had even been on the brink of committing suicide. . . . But then it got to be just like it is with a drug addict or an alcoholic . . . trying to smother his spiritual pain . . . again and again . . . indiscriminately . . . new sex partners all the time . . . and his disease was the result. He got what he needed from them, but did everything mechanically, caring only about the physical part of the encounter. . . . Some of his partners even felt slighted.

And so Seryozha also, it seemed, hadn't liked it too much. . . . He, apparently, had expected something more. . . .

He did everything distractedly, as if he had no control over it. He could, of course, have decided not to have sex. . . .

Sergei, sure enough, seemed like a decent sort of guy, good-hearted. . . . Only what did he really matter to him? What did either of them really matter to one another?

Would he come by again?

He'll come.

And if he doesn't, that doesn't mean anything.

The phone kept ringing insistently. . . .

Kolya didn't pick up.

He just let it ring and ring.

Finally he fell asleep.

Today Seryozha asked him:

"Kolya . . . you're upset about something, aren't you . . . it seems to me like something's upset you . . . and you're not talking because for you I'm an outsider, someone who's just passing through. . . . Right? . . . is that why you're not talking?"

Kolya grinned and shrugged his shoulders.

"You think I'm upset? No. Everything's fine. I don't have any problems at all."

"You're so reserved. . . . And you do everything as if you really didn't want to be doing it. . . . It's as if you were being forced to do it. . . . Is something wrong?"

"I told you . . . everything's okay."

"I understand. . . . I don't have any right to get so personal. But you know . . . I'm so lonely. . . . It seems to me like you might also be . . ."

"Me? . . . What are you implying?"

Sergei didn't answer.

Kolya looked about disinterestedly, scornfully, indifferently.

Kolya didn't refuse the money Sergei offered him the next day.

But he took it indifferently, coldly.

As if it was what was supposed to happen. Whenever someone offered him money, he always took it.

"I don't know what else to offer you. . . ." Sergei said in a strange tone that reflected both caution and awkwardness.

Kolya kept silent.

That afternoon two men came by.

Kolya gave himself up to each of them in turn. And then satisfied both of them together.

He also got really wasted, and didn't even hear them as they left. . . .

He was tired and nothing mattered to him. . . .

And then there was this insistent ringing at his door.

From morning on, again the telephone. . . .

His head was splitting.

Kolya, not really answering the phone, simply swore into the receiver and slammed it down . . . he was lucky he didn't break the phone.

Then a short while later the phone began to ring again.

He answered, a bit calmer this time.

It was Seryozha calling; his voice was agitated. "What the hell's going on. . . ?" he asked.

"Nothing's going on. . . . Nothing."

And then he put the receiver back onto the cradle.

It was quiet. . . . Silence. No one was calling anymore.

That evening, at his door. . . .

Why can't you all just disappear. . . .

But it was so persistent.

He went to open it up.

Seryozha . . .

He was frightened and feeling somewhat guilty. . . .

"What's going on? . . ." he asked that question again. "Can I come in?"

"Sure."

"What's going on with you. . . . Why did you freak out like that on the phone? . . ."

"I felt like sleeping this morning. . . ."

"And last night I was ringing at your door. . . . Weren't you here? The light was on. Was there someone here with you? . . ."

"I was asleep, understand. . . . Asleep! I didn't hear anything."

"Oh all right, never mind. . . ."

It was kind of funny to Kolya that Sergei took this all to heart. He was in a hurry, after all—he'd be leaving soon. And of course he'd given him money. And here he is, messing around with other guys. It was, to be sure, insulting. . . . But was he to blame that the guys had come around?

They lay next to one another, naked . . .

"Do you like me?" Kolya asked calmly. . . .

Kolya was asking him . . . and looking at him with interest, but somehow as if from afar. . .

Sergei turned his head. He looked into his eyes. . . . And then averted his gaze and quietly, with tenderness and care, looked at Kolya's shoulder, his hand . . . his fingers slowly slid down his body.

He kept silent.

"Will you see me off at the train station?" Sergei asked, already dressed, his briefcase in hand.

Kolya looked at him, propping his head up while lying in bed, curled up under the covers.

Then he slid back onto the pillow, smiled and shook his head, closing his eyes . . . as if luxuriating.

Kolya heard footsteps.

Sergei was leaving. He was leaving, not even having said good-bye.
The door slammed.
Kolya continued to lie in bed. But now he was just staring at the ceiling.
His gaze was frozen. . . .
Then he got up and began pacing the room. . . .
There was a farewell souvenir on the table . . . a little gray downy swan
. . . a children's toy. . . . But so touching.
Kolya stroked it cautiously. . . . He liked it. . . . It was soft . . .
pleasant. . . .
Then he went into the kitchen to drink some water. . . . He looked out
the window. . . .
It was a gloomy day . . . soon his life would end . . . altogether.
Kolya slowly wandered back to his room, opened his dresser door and
looked at himself in the mirror. . . .
He was still naked. . . .
Again he lay down on the bed.
And shuddered. . . .
In the stairwell he heard some footsteps . . . a shuffle. . . . Was some-
one coming to see him again?
What was he so afraid of? . . .
The noise passed by . . . passed by. . . . He didn't get a lot of guys com-
ing by to see him. . . . The neighbors would take note of something like
that. . . . Visitors. . . .
He closed his eyes. . . .
No, he didn't want to sleep at all. . . .
Like Seryozha had just said to him. . . . "You're so young . . . hand-
some . . . why are you so detached from everything . . . so cold . . . can
it be that you never loved anyone? . . . You're indifferent to everyone.
Why do you give yourself up as if it were an act of kindness, as if you had
no need of it, and were doing it only for the other person . . . can you
really be so totally apathetic . . . with everyone? Completely indifferent?"
And he then, maybe wanting to defy his depravity, or maybe in fact it was
how he really felt, answered: "Yes. I am indifferent. I need only a pr***
. . . who it belongs to . . . that doesn't matter. . . ." "So you'll give it to
anyone, huh? . . . Whoever wants it?" Sergei had asked, it seemed, even
with a certain sort of horror. "Yes . . . I'm a humanist," Kolya joked.
What did he want from him, why did this guy on a business trip keep
asking him about these things?
Then he left, without even saying good-bye.
Once again the phone rang.
Who needed him now?
"Yes . . ."
". . . it's Seryozha. Kolya . . . listen to me. Come to the train station,
okay? There's still time . . . it's almost an hour before my train. Come
down. . . ."

"Why?"

"You know which train it is. I'm in car number fifteen. I'll be waiting for you. . . . I'll tell you why . . . if you come . . . otherwise it wouldn't make any sense. . . . Will you come? . . ."

"Why?"

On the other end of the line he heard the receiver slam down.

But in point of fact, why? . . .

Kolya slowly put down the phone and once again lay on his bed.

He wasn't going anywhere. . . .

Anyhow, he knew what the other guy would say. . . .

Kolya smiled, almost mockingly. . . .

He turned his head to the side and lay there ever so quietly. . . .

How much time passed by like this?

Even if he left for the train station right now . . . he'd still be late.

Besides, he knew what that guy would say to him.

Kolya slowly got up from his bed.

Well, what did he want to say to him? . . . What? . . .

Wasn't it all the same anyhow? . . .

Kolya got up. Slowly, lazily, he moved about his room as if still half-asleep. . . .

He stumbled into the chair he'd left his clothes on. . . .

A shirt slid to the floor. . . .

If he got dressed right away . . . then maybe he could still make it in time . . . he'd get there . . . run there. . . . But no. . . . It wasn't worth it. . . . It wasn't worth doing.

Again he moved slowly about his room.

Again he sat down on his bed, sort of hunching over, his head bent down. . . .

Now he surely couldn't make it on time. . . .

Even if he had wanted to.

Minutes, seconds slipped by, flying by without pity, quickly becoming history. They disappeared forever. There remained only the present. . . . It swallowed itself up and became eternity. . . .

Again some sort of sudden ringing brought him back from his distanced and torpid state.

Again Kolya, for the second time that evening, shuddered and, surprising himself, picked up the receiver right away.

"Kolyukha, is that you? Hi! It's Slavik. Have you missed me?"

A malicious smile spread across his mug, that much was certain. He knew there'd be no refusing, he knew . . .

Kolya silently threw down the receiver. He had expected a completely different voice.

He looked at the clock.

One minute before his train left! . . .

He wouldn't be able to get there in time. . . . Of course now there was no way he could have made it there! . . . And he wasn't even dressed. . . . But if the train was late, then wouldn't he be leaving later? . . .

No . . . No . . . No!

No!!!

Now he clearly understood . . . it was too late.

He slowly lay down on his bed, wrapping himself up in the sheet . . . and calmed down . . . curling up into a ball, burying his face in the pillow.

No!!!

. . . He shouldn't have let him go.

This Seryozha . . . it must have been his destiny. He would never find a gentler, kinder, more sensitive man. . . . How that man had wanted to know who he was . . . to know the truth . . . his soul . . . to become his friend.

Couldn't it have happened? . . .

Why had he been so cold, indifferent, so cynical? . . .

Oh God . . .

They simply hadn't had the time . . . to get to know one another better. That's not true . . . there had been time. Had it really been so short?

He almost didn't hear the bell. . . .

But someone was now ringing again, insistently. . . .

He wouldn't go see who it was, he didn't need anyone. . . .

And then there was a ringing at his door.

Let them ring all they like.

Let them break the door down, he wasn't going to open up.

Let them . . .

But why were they ringing with such insistence? . . .

Who could it be?

The scum . . . Bastard . . .

It was that Slavka . . . so what . . . to hell with him. . . .

But maybe Seryozha hadn't left after all?

Why had such a strange thought entered his head?

Probably because he wanted him so much right now . . .

And Kolya got up slowly and went to the door.

Blood pounded to his temples. . . .

Cautiously he opened the door.

No, behind the door it wasn't Seryozha at all. . . .

It was Slavka. And a couple of other guys who'd been drinking.

He stepped back slowly.

His next-door neighbors were having a drunken row. . . . What a racket and din . . . singing. . . .

The three of them entered the apartment. The door closed.

He kept backing up, into the depths of his apartment . . . a shudder came over him . . . he broke out in a cold sweat . . . everything went dark. . . .

I beg you . . . Oh my God . . . help me! . . . I beg you . . . Dear Lord.

Photo by Alexei Sedov.

Yaroslav Mogutin (b. 1974)

THE DEATH OF MISHA BEAUTIFUL

[Smert' Mishi B'iutifula, 1996]

Translated by Vitaly Chernetsky

YAROSLAV MOGUTIN (b. 1974) is probably the best known "out" gay literary figure among Russians today. Since 1991 he has been publishing essays and articles on literary and cultural topics in both the mainstream and the alternative Russian media. Mogutin became the first to confidently speak out in Russia from the point of view of a gay man comfortable with his sexual identity. His poetry has appeared in a number of literary journals, and he has also edited several editions of gay literary classics, notably the collected works of Yevgeny Kharitonov and the Russian translations of *Giovanni's Room* and *Naked Lunch*. Mogutin's articles, frequently dealing with controversial issues, earned him the honor of being named cultural critic of the year by *Nezavisimaya gazeta* in 1994, but they also provoked the displeasure of the Russian authorities and increased harassment by them. In 1995 the threat of persecution forced him to leave Moscow for New York, where he applied for political asylum.

SOME FRIENDS from Moscow who recently passed through New York relayed the shocking news: Misha Beautiful was killed in prison. The story of his brief life could provide excellent material for a book or a movie. His name did not appear in the society chronicles. Actually, nobody even knew either his real name or his age. People were saying at the time of his death he was nineteen. His death wasn't reported in newspaper obituaries, and it is unlikely that anyone except me would write about him.

Not a single drug or rave-related party could take place without Beautiful. Almost everybody knew him. He was one of those exotic nocturnal creatures, those girl-boy club kids who keep it all going in any one of the world's capitals.

We met at Michael Jackson's concert at the Luzhniki Stadium in Moscow, where I was taken by Vladik Monroe who had free tickets (of course I wouldn't have gone to watch this American gnome with my own money). There was an incredible number of cops there, one of whom displayed rather aggressive interest in me, catching me taking a leak in an inappropriate place. Only my journalist ID saved me from his insistent pestering. At the stadium entrance several lines of cops thoroughly searched and felt everyone. This got Monroe very excited and he went back and forth about three times to prolong the pleasure.

The concert was a flop, the weather was nasty, the rain was pouring, and people were standing up to their ankles in water. Misha came up to us and asked for a smoke. It turned out that previously, back in St. Petersburg, he tried to "get" Monroe for a long time and claimed to be in love with him. Don't know what ever happened between those two, but Vladik told me he was now trying to avoid Misha.

Monroe and his retinue left, and I remained standing in the rain with Misha, who was high and seemed to have some difficulty understanding what was going on around him. Later I never saw him completely sober, looking normal; his pupils were always dilated. Misha was a clear case of a teenager who grew too quickly—tall, dystrophically thin, boyishly awkward, with long arms and legs and with shoulders and chest that had not shaped up yet. He truly was *beautiful* with the innocent childish expression of his face, wide open eyes and long lashes, with a short haircut, always in a baseball cap turned backwards and with rings in both ears, nose and one eyebrow (piercings always excited me!).

He slightly stuttered and slurred when he spoke, and his vocabulary was full of slang and Russianized English words. Later he became for me a walking dictionary of this simultaneously entertaining and somewhat stupid language that served as a password of sorts for the "in" crowd. His head was an utter mess, he jumped from one thought to another, and his speech frequently resembled a Joycean stream of consciousness. I liked his stories and fantasies; to me they looked like good material for an absurdist play yet to be written.

After the concert he had to go back to St. Petersburg. In a kiosk by the metro station I bought a bottle of vodka which we drank right there, chasing it down with some nasty franks. He got drunk in an instant and was overflowing with tenderness toward me. He wrapped himself around me, grabbed and kissed my hands, felt my cock, whispering excitedly, "Wow! So big!" We embraced, kissed and rubbed against each other like lusty wild animals, cold and wet from the rain. Old drunkards standing nearby watched us with both hate and surprise.

Catching the last metro train, we found ourselves in an empty car and lay down on a bench, still kissing and embracing. He unbuttoned my fly, got his hand inside, and started squeezing and caressing my cock. At the moment when he was about to take it in his mouth, two Georgian men walked into the car. I understood by their reaction that they could have easily killed us right there if we did not manage to jump out of the car an instant before the doors closed. When I saw him off at the train station, we parted as if we had been lovers for a long time: we only had known each other for about three hours!

He called me all the time, often leaving some ten messages a day in his bird language on the answering machine. The messages were about him loving me very much, him thinking about me all the time, wanting to see me, feeling bad without me, deciding to kill himself, overeating magic mushrooms and thinking he was about to die, having some girl and imagining I was doing to him what he was doing to her, and so on. At the time I was already a well-known journalist and regularly received calls and letters from the fans that I suddenly acquired. But Misha differed from them in that he hadn't the slightest idea about the things I did or the origin of my fame and wasn't at all interested in that. In any case, I am certain that he never read a single line of what I had written (if he knew at all how to read). However, occasionally he became the inspiration for some of my writing. In the pornographic poem "Seize It!" dedicated to him there are the following lines:

> and that boy in a baseball cap
> with a shelf that sticks out
> takes and swallows like a god
> nobody else could do it like him

The parents of Misha Beautiful are well-known and respected in St. Petersburg. I believe his father is the director of some large department store. And, as it often happened in well-off Soviet families, he grew up "difficult," a "problem child." He told me about doing *fartsovka* (trading with foreign tourists) next to the "Intourist" hotel. The queers who "picked up" foreigners also hung out there. Misha and his trader friends periodically bashed the queers: beat them up and took away money, watches, jewelry and such. Misha did not consider himself queer.

From his other stories I found out that as a child he fell down a staircase and suffered a severe concussion. Apparently this was the reason why his mind was clearly slow. I was only older than him by some two years, but it seemed to me that a veritable age gap divided us, turning our communication (when his mouth wasn't busy with something else) into some inarticulate babbling. He had the intellect of a five-year-old child, with only two passions: drugs and parties. And, of course, beautiful and expensive clothes. He didn't like to work and didn't know how, and when he ran out of his parents' money he stole or begged his friends for money; many of them used Misha as a prostitute in return. If one were to try to count his lovers or just fleeting partners, the result would appear as a rather long list of names, with many celebrities among them. For Misha sex was the only way to earn income, and he had all he needed to become a successful hustler.

Misha did not have a strong will or character, which is why, like some "son of the regiment,"* he had a need for elder comrades. Having found

---

*A term used to describe orphans found and taken care of by Soviet army regiments during World War II, an important element of Soviet cultural mythology.

himself in the coterie of Timur Novikov, Beautiful became a student at his New Academy of Fine Arts. Timur himself had admitted that one of the main criteria he used for selecting students was attractive appearance—a quality thanks to which Misha, like other beautiful creatures, successfully passed the "face control" and became a pupil at this unique educational institution above which hovered the sinful spirit of Baron von Gloeden and Oscar Wilde. Timur's boys served as naked models for each other, had their pictures taken in ancient garb and poses on roofs or at the Academy itself, located in a large communal apartment, one of the walls of which was covered from floor to ceiling by satin of the symbolic sky blue color.

Timur (whom Misha referred to respectfully as Timur Petrovich) was for him for a while a true idol and figure of authority. But even he, despite his definite organizer's talent and his skill in (let's say) "working with the young," managed to divert Misha from the lifestyle he had been leading only for a short while. Fine Arts interested him far less than drugs and parties. Timur Petrovich sincerely tried to bring him to reason and to take him back to the realm of beauty, but his efforts were in vain. . . .

Misha gave me a big surprise by showing up in Moscow on one of the days of the October 1993 putsch, during the state of emergency. He must have been the only person in the world who knew nothing about it. He had no papers with him. He called me from the train station. He had tons of acquaintances in Moscow, but he called me and no one else since, according to him, he came down to see me. And I felt some responsibility for him. Dropping everything, I grabbed a pack of my journalist IDs and went to meet (or, rather, save) him.

The previous night Monroe had been arrested when he was wandering around Moscow, having his pictures taken for his magazine *Ya* and making indecent poses in front of the tanks. Vladik and a friend of his had to spend a night in pre-trial detention. This probably was the best possible scenario of what could have happened to Misha. I did not know what to do with him or where to take him. I could not even bring him home, since my pathologically jealous and hysterical lover was there, and he could have easily killed me, Misha, himself, or all three of us.

Having found out that something scary and incomprehensible was happening in Moscow, Misha went into raptures and begged me to take him to the White House. The most surprising thing was that he succeeded in that. The invisible evil snipers followed us desirously with their eyepieces, stray bullets whizzed by, the level of adrenalin in our blood exceeded all the Health Ministry's norms, people wandered in the streets, ogling and dumbfounded; all of this served as an arousing backdrop. Like homeless teenagers forced to engage in public sex, we found ourselves in alleys and doorways, and Misha used every opportunity to directly communicate with the object of his desire. Several times we were caught in the middle of it, but in that extreme situation our pranks did not cause particular reactions in anyone. (Queers on barricades!) So this was my baptism by fire. I will always remember that sharp feeling of sex in the midst of war, and I understand very well why shooting, war, occupation have been depicted in such desirous ways in Genet, Liliana Cavani, Tom of Finland and many others.

I am writing about Misha in such detail, trying to recall all that I know and remember about him precisely because he is no longer in this world, and I am getting excited under the pressure of some cruel and dark necrophiliac fantasies. I know this is blasphemy, that *de mortuis aut bene, aut nihil,* but I am describing him the way he was, portraying him as a tender exotic plantlife, a delicate blossom, unadapted and unprepared for life. He was doomed. He had it imprinted on him, and it was difficult not to notice that. I knew that, sensed that, and repeatedly tried to do something to influence his fate. But I had not fallen for him that badly. I had a life of my own into which he intruded from time to time; we met periodically and made love, he was always somewhere nearby, and it seemed things would stay like this forever. As I was moving across Moscow, changing addresses and lovers, Misha somehow managed to find my phone numbers and called me, giving me more material for the absurdist play I had conceived and running into my jealous boyfriends from time to time.

On April 12, 1994, the day of my twentieth birthday and of the legendary attempt to register the first same-sex marriage in Russia I undertook with my American friend Robert, Misha's half-ghostly figure suddenly appeared in the crowd of reporters armed with erect cameras and microphones. As is well known, our marriage wasn't registered, but we managed to make enough noise for all the world to hear, and we bravely withstood the marathon of endless filmings and interviews that followed. As in the case of the putsch, Misha was probably the only person unaware of this historic event. He fluttered his eyes and wrinkled his forehead in surprise, failing to understand who was marrying whom and why there was such commotion.

I had neither the opportunity nor the desire to explain things to him and deal with him at that moment, and I decided to give Misha away to my friend Fedya P., the son of a famous woman writer. Fedya was a cute young man and a novice journalist with good brains and a kind heart; prior to this the two of us "did it" somewhat awkwardly a couple of times (on his initiative, in spite of Fedya usually acting straight and repeatedly trying to lecture to me about my "sinful" way of life). I knew he wouldn't mind "doing it" with someone else. Misha was an ideal character for that, and he obediently went with Fedya as he was told.

After the noisy party at Robert's studio Fedya took Misha to the apartment he was renting separately from his parents. Having slept with him that night, Fedya departed either for work or for college, leaving Beautiful at his place and making the noble jesture of leaving him the only key. He promised to get Misha a journalist ID so that he could attend any cultural event without problems. More than a month passed before the trusting Fedya managed to catch Misha and get the key back from him. He had to pay for the apartment he couldn't even get in, while Misha turned it into a drug den, did not answer calls and hid from the naive Fedya. But an even greater surprise was still awaiting Fedya: his landlord demanded that he pay for Misha's long distance and international calls (he must have been leaving numerous messages on his lovers' answering machines). "But I tried to help him, to drag him out of this swamp!" Fedya later complained to me, frustrated in his best feelings.

Several times I ran into Misha in various clubs, and by then he was already so high he could hardly recognize me. His speech consisted of half-senseless interjections à la futurist *zaum*. Later Misha disappeared somewhere, and different stories about him reached me from time to time: he had hung out with some Scandinavian DJs who drugged and "gang-banged" him; he had to move completely to Moscow since in St. Petersburg people from whom he "borrowed" various valuable things were trying to hunt him down; that people were beginning to look for him in Moscow for the same reasons as well. Once an acquaintance of mine called me to ask where one could find Misha to ask him to return the video camera that had disappeared after his visit. Misha had gone too far: for the majority of people he stopped being "beautiful," and clouds were beginning to gather above his head.

Our last meeting took place when he called and found me in a kind of sentimental and lyrical mood. I missed him and his silly stories. We walked around town and he entertained me with stories about his parents frying some mushrooms and him adding some of *his own*, and then his parents started seeing things, and his grandma had the most serious hallucinations. "I don't understand what's happening to me!" exclaimed grandma. "I feel like a completely different person!" Another story, completely unrealistic, was about some rich mistress Misha had who liked anal sex and Misha satisfying her. Misha himself confessed he grew to like anal sex as well. He said he'd been invited to go work as a model either in Italy or Spain, and that he would go there "as soon as he's ready."

Having bought a couple of bottles of champagne, we dropped in at the studio of my friend Katya Leonovich, on the Garden Ring. She was having a business meeting with a couple of obscure journalists who nearly fainted at hearing my name. Having gotten drunk on champagne, we started behaving in a rather unrestrained manner. Just like the first time, Misha wrapped himself around me and our fit of tenderness finished in the bathroom where I resolutely brought him down on his knees and pushed my cock into his mouth. He diligently and skillfully sucked and licked it, stopping from time to time, looking puppy-like into my eyes, saying pitifully and devotedly, "Please don't abandon me! I beg you! I want to be with you!'' At that moment I wanted only one thing—to come—and could easily promise anything. When it was all over, we came out of the bathroom to meet the frightened gaze of the obscure journalists. Then Misha undressed to show his tattoos, and Katya had him try on one of the outfits from the collection she was working on. Being at the center of attention, Misha was shy and at his best. One could do anything one wanted with him, like with a doll or a mannequin—he was so obedient-malleable-passive.

On the eve of our departure (or, rather, escape: I had to flee from another case that was brought against me) from Russia, literally a few hours before our plane, when Robert and I were hurriedly trying to pack at least something, Monroe burst into our place with his friend Ivan Tsarevich and the conceptualist artist Sergei Anufriev. Monroe and Ivan were then renting an apartment on the Arbat, a two minute walk from us, and whenever they completely ran out of money they would come to our place to eat. We thus had to put off the packing until the very last moment and feed the hungry artists. It was then, at our last supper, that I learned from Vladik that Misha Beautiful had gone to jail for theft and drugs. We made a bad joke about "Misha now going to feel good and having an intense sex life in prison" and so on. But since I had a good chance of finding myself behind bars as well, I understood perfectly well the seriousness of what had happened.

For a homosexual prone to sadomasochist fantasies, prison sometimes appears as an enticing sexual paradise, a place where the most daring dreams and fantasies come true. Such beliefs are usually taken from the porn films of Jean-Daniel Cadinot, the books of Genet, or even domestic prison folklore. One can fantasize about this for a long time, and these fantasies can be tempting and beautiful. But I have seriously investigated the topic of homosexuality in Soviet prisons and detention camps, and I know what happens *there* up to this day to those like myself and especially like Misha Beautiful. It doesn't matter that he didn't consider himself queer.

The story of his life and death could easily be reworked into a moralizing oration: look what drugs, homosexuality, parties, idleness and loose nightlife do to a person! He started out with *fartsovka* and mushrooms, and finished in prison, among the criminals! But one can also present it in a completely different way: it's a pity that there did not appear a Michael Jackson who could have saved him and turned his life into One Big Disneyland. It's a pity that neither Monroe nor Timur Petrovich, nor me nor Fedya became his Michael Jackson.

Poem: THE ARMY ELEGY

[Armeiskaia elegiia, 1994]

Translated by Vitaly Chernetsky

*To the soldier Seryozha, whom I discharged from his
post at four o'clock in the morning, having introduced
myself as the son of Russia's Defense Minister.*

The scent of a soldier's cock is beyond comparison
Which is well known in New York Berlin and Nice
There they know all about tenderness
When taking a sniff of the crotch

Terrains of alien pillows
Stains of alien sheets
The disparity of guns' caliber
Grows in viciousness and length

I did not have anyone except the Army
Rosy-cheeked soldiers fall out of windows
Like Kharms's old women*
When they try to gaze at the sky
Their resilient bodies are dragged away
(And there's something farcical in it)

The intoxicating smell of the barracks and dirty feet
The creaking tenderness of several pairs of entangled combat boots
(What to do—I couldn't do otherwise any more)

Foreign queers are aroused by Russian soldiers
Russian soldiers are not afraid of foreign queers
They bravely gaze at the sky
Many of them did not have anyone except the Army
They fall out of windows
And their able young bodies fall into foreigners' hands
They are dragged across the border
usually to Paris Berlin New York or Nice
Smuggled by a firmly united lusty gang
Getting through customs with difficulty
(The creaking and scent alone could drive one crazy
Were it not for the tenderness
That squeezed the crotch in the final gasps
Of disparate guns alien sheets and pillows)

---

*An allusion to "Old Women," by Russian absurdist writer Daniil Kharms (1905–1942).

Dimitri Bushuev (b. 1969)

POEM: "The night will burst with hail, and the rain"

Translated by Vitaly Chernetsky

DIMITRI BUSHUEV (b. 1969) studied at Ivanovo University, north of Moscow and the Gorky Literary Institute in Moscow. His poems have appeared in various literary journals in Russia, and he won the *Yunost* literary award for best poem of the year. His book collection of poems *Usad'ba* (*Country Estate*) was published in Yaroslavl in 1991. Of recent years he has been living in England and working as a Sports Commentator (Russian speaker) for the Satellite Telesport Ltd., London, while continuing his writing. The prose printed here is from a long, unpublished novel, *Echoes of Harlequin*.

The night will burst with hail, and the rain
Will pour down, like sayings from the Cabbalah,
While Autumn carries slender glasses
Filled with hot amber.

A different, brightly colored wine
The harlequins once brought me,
With stars and rubies all inside it,
And ships sinking down to the bottom.

Like under a chimera's wing
I sit alone next to an old book
Where three pages of wild strawberries
Are blooming under a bronze cross.

I am gay, and hence I know the magic
Inside the sealed sea bottles and under the roots—
But you have called it all
Boyish pranks and tomfoolery.

I might be going down to hell
Through the dark windowless cabins
And there I kiss Demon himself on the lips,
Dictating a tale amid falling leaves.

Photo by Alexei Sedov.

Dimitri Bushuev (b. 1969)

ECHOES OF HARLEQUIN

[Na kogo pokhozh Arlekin]

Selections from the unpublished novel

Translated by Vitaly Chernetsky

I SENSED YOUR FIELD of energy, the currents of warmth, the peculiar vibration of the air, mixed with your familiar scent; my chakras exuded golden balls, the cod liver oil of constellations floating around me. The root of my life hardened painfully, I could barely restrain myself from hugging you and whispering in your hot little ear, "I love you, Dennis." I was screaming in my thoughts, screaming for all the Universe to hear; the blood pulsated in my temples; I wanted to loosen my tie, raise my head and whistle like a nightingale! I sensed fantastic blips and explosions of energy—it seemed to me that I could overturn a train, tear a wing off a plane, saddle a rhinoceros or even screw a crocodile—for you. And how much verse, mountains of verse of the highest standard I composed, burning in my flame! You won't be able to read them. . . . And in the meantime, hold your pants better and button up your fly so that your sparrow doesn't fly out. And has it even grown its feathers yet, this little bird? And generally, keep your ass close to the wall, you little squirrel. . . . You lick your dry lips, the poisonous tip of your tongue glides over the pearls of the two wide front teeth. Lord, Lord, what do I do with my beastly tenderness, the burning bush of passion, what do I do with my beauty, my youth and strength? Look how much champagne sparkles in my blood, how my flute sings in the warm nights of the East, how eternity, immortality, peacefully spends the night inside me—only the swallow of black eyebrows flies over the sea of life. When Judgment Day comes I shall look for Dennis in the crowd—Lord, put a red band on his forehead so that I can find him faster.

After class you came up to me to double check the numbers of the homework exercises, but why then, you sly little thing, were you casting glances out the window where you could see my mustang in the bike lot? Triumphantly I opened the door of the closet where the two brand new helmets were sparkling: one orange, the other purple, with a fantastic butterfly upon it! The fragile boy in this huge helmet looked like an extraterrestrial from the constellation of Aquarius—where, but where is the highway knight in black leather carrying him, have you seen by any chance where they went? Police! Firemen! Witnesses! The first lanterns lit up on the embankment, lights floated down the river, a fisherman's figure grew still on top of a bridge. I stopped and asked where we should go now. With unexpected abruptness, you answered, seriously. "To the park!" At that mo-

403

ment you seemed strangely adult and sullen, like a pigeon with its feathers ruffled up.

Having noticed the lit archway of the park entrance, you grabbed my jacket even more tightly; I slowed down, and we softly rustled over the fallen leaves of the old alley, already dusted with snow. In the distance burned the lights of the show booths, explosions of neon flashed, and the floodlights lit the enormous inflated Mickey dancing in the wind in the lead-colored sky. The air was charged with the overwhelming beat of computerized muzak. We left the motorcycle and went where there was more light and more music. The cheerful hell of the carnival burned us with its multicolored flame. There was a smell of roasted chestnuts which the Chinese were selling; the muzak hurt our ears; over the entrance to the "Cave of Horrors" a plastic skeleton dangled in the air; enormous teacups whirled, with children screaming delightedly inside them. Airplanes looped the loop, and at the shooting-gallery portraits of Saddam Hussein hung instead of regular targets. Snow was mixing with dirt under our feet, and the wind was tearing off the sails of tarpaulin roofs. . . . but you, Dennis, seemed not to be excited by the festive atmosphere. I bought you a little teddy bear, as a gift to remember this evening, and suggested taking a ride on the roller coaster. I persisted in suggesting it and even started dragging you by the hand, but you were stubborn and then broke free and ran back into the alley like a madman, not turning back to my cries . . . I was barely able to catch up with you in the dusk, pulled you by the sleeve and saw your huge eyes filled with tears. . . . A teardrop rolled down your inflamed cheek, and I immediately wanted to lick it, so hot, so salty, so alive. Puzzled, I embraced your shoulders and carefully caressed your hair, you put your face into my sweater and started crying even harder, only your fragile shoulders shuddered in my embrace. Totally at a loss, I did not ask questions, but the answer came by itself when you uttered, sobbing, just one word, "Daddy." Stuttering from agitation, swallowing cold air, you told me the story of that dramatic day when your father passed away. It's good you got to talk about it, cry about it into my prickly sweater.

Death found the simple assistant from a chemical laboratory in a most appropriate place, in the sea of lights and music, in this earthly model of hell with its wheels, ropes, shining cables and neon lamps. It likes carnivals. Mr. Semyon Belkin died on a Sunday evening at one of the rides in an amusement park where he brought his son to properly end the weekend. The Loop of Death, with its sharp drops and quick turns, with the fantastic incline of the car among the blue stars, turned out to be his last journey. There is black humor in the very name of this ride onto which I so mistakenly tried to drag Dennis. This was chemist Belkin's third and last heart attack. At this most important, final moment of his life, he was trying to swallow a nitroglycerin tablet with one hand, while hugging his son with the other and attempting to smile all the while. . . . The music was loud, and at first nobody heard the cries of the pubescent froglet, holding on in horror to his father's dangling head. The dead, pale head. "Stop the motor! Sir, stop!"—a film director might cry like this, dissatisfied with the scene just filmed, but life doesn't allow second takes. The flashing lights of the ambulance were only a small addition to the big illumination.

Electric shock.

The underpants' elastic cut into the plump stomach.

It seemed to you that a smile passed over your father's lips. . . . Then— mother's endless crying, pennies in the bank account, some kind old women. . . . Kids of your age already have racing bikes, computer games, clothing from latest catalogs, and you are dressed in the style of dignified poverty and shy away from school dances.

I gave you a ride home and, having worked up the courage, offered a Sunday game of tennis, at the "Dynamo" sports complex; you nodded and looked closely into my eyes. . . . I got embarrassed and said a quick good-bye.

In the evening I stand in front of the mirror for a long time. An unfamiliar pale face of a specter double with bright lips, as if I'm wearing lipstick. The face of a dummy in a Broadway shop window, calculated by the computer to be the most sexually appealing. I put on some mascara, lined the eyebrows and covered half my face with a Chinese fan. Very, very stylish. . . . If only I could also change the color of my eyes, put in blue contact lenses. . . . Where is this magnetism in the eyes from?

Look carefully at the double.

Put the fan down.

How old are you, moon man? A thousand years? Two thousand? Was it your horse, covered with brocade and bronze, that entered Rome through the triumphal arch?

You were burnt at the stake in Scotland, do you remember the long-haired youth with a model sailboat and a compass in his hands?

Was it you that covered yourself with penitent chains at an Italian monastery and still sinned with the novice?

The gorgeous bartender on the *Titanic*?

A Chinese conjurer?

A French actor?

A German officer who tortured a Polish boy?

A landscape architect consumed by liver cancer?

Be silent. Be silent, dear scoundrels. Shut up! Go to hell, I'm Andrei Naitov, I don't know you, this is blood muttering insane verse, my structure is cracking up at the seams, and I'm even afraid to unbutton my shirt! But the clown behind the mirror winks with his painted eye, "It's even surprising such a small, feeble, weak-willed creature can drag along this coal train of horrible karma?" . . . I covered my face with my hands . . . brushed off all the makeup from the dressing table, broke the fan and crisscrossed the mirror with lipstick!

For some time now I never part with my Minolta, trying to capture your fleeting and transient presence. The entire desk is covered with your photographs, and here is one of my favorite pictures: you are standing with your legs apart and hands in pockets, your head bent, a smile, a sly glance, your bangs to one side. . . . Still you are posing for me, you little devil! But that's good. The bulge in your trousers is too well defined for your age, like a ballet dancer's. There is something in you of a sweet Gavroche, charming clownishness, liveliness, pure boyish tomfoolery. . . .

2:0. Your serve. With what amazing anger you toss up the spinning balls; if only you were so lively when dealing with verb endings. . . .

3:0. Your serve. . . . The fluorescent green ball reached me from Russia, sent by your well-aimed stroke. . . .

3:1—good thing the window into the garden was open.

The game is finished. You rush into the shower, a pink towel over your shoulder. I feel lost, spend a long time searching inside my gym bag and feel hot blood rushing to my thighs. . . . How I want you! It must be done! I will slowly kiss your chapped, full lips, your nipples, shoulders (a mole on the left one), thighs, knees, drink your breath, swallow your tears, slide my palms down your well-shaped buttocks, and, forgetting myself in purple sweat, I shall possess this milky shivering body. . . . Steam in the shower room, I see only your silhouette and the swimming trunks hanging on the wall of the shower stall. I get an erection and shower myself with ice-cold water. The rainbow-colored St. Elmo's lights around the dim lightbulb, hot steam from a hole in the pipe—we are inside clouds and rainbows, now we'll fly away to other clouds, into the stream of light and music. . . . Pearls drop on marble, fountains ring—over there are the Roman thermae, stained glass, libraries, lush greenery and wicker armchairs, there Pilate hasn't yet met Christ; two little moors play in the pool with a sea turtle, and the corpulent legislator lazily watches their game; wine doesn't cheer him up, only makes the headache go away for a short while. And when the flutes grow silent, he painfully tries to recall a forgotten name, but just as the sound begins to gain shape, it slips frustratingly out of reach. One of the boys comes out of the pool, shakes his wet curls and cuts a melon. A bee is hovering above the melon, as if time has stopped for a little while.

. . . I have invited you over to my place to look at the slides I took on the island of Valaam, where I spent the end of August: the bay, the monastery . . . Domes. Clouds. Clouds. Oily dragonfly upon a yellow water lily. Overturned boats and two teenagers. A seagull on a rock. Clouds. Ivy on a brick wall. A spring with an icon. Sunset. Clouds again. A hobbled horse. Lights over the river. . . . You are on the floor, your feet tucked in. You ask to keep on the slide with the horse. The stallion looks at you with sad eyes—he is old, with a matted mane and sore sides. You ask why I photograph clouds so much—at sunset, ink-colored before a thunderstorm, or in the watercolor of the morning, with a barely noticeable rainbow, smoky and well defined, scattered, sheep-like, dispersed. . . . I don't know. I have never encountered anything more interesting; I feel easy and free in the clouds, there is light, breeze and calm there, there's a seagull and a hawk, a burned-out propeller, mirages and rejoicing souls, wind and flutes, aeolian harps, choirs and ether. . . . There's a cloud, look, Dennis, it looks like a dolphin, right? And behind it an elephant, a turtle and a sky dog. I close my eyes. Childhood. The Volga. A colorful box kite stretches the fishing line, rushes about in the clouds; I stand up on the tips of my toes, but still cannot get off the ground, and it is so interesting in the sky! Butterflies and God live there. There certainly must be some kind of holiday going on up in the sky, and I'm a little bored down here. . . . Hey, throw me down some goodies and candy, and toys, and new boots! Here, Lord, I'm here! Hey, Lord, do you see my multicolored kite? Here I am! Hello! A ladybug crawls up a tall grass stem. A gust of wind. The noise of the trees. Dry leaves fall into the puddles, where clouds are reflected. "Mommy, mommy, pour into this clay mug some stormy sky with the smell of wild lilies of the valley, with lightning and rainbow! Angel, my angel, drop me at least a feather. . . ."

I rolled up the screen and did not know what else to entertain you with, realizing with regret that I'm not a conjurer and not a magician. I suggest for fun a home-made test, and you spend a long time thinking over my "questionnaire." Here's this crumpled document, your letters, carefully outlined on the back side of my ancient award for first place in the shooting competition at the university.

FAVORITE HERO—the Little Prince.

MOMENT OF GREATEST DELIGHT—the overcoming of the insurmountable.

MATERIALIZED IMAGE OF FEAR—dentist's chair.

FAVORITE ANIMAL—the dolphin and the horse.

PERSISTENT SEXUAL FANTASY—you didn't answer this question, blushed, and returned the pen to me.

You put your hands in your pockets and came up to the window; in the sunset light your blond bangs turned orange. A soft, pastel-colored sunset. You have a sad smile on your face. What are you thinking about? I came up behind you and carefully embraced your shoulders; you shuddered, but didn't try to get out of the clumsy embrace. The little squirrel's heart was beating very fast, and you held your breath. I already almost did not belong to myself. I had run away from myself, forgot my name, my street, my town—I'm afraid even my planet. . . . Something winged and unbelievably tender in my embrace. . . . I kissed you from behind, on your neck—didn't even really kiss, but touched with my lips the barely noticeable down—you shuddered again, turned around, and we looked into each other's eyes for a long time. Yours—sea splashes, wet leaves, juicy greenery in the sun, in them puzzlement and sober tipsiness. I felt your strange fear, as if on the edge of an abyss of dancing stars, and if this fear materialized into an old dentist's chair then. . . . Dennis first tried to move away from my kisses, as if he was afraid "to overcome the insurmountable," but in a moment he kissed me on the lips himself, HIMSELF! A bittersweet kiss. I don't know how many worlds burnt down inside me during those precious minutes. Your shirt is getting wet at the armpits. . . . The boundary between heaven and hell passes through the bedroom, and after the orgasm we fall from the sky onto the rocks, having just been driven out of the heavenly garden to follow our ancestors. You have the beauty of Vrubel's Demon (even in my mind your image appears on a purple background); which wandering and forgotten spirit chose this perfect body, or which prodigal spirit got it as a gift? Your time became mine, and right now a boy with a briefcase stands in front of my eyes in the Russian New Year snowstorm. . . .

The sunny frozen morning unexpectedly fell to earth with the ringing of all the icicles, like a heavy crystal chandelier from a stucco ceiling; the clouds looked exactly like stucco molding, done in a rush by a mad sculptor possessed with a *mania grandiosa*. The sun found us exhausted on crumpled sheets. . . .

The same day, before leaving, I visited auntie Elizabeth. My aunt, my dear lonely aunt, the only one among all my relatives who understood me and accepted me the way I am. Why, why didn't I spend more time with you when you were alive? A window on the fifth floor of the house on Kotelnicheskaya Embankment shines through the night—the Stalinist house swims through Moscow like an ice-breaker, through time and timelessness, the Flying Dutchman of lost generations. The chains jingled, and my good fairy opened the door, having specially put on for this long-awaited meeting her old satin dress. Funny. Old-fashioned. I kiss her dry vein-covered hands; polish has been coming off her nails. She hugs me and cries, "Andryusha, my dear boy, today is such a happy day for me!" . . . Auntie is so thin, almost transparent, she seems nearly weightless—a white cloud in a lavender dress, a dandelion. My auntie was widowed three times! The first husband died at the front; the second, an NKVD officer, perished in the purges when the machine of dictatorial paranoia began devouring its very self; the last one, a well-known party boss, famous for his jokes and stories, hanged himself after one of his drinking sprees, not having accepted the climate of Gorbachev's thaw. We never talked about all this, and the real auntie Elizabeth remained in my childhood when she took me to the capital for holidays, stuffed me with various goodies and bought expensive gifts. She spoiled me, probably because she was kind and childless, and all her love and motherly care she projected onto the little Andrei with his runny nose, who loved to ride the pony at Gorky Park for hours. All the children envied my sailor hat and the gilded dirk on a leather belt with a real soldier's buckle. More pictures from memory: the rainy Tsvetnoi Boulevard through which we rush in a white Pobeda car; the river boat, all covered with colored lights, slowly moving between the granite-covered banks of the Moscow river. . . . My mother was jealous of me because of auntie, and one summer they even quarreled when my mother refused to let me go with her to the Black Sea for the holidays. But the next season my aunt finally took me to the coast. We lived in the former Empress Catherine's palace near Swallow's Nest; this was a resort for the party elite. I was of the age when boys already get *1001 Nights* as a birthday present, and the bittersweet magnolias make your head spin so much that you want to run away into the moonlit southern night, to the sea, to watch lovers' night bathing. I was fantastically susceptible to love. Together with one of the locals, a long-legged tanned teenager named Aslan, we threw wild cucumbers at each other, caught crabs and went diving from the basalt rock for sea shells from the underwater sandy spit. Auntie Elizabeth always took opera glasses with her, so that our "dangerous swimming" wasn't out of her sight. Luckily, our erotic games didn't fall within her field of vision. . . . He was the same age as me, and I sincerely envied him for having a dick larger than mine; I was particularly distressed that my little bird hardly had any feathers yet, while Aslan already had thickets! We had our secret gazebo in a vineyard where we "fantasized about girls" together and helped each other masturbate; however, his muscular body and the jumping pulsating little column excited me more than comments about girls. Aslan definitely was attracted to me as well, since it was he who first asked me to kiss him on the lips, saying he'd close his eyes and think about some girl named Esmigyul. I am certain that no Esmigyul has ever existed. . . . In the mornings, in my bed, I persistently masturbated, again and again recreating in my fantasy my games with Aslan, anticipating new meetings at the gazebo; there we also smoked the strong "Herzegovina Flor" cigarettes and together dreamed of sea voyages. . . . On the day of my departure I cried, and my boy gave me a coral necklace to remember him by; I have kept it to this day.

My dearest auntie, I enter your shadowy rooms as if I am entering my childhood; all the objects are in their places, even the tortoise-shell comb is lying on the dressing table in front of the mirror in a carved frame, as if time has stopped here. I wouldn't be surprised if my reflection in the mirror turned out to be the freckled boy in a sailor's hat; I wouldn't be surprised if early February produced a warm rain with roaring thunder, and the piano in the living room would start playing by itself, and we would make jokes and laugh like then. . . . Why, why can't we joke and laugh like that now? Why?

All her life auntie was a staunch atheist, but everybody knows that it is precisely the atheists who, having passed the dialectical stage of rebelling against God, most often become devout believers or simply are infected with various forms of mysticism—that's what happened to my aunt; in her declining years she joined some strange esoteric society. This was a kind of a New Age group with a Russian twist, where everything went into the mix: the manuscripts of unrecognized messiahs, silver-maned unicorns, the poetry of ancient Russian spells, the horoscopes of the Druids, the ritual laments of southern Croatians and Australian didgeridoo. . . . Now as well, during our good-bye dinner, auntie smokes a lot, talking about Atlantis, Glob's prophecies and the latest book by David Ike, of which she suddenly decided to do a pirated translation. . . . I couldn't restrain myself from laughing when auntie declared that there are little people living inside mountain crystals: it appeared that my Elizabeth was reaching the stage of infantile mysticism. I was even more convinced of that when she showed me a strange device resembling a primitive tennis racket hanging above her bed; there were crystals and feathers hanging from it on threads.

"My God, what is this?" I couldn't restrain my puzzlement.

"Andryusha, this is an amazing thing! It's a Mexican dream catcher! Just look: these are real owl feathers! By the way, I have been writing down my dreams for some time—do you see those notebooks? When I die . . ."

"Auntie!"

"Yes, when I die don't be lazy, have a look at them. I know, you'll be interested, you have always been an unusual boy. . . . By the way, I always knew you were gay. . . ."

"???!"

". . . Yes, I knew. And always understood. You know, when I was young I took ballet lessons, and some of the guys were like that too. Do you know how I recognize people of your type? By their eyes! By the way, now I'm reading Erich Fromm's *The Soul of Man*, he keeps referring to a paper by Freud entitled 'Character and Anal Eroticism' where the latter writes that such persons show three qualities in consistent combination: they are particularly thrifty, neat and . . . eccentric! Funny, isn't it? And Fromm himself thinks that an anal character is that of accumulation. There you have it, sir!"

Auntie again keeps me in the hallway for a long time and doesn't want to let me go, she keeps on crying and hugging me, crying and hugging. . . . My God, how lonely she is! It smells of lilies of the valley. I feel very, very sad. I took two books to read from her extensive library, Madam Blavatsky's *The Secret Doctrine* and Daniil Andreyev's *Rose of the World*. But I didn't get to give them back to her.

The following day Dennis and I are planting apple trees next to a church. Amazing vistas stretch out from the cliff here. What an expanse! Eternal peace. A seagull circles above our heads, and for some reason its cries make the heart skip a beat. I dig into the earth with a rusty shovel, and the earth is alive and warm . . . something jingles under the spade . . . wow! A coin! I wipe it with the edge of my jacket—two copecks from 1892! A nice heavy little coin. I give it to Dennis saying, "Here, the times have been reconnected." Indeed, maybe this closes a chain of events that stretched several centuries? Who knows? It turned out Dennis knew it all. We finished planting our apple trees. Let them grow. I stuck the shovel into the ground, wiped my sweaty forehead with my sleeve, and then, holding my knees, I watched a little steamboat going down the river. Dennis sat down next to me and asked, tossing up the coin,

"Heads or tails?"

"Heads."

"No, tails . . . tails." Dennis somehow immediately grew sadder and pensive, his eyes started filling with tears, but in a moment he smiled—an enigmatic, strange half-smile, like that of the Sphinx. . . . My love with the smile of the Sphinx. . . . And I once stood feeling all lost on the cliff next to the half-destroyed little church, broken bottles on the old graves and pieces of rocks with imprints of prehistoric shells. . . . I was standing in the wind, and the crazy seagull circled and sobbed above me. An inexpressible melancholy joy filled my soul, and I was thinking about the most important thing. And do you know what I wanted to do then, Dennis? To get lost in these shy places, cross myself out of my own narrative and get a job on the village ferry.

We return to Rafik's estate along a sunny path, holding hands; halfway there, we stop by the well—you follow me in taking off your shirt, and we pour icy water over each other. The water glistens in the bucket, and I pour pure silver over you.

Take my baptism.

Take my silver.

The house greets us with open windows; in the bedroom we again make love. Dennis and I made love in every country of the world, in every continent: we were on the floor, and the colored patchwork of the political map of the world was beneath us. I kissed you in America, and the fountain of the orgasm shot up somewhere in Africa, but a few hot drops also fell on Europe. Amsterdam got completely flooded. What a disaster!

. . . Exhausted, you fell asleep, covering yourself with a plaid blanket, your knees close to your stomach; I wanted to take a picture, but I had run out of film. . . . A roll of thunder came from somewhere far away. . . . When I was little and it thundered, my grandmother always said, "That's Elijah the prophet driving his chariot"—and I believed her. I believed, and peered into the stormy sky, trembling. . . . I want to be taken to heaven in my body. With Dennis. What if we put together an enormous hot air balloon, I would take with me Dennis, Rafik, Oleg, Arseny, well, and perhaps also Gelka—for ballast—and we would burst into the stormclouds with balloons, sparks and laughter, accompanied by the explosions of my heavenly harlequins' firecrackers!

I lit a fire in the fireplace and realized that I was hopelessly happy—right then, that very minute. I knew that right then you couldn't find a man happier and guiltier than myself, that my life was carefree and full of light; and despite its unexpected turns, I shall only thank the Lord, only thank Him— for the enormity of my space, for the pain of passion, for the dancing stars of my love, for poetry in heart's excess, for the fresh bright red roses of the harlequins, of their nonsense and silliness, for my sublime madness, for Russia to which there is no return—just as there is no return to the days of youth and childhood; I thank Him for the Demon's kiss, for the saxophone and the flute, for strawberry paths and the morning birch fog, for the drop of rain on a forest spiderweb, for everything, for everything . . . for that which is most important, elusive and unaccountable.

Photo of Dimitri Bushuev from his poetry collection *Usad'ba* (Yaroslavl, 1991).

TRANSLATORS

(The author/work translated is given in brackets after each translator's name)

MICHAEL BIGGINS [Makanin: Prisoner of the Caucasus; Rybikov: Lays of the Gay Slavs—both co-transl.] has translated widely from contemporary Slovenian poetry and prose, with work appearing in *American Poetry Review, Grand Street, Paris Review*, and elsewhere. His translation of a book-length Holocaust memoir (*Pilgrim Among the Shadows*) by Slovenian-Italian author Boris Pahor was published in 1995 by Harcourt Brace. Together with Anatoly Vishevsky he has also produced an anthology of contemporary Russian ironic prose in English translation (University Press of Florida, 1993). He lives in Seattle, where he works as librarian for Slavic and East European collections at the University of Washington.

VITALY CHERNETSKY [Lermontov: Poems; V. Ivanov: Poems; Esenin: Poems; Ivnev: Poem; G. Ivanov: The Third Rome; Pereleshin: Twelve Sonnets; D. Kuz'min: Poems; Mogutin: The Death of Misha Beautiful; and Poem; Bushuev: Poems and Echoes of Harlequin] was born in 1970 in Odessa, Ukraine. He was educated at Moscow State University and Duke and has a Ph.D. (University of Pennsylvania, 1996). He has published several essays on contemporary Russian literature and art and translations of Russian fiction. He is now working on a book-length study, *Towards a Soviet Postmodern: Paradigms of Late Soviet Culture*. He now teaches Slavic and East European literature and culture at Columbia University.

SAMUEL D. CIORAN [Sologub: The Petty Demon] is Professor of Russian at McMaster University (Hamilton, Ontario, Canada). He is author of several monographs on the Silver Age of Russian literature, as well as translator of some dozen major works of Russian fiction. He is also the creator of the instructional multimedia Russian language program titled "RussianAlive!"

MICHAEL GREEN [Pushkin: Poem; Kuzmin: All stories and poems] currently teaches Russian at the University of California, Irvine. He is an authority on 18th century Russian theatre and has published numerous articles on this period. His works of translation include Mikhail Kuzmin's *Wings: Prose and Poetry* (1972) and *Selected Prose and Poetry* (Ardis, 1980), and (with Vera T. Rech) a translation of Boris Pilnyak's stories, *Chinese Story and Other Tales* (University of Oklahoma Press, 1988). He is currently working on the second volume of *The Unknown Russian Theater* (previously untranslated plays of the post-Revolutionary period). The first volume, published in 1991, consists of previously untranslated plays of the pre-revolutionary period.

DAN HEALEY [Letters about Prison Life] has a Ph.D. from the Department of History, University of Toronto, on the history of homosexuality in Soviet Russia. Before returning to his native Canada in 1991 he lived for eight years in England, where he served on the Board of Directors of the London Lesbian/Gay Switchboard. In Canada he was a director of the Toronto Centre for Lesbian and Gay Studies for two years. He has presented extracts from his research at the Moscow AESOP Centre.

DIANE NEMEC IGNASHEV [Past: No Offense in Love] teaches Russian literature and courses in gay studies at Carleton College, Minnesota. She met Iura Past through a mutual friend, just as Iura was beginning to realize that literature *was* his fate. Though their research interests do not coincide—she is working on a revisionist history of Russian theater and the role(s) women played in forming a canon—Iura has been a source of ideas and a good listener. Beside Iura's work Diane Nemec Ignashev has published translations of poetry and prose by Galich, Ratushinskaia, Soloukhin, Vaneeva, and Pristavkin.

SIMON KARLINSKY [Gogol: Nights at the Villa; Klyuev: Two Poems; Pereleshin: Selected Poems; Trifonov: Poems] is Professor Emeritus (Slavic Languages) at the University of California, Berkeley and currently lives in the Bay Area. His major works include *Marina Tsvetaeva: The Woman, Her World, and Her Poetry* (Cambridge Univ. Press, 1985), *The Sexual Labyrinth of Nikolai Gogol* (2nd ed.: Univ. of Chicago Press, 1993) and works on Nabokov and Chekhov. His groundbreaking article on Russia's gay literature, history and culture first appeared in *Gay Sunshine Journal* in 1976 and makes him the founding father of gay studies in Russian.

J. KATES [Gubin: Poems] is a poet and translator who lives in Fitzwilliam, New Hampshire.

SUSAN LARSEN [Kolyada: Slingshot] is a writer, translator and Assistant Professor of Russian Literature at the University of California, San Diego. She was also rehearsal interpreter for Roman Viktiuk's staging of *Slingshot* at the San Diego Repertory Theater in 1989.

GERALD M. MCCAUSLAND [Leontiev: Khamid and Manoli] was born in 1961 in Philadelphia. He holds an M.A. in Russian from Middlebury College, Vt., and is a doctoral candidate in the Dept. of Slavic Languages/Literatures at the University of Pittsburgh—on experimental prose and cinema in contemporary Russia.

MICHAEL MOLNAR [Ivnev: Diaries; Trifonov: Two Ballets by George Balanchine] lives in London where he is Research Director of the Freud Museum. He has published a monograph on Andrei Belyi and articles on Freud, whose diary of the 1930s he has also edited. His translations of contemporary Russian writers have appeared in journals and anthologies in the U.K. and U.S.A.

KEVIN MOSS [Tolstoy: The Ivins, Pages from Diaries; Kharitonov: Four stories; Trifonov: Open Letter; Letters to *Tema* and *1/10*] was born in 1955. He currently teaches Russian language and literature at Middlebury College, Vermont, where he also conducts the Middlebury Russian Choir. He has written on Bulgakov, Russian and East European film, and the Russian classical scholar Olga Freidenberg. He is currently working on a translation of the short fiction of Yevgeny Kharitonov supported by the National Endowment for the Humanities.

SPENCER E. ROBERTS [Rozanov: People of the Moonlight] is Professor Emeritus at the City University of New York (Brooklyn College). In the past he has been Cultural Attache in the American Embassy, Moscow, an actor in summer theater, and a professional pianist and organist. His other translations include Rozanov's *Doestoevsky and the Legend of the Grand Inquisitor* (Cornell U. Press) and *Essays in Russian Literature: Leontiev, Shestov, and Rozanov* (Ohio U. Press).

PAUL SCHMIDT [Steiger: Poems] holds a Ph.D. in Russian from Harvard University. His translation of all of Chekhov's plays was published by HarperCollins, 1996; he has also translated the *Complete Works of Arthur Rimbaud* (Harper & Row) and *The King of Time* (Harvard University Press), selections from the Russian futurist poet Velimir Khlebnikov. His play *Black Sea Follies* was produced off Broadway and won the 1987 Kesselring Award. His translation of Chekhov's *The Cherry Orchard* was produced in San Francisco by A.C.T. (Spring 1996).

ANTHONY VANCHU [Yeliseev: The Bench; Yasinsky: A Sunny Day at the Seaside; K.E.: The Phone Call] received his Ph.D. from the University of California, Berkeley in 1990. He is currently Assistant Professor in the Dept. of Slavic Languages/Literatures at the University of Texas, Austin, where he teaches courses in 20th century Russian literature and culture. His scholarly work focuses on early 20th century prose and drama, contemporary prose, and issues of gender and sexuality in Russian cultural history. He lives in Austin, Texas with his partner Seamus and their dog Phydeaux.

ANATOLY VISHEVSKY [Makanin: The Prisoner of the Caucasus; Rybikov: Lays of the Gay Slavs; both co-trans.] is a native of Chernivtsi, Ukraine and currently teaches Russian language and literature at Grinnell College, Iowa. He has authored several articles on 19th and 20th century Russian literature. Vishevsky is also author of two books: a collection of original stories in Russian, *Sobach'e delo* (in co-authorship with Boris Briker), Third Wave Publishers, 1985; and *Soviet Literary Culture in the 1970s: the Politics of Irony*, University Press of Florida, 1993.

ALLA ZBINOVSKY [Aksyonov: Around Dupont] is a freelance translator currently living in Moscow. She has a Master of Arts in Russian literature from Columbia University.

PUBLISHER

WINSTON LEYLAND was born in Lancashire, England in 1940 and has lived in the U.S. since childhood. For the past twenty-five years he has been publisher of Gay Sunshine Press in San Francisco: first of the cultural/literary publication *Gay Sunshine Journal* (1971–1981) and, since the mid 1970s (via Gay Sunshine/Leyland), of some 120 books covering a wide range of gay sexuality and culture—from anthologies (*My Deep Dark Pain Is Love*; *Partings at Dawn*; *Angels of the Lyre*; *Black Men/White Men*), to novels and short story collections (Pai Hsien-yung's *Crystal Boys*; Joseph Hansen's *Pretty Boy Dead*; Gore Vidal's *A Thirsty Evil*), to poetry collections (Allen Ginsberg's *Straight Hearts' Delight*; Luis Cernuda's *The Young Sailor*; Jean Genet's *Treasures of the Night: Collected Poems*). He initiated the present Russian anthology project in the 1980s and has worked with chief editor, Kevin Moss, in choosing and editing material submitted. He currently lives in San Francisco and is working on several book projects: among them, an Israeli gay anthology, a Buddhist gay anthology and a collection of gay love letters through the centuries. An in-depth autobiographical interview on his life is printed in *Gay Roots: An Anthology of Gay History, Sex, Politics and Culture, Vol. 1* (Gay Sunshine Press 1991). His own translations, essays and poetry were also gathered in this same volume, along with work by 100-plus authors, artists.

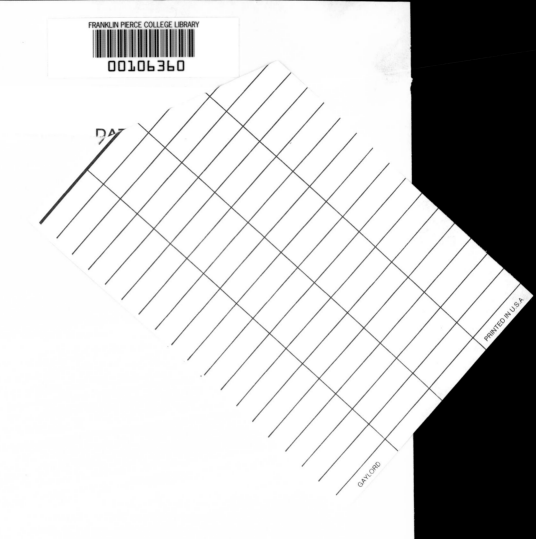

OUT OF THE BLUE is published in paperback and limited hardcover editions.
There is also a special edition of 26 lettered copies,
handbound in boards.

HUNTINGTON LIBRARY PUBLICATIONS